MW00780250

CHRISTIAN INTELLECTUALS AND THE ROMAN EMPIRE

INVENTING CHRISTIANITY

Series Editors

L. Stephanie Cobb

David L. Eastman

In the second and third centuries, insiders and outsiders alike were grappling with what it meant to be Christian. In this period, there were shifting and competing centers of clerical and textual authority and disagreements over group boundaries, interpretive strategies, and ritual practices. Inventing Christianity examines the numerous ways in which early Christianity was "invented"—that is, given definition and boundaries—by different people in different times to different ends. The series contributes to the study of second- and third-century Christianity by exploring how the very notion of Christianity developed and redeveloped in multiple forms and through cultural interactions.

OTHER BOOKS IN THE SERIES:

Michael Flexsenhar III, *Christians in Caesar's Household: The Emperor's Slaves in the Makings of Christianity*

ADVISORY BOARD

Nicola Denzey Lewis

Kim Haines-Eitzen

Robin M. Jensen

David Konstan

Jeffrey Siker

Jeanne-Nicole Mellon
   Saint-Laurent

CHRISTIAN INTELLECTUALS AND THE ROMAN EMPIRE

From Justin Martyr to Origen

JARED SECORD

The Pennsylvania State University Press
University Park, Pennsylvania

Portions of chapter 4 appeared earlier as "Julius Africanus, Origen, and the Politics of Intellectual Life
Under the Severans," *Classical World* 110, no. 2 (2017):
211–35. Copyright © 2017 The Classical Association
of the Atlantic States.

Library of Congress Cataloging-in-Publication Data

Names: Secord, Jared, author.
Title: Christian intellectuals and the Roman Empire :
    from Justin Martyr to Origen / Jared Secord.
Other titles: Inventing Christianity.
Description: University Park, Pennsylvania : The
    Pennsylvania State University Press, [2020] |
    Series: Inventing Christianity | Includes bibli-
    ographical references and index.
Summary: "A novel treatment of a group of early
    Christian authors, demonstrating that their be-
    havior and self-presentation were shaped by the
    norms of Roman intellectual culture, and not
    simply by factors internal to Christianity"—Pro-
    vided by publisher.
Identifiers: LCCN 2020017343 | ISBN
    9780271087078 (hardback)
Subjects: LCSH: Church history—Primitive and
    early church, ca. 30–600. | Intellectuals—Rome. |
    Christianity—Rome. | Rome—Intellectual life.
Classification: LCC BR170 .S43 2020 | DDC 270.1—
    dc23
LC record available at https://lccn.loc.gov
    /2020017343

Published by The Pennsylvania State University
    Press,
University Park, PA 16802–1003

The Pennsylvania State University Press is a member
of the Association of University Presses.

It is the policy of The Pennsylvania State University
Press to use acid-free paper. Publications on uncoat-
ed stock satisfy the minimum requirements of Amer-
ican National Standard for Information Sciences—
Permanence of Paper for Printed Library Material,
ANSI Z39.48–1992.

CONTENTS

PREFACE AND ACKNOWLEDGMENTS

This book derives in part from research that I conducted as part of graduate studies at the University of Michigan. My research then focused on Greek intellectual culture in the city of Rome from 100 BCE to 200 CE. Some of this focus remains in the present book. But much of the rest of the book represents a considerable departure from and expansion of my earlier research, offering more substantial coverage of a group of Christian intellectuals with connections to the city of Rome who wrote in Greek. I focus on this group as a way to probe the engagement of early Christians with the intellectual culture of the Roman Empire.

I approach this topic primarily as a historian of the Roman Empire and a scholar of the Greek literature that it produced. One of my major goals with this book is to encourage scholars of Greek imperial literature to spend more time with works of this period authored by Christians. I have therefore focused my attention on a group of early Christian authors who should be of interest to scholars who might otherwise have no desire to read early Christian literature. I recognize that the book will have a larger readership among students and scholars of early Christianity, but I have tried to explore questions that will also engage other audiences.

I have also tried to make the book's arguments accessible for readers with little to no knowledge of Greek or Latin. All passages quoted from ancient literature include a translation, most often my own. But I have also included the original Greek or Latin texts for readers with knowledge of those languages. In some instances, for the benefit of readers who have little to no knowledge of Greek, I include transliterated forms of Greek words (e.g., *eugeneia, poikilia*) that I deem especially significant for the book's arguments. This sometimes has led to the presence of transliterated and untransliterated Greek in the same sentences, but this seeming inconsistency was unavoidable.

I am grateful to a long list of people who supported or guided me during the writing of this book. First, I owe a large debt to the University of Michigan's Interdepartmental Program in Greek & Roman History. Sara Ahbel-Rappe and Ellen Muehlberger were both generous in sharing their

PREFACE AND ACKNOWLEDGMENTS

respective expertise in ancient philosophy and Christianity. David Potter encouraged me to read widely across different genres of ancient literature and provided me with my first introductions to several of the authors I discuss in this book. Ray Van Dam pushed me at a preliminary stage in my research to think about early Christian authors as intellectuals in the Roman Empire, and not just as Christians.

Many friends and colleagues read and commented on one or more chapters of the book: Matt Crawford, Allan Georgia, Lawrence Hatter, Jesse Spohnholz, Charles Weller, and Sean Wempe. I owe special thanks to Matt Unangst for reading multiple drafts of every chapter. Kendra Eshleman served, twice, as the respondent to papers that became part of chapters in this book. The standard disclaimer applies: any mistakes in facts and errors in judgment are my own and cast no shade on those who read the manuscript. The same comment applies for the two anonymous readers for the press, who provided much helpful feedback, and the editors of the series, David Eastman and Stephanie Cobb.

I also want to thank friends who offered advice, assistance, or support, sometimes by sharing advance copies of forthcoming publications: Nate Andrade, Rob Chenault, James Corke-Webster, Matthijs den Dulk, David DeVore, Jackie Feke, Jenn Finn, Theresa Jordan, Adam Kemezis, Dawn LaValle Norman, Katherine Lu Hsu, Heidi Marx, Krissy Nasse, Ray Sun, Kristi Upson-Saia, and John Vanderspoel. Work on this book could not have proceeded without help from library staff at the University of Michigan, the University of Chicago, Washington State University, and now the University of Calgary. Apologies go to all whose names I have forgotten or neglected to mention.

Finally, I need to acknowledge the immense amount of love and support that Carolyn Gersh has provided. She knows just as well as I do how much work on this book has shaped our lives for the past decade, leading us first from Ann Arbor to Chicago, then to Pullman, and now to Calgary. I am happy to say that the coming decades should be more stable for both of us. I am also grateful to my immediate family, and to Carolyn's, for supporting me in pursuit of an academic career in the humanities at a time when the prospects for such a career began to seem increasingly remote.

Portions of chapter 4 appeared earlier as "Julius Africanus, Origen, and the Politics of Intellectual Life Under the Severans," *Classical World* 110, no. 2 (2017): 211–35, copyright © 2017 The Classical Association of the Atlantic States.

Calgary

ABBREVIATIONS

Titles of journals and series that appear only once or twice in the bibliography are given there in unabbreviated form. For works of ancient authors that appear more than once or twice in the notes, I use the abbreviations of the *Oxford Classical Dictionary*, edited by Simon Hornblower, Antony Spawforth, and Esther Eidinow, 4th ed. (Oxford: Oxford University Press, 2012), supplemented by *The SBL Handbook of Style*, 2nd ed. (Atlanta: SBL Press, 2014), occasionally with slight modification. For works by Galen cited frequently, I use Hankinson's (2008a) abbreviations. References to *Brill's New Jacoby* in the notes include parenthetical identification of the author(s) responsible for that entry in the first citation of it.

Journals, Series, Collections

AJP	*American Journal of Philology*
ANRW	*Aufstieg und Niedergang der römischen Welt: Geschichte und Kultur Roms im Spiegel der neueren Forschung*. Pt. 2, *Principat*. Edited by Hildegard Temporini and Wolfgang Haase. Berlin: de Gruyter, 1972–.
BICS	*Bulletin of the Institute of Classical Studies*
BNJ	*Brill's New Jacoby*. Edited by Ian Worthington.
CCAG	Francisco Boll et al. *Catalogus Codicum Astrologorum Graecorum*. 12 vols. Brussels: H. Lamertin, 1898–1953.
CMG	Corpus Medicorum Graecorum
CMG Suppl. Or.	CMG Supplementum Orientale
CP	*Classical Philology*
CQ	*Classical Quarterly*
CW	*Classical World*
FGH	*Die Fragmente der griechischen Historiker*. Edited by Felix Jacoby. Leiden: Brill, 1954–64.
GCRW	Greek Culture in the Roman World
GCS	Die griechischen christlichen Schriftsteller der ersten Jahrhunderte
GRBS	*Greek, Roman, and Byzantine Studies*
HTR	*Harvard Theological Review*
JECS	*Journal of Early Christian Studies*
JRS	*Journal of Roman Studies*
JTS	*Journal of Theological Studies*

OECT . . . . Oxford Early Christian Texts
P.Oxy. . . . . *The Oxyrhynchus Papyri.* Edited by B. P. Grenfell and
A. S. Hunt. London: Egypt Exploration Fund, 1898–.
REG . . . . *Revue des études grecques*
SC . . . . Sources chrétiennes
SHA . . . . Scriptor Historiae Augustae
SP . . . . *Studia Patristica*
SVF. . . . . H. von Arnim. *Stoicorum veterum fragmenta.* Leipzig:
Teubner, 1903–24.
VCSup . . . . Supplements to *Vigiliae Christianae*
WUNT . . . . Wissenschaftliche Untersuchungen zum Neuen
Testament
ZAC. . . . . *Zeitschrift für Antikes Christentum*
ZPE. . . . . *Zeitschrift für Papyrologie und Epigraphik*

Frequently Cited Ancient Authors and Works

Aristides, *Or.* . . . . Aristides, *Orationes* (*Orations*)
Aulus Gellius, *NA* . . . . . Aulus Gellius, *Noctes atticae* (*Attic Nights*)
Clement, *Ecl.* . . . . Clement, *Eclogae Propheticae* (*Selections from the Prophets*)
Clement, *Paed.* . . . . . . Clement, *Paedagogus* (*The Teacher*)
Clement, *Protr.* . . . . Clement, *Protrepticus* (*Exhortation to the Greeks*)
Clement, *Strom.* . . . . . . Clement, *Stromateis* (*Miscellanies*)
Dig. . . . . *Digesta* (*Digest of Justinian*)
Dio Chrysostom, *Or.* . . . . Dio Chrysostom, *Orationes* (*Orations*)
Dionysius, *Ant. or.* . . . . . Dionysius, *De antiquis oratoribus* (*On the Ancient Orators*)
Dionysius, *Ant. Rom.* . . . . Dionysius, *Antiquitates Romanae* (*Roman Antiquities*)
Dionysius, *Comp.* . . . . . . Dionysius, *De compositione verborum* (*On Literary Composition*)
Dionysius, *Pomp.* . . . . . Dionysius, *Epistula ad Pompeium* (*Letter to Gnaeus Pompeius*)
Eusebius, *Hist. eccl.* . . . . Eusebius, *Historia ecclesiastica* (*Ecclesiastical History*)
Eusebius, *Praep. ev.* . . . . Eusebius, *Praeparatio evangelica* (*Preparation for the Gospel*)
Galen, *AA* . . . . Galen, *De anatomicis administrationibus* (*On Anatomical Procedures*)
Galen, *Hipp. Epid.* . . . . . Galen, *In Hippocratis epidemiarum libri, I–VI* (*On Hippocrates's Epidemics*)
Galen, *Loc. Aff.* . . . . . . Galen, *De locis affectis* (*On the Affected Parts*)
Galen, *MM* . . . . Galen, *De methodo medendi* (*On the Method of Medicine*)
Galen, *Pecc. Dig.* . . . . . . Galen, *De animi cuiuslibet peccatorum dignotione et curatione* (*On the Diagnosis and Cure of the Errors of the Soul*)
Galen, *Praen.* . . . . Galen, *De praenotione ad Epigenem* (*On Prognosis*)
Gregory Thaumaturgus, *In Origenem oratio panegyrica* (*Oration and Panegyric to
Orat. paneg.* Origen*)
Irenaeus, *Adv. haer.* . . . . Irenaeus, *Adversus haereses* (*Against the Heresies*)
Josephus, *AJ.* . . . . Josephus, *Antiquitates judaicae* (*Jewish Antiquities*)
Josephus, *Ap.* . . . . Josephus, *Contra Apionem* (*Against Apion*)

Josephus, *BJ*. . . . . . . Josephus, *Bellum judaicum* (*Jewish War*)

Justin, *1 Apol.* . . . . Justin, *Apologia i* (*First Apology*)

Justin, *2 Apol.* . . . . Justin, *Apologia ii* (*Second Apology*)

Justin, *Dial.* . . . . Justin, *Dialogus cum Tryphone* (*Dialogue with Trypho*)

Lucian, *De mort. Peregr.* . . . Lucian, *De morte Peregrini* (*On the Death of Peregrinus*)

Marcus Aurelius, *Med.* . . . Marcus Aurelius, *Meditationes* (*Meditations*)

Philo, *Leg.* . . . . Philo, *Legatio ad Gaium* (*Embassy to Gaius*)

Philostratus, *VA* . . . . . . Philostratus, *Vita Apollonii* (*Apollonius of Tyana*)

Philostratus, *VS* . . . . . . Philostratus, *Vitae sophistarum* (*Lives of the Sophists*)

Photius, *Bibl.* . . . . Photius, *Bibliotheca* (*Library*)

Phrynichus, *Ecl.* . . . . . . Phrynichus, *Eclogae* (*Selections*)

Pliny, *Ep.*. . . . . Pliny, *Epistulae* (*Letters*)

Pliny [the Elder], *HN*. . . Pliny [the Elder], *Naturalis historia* (*Natural History*)

Plutarch, *De gen.* . . . . . Plutarch, *De genio Socratis* (*On the Sign of Socrates*)

Pollux, *Onom.* . . . . Pollux, *Onomasticon* (*Vocabulary*)

Porphyry, *Plot.* . . . . Porphyry, *Vita Plotini* (*Life of Plotinus*)

Ptolemy, *Tetr.*. . . . . Ptolemy, *Tetrabiblos* (*The Quadripartite Mathematical
        Treatise*)

Quintilian, *Inst.* . . . . . . Quintilian, *Institutio oratoria* (*The Orator's Education*)

Rufinus, *Adult. libr. Orig.* . Rufinus, *De adulteratione librorum Origenis* (*On the Falsifi-
        cation of the Books of Origen*)

Sextus Empiricus, *Math.* . Sextus Empiricus, *Adversus mathematicos* (*Against the
        Mathematicians*)

Suetonius, *Aug.* . . . . . . Suetonius, *Divus Augustus* (*The Divine Augustus*)

Syncellus, *Ecl. chron.* . . . Georgius Syncellus, *Ecloga chronographica*
        (*Chronography*)

Tacitus, *Agr.* . . . . Tacitus, *Agricola* (*Agricola*)

Tacitus, *Ann.* . . . . Tacitus, *Annales* (*Annals*)

Tacitus, *Hist.*. . . . . Tacitus, *Historiae* (*Histories*)

Tatian, *Ad Gr.*. . . . . Tatian, *Oratio ad Graecos* (*Against the Greeks*)

INTRODUCTION

According to Eusebius of Caesarea, the reign of the emperor Commodus (180–92 CE) marked a change in fortunes for Christians, whose ranks grew in this period to include some of the wealthiest and most powerful people in the Roman Empire: "The word of salvation was leading every soul from every race of humanity to the pious worship of the God of the universe, so that now many of the people in Rome conspicuous for wealth and breeding turned to their salvation with all their households and families."[1] In Eusebius's narrative, one sign of the newfound interest in Christianity among the empire's elite classes came from the trial of a Christian named Apollonius during Commodus's reign. This Apollonius, Eusebius says, was "celebrated for his culture and philosophy" (παιδείᾳ καὶ φιλοσοφίᾳ βεβοημένον) and offered a "most learned" (λογιωτάτην) defense of Christianity in front of the praetorian prefect and senate in Rome.[2] Despite his learning, Apollonius was put to death.[3] But Apollonius's example, and the defense he provided of Christianity, helped demonstrate the growing prominence and learning of Christians toward the end of the second century. Wealth, breeding, and education went together, and people who possessed all three things were accustomed to speak in front of imperial authorities.

This book tells the story of how Christian intellectuals became more prominent and learned, and how they eventually came to be associated with imperial authorities in settings that did not end with their deaths by execution, as was the case for Apollonius. The story extends from the 150s to the 230s, by which point a small group of Christian intellectuals had succeeded in gaining close connections to the imperial household and in being taken seriously as intellectuals. This did not mean the end of persecution for Christians, which would come only with greater changes in the fourth century. But the breakthrough for Christianity in the third century was still an important transition. It meant that, for the first time, Christian intellectuals had joined the mainstream of the Roman Empire's elite intellectual culture.

Following the norms of scholarship in study of the early church, this breakthrough seems like it should have much to do with changing attitudes toward Christianity. The guiding assumption at work here is that Christianity was the key factor for how Christian intellectuals presented themselves and how they were perceived. Justification for this belief comes, in large part, from the narratives found in accounts of Christian martyrdom and persecution, including the likely spurious *Acta* of Apollonius's trial before the praetorian prefect, the senate, and an audience of intellectuals.[4] In this text, Apollonius is asked if he is a Christian, and he responds without hesitation, "Yes, I am a Christian" (Ναί, Χριστιανός εἰμι).[5] The trial and the text continue, but this is the decisive point and the moment at which Apollonius's fate was determined, in spite of the learned defense he offered of Christianity. The phrase "I am a Christian" appears in many other early texts relating to persecution, including some that are more likely to be authentic than the *Acta* of Apollonius.[6] Documents like these condition readers to believe that Christianity was the most important consideration when a Christian intellectual met with an imperial authority and interacted with non-Christians. Readers come away with the assumption that the only way for the outcome of such meetings to change was increased sympathy to Christianity on the part of imperial authorities.

My aim is to challenge this assumption. I do this by suggesting that Christianity was not always the defining factor in how Christian intellectuals were regarded by imperial authorities and other elite figures in the Roman Empire.[7] Christian intellectuals were also regarded as intellectuals and judged for the "culture and philosophy" that they displayed. In some contexts, they placed more emphasis on culture and philosophy than on Christianity in terms of how they presented themselves. In short, Christian intellectuals often behaved in ways that avoided, deemphasized, or complicated the simple claim of "I am a Christian." Rather than marking themselves off from others, they depicted themselves as full participants in the intellectual culture of the Roman Empire and were judged on this basis.

My argument to demonstrate this claim is based on an expansive view of Roman intellectual culture that resists the traditional tendency to keep different types of intellectuals segregated from each other. This tendency has increasingly been challenged in scholarship, which now is more eager to group together philosophers, physicians, and sophists, among others.[8] A key emphasis in this more expansive view is on "ways of knowing," an approach that identifies patterns throughout the Roman Empire in how self-proclaimed experts tried to demonstrate their expertise, regardless of their specialty.[9] This, in turn, provides the basis for my definition of intellectuals, by which I simply mean people who presented themselves as authority figures because of what they knew or claimed to know, especially if this knowledge was based on the possession of high-level literacy.[10] The definition I offer sets aside the requirement of past studies that intellectuals were defined by being "learned . . . according to ancient standards."[11] This definition speaks to the idea that intellectuals had to convince people that they had expertise, which was a fundamental concern for intellectuals. But the definition takes for granted the concept of ancient standards, as if there were unanimous agreement on this point within the Roman Empire.[12] I dwell on this point because some of the figures I term intellectuals may not have measured up to more restrictive ancient standards of learning and education, especially as they were applied by the wealthiest and best-educated figures in the Roman Empire. Some of the intellectuals who may have failed to measure up include Christians, but also figures with expertise in fields like astrology and dream interpretation who had ambivalent reputations, despite the obvious learning and technical skills of some practitioners.[13] This situation, in short, points to the variability in standards of learning and education in the Roman Empire. Not all intellectuals may have been successful in demonstrating to everyone that they possessed expert knowledge, but this does not disqualify them as intellectuals by my definition.

Christians fit into this competitive world, in spite of the long-standing tradition of their being exceptionalized or ignored in studies of Roman intellectual culture. Exceptionalism of this sort owes something to the force of the statement "I am a Christian," which implies that Christians were different from everyone else. But it also has been reinforced by tendencies within early Christian studies and classical scholarship, two overlapping fields that have nonetheless often operated in isolation from each other.[14] This is reflected in the myopic tendencies of much scholarship on the early church, which makes Christianity the exclusive focus, zooming in on it so closely that all other considerations fade into a distant background.[15] Isolation is also apparent in the general absence of Christian authors and literature from the works of classical scholars treating Greek imperial literature.[16] Attitudes are evolving within both fields, but it is still notable that early Christian authors have been basically excluded from the new series of volumes focusing on ways of knowing in the Roman Empire.[17] Scholars of early Christianity, at least, are now doing more to highlight commonalities between Christian and non-Christian intellectuals, particularly in recent studies that group Christians with other religious or ritual experts of the Roman Empire.[18] This approach comes close to my own, but I expand the category of experts further to link Christians with a wider intellectual culture.

Christian intellectuals offer many signs of their place within this culture. Some of these are so basic that they can easily be missed or ignored.

The city of Rome is one. It was all but an obligatory destination or a longer-term home for Christian intellectuals, including many of the most significant authors and intellectuals of the second and third centuries.[19] The same was true for non-Christian intellectuals, who had been regular visitors and inhabitants of Rome since the Hellenistic period.[20] Another basic factor linking Christian and non-Christian intellectuals was their preference to work and communicate in Greek, even when they were in Rome.[21] It was not coincidental that the primary language for Christian literature written in Rome continued to be Greek well into the third century, just as it was for some of the city's non-Christian intellectuals, including Aelian, a native of Italy who nonetheless wrote exclusively in Attic Greek.[22] One final significant feature of Roman intellectual culture was the prominent role the emperor and other imperial authorities played in it. When Christians addressed apologetic works to the emperor, they were following the same pattern as their non-Christian counterparts, who were equally interested in attracting imperial attention and favors.[23] In short, there was much linking the Christian and non-Christian intellectuals of Rome, even if disciplinary boundaries and traditions have predisposed scholars to keep them apart.

Among the Christians who came to Rome or addressed themselves to imperial authorities, I am interested in a select group of intellectuals whose careers mark out key developments in Christian engagement with Roman intellectual culture. These are Justin Martyr, Tatian, Julius Africanus, and Origen. In the 150s and 160s, Justin's works provide the earliest extant and detailed evidence of a Christian intellectual making himself known to his non-Christian counterparts and the imperial household.[24] His pupil Tatian, meanwhile, reveals the increasing complexity of Christian intellectual culture in the 170s and after, and the diverse ways in which Christian intellectuals responded to the norms of their non-Christian counterparts. Then, in the 220s and 230s, Julius Africanus and Origen were among the first Christian intellectuals to gain close connections to the imperial household and to enjoy a wider reputation in non-Christian intellectual culture. Other Christians will be part of the story, and this book could well have been expanded to include coverage of additional Christian intellectuals with connections to the city of Rome or who addressed themselves to the imperial household.[25] But the four figures of Justin, Tatian, Africanus, and Origen are key for offering a contextualized historical narrative. They can all be situated in particular places at particular dates, and substantial portions of their works survive. They may have been anticipated in some of what they did by earlier Christians, but the evidence for this suggestion can be derived only by inference from fragments and scattered hints in the works of other authors.[26] This sort of exercise would introduce much uncertainty to the discussions and arguments of this book, which is not designed to be an exhaustive treatment or catalogue of Christian intellectuals in Rome.[27] Instead, I work with what survives, and what can show with more certainty important steps in the development of Christian intellectual culture within the context of the Roman Empire.

The point of this approach is to emphasize similarities between Christian and non-Christian intellectuals and their common engagement with the same intellectual culture. This, it must be emphasized, is different from pointing out that both Christians and non-Christians had similar interests in philosophical thought.[28] It is likewise different from noting parallels between Christian and non-Christians genres of literature, such as the clear similarities between works of heresiology and doxography, both of which reported the doctrines of a succession of philosophers or teachers.[29] My aim, instead, is to show the interest of Christian intellectuals in the same issues and topics that were engaging their non-Christian counterparts. Both groups were participating in the same debates that characterized intellectual culture in the period, including those concerning the proper relationship of an intellectual with imperial authorities and the significance of Greek culture in the broader history of the world. The engagement of Christian intellectuals with these issues was part of their larger attempt to be taken seriously and to seek out favors and privileges from imperial authorities. Christian intellectuals were even engaging in a characteristic tendency of the period—namely, claiming that the learning they possessed was superior to that of their rivals who had different specialties.[30] All of this highlights the wide-ranging engagement of Christian intellectuals with the culture of their time, and the lack of clear boundaries between intellectuals of different specialties.

Christian engagement with intellectual culture extends beyond the Second Sophistic, a concept that has sometimes been emphasized in studies of Christian intellectuals of the second and third centuries.[31] The elusiveness of the Second Sophistic, however, limits its helpfulness as a means to approach and contextualize Christian intellectuals. In a strict sense, the Second Sophistic refers only to a small group of famous sophists identified by Philostratus in his *Lives of the Sophists* who were active from roughly the time of Nero (r. 54–68 CE) to the early third century.[32] But the concept of the Second Sophistic is often applied much more loosely to nearly any type of Greek literary production in the Roman Empire, and even to some Latin authors of the second and third centuries who seem especially sophistic.[33] The term does retain some value as a useful shorthand to describe characteristic aspects of elite Greek intellectual culture of the Roman Empire, including an emphasis on classicism and extemporaneous speech.[34] But the Second Sophistic offers little utility as an analytical or conceptual category when approaching Christian intellectuals. A broader focus on Christians alongside intellectuals of many different specialties is more productive than grappling with the murky concept of the Second Sophistic.[35]

What results from this approach is a new set of conversation partners for Christian intellectuals and a new appreciation of the challenges they faced fitting in with the competitive intellectual culture of the Roman Empire. In traditional scholarship on early Christian intellectuals, they tend to be associated almost exclusively with their coreligionists, particularly in studies that trace the development of a specific theme or topic of significance in a range of Christian authors over time.[36] This type of scholarship is insular, fostering the attitude that Christians were exceptional and kept to themselves. Even when Christian intellectuals are studied with reference to their non-Christian counterparts, much of the focus tends to be on the small collection of passages where a Greek or Roman author makes an explicit reference to Christianity.[37] These passages are of interest to me, but my method allows for an expanded pool of relevant evidence, dealing with authors and texts that rarely appear in scholarship on early Christianity. My method focuses on how emperors and other members of the empire's elite intellectual culture regarded other intellectuals who shared key features in common with Christians. I thereby show that Christians were regarded not simply as Christians but also as intellectuals. In the process, I reveal why they may have had their credentials and expertise challenged for reasons that had little or nothing to do with Christianity.

The book's argument proceeds in four chapters, first setting out the challenges facing Christian intellectuals in the second century and then showing how their successors in the third century were able to gain some degree of acceptance and legitimacy. Chapter 1 describes the general intellectual climate of the Roman Empire, and the emergence of an exclusive partnership between Greeks and Romans based on a shared fascination with the classical Greek past. Fascination with Greek culture and history led to the exclusion of other civilizations, and the marginalization of intellectuals linked with regions of the world that were associated with barbarians. The result was a competitive and homogeneous intellectual culture supported by the close relationships of elite Greeks and Romans. This context posed challenges for Jews, Christians, and any other intellectuals who might challenge the prevailing fixation on classical Greece.

Chapter 2 focuses on Justin Martyr, presenting him as a pioneering figure in the development of Christian intellectual culture and examining the attempts of subsequent Christian intellectuals to gain public reputations and imperial connections. His efforts to become known to the imperial household fit in with a normal trend for intellectuals who came to Rome. The emphasis he placed on persecution by imperial authorities was likewise not unique to Christianity, as conventional wisdom suggests. Rather, his claims that philosophers gained legitimacy by being persecuted by secular authorities formed part of a larger conversation in his time about the proper way for an intellectual to behave when faced with the emperor. Some of his contemporaries shared Justin's views on this point, but others were more impressed by intellectuals who managed to survive their encounters with imperial authorities. Justin mostly failed in his attempt to gain the sort of attention he seems to have wanted, but he also offered a model for later Christian intellectuals about how to present themselves.

Chapter 3 shifts attention to Justin's pupil Tatian, demonstrating the growing complexity of Christian intellectual culture in the later second century. It shows that Tatian built on the example of Justin in presenting himself as an intellectual. Tatian suggested that he was not simply a philosopher but also a man of culture, with encyclopedic knowledge of all the subjects that might interest intellectuals of his time. In the process, he claimed to reject the norms of Greek culture, while nonetheless demonstrating his mastery of it. This pose was key to Tatian's attempt to show that he possessed greater expertise and superior knowledge than his Greek contemporaries. It likewise provided part of the basis for why he was dismissed as a heretic by many later Christians, who were less aggressive in their rejection of Greek culture and little inclined to call themselves barbarians, as Tatian did. Tatian's career consequently shows the increasing extent of Christian engagement with Roman intellectual culture in the second century, and the internal controversies that resulted from it.

Chapter 4 then addresses Julius Africanus and Origen, and the breakthrough of Christian intellectuals in the third century. It challenges the idea that the successes gained by these intellectuals in gaining connections and respect were related to growing sympathy toward Christianity. Instead, the chapter shows that Africanus and Origen were better able than previous generations of Christian intellectuals to fit in with the competitive norms of Roman intellectual culture and to make themselves useful to members of the imperial household. The connections they gained to the emperor and his family were likewise a consequence of major changes for the empire that resulted from the transition of the Antonine to the Severan dynasty around the turn of the century. Civil wars and instability led the Severan emperors to open themselves up to a larger and different group of people than their Antonine predecessors had. The Severans' intellectual interests also reflected a larger shift toward more focus on the ancient history and culture of non-Greek civilizations, subjects where both Africanus and Origen could demonstrate real expertise. Africanus and Origen shared many of the same interests and tendencies as Justin and Tatian, but they were in a better position to take advantage of these, thanks to the changes that the empire experienced under the Severans.

This book challenges traditional narratives about the development of Christianity that pay little attention to the context of the Roman Empire, especially as it relates to intellectual culture.[38] Justin, Tatian, Julius Africanus, and Origen emerge as intellectuals who seem less exceptional than scholars have been accustomed to see them. Like other intellectuals in the empire, they were interested in building reputations for themselves and in capturing the attention of the imperial household. In the process, they became caught up in debates and controversies that were engaging the great majority of intellectuals in the Roman Empire and that were shaping how Christians thought of themselves and their relationship to the empire. If we seek to explain how Christian intellectuals behaved and how they ultimately gained more prominent positions in the Roman Empire, we need to start from the premise that they were little different from their non-Christian counterparts. The successes that they eventually experienced were predicated on these similarities and on larger transitions that the empire underwent in the early third century, rather than growing sympathy for Christianity.

In simple terms, we will gain a greater understanding of the careers and works of Christian intellectuals if we understand what it was like to be an intellectual in the Roman Empire. This is a fundamental point in the following chapters, and the reason why so much space is devoted to non-Christian intellectuals, particularly in chapter 1. The careers and experiences of non-Christian intellectuals in Rome provide a context that has largely been ignored for Justin Martyr and his successors in the Roman Empire, and a less insular way to approach the development of Christian intellectual culture.

CHAPTER 1

EMPERORS, INTELLECTUALS, AND THE
WORLD OF THE ROMAN EMPIRE

Toward the end of his reign, the emperor Claudius granted special privileges to the people of the island of Cos. We learn this from Tacitus, who
offers details about what the emperor said on the occasion regarding early
Coan history: "The most ancient inhabitants of the island were Argives,
or Coeus, the father of Latona. Then, with the arrival of Asclepius, the
art of healing was introduced, and this was extremely famous among his
descendants."[1] The report of Claudius's speech is interrupted here, as he
evidently offered a long list of Asclepius's descendants, generation by generation. Tacitus then resumes the speech, highlighting the praise Claudius
offered of C. Stertinius Xenophon, a native of Cos who served as his personal physician: "'Xenophon,' whose knowledge [Claudius] himself used,
'was sprung from this same family [sc. Asclepius's], and as a grant to his
requests, the Coans should be free of all tax in the future, and allowed to
inhabit the island as a sacred place dedicated only to the god.'"[2] Tacitus
suggests that Claudius might have been able to emphasize other services
that the people of Cos had provided to Rome. But the emperor instead
presented the grant of immunity as a favor to his physician. In the process,
he offered what amounted to an encomium of Cos, exploring at length the
distinguished people who first settled the island and the line of descent that
connected his physician Xenophon back to Asclepius, who was regarded
by Greeks as the founder of medicine.

Claudius's speech was a product of the Greek education that he had
received and of the emphasis placed by Greeks of his time on ancestry. The
key concept underlying his speech is *eugeneia*, a Greek virtue that can be
translated both as "nobility" and as "good birth," linking the word directly
with a person's or a people's ancestry.[3] Aristotle's definition of *eugeneia*
reveals this latter sense of the word: "Good birth, for a people or a city, is

being autochthonous or ancient, with distinguished first rulers, and many of those born from them famous for qualities that are admired."[4] Claudius, one of the more learned of the Roman emperors, was undoubtedly familiar with this concept and its significance for Greeks.[5] He had surely encountered it in his training as an orator, which must have involved a set of preliminary exercises in composition called *progymnasmata*.[6] Claudius's speech in praise of Cos and Xenophon precisely follows the advice found in extant works of *progymnasmata* about how to write an encomium. The earliest of these works, attributed to Aelius Theon (first century CE?), suggests that an encomiast should turn immediately to the subject of *eugeneia* after the speech's introduction.[7] And this is what Claudius's speech does, touching on the antiquity of the city's distinguished founders, before providing a detailed list of Xenophon's ancestors. The list Claudius offered likely came from information provided by Xenophon. Epigraphic evidence from Cos shows that members of Xenophon's family claimed Hippocrates, Asclepius, and Hercules among their ancestors.[8] One inscription even says that the dedicatee was thirty-five generations removed from Asclepius and fifty from Hercules.[9] Claudius's speech evidently offered a similar genealogy, showing his familiarity with the family's claims to *eugeneia*. Clearly, both Claudius and his physician were part of a culture and educational system that valued ancestry.

This emphasis on ancestry challenges suggestions about the inclusiveness of Greek intellectual culture in the Roman Empire. Claims about this point are tied up with the idea that culture, more than ethnicity, was the key factor in how Greeks of this period conceived of themselves.[10] A focus on culture implies that people could transcend their barbarian birth by receiving a Greek education and behaving like a Greek. Some support for this idea comes out in a comment by the physician Galen, who suggests in his treatise *On Hygiene* that he is writing not for "wild or barbarian people" (ἀγρίοις ἢ βαρβάροις ἀνθρώποις) but for "Greeks and those born as barbarians by race who emulate the customs of the Greeks."[11] Galen's comment seems to imply some openness to people who lacked Greek ancestry, provided that they tried to act like Greeks. But this remark cannot be read in isolation, as it often has been. Another passage from Galen's works reveals the significance he placed on ancestry and *eugeneia*. This concerns Galen's view on the superiority of medical education in the time of Asclepius, the same divine figure from whom Xenophon claimed descent. Of doctors in this early period, Galen says, "It was superfluous for them to write works for themselves or others, because they practiced dissections from childhood with their fathers by their sides."[12] Over time, however, "the art became known outside the family of the Asclepiadae and became ever worse with each succeeding generation."[13] Galen's perspective here matches the emphasis placed on ancestry by Claudius and Xenophon. All three suggested that there was inherent value in a family tradition of education and scholarship—in this case the practice of medicine. Barbarians might learn to act like Greeks, but they might still be marked out as different in a culture that placed so much value on *eugeneia*.

Eugeneia and the exclusive attitudes that accompanied it were key features in the relationship between Greek intellectuals and powerful Romans, including the emperor and his household. This is not something that has received much attention, perhaps in part because of how obviously fictional claims about ancestry could be, including the suggestion in an inscription of the first century BCE that two Greek cities were linked by their shared descent from the centaur Chiron.[14] From this sort of example, scholars have come away with the idea that ancient intellectuals were simply playing lip service to the idea of *eugeneia* and that they were using the word more in the sense of "nobility" than "good birth."[15] What ancient intellectuals really thought about *eugeneia* is unknown to us, but we can still discern in our ancient sources a major emphasis on the importance of ancestry.[16] This comes out especially in the efforts of intellectuals to link themselves to Greek cities that possessed *eugeneia*. What this all implies is that some intellectuals acted as if the possession of *eugeneia* would be helpful for their careers, as Claudius's speech regarding Xenophon suggests. It likewise suggests that intellectuals who rejected this emphasis on Greek ancestry might struggle to receive recognition from their peers and from Romans like Claudius, who had been educated to praise people for their good birth. There were some exceptions to this pattern, such as when Claudius criticized the exclusive citizenship policies of Athens and Sparta whereby conquered peoples continued to be regarded as "foreign" (*alienigenis*), rather than being accepted as citizens and even as senators, in keeping with his own policies toward some groups of Gauls.[17] Even Aelius Theon, who emphasized the importance of mentioning *eugeneia* immediately in a speech, offered advice about how to praise someone who lacked "good birth."[18] In short, different contexts might lend themselves to different attitudes about how open Greeks and Romans should be toward people who might be described as barbarians. But an emphasis on *eugeneia* nonetheless emerges as a significant factor within Roman intellectual culture, and especially in debates between rival intellectuals. The possession of good birth helped dictate which intellectuals were able to gain connections—and the privileges that accompanied them—with powerful Romans.

The significance placed on good birth by Greeks and Romans alike led to some basic strategies for intellectuals seeking to attract attention to themselves. These strategies revolved around trying to claim some special access to the Greek past, as the physician Xenophon and his family did. The first section that follows explores how this emphasis on the past led some intellectuals to disown their places of birth and claim instead to be from Greek cities that had ancient and autochthonous founders. This fascination with the past, in turn, led to the development of exclusive family traditions of scholarship, shaped by hereditary bonds and links to the Greek past. The second section considers how a fixation on the Greek past was shaped by the belief that Greek culture had been corrupted in more recent periods by the negative influence of barbarians. Amid these narratives of barbarization, Greek intellectuals claimed that they were trying to restore the purity of the Greek past, often with the help of Romans. As the third section shows, this fixation on the Greek past led to Hellenocentric views of the history of the world. Both Greeks and Romans displayed only a limited interest in the history of other regions of the world, and they were often skeptical of claims that made barbarian civilizations older than Greece. The final section of the chapter shows how this attitude limited opportunities for intellectuals who identified with other cultures and regions of the world. Though they came from places that had their own ancient histories and traditions of literature, their credentials and legitimacy were questioned, and they struggled to gain close connections to the Roman elite. Intellectuals who lacked obvious ways of linking themselves to the Greek past found themselves disadvantaged by this insular view of world history.

Consequently, an exclusive Greco-Roman partnership and intellectual culture emerged in the Roman Empire. This culture was largely homogeneous, especially in terms of how intellectuals sought to gain attention and patronage from powerful Romans. Claiming special access to the Greek past was a basic strategy for intellectuals seeking to attract attention. Such claims were a challenge for intellectuals who lacked plausible connections to the Greek past, especially if they wished to say that they were anything but Greeks themselves. These claims, challenges, and conflicts were basic components of Roman intellectual culture from the late republic well into the second century and beyond.

Genealogies of Power

A fascination with the past characterized the intellectual culture of the Roman Empire.[19] This was, in part, a legacy of the Hellenistic period, manifested in the efforts of Alexandrian intellectuals to collect and edit Greek texts that had already gained the status of classics.[20] Greek intellectuals brought these same interests with them when they came to Rome in increasingly large numbers during the first century BCE.[21] Intellectuals in this period were largely concerned with linking themselves to the past, particularly by means of a succession narrative, tracing their own connections to Greek antiquity back generation by generation to demonstrate their possession of *eugeneia*. Good birth consequently became a major feature associated with intellectual success. Some controversy did surround claims of good birth, but even the intellectuals who disdained the obviously false claims of their peers show that they were implicated in the system.[22] Intellectuals who could make plausible claims about their links to the past were often rewarded by members of the Roman elite. This recognition was part of a larger system whereby Greeks of distinguished standing in the eastern regions of the Mediterranean represented themselves and their communities, seeking and receiving privileges and rewards for both from Rome. Genealogical claims provided the foundation for an elitist and exclusivist intellectual culture, developed through the partnership of Greeks and Romans with similar interests in the past.

Some of the different strategies used to claim ownership of the Greek past come through in a short piece of evidence that highlights the competition among Greek intellectuals to earn a place close to the Roman imperial family. This evidence is found in an entry in the *Suda*, the tenth-century Byzantine encyclopedia, concerning Theodorus, one of the more famous orators of the first century BCE: "Theodorus, from Gadara, a sophist of servile birth [who] became the teacher of Tiberius. Since he was examined while competing in sophistry with Potamon and Antipater in Rome itself, his son Antonius became a senator under Caesar Hadrian."[23] The passage makes this point only implicitly, but the sophistic competition was evidently meant to decide which of the three orators would become the teacher of Tiberius. When exactly this happened is unclear, but a date around 30 BCE recommends itself, when Tiberius was still quite a young man and in need of a teacher of rhetoric.[24] The passage does contain one chronologically impossible suggestion—namely, that Theodorus had a son who became a senator during the reign of Hadrian.[25] Apart from this detail, though, the passage's suggestion of a competition in Rome between three orators is entirely plausible, despite there being no mention of it in other sources.[26] Such a competition, evidently organized by Tiberius's adoptive father, Augustus, fits the attested habit of this emperor in bringing together rival intellectuals to debate.[27] The Elder Seneca offers one illustration of this in his reference to the combative orator Craton, who "often used to clash in front of the emperor with Timagenes, a man of acid tongue who was also excessively free with it."[28] Augustus seems to have derived some entertainment from watching outspoken intellectuals argue with one another. This reference in Seneca provides a context for the debate between Theodorus, Potamon, and Antipater, and their efforts to earn a place close to the imperial family.

The three orators involved in the contest used genealogy in a variety of ways to present themselves and claim *eugeneia*. Theodorus, the winner of the contest, reveals the pressures intellectuals faced to link themselves to a major center of Greek culture, regardless of where they were born. Theodorus was from Gadara, a city in Syria that had produced several distinguished intellectuals in the period before his lifetime.[29] After leaving Gadara, however, Theodorus found reason to deemphasize his connections to the city and to Syria. He became best known as a resident of Rhodes, where he established a school of oratory.[30] Theodorus evidently came to associate himself with the island of Rhodes more than with his native Gadara. Quintilian says in simple terms that Theodorus "preferred to be called a Rhodian," which likely means that he became a citizen there.[31] This choice was based on some fundamental contrasts between his place of birth and his adoptive home. Syria and Gadara both lacked associations with the ancient Greek past and were regions that seemed foreign to Greeks, linked with corruption and excess.[32] By contrast, Rhodes was a place that possessed a reputation for *eugeneia*, including claims about the autoch-thonous origins of its ancient founders, just as Aristotle's definition of the word stipulated.[33] The island was likewise a major center for philosophical activity and the teaching of rhetoric in the Hellenistic period.[34] In the late fourth century, Rhodes became the new home of the famous Athenian orator Aeschines, who may have had some hand in the development of a Rhodian school of rhetoric that attracted powerful Romans as students.[35] Theodorus became a successor to this school in Rhodes, attracting a large crowd of pupils.[36] Though he did write a work of uncertain contents called *On Hollow Syria*, he presented himself as a Rhodian first.[37] This simply made sense in a competitive culture that placed much emphasis on a person's origins and ancestry.

Theodorus's choice to deemphasize his connections to Syria was likely a source of tension when he interacted with his rival Antipater in the sophistic contest. The identity of this Antipater is uncertain, but there is a strong possibility that he was also from Syria and more eager than Theodorus to acknowledge this. This supposition is based on his proba-ble identification with Antipater the father of the historian and polymath Nicolaus of Damascus, who enjoyed a distinguished career of his own, including connections with Augustus and other powerful Romans.[38] From Nicolaus, we learn that Antipater was "superior in his eloquence" (λόγου δεινότητι προὔχων) and that he had become "wealthy and famous" because of his education.[39] Antipater also went on "many embassies" (πλείστας . . . πρεσβείας) for his native Damascus, besides serving his city in several other capacities.[40] Nicolaus's report concerning his father's life is encomiastic in character, but the basic profile it offers of Antipater still makes much sense, especially considering how well it matches what is known of his son. Antipater therefore emerges as a good candidate to have participated in the sophistic contest. His service on behalf of Damascus also suggests that he was more eager than Theodorus to identity himself with Syria. There was real potential for disagreement between these two men, something that may be reflected in Dio Chrysostom's choice to group Antipater and Theodorus together in a list of famous orators close to his time.[41] They may have been rivals who would have offered much entertainment to the contest's audience.

Confirmation of the possible issues between Theodorus and other Syrians comes through in a key fragment from Nicolaus that critiques people who denied their places of birth. This passage helps provide a context for Theodorus, even if the Antipater involved in the contest was not the father of Nicolaus. The brief passage comes from Nicolaus's auto-biography, which was written in the third person: "He never thought it necessary to call himself the citizen of a city other than his own, and he laughed at the sophists of his time who paid great sums to be called Athenians or Rhodians, ashamed by the obscurity of their ancestral homes (πατρίδων). Some of them even wrote works to explain that they were not from their cities of birth, but rather from a notable Greek city. These men he declared were like those who are ashamed of their own parents."[42] Theodorus, is almost certainly included among the "sophists" who wished to claim that they were from Rhodes.[43] Nicolaus likely also was alluding to the philosopher Posidonius, a native of Apamea in Syria who later became a citizen and office holder in Rhodes.[44] Fragments of Posidonius's history offer a negative view of Syria, attacking the degeneracy of its inhabitants and suggesting that he had no interest in linking himself with his place of birth.[45] No evidence survives to suggest that either Theodorus or Posidonius "paid great sums" to gain status and citizenship in Athens or Rhodes, much less wrote works disowning their places of birth. But their examples lend credence to Nicolaus's suggestion about intellectuals in his time labeling themselves as Athenians or Rhodians, regardless of their actual places of birth.

Apart from Theodorus and Posidonius, Nicolaus was targeting a larger phenomenon of the late Hellenistic period, when many intellectuals were faced with a choice of self-identifying with an adopted home rather than their place of birth. This dilemma was especially common among the many philosophers who took up residence in Athens and were often faced with the question of whether to accept citizenship in the city.[46] The issue extended back before Nicolaus's time into the early Hellenistic period. Plutarch mentions the phenomenon, citing an earlier discussion of it by the Stoic Antipater of Tarsus, who was referring to the choices faced by the first three heads of the Stoic school in Athens: "Antipater in his *On the Difference Between Cleanthes and Chrysippus* has reported that Zeno and Cleanthes did not wish to become Athenians lest they seem to do wrong to their ancestral homes (πατρίδας). But if they did well in this, Chrysippus was wrong to be enrolled in the body of citizens."[47] Plutarch's subsequent conclusion on the issue suggests that Chrysippus was right to link himself with Athens, challenging the opinions of Zeno, Cleanthes, and Nicolaus.[48] This disagreement speaks to the continuing resonance of this issue into the imperial period, when intellectuals who moved away from home were still faced with the dilemma of how to identify themselves.

This issue was also a factor for the third participant in the contest, Potamon, who emphasized his links to the early history of his place of birth, the city of Mytilene. Potamon's overall profile was similar in this respect to what Nicolaus reports about Antipater. Like Antipater, Potamon served on embassies for his home city, including multiple encounters with Julius Caesar during the early 40s BCE.[49] He was one of several intellectuals from Mytilene who served the city and helped it gain privileges from Rome, though it had initially supported the losing side in the civil war between Pompey and Caesar.[50] For his services, Potamon was honored by his city with a monument that included a collection of inscriptions listing his accomplishments.[51] One of these inscriptions reveals how closely Potamon identified himself with Mytilene. It identifies him as the "descendant of Penthilus" (τὸν ἀπύγονον Πενθίλω), who was the son of Orestes, and someone credited as the first Greek to settle the region of Aeolis and the neighboring islands, including Lesbos, where Mytilene was located.[52] With this claim, Potamon was consequently linked to the founders of his city, and through them to heroes of Greece's mythical past. Mytilene's ancient past as a Greek city was evidently something that Potamon could emphasize in presenting himself. Unlike Theodorus, he felt no need to hide or disown where he was from. Potamon therefore demonstrates similar concerns with genealogy apparent from the examples of Theodorus, Antipater, and Nicolaus.

These intellectuals likewise demonstrate the significance of genealogical claims for their descendants, whether these happened to be family members or students. Theodorus illustrates both points. He became the

founder of a new school of oratory, with its followers identifying themselves with him. This school of Theodorus's followers had a rivalry with
a school associated with his contemporary Apollodorus of Pergamum,
who had himself been the teacher of the young Octavian.[53] As Quintilian explains, the pupils of these two men were called "Apollodoreans
and Theodoreans, following the fashion of certain philosophical sects."[54]
Orators of this period could be asked if they were either an "Apollodor-
ean or a Theodorean," as if there were no other possibilities.[55] Even the
emperor Tiberius could be called a Theodorean, signaling his continuing
links with Theodorus following the contest.[56] This philhellenic emperor
evidently became part of the competitive world of Greek intellectuals and
their emphasis on successions.[57] Theodorus's descendants likewise became
powerful members of the Roman world themselves, if we can put any trust
in the *Suda*'s confused suggestion that his son Antonius "became a senator
under Caesar Hadrian."[58] This Antonius may have been a grandson or
great-grandson, or the emperor involved may have been one of Hadrian's
predecessors. The name Antonius even hints that Theodorus may have
been linked at some point to Augustus's rival Marcus Antonius.[59] Theodorus consequently stands as the forebear, at least, of a group of students
who presented themselves as his successors, and perhaps also of a descendant who became a senator.

More definite signs of the significance of genealogy come from evidence relating to the descendants of Antipater via his likely son Nicolaus.
This evidence points to the status and fame that Nicolaus achieved, something that his family kept alive in Damascus some six centuries later. We
learn of this in a work by the Christian sophist and monk Sophronius of
Damascus, who was patriarch of Jerusalem from 634 to 638.[60] He identifies
Nicolaus as the ancestor of a man of his time: "Dionysius was one of the
famous magistrates in Damascus, having been born to a family that was
always illustrious. Its origin and root was Nicolaus the philosopher, who
was the instructor of Herod and the teacher of the children of Antony
and Cleopatra. From him bloomed twelve Nicolauses in succession, who,
priding themselves in philosophy, illuminated the family and brought it
into great fame and glory."[61] There is no mention here of Nicolaus's father,
whose fame was eclipsed by that of his son, as judged by the fact that
the name Nicolaus continued to be passed down for many generations.
As Sophronius reports, these later men named Nicolaus were all philosophers, continuing the tradition of their ancestor. One of them may even
be responsible for a work called *On the Philosophy of Aristotle* that has traditionally been attributed to the first Nicolaus.[62] Nicolaus's later descendants
followed his example of combining learning and service for the city of

Damascus, as Dionysius's status as a magistrate attests. This sort of family tradition seems to have been a relatively common occurrence for philosophers, if not for thirteen generations. One good example on a smaller scale is the philosopher Alexander of Aphrodisias, who shared a name, T. Aurelius Alexander, and profession with his father.[63] Like Nicolaus and his descendants, they combined the succession of teacher and pupil with that of father and son.

Potamon is another example, with a similar pattern and more details that confirm the legacy that he left for his descendants. Though he was not the victor in the sophistic contest, Potamon still maintained close connections with the imperial household, traveling to Spain in the mid-20s BCE to gain an audience with Augustus.[64] His entry in the *Suda* likewise suggests a connection with Tiberius, by then the emperor, who provided Potamon with a letter of protection for a journey home to Mytilene: "If someone should dare to harm Potamon, son of Lesbonax, let him consider if he should be able to go to war with me."[65] Potamon's significance to the imperial household is apparent in the position he held as priest for life in the new cults of Roma and Augustus established in the province of Asia in 29 BCE.[66] Potamon is identified explicitly as such in one of the inscriptions that appears on the monument set up for him in Mytilene.[67] Another inscription demonstrates that his son, G. Claudius Diaphenes, held the same title, gaining it as a hereditary position from Potamon.[68] Other evidence, both textual and epigraphical, identifies male and female members in Potamon's family, demonstrating continuity with their ancestor in terms of both learning and cult positions.[69] The latest piece of evidence relating to this family comes from the late second or early third century CE in the form of an inscription commemorating the priestess Aurelia Artemisia that identifies Potamon as her ancestor (ἀπύγονον).[70] This may not match the family tradition of Nicolaus, but it still demonstrates the impact that a famous ancestor could have on the lives of his descendants.

The sophistic contest between Antipater, Potamon, and Theodorus provides a sign of the emerging links between Greek intellectuals with claims to *eugeneia* and powerful Romans. The three speakers involved were part of a culture that placed great value on where people were from and who their ancestors were. This encouraged people to emphasize or invent connections to important centers of Greek culture and to heroes of the ancient Greek past. Though these connections were sometimes dismissed as fictional, they still played a role in how intellectuals built reputations for themselves and attracted the attention of powerful Romans. In turn, intellectuals like Antipater, Potamon, and Theodorus became part of a cycle whereby the same emphasis on *eugeneia* was passed along to their

Roman pupils, encouraging them to value people who claimed to have ancient and autochthonous ancestors. This cycle provided a strong foundation for a partnership between elite Romans and a select group of Greek intellectuals.

Barbarization, Purity, and Classicism

The partnership between these Romans and Greeks received additional support from Rome's growing role in Greek intellectual culture, particularly during the first century BCE, when a new fascination developed with the oratory of Athens in the fifth and fourth centuries, labeled Attic after the dialect of Greek used by Athenians. Much scholarly interest has been devoted to figuring out the origins of this movement and whether it began with Greeks or Romans.[71] Debates on this point are based on the long-standing tendency of Hellenists and Roman historians to claim authors of Greek imperial literature as their own.[72] However, such attempts to segregate Greeks from Romans in the development of this Attic movement are unproductive. Arguments of this sort gloss over the extent to which there was a partnership between Greeks and Romans, who were linked by their shared fascination with the classical Greek past and its literature, and by the type of teaching relationships described in the previous section. More to the point, though, the debate about the Greek or Roman origins of Atticism pays insufficient attention to the presence of a third group, barbarians. The threat of barbarians, real or imagined, was a key factor in the development of fascination with classical Athenian literature. Greeks and Romans were united in believing that Greece and Greek culture had been corrupted by the influence of barbarians, causing Greeks to fall away from the high standards of Athens's classical period, and of their ancient and autochthonous ancestors. They likewise shared the goal of restoring Greece to the lost purity of its classical period and overcoming the barbarization that Greece, together with its language and literature, had undergone in the previous three centuries. In the first century BCE, Greeks and Romans imagined a future that was based on Greece restored to its classical past, with Romans as its leaders, who proved to be much more Greek in their ancestry than had previously been believed.

The key figure tying together all of the threads for this partnership of Greeks and Romans is Dionysius of Halicarnassus, whose career in Rome highlights the growing interconnections between the two peoples. Dionysius was a resident of the city from 30 BCE, soon after Augustus's victory at Actium, until at least 7 BCE.[73] He was busy with many activities during this time, as both a teacher and a writer. Dionysius evidently conducted daily exercises with pupils, including the dedicatee of one of his works, a certain Rufus Metilius.[74] But Dionysius also spent much time working through the many speeches attributed to a group of Athenian orators active in the fifth and fourth centuries, identifying works that he believed to be spurious. In the case of one of these orators, Lysias, Dionysius had to review 425 speeches, only 233 of which he believed to be genuine, based on a rigorous series of stylistic and historical tests that he applied to each oration.[75] This close engagement with Greek literature resulted in a series of literary critical essays. Dionysius also found time to write a twenty-book treatment of the history of Rome from the city's foundation down to the time of the First Punic War (264 BCE), called *Roman Antiquities*. Though his history may seem to be a separate project from his literary-critical activities, there are major links between them. In *Roman Antiquities*, Dionysius explored the connections of Rome to ancient Greek history, investigating who exactly Rome's founders were. He likewise framed his literary-critical essays with an introductory piece that emphasized the impact of Rome on recent developments in the study of Greek oratory. Dionysius's works therefore demonstrate the close connections of the Greek and Roman worlds.

The same is true of Dionysius's life, and that of his descendants, following a pattern familiar from the intellectuals discussed in the previous section. Details of Dionysius's life are sparse, but we learn from his entry in the *Suda* that he was "the ancestor of the Atticist who lived under Hadrian."[76] This refers to the grammarian Aelius Dionysius, the author of an Attic lexicon, fragments of which survive in later works of lexicography.[77] Aelius Dionysius's name contains a significant clue regarding the life of his ancestor. Dionysius's patron in Rome was named Q. Aelius Tubero, which implies that he or one of his descendants gained citizenship from one of the Aelii.[78] Dionysius evidently represented the start of another family tradition of scholarship and privilege, built by the close connections he enjoyed with elite Romans.

The idea of purity was a basic feature of Dionysius's scholarship on both Greece and Rome, and his close engagement with the works of classical Athenian orators reflects this. Identifying spurious and genuine works of the orators would produce a pure corpus of texts that Dionysius and his pupils could imitate in their study of classical Athenian literature. Dionysius reveals his interest in purity explicitly in a comment about the study of literature in which he claims that the "chief virtue" of literature is "the purity of [its] vocabulary" (ἡ καθαρὰ τοῖς ὀνόμασι) and its "preservation of the Greek character of speech" (τὸν Ἑλληνικὸν χαρακτῆρα σῴζουσα διάλεκτος).[79] He illustrates this remark with reference to two historians, suggesting that "Herodotus is the best standard (*kanon*) of the Ionic and Thucydides of the Attic dialect."[80] Dionysius reveals himself to be a historical linguist with this comment, using the texts of both historians to reconstruct how the Attic and Ionic dialects were used in the classical period. Imitating Herodotus and Thucydides could help Dionysius and his pupils recapture the purity of the Greek in which they wrote.

This emphasis on purity of speech was linked to larger concerns about ancestry and *eugeneia*. In Dionysius's view, Athenian literature of the classical period was excellent because of the city's ancient origins and the ancestry of its leading families. He reveals this by referring to the "ancient and autochthonous Attic Muse" (Ἀττικὴ μοῦσα καὶ ἀρχαία καὶ αὐτόχθων) who had served to inspire the best Athenian authors when they spoke and wrote.[81] The adjectives that Dionysius uses here match exactly key elements of Aristotle's definition of *eugeneia*. In effect, then, Dionysius was suggesting that the excellence of Athenian literature in its classical period was linked to the autochthonous origins of the city's ancient founders. Thus classical Athenian literature could provide access to this ancient purity. In Dionysius's view, the purity and the excellent style of classical Athenian literature were products of the city's ancient and autochthonous origins.

Dionysius, however, joined a large group of intellectuals who believed that the *eugeneia* of Greece had been corrupted, and with it the purity of how Greek was spoken and written. This was an idea that Dionysius had certainly encountered in his reading of earlier authors, including some from the classical period of Athens. The key vocabulary for this process of corruption was the relatively rare verb *ekbarbaroō*, "to barbarize completely." Dionysius was certainly familiar with the verb's use in Athenian classical literature, particularly in the works of Plato and Isocrates.[82] Both authors reveal concerns about what might happen to Greeks if they were ruled by barbarians. In these circumstances, Greek culture was in constant danger of being corrupted.

The concept of barbarization and the word *ekbarbaroō* became more common in the Hellenistic period, reflecting the concern displayed in much Greek literature about the negative influence of barbarians. A review of Greek literature shows that the word *ekbarbaroō* enjoyed its greatest popularity during the first centuries BCE and CE.[83] What this frequency masks, however, is how much the concept seems to have been a major part of Hellenistic historiography, little of which survives. But Dionysius was familiar with this literature, even if he was quite dismissive of it.[84] And his own use of the word *ekbarbaroō* offers additional insight into how the process of barbarization was believed to work. Barbarization was an almost inevitable result when Greeks were outnumbered by barbarians,

as Dionysius explains: "For many other [Greeks] dwelling among barbarians forgot all of Greek culture (τὸ Ἑλληνικὸν) in a short period of time,
so that they neither speak the Greek language nor practice the customs of
the Greeks, nor honor the same gods and equitable laws—in which area
Greek nature is especially different from barbarian—or are they alike in any
other respect."[85] Dionysius here emphasizes Greek language, customs, and
laws as markers of Greekness. Greeks in the Hellenistic period believed
that all of these were features that had been corrupted by the influence of
barbarization, which was something to be constantly feared.

Given Dionysius's interest in classical literature, language is an especially significant feature of Greekness. Dionysius was drawing from a
popular belief that Greeks would lose the purity of their language if they
traveled abroad or lived among a majority of barbarian peoples. This principle was set out long before Dionysius by Solon, with reference to Athenian
exiles whose travels led them no longer to speak "the Attic tongue."[86] The
same idea prevailed in scholarly discussions of language from Dionysius's
time. His contemporary Didymus seems to have been the source of the
following lexicographical comment about the Greek spoken by residents of
Ionia, drawn from a work written by Dionysius's relative Aelius Dionysius:
"Through the proximity of non-Greek speakers they spoiled their native
language, meters, and quantities."[87] Changes in custom were important, but
linguistic changes were quite significant and obvious signs of barbarization
for Dionysius and other Greek intellectuals.

Dionysius believed that such changes had taken place in Athens and
throughout the Greek world thanks to barbarization, whose negative
impact had begun some three centuries before his time. The programmatic
essay introducing his literary-critical works explains the circumstances of
these changes. According to the essay, the death of Alexander the Great
(323 BCE) marked the onset of the decline of Greek culture and the negative influence of barbarization.[88] The once-pure Attic style of Athens, which
Dionysius links with the "ancient and autochthonous Attic Muse," fell out
of favor at that time and was replaced by a style that he called Asiatic—a
process that he likens to that of "some shameful courtesan" (ἑταίρα . . . τις
ἄφρων) supplanting the place of a lawful wife in her own home.[89] Dionysius
emphasizes that the Asiatic style was of recent origin and that it had sprung
up in regions on the outskirts of the Greek world that had the reputation
of being unrefined and even barbaric: "It arrived just yesterday or the day
before from some Asian pit, a Mysian, a Phrygian, or a wicked Carian."[90]
Dionysius himself was from Caria, but this passage makes it clear that he
dissociated himself from the region, which stands in here for the barbarian
world. The Asiatic style therefore acts as an opposing force to Atticism, and

the excellent style associated with it. Attic was ancient and of legitimate birth, making it a natural outgrowth of Athens's *eugeneia*. The Asiatic style, by contrast, was a recent development originating in places that Dionysius links with the non-Greek world. It consequently represented a corruption and a barbarization of the Greek world and its *eugeneia*.

This idea of an Asiatic style was shared by Greeks and Romans, based on their shared distaste for regions to the east. By the time Dionysius was writing, Romans had been labeling themselves Attic and their rivals Asiatic for decades, however arbitrary and meaningless these terms were, especially when applied to people speaking Latin, rather than Greek, as Cicero noted.[91] But these labels gained additional currency from their use by Augustus in his propaganda campaign against his rival Antony, whom he linked with the Eastern designs of Cleopatra VII.[92] Augustus associated himself with the Attic side, as Dionysius did, and branded Antony with the label Asiatic. Suetonius quotes Augustus speaking to Antony directly in an unidentified context or work: "Or would you [prefer] that the fluency of the Asiatic orators with their empty thoughts be brought over into our speech?"[93] Traces of similar charges appear in later authors, including Plutarch, who records simply that Antony "used to employ the so-called Asiatic style of speech, which was flourishing especially at that time."[94] Augustus's labels, together with Dionysius's inflated suggestions about the popularity of the Asiatic style, had won out in later characterizations of Antony and this period. Although at least one orator, Craton, willingly labeled himself Asiatic and even debated in front of Augustus,[95] this was otherwise a label that Greeks and Romans applied to rivals who were meant to be excluded from an emerging Greco-Roman culture that venerated classical Athens.

Dionysius even had reason to believe that the barbarization associated with the Asiatic style had recently come to an end thanks to the influence of Rome. As he reported, the "ancient and autochthonous" Attic style was in the midst of being restored to its rightful place, and the Asiatic harlot was being rejected by all but a few cities in Asia Minor.[96] There was a straightforward reason for this, Dionysius explained: "I think that the cause and origin of this great change has been the conquest of the world by Rome, who compels all cities to gaze upon her."[97] This view paralleled Augustus's victorious campaign against Antony, which ended just before Dionysius arrived in Rome. Dionysius even emphasizes the influence of Rome's leaders in this transition. He suggests that they were "extremely well-educated and noble in their judgments; under their rule, the sensible part of the city has progressed still further, and the foolish part has been compelled to see reason."[98] Thanks to the wisdom of these unnamed leaders, contemporary

Greeks and Romans alike have produced excellent works of history, philosophy, and political theory in a style that befitted the classical period of
Athens.[99] This was proof for Dionysius that a renaissance was truly under-
way thanks to Rome, with most of the Greek world restored to its former
state of purity, driving out the negative influence of Asia.

Dionysius's celebration of the Greco-Roman triumph over Asianism
depends implicitly on his larger claim that the founders of Rome were
Greek by descent and possessed of *eugeneia*. He set out this argument at
great length in the first book of his *Roman Antiquities*, which functions
almost as a separate treatise from the rest of the work.[100] Dionysius frames
his argument as a response to the ignorance of Greeks about the origins
of the Roman people and to the insistence of some historians that the
founders of Rome were barbarians.[101] Challenging this point, Dionysius
argues not simply that the founders of Rome were civilized and followed
some Greek customs—a point that was accepted by some Greek authors.[102]
In Dionysius's argument, the Romans were Greeks because their ancestors were Greeks, and of a distinguished and ancient pedigree at that.
According to Dionysius, "one will find no nation that is more ancient or
more Greek than" the several groups of settlers who founded Rome.[103]
He likewise offers the hope in the opening sections of the book that the
present-day descendants of Rome's founders would choose to live "most
well-born" (*eugenestaton*) lives, employing the root of the word *eugeneia*.
The Greek emphasis on *eugeneia* in education comes through in this passage. Dionysius no doubt had taught his pupils, Greek and Roman alike,
to place similar emphasis on a person's *eugeneia* when they delivered enco-
mia. Thanks in large part to teachers like Dionysius, the Greek and Roman
worlds were coming closer together, even if this involved reconsidering
past views about the historical relationship of the two peoples.

Dionysius's views about Rome's Greek founders were supported by
an emerging consensus that the Latin language was closely related to
the Aeolic dialect of Greek. This theory about Latin's origins, now called
"Aeolism" in modern discussions, depended at its root on the belief that
there were Greeks among the founders of Rome.[104] Details about Aeolism vary in different authors, and most of our evidence for the theory is
fragmentary, but there still was a basic consensus that Latin was a hybrid
language resulting from a process of what might be called the barbarization of the Roman people.[105] This was a fundamental point for Dionysius
in his characterization of Latin: "The Romans speak a language that is
neither completely barbarous nor entirely Greek, but a mixture of both,
the greater part of which is Aeolic."[106] Latin was necessarily changed when
Rome accepted into its population a large group of barbarian peoples,

listed at some length by Dionysius: "the Opicans, the Marsians, the Sam-nites, the Tyrrhenians, the Bruttians and many thousands of Umbrians, Ligurians, Iberians, and Gauls, besides innumerable other nations."[107] Latin was consequently a hybrid language formed from the mixture of Greek with a number of other barbarian languages, just as the Roman people themselves came from a mixed stock of Greeks and barbarians.

The hybridity of the Roman people did not detract from their identity as Greeks, however, according to Dionysius. To make this claim, Dionysius turned to both language and customs. In the first place, on the subject of Latin, Dionysius claimed that the only sign of Roman "intermingling" (ἐπιμιξιῶν) with barbarian peoples was that Latin speakers "do not pro-nounce all their sounds properly" (τὸ μὴ πᾶσι τοῖς φθόγγοις ὀρθοεπεῖν).[108] This is a remarkable suggestion, and one that goes beyond what other adherents of the Aeolic theory were willing to claim.[109] But it nevertheless fits in with Dionysius's suggestions about Roman customs. However tenu-ous Dionysius's claim about Latin may be, he was able to offer a number of other proofs to support it, drawing on the "customs, laws, and institutions which [the Romans] preserve down to [his] time just as they received them from their ancestors."[110] Studying a people's customs, Dionysius believed, could help confirm the claims they made about their own history.[111] Reli-gious rites were especially important in this respect, for, as Dionysius says, "these both the Greeks and barbarian world have preserved for the greatest length of time and have never decided to change them, restrained from doing so by their fear of divine anger."[112] People only change their religious rites if they are "subdued by a foreign power and compelled to exchange their own institutions for those of their conquerors."[113] But this had never happened to Rome, Dionysius insisted. So it stood to reason that Roman religious rites practiced in his time should be the same as those practiced at the foundation of Rome. And, as it happens, Dionysius was able to find parallels between Roman customs and the habits of Greek heroes attested in Homer.[114] One such custom was the Roman practice of athletes competing in loincloths, which was something the Greek heroes in Homer did, too.[115] Dionysius's conclusion is revealing: "Thus it is plain that the Romans, who preserve this ancient Greek custom to this day, did not learn it from us afterward nor even change it in the course of time, as we have done."[116] It was not enough that Romans of his day practiced an ancient Greek custom. The practice of this custom, Dionysius argued, proved that the Romans had been and remained of Greek ancestry, possessing *eugeneia*.

Dionysius's claim about the Greek ancestry of the Roman people mat-tered because it meant Rome was not going to barbarize the Greeks under their rule. Romans, after all, were in control of the Greek world, and it would have been natural for them to have their subjects take up Roman customs, following the normal practice of conquerors forcing their subjects to change their ancestral practices.[117] But barbarization had not resulted, and this provided a final proof for Dionysius that the Romans were really Greek: "Nothing could have hindered the whole Greek world, which is now subject to the Romans for already the seventh generation, from being barbarized completely if the Romans had indeed been barbarians."[118] One generation for Dionysius seems to equal roughly twenty-seven years, which means that he seems to be looking back from his own day to around 196 BCE, when the Macedonians were defeated at Cynoscephalae.[119] With so much time under Roman rule having elapsed already, Greek fears about barbarization were groundless. Dionysius does acknowledge that some Romans in his time were abandoning the old customs of their ancestors.[120] But, he says, a few Roman men were still preserving the Greek ancestral customs of the city, and it was through these men that "the dignity of the commonwealth is still maintained and a resemblance to those men [sc. their virtuous ancestors] preserved."[121] The Romans were Greek by ancestry, and this meant that the expected pattern of barbarization had not happened and would not happen in the future.

Dionysius's perspective on the relationship between Greeks and Romans points to a growing partnership, based on the consensus that there was close kinship between the two peoples. By this point, Greeks were identifying Romans as allies in the struggle against barbarization, and in the restoration of Greece to the great days of its classical period. The lost purity of Greece's past and the *eugeneia* of its ancestors were concerns for both Greeks and Romans in this process. Amid claims that a Greek renaissance was beginning, led by the leaders of Rome, it becomes difficult to determine how much Greeks or Romans were responsible for its development. Boundaries between the two peoples were disappearing, even as the Atticists among them labeled their rivals as Asiatics and, therefore, barbarians. This points to an exclusive partnership between Greeks and Romans, who shared the same ancestors and spoke dialects of the same language, according to a growing consensus around the time of Dionysius.

The Marginalized Barbarian Past

Even as a combined Greco-Roman culture emerged, Greeks and Romans were interested in the place of both of their civilizations in the history of the world. This comes out in works of ecumenical character, including works of universal history and geography, both of which were popular genres in the late Hellenistic and early imperial periods.[122] Similar universalizing

rhetoric features prominently in the self-presentation of Rome's political elite, as is clear to any reader of Augustus's *Res gestae*, among other
sources.[123] This sort of interest in universal history has sometimes been
taken as a sign of deep Roman interest in the world and respect for the
antiquity of barbarian civilizations.[124] Some signs of these attitudes do
exist, but they should not be taken as representative of the prevailing
views toward people outside of the Greek and Roman partnership. Rather,
much of the seeming ecumenism displayed by Greeks and Romans was
more concerned with exploring the relationship of the rest of the world to
Greece and Rome. Greeks and Romans were consequently less interested
in hearing about history told from a perspective that challenged theirs,
especially if it seemed to minimize the significance of Greece. The result
was a view of the world's past in light of the Greco-Roman present and
the fixation on Greece's past that characterized it. Barbarian history was
of little interest to Greeks and Romans, who were eager to overcome what
they saw as the negative impact of barbarization on Greek culture.

A typical attitude toward barbarian history is on display in the universal history of Diodorus of Sicily. Diodorus, who came to Rome during
the mid-first century BCE, breaks some of the patterns evident in the lives
of Greek intellectuals discussed in the previous two sections. There is no
explicit evidence connecting him with a Roman patron, much less any
indication that he was part of an expansive family tradition of scholarship.
But this lack of evidence should not be taken as a sign that Diodorus
remained outside the norms of intellectual culture in Rome, contrary to
suggestions that he was an independent, isolated figure.[125] A range of
comments by Diodorus himself hint at his engagement with the norms of
intellectual culture in the first century BCE. He notes that he "acquired
great experience with the language of the Romans" by interacting with
people in his native Sicily, which suggests that he had connections to
Roman visitors and magistrates on the island.[126] He likewise displays first-
hand knowledge of a Roman embassy to Egypt around the year 60/59
BCE.[127] This came before his "long residence" in Rome, which evidently
involved engagement with other intellectuals in the city.[128] We find some
indications of the latter in Diodorus's claim that unfinished portions of his
work were stolen and published by unnamed rivals.[129] This comment is not
indicative of a person who remained aloof from Roman intellectual culture, despite a lack of evidence situating him more squarely in this context.
Recent scholarship on Diodorus has even tried to link him with Pompey
and his supporters, or Julius Caesar, who had emerged as victor in the
civil war at what was a significant time in the composition of the *Library
of History*.[130] Even if much about his life remains uncertain, Diodorus still

offers abundant evidence to confirm that he fit in with Roman intellectual culture of the first century BCE.

In this culture, little regard was given to the history of the barbarian world, something that the extant sections of Diodorus's *Library of History* demonstrate better than any other source. The fact that this work is a universal history has lent itself to the view that Diodorus offered a cosmopolitan outlook in it and that he was consequently receptive to what barbarians claimed about their own histories.[131] Reading parts of his work in isolation can lead to this opinion, but a full reading of the extant sections of the *Library of History* reveals a thoroughly Hellenocentric outlook. A general indication of this outlook comes from Diodorus's choice to segregate the early history of non-Greek peoples in the first three books of his *Library*, devoting the remaining thirty-seven to how Greece and Rome interacted with the rest of the world. Putting the barbarians first might suggest that Diodorus regarded them as more ancient than the Greeks. But he disabuses readers of this notion in a telling prefatory comment: "The first peoples which we shall discuss will be the barbarians, not because we think them to be more ancient than the Greeks."[132] Instead, Diodorus elected to treat them before Greece and Rome "because we wish to discuss first the majority of the material about the barbarians."[133] This was simply an organizational decision, allowing Diodorus to let Greece and Rome be the main focus of his narrative. Barbarian history was subsequently marginalized in his work, despite its appearance in the first three books.

Even in these first three books, Diodorus offers a Hellenocentric perspective, making skeptical comments about barbarians past and basing his account on sources written by Greeks. For these opening books, Diodorus should have been able to access works written in Greek by two priests about the history of their countries—one an Egyptian named Manetho and the other a Babylonian named Berossus.[134] Instead, Diodorus cited the Greek authors Hecataeus of Abdera and Ctesias of Cnidus as sources for his accounts of Egypt and Assyria, respectively.[135] This choice fits in with Diodorus's tendency to deny claims that would make barbarian civilizations earlier than Greek. One telling example comes in a long list of cities that Diodorus says the Egyptians claimed to have founded, including the Greek cities of Argos and Athens.[136] Diodorus simply rejects this: "It seems to me that [the Egyptians] speak more from a love of glory than of truth, and claim that [Athens] was their colony because of the city's fame."[137] He was similarly doubtful of the validity of all of the other colonies claimed by Egyptians: "They offer no precise proof for their claims, and no historian worthy of trust gives evidence in their support."[138] There is no cosmopolitanism on display here. Instead, Diodorus displays an attitude of defensive

Hellenism, rejecting out of hand the idea that Athens might have been founded by Egyptians.

Diodorus's defensiveness on this point reflects a larger trend of Greek and Roman authors limiting or denying the great antiquity of barbarian civilizations in works of chronography, including those of a universal character. This tendency is on prominent display in the fragments of the chronographical work of Diodorus's Roman contemporary Varro, who used Greek authors as sources.[139] The basic chronological point of reference for Varro was the first Olympiad of 776 BCE, which for him began the "historical" (ἱστορικόν) period, so called "because the events that transpired in it are contained in actual histories (*veris historiis*)." The period of 1,600 years before 776 was called "mythical (μυθικόν) because many legends are assigned to it." Before the beginning of the mythical period, around 2376 BCE, there was only the "unknown" (ἄδηλον), so called because of sheer ignorance.[140] Varro's scheme for chronology equated the historical period with Greek history and effectively consigned all earlier events in non-Greek history before 776 BCE to the realm of mythology. As he said, it was only for this historical period that there existed "actual histories"—a reference that dismisses the works of Berossus, Manetho, and others like them as unreliable, or at least irrelevant. The chronographic data from non-Greek civilizations that Varro did include fit into what he called the "historical" period following 776 BCE, meaning that it offered no real challenge to Greek views about the past.[141] Varro's perspective on the history of the world was shaped at a basic level by the Hellenocentrism of his Greek sources.

Signs of a similar attitude come through in the fragments of a Greek chronographer who shared Diodorus's view that barbarian history was less ancient than sometimes believed. This was Castor of Rhodes, who was roughly contemporaneous with Diodorus.[142] Little is known about Castor's life, though the epithet he gained of "Roman-lover" may suggest that he, like Diodorus, spent some of his career in Rome.[143] His chronography ends in 61/60 BCE, which was around the same time that Diodorus began writing his *Library of History*, and also the end point of the history, though it is agreed by scholars that Diodorus made no use of Castor's work.[144] Nonetheless, the two authors did share a universal focus, though Castor lived up to this standard better than Diodorus did.[145] Castor's work brought together the histories of different peoples into a single work in a way that Diodorus's ostensibly universal work simply did not. But Castor still agreed with Diodorus's claim that barbarian peoples were no more ancient than the Greeks, and he did so by means of an unusual solution. He simply claimed that the relatively obscure Greek city of Sicyon had kings who were just as ancient as Ninus, the first king of Assyria, circa 2090 BCE.[146] This solution evidently recommended itself because the chronology of other Greek cities and their kings was already firmly established in the works of his predecessors.[147] So Sicyon, of all places, was left to support claims of Greece's great antiquity. Castor did grant the ancient past of non-Greek civilizations the status of real history, assigning precise dates to their events and synchronizing them with other civilizations. But he nonetheless shared Diodorus's belief that the Greeks were just as ancient as any barbarian people. Data from barbarian history had little impact on how Greeks and Romans viewed the history of the world and the relative antiquity of its various civilizations.

Instead, barbarian history tended to be little more than a curiosity for a small subset of Greek and Roman intellectuals with interests in obscure, specialized subjects. One such intellectual was Alexander Polyhistor, a slightly older contemporary of Diodorus at Rome.[148] His entry in the *Suda* simply says that "he wrote innumerable books."[149] Fragments surviving from these show that Polyhistor was mostly interested in quoting passages from ancient and obscure authors, with seemingly little concern for what they had to say.[150] This helps explain why Polyhistor was one of the very few Greek intellectuals to show awareness of the Babylonian Berossus, not to mention several Jewish authors who wrote in Greek during the Hellenistic period.[151] Polyhistor's choice to quote from these latter authors was vital for their survival, demonstrating how rarely read and used they seem to have been among Greek and Roman intellectuals.[152] A similar pattern is apparent in a technical glossary found on papyrus (*P.Oxy.* 15.1802 and 71.4812), which includes some rare references to the works of Berossus.[153] This probably emerged from the school associated with Pamphilus, who was active at Alexandria in the first century CE.[154] The glossary's purpose was to explain the meaning of foreign words and rare dialect forms of Greek words that were found in literature of the classical and Hellenistic periods (e.g., "Menemani [μενεμανι]: water among the Persians. D(e)inon in Book . . . of the *Persica*").[155] As Francesca Schironi notes, the glossary does not show a real interest in foreign cultures, or even in non-Greek languages, but instead is a pedantic effort to explain words of foreign origin that might confuse monolingual readers.[156] It was an insular, scholarly project, and it serves only to highlight how little interest there was in barbarian history and literature. Only specialists had any interest in this subject, and even that came from a desire to aid their understanding of Greek literature.

Barbarian antiquity thus lacked the standing that the ancient pasts of Greece and Rome possessed. Barbarians were marginalized or excluded from works of ostensibly universal focus. Evidence suggestive of the great antiquity of barbarian civilizations was likewise deflated or dismissed. This was a consequence of Hellenocentric attitudes held by both Greeks and Romans. These attitudes were supported by the partnership of Greeks and Romans, which effectively suggested that the past of the barbarian world had little value, especially when it might challenge views about the significance of Greece or Rome.

Barbarian Intellectuals in Rome

The dismissive attitude toward barbarian history carried over to barbarian intellectuals, by which I mean intellectuals who associated themselves with, or who were regarded as representatives of, a civilization or cultural tradition besides Greece or Rome. Intellectuals of this type found it difficult to gain recognition from their Greek counterparts and members of the Roman elite. Their examples help demonstrate how misguided it is to seek in Greek literature of the imperial period what Tim Whitmarsh calls "a coherent articulation of subaltern resistance through literature."[157] In other words, Greek intellectuals like Theodorus, Dionysius, and Potamon, among many others, were complicit in Roman imperialism and helped further the development of an exclusive Greco-Roman partnership.[158] Barbarian intellectuals, by contrast, faced challenges that their Greek counterparts never experienced. They were expected to display mastery of Greek culture and literature, even as they tried to demonstrate the antiquity and value of other cultures and traditions. They likewise had to face the stereotypes of a Greek and Roman audience that had fixed ideas about barbarians and was sometimes skeptical about the validity of barbarian wisdom. Greeks and Romans tended to expect exoticism from the barbarian world, even as they took for granted that intellectual culture should revolve around classical Greek culture and literature.[159] Thus there were major barriers for the barbarian intellectuals who came to Rome seeking to gain recognition from the imperial household and the elite intellectuals associated with it. Their potential for success was limited and depended on presenting themselves in ways that fit in with Greek and Roman expectations for barbarian culture and history, while often denying their barbarian heritage.

The experiences of a group of ambassadors who spoke before two Roman emperors, some seventy years after Antipater, Potamon, and Theodorus debated in front of Augustus, offer an illustration of the challenges facing barbarian intellectuals. The debates in which these ambassadors participated were the result of controversies surrounding the large Jewish community of Alexandria and its increasingly difficult relationship with the Greek residents of that city.[160] Alexandria's Greeks and Jews were attempting to determine their relative status and seeking to differentiate themselves from the native Egyptian population, who were excluded from being full Alexandrian citizens. This mattered for several reasons, including the simple fact that only Alexandrian citizens, and not Egyptians, could become Roman citizens.[161] The controversies between Jews and Greeks in Alexandria were therefore bound closely to the city's Roman rulers. Many sources discuss this controversy and the rival embassies sent to Rome by the Jewish and Greek communities of Alexandria, initially in the reign of Caligula (r. 37–41), and spilling over into the time of his successor Claudius (r. 41–54). We likewise possess information about several of the ambassadors. Only one member of the Jewish side is known with certainty. This was Philo, the leader of the embassy to Caligula, who wrote an account of his experiences in Rome. On the Greek side, we have the names of sixteen members of two embassies: four from the group that met with Caligula and twelve more listed in the letter Claudius wrote setting out the terms of his resolution to the controversy.[162] Three of these ambassadors are intellectuals we know much about from other sources: Apion, Tiberius Claudius Balbillus, and Chaeremon. Comparison of these three intellectuals with Philo reveals that they were treated in substantially different ways by Roman authorities.

The different treatment Philo received occurred despite many similarities between him and his rival ambassadors. His profile is typical for Greek intellectuals who came to Rome seeking imperial attention. A report from Josephus highlights the key attributes contributing to this profile: "Philo, the leader of the embassy of the Jews, a man of high reputation in all respects, brother of Alexander the Alabarch, and a philosopher of much experience."[163] Josephus identifies Philo as Jewish, but also as a distinguished and learned man representing his community to the emperor, much like Antipater and Potamon before him. The reference to Philo's brother Alexander shows that he belonged to a family that had connections to powerful Romans. Alexander's title of Alabarch is synonymous with Arabarch and identifies him as the superintendent of customs on the eastern, or Arabian, side of the Nile.[164] Another passage from Josephus reveals that Philo's brother Alexander had served as an administrator (*epitropos*) for Antonia, the mother of Emperor Claudius.[165] Philo was consequently a logical choice to lead the Jewish embassy, possessing the learning and connections that Greek ambassadors to Rome tended to have.

Philo's works likewise display his close connections to Greek culture, even in terms of how he presented the ancient history of the Jewish people. In the first place, Philo seems to have known little Hebrew and to have

regarded the Septuagint translation of the Hebrew Bible as authorita-
tive.[166] Greek, rather than Hebrew, was his language—something that he
reveals when he mentions translating Hebrew names into what he says is
"our tongue" (τὴν ἡμετέραν διάλεκτον).[167] Greek culture and learning even
have a place in Philo's account of the life of Moses, which suggests that
Greeks gave him a "general education" (ἐγκύκλιον παιδείαν).[168] In Philo's
view, Greek culture was at the roots of Judaism, underlying Moses's composition of the Pentateuch. This emphasis on Greek culture continues in
Philo's discussion of the Roman Empire of his time. He assigns Athens a
special status, suggesting that its residents are "the sharpest in thinking of
the Greeks," and therefore conforming to prevailing Greek views about the
exceptionality of the city.[169] Philo even describes the recent history of the
empire in terms that resonate with Dionysius's views of a Greek renaissance
taking place under Roman rule. Philo suggests that the emperor Augustus "gentled and governed all the savage and brutish peoples, expanding
Greece [by adding] many Greeces to it, and hellenizing the barbarian
[world] in its most significant regions."[170] There is no mention here of
Atticism and Asianism, or the triumph of one over the other. But Philo
nonetheless links the expansion of Greek culture with Roman rule. Like
Dionysius, he points to the existence of a close partnership between Greeks
and Romans—one in which he held a share.

Yet Philo claims his Alexandrian rivals should be excluded from
this partnership. His support for this claim is the suggestion that these
rivals were more Egyptian than Greek, a basic point of contention in the
controversies between Jews and Greeks in Alexandria. From Philo's perspective, his rivals were decidedly non-Hellenic, regardless of how much
they insisted they were Greek. Philo presents them, instead, as native Egyptians, a people he treats in almost universally negative terms throughout
his works.[171] Much of this negativity focuses on the Egyptian predilection
to worship animals as gods, a feature of Egyptian religion criticized by
Greek and Roman observers.[172] Philo employs this motif when he suggests
that his Alexandrian rivals were willing to regard Caligula as a god because
they were basically Egyptians, who applied the name "god," he says, to
"indigenous ibises, poisonous snakes, and many other wild beasts."[173] This
fits in with Philo's claims that Caligula was disposed against Jews because
of the influence of Egyptian domestic slaves serving in his household.[174]
Animal language appears in Philo's description of these slaves, suggesting
that they had "received in their souls the venom and temper of the native
crocodiles and asps."[175] From this presentation, Philo asserts that he was
emphatically not Egyptian, while his rivals who claimed to be Alexandrians
and Greeks were.

Philo's Alexandrian rivals made similar charges against the Jewish people, emphasizing that they were neither Alexandrian nor Greek. In some cases, this type of allegation meant simply offering the converse of Philo's charges, and suggesting that the Jews were more like Egyptians. One such charge appears in a text celebrating the life of Isidorus, who served on the Alexandrian embassy to Caligula.[176] This text emphasizes that the Jewish people were different, and not Alexandrian: "They are not of the same temperament as the Alexandrians and live rather in the manner of the Egyptians. Are they not equal to those who pay the poll-tax [i.e., the Egyptians]?"[177] Other Alexandrians participating in the embassy similarly emphasized that the Jewish people were not Alexandrians but had close links to Egypt. One proponent of this view was Apion, whose remarks are reported and critiqued by Josephus.[178] Apion evidently expressed amazement that Jews could be called Alexandrians though "they do not worship the same gods as the Alexandrians."[179] This was part of a larger strategy apparent in the works of Apion and Chaeremon, whereby the Jewish people are linked closely with Egyptian history. Both presented forms of the older story that identified Jews as a group of people expelled from Egypt because they were suffering from leprosy.[180] This tradition sought to explain how Jews were different from other peoples and why they marked themselves off from others, notably by the practice of circumcision.[181] The result of this claim was the accusation that Jews were willfully different from everyone and therefore not worthy of the status held by Greek citizens of Alexandria, as Philo claimed.

Faced with this debate between rival communities in Alexandria, both Caligula and Claudius came down on the side that emphasized the foreignness of the Jewish people, excluding them from the Greco-Roman partnership. Caligula's response is clear from Philo's report of his encounter with the emperor, who seems to have made the Jewish ambassadors wait for months in Rome before meeting with them.[182] When the ambassadors finally gained an audience, Philo describes how he and the other members of his party were forced to follow the distracted emperor around as he conducted other business.[183] Along the way, Caligula asked them questions about their customs, trying to understand some of the characteristic features of Jewish culture: "Why do you abstain from the flesh of pigs?"[184] Otherwise, he had no interest or time for Philo and his fellow ambassadors. Caligula's successor Claudius seems, at first glance, to have been more receptive to the Jewish ambassadors, to judge from the letter he sent back to Alexandria explaining his solution to the controversy. In this, he instructs the Alexandrians "to behave gently and kindly towards the Jews who have inhabited the same city for many years, and not to dishonor any

of their customs in their worship of their god."[185] But he follows this instruc-
tion with a series of warnings for the city's Jewish community, including
one with ominous undertones: "If they disobey, I shall proceed against
them in every way as fomenting a common plague for the whole world."[186]
Alongside this warning, Claudius emphasizes to the Jews that they live "in
a city that is not their own" (ἐν ἀλλοτρίᾳ πόλει).[187] Claudius's letter therefore
offered to the Alexandrian Jews the prospect of peace but at the same time
told them that they were foreign to "the whole world" and that Alexandria
was not really their city. Both Caligula and Claudius evidently regarded
the Jews as foreigners, rather than potential partners.

The close relationship of Claudius to some of the Alexandrian ambassadors emphasizes this point, confirming that they were treated as partners,
and sometimes even as trusted members of the imperial household. A first
sign of this is simply the names of the twelve ambassadors listed in Claudius's letter to the Alexandrians. Six have the *tria nomina* of Roman citizens,
and two of these, Ti. Claudius Phanias and Ti. Claudius Archibius, seem
even to have been made citizens by Claudius himself.[188] A third ambassador, Ti. Claudius Balbillus, shares the same *praenomen* and *nomen*, but this
may have been inherited from his likely father, Ti. Claudius Thrasyllus,
who was the personal astrologer for the emperor Tiberius and received
citizenship from him.[189] Balbillus himself evidently served as an astrologer to Claudius and Vespasian, too.[190] He is identified in Claudius's letter
as a "friend" (ἑτέρωι), hinting at the closeness of his connections to the
emperor.[191] He was also joined in the embassy by Chaeremon, who served
as tutor to Claudius's adopted son, the future emperor Nero.[192] These connections dwarf those that we know of for the Jewish ambassadors. Philo
himself may not have been a Roman citizen, despite his brother the alabarch's connections to the imperial family.[193] More to the point, there was
no possibility of Philo or the other Jewish ambassadors gaining the sorts
of connections Balbillus and Chaeremon had to the imperial household.
The emperors had no interest in having people who refused to eat pork
teaching members of the family, regardless of how Greek they may have
seemed in other respects.

The greater success of the Alexandrian ambassadors reflects their ability and willingness to conform more to the norms and expectations of
Greco-Roman intellectual culture, despite their connections to Egypt and
other non-Greek civilizations. Their efforts reflect the larger concerns of
Alexandrians in this period to establish their credentials as Greeks, amid
doubts that they had become more like Egyptians, as Philo charged. Centuries earlier, Polybius underlined their ambivalent status in the eyes of
outsiders when he observed that the Alexandrians were a "mixed" (μιγάδες)

people, though they remained "mindful of the customs common to the Greeks."[194] In response to the claim that they may have been less than Greek, Alexandrian intellectuals offered technical discussions of the Greek language. Little of this sort of work survives from the first century CE, but the *Suda* entries for the Alexandrian grammarian Irenaeus help reveal some of its major features.[195] Amid a number of works he wrote about the Attic dialect, one title makes Irenaeus's argument about the origins of Alexandrian Greek clear: *On the Dialect of the Alexandrians, That It Is Derived from Attic*.[196] The same work also had the subtitle of *On Hellenism* (Περὶ Ἑλληνισμοῦ), suggesting that Irenaeus was defining Greece primarily through the language spoken in Athens.[197] A fragment from his works shows that he dismissed usages of Greek words as "barbaric" (βάρβαρον) if they were not found attested "in any of the ancients" (παρά τινι τῶν παλαιῶν).[198] Like Dionysius, Irenaeus turned to classical Athens to define acceptable usage of Greek, dismissing anything else as barbaric. He then applied this standard to the language spoken by Alexandrians in his time, demonstrating the city's Greek origins and the claims of its residents to *eugeneia*. Irenaeus conducted all this research and work while at some point acquiring the additional name of Minucius Pacatus, demonstrating that he had gained Roman citizenship.[199] He emerges as a member of the Greco-Roman partnership, fitting in with the prevailing fascination among both Greeks and Romans with Athens and Atticism. Irenaeus consequently provides a prime example of the sorts of strategies used by his contemporaries and compatriots, the Alexandrian ambassadors who represented the city to the emperors.

Apion, who gained a reputation as a highly cultured Greek despite his likely origins as an Egyptian, shows similar concerns about finding the right balance between Greece and Egypt. Apion may have been something like Theodorus, Posidonius, and the other "sophists" critiqued by Nicolaus (as noted previously) in that he seems to have denied his origins in an obscure place and claimed instead to be from somewhere else. Josephus is our source for this: "Though [Apion] was born in Oasis of Egypt and, as one might say, was foremost of the Egyptians, he denied his true homeland and people, claiming falsely to be Alexandrian, and acknowledging the wickedness of his people."[200] Some of this accusation may certainly be slander, but Apion's own name suggests an Egyptian background, being theophoric of the sacred Apis bull, about which he wrote a work.[201] This implies that Apion was from somewhere in Egypt but that he became a citizen of Alexandria, evidently on the basis of his literary and poetic skills.[202] The works he wrote demonstrate his expertise in Egyptian history, not just in his treatment of the Apis bull but also in a work called *Egyptian*

Matters that included coverage of the country's very early history.[203] Apion, however, seems to have gained a reputation mostly for his Homeric scholarship, producing a glossary to the poet's work containing many fanciful etymologies.[204] A papyrus from Oxyrhynchus also shows that Apion traveled extensively throughout the Roman Empire, competing in and winning many poetic competitions.[205] This was evidently how Apion became known to many powerful Romans, including the emperor Tiberius, who called him "the cymbal of the world" (*cymbalum mundi*) because of his boastfulness.[206] Apion clearly fit into the emerging Greco-Roman culture of the first century CE, even authoring a work called *On the Roman Dialect* in which he subscribed to the consensus view that Latin was derived from Aeolic Greek.[207] For another later observer, Aulus Gellius, Apion even qualified simply as a "Greek man" (*Graecus homo*).[208] All of this helps explain why Apion was part of the Alexandrian embassy, demonstrating that he was received as an Alexandrian and a Greek, regardless of his likely origins in an out-of-the-way region of Egypt.

Chaeremon, who served in the embassy to Claudius, provides a similar example of an intellectual whose profile leans further in the direction of Greek culture, despite his evident expertise in Egyptian history. A relative lack of evidence makes it difficult to say much with certainty about Chaeremon, especially compared to Apion.[209] But a few details in his fragments stand out, attesting to his engagement with both Greek and Egyptian traditions. Later authors refer to him as a "sacred scribe" (ἱερογραμματεὺς) and as a Stoic philosopher.[210] The former term reflects Chaeremon's claims to expertise in Egyptian history and culture, demonstrated by his works on Egyptian history and hieroglyphs.[211] These works were themselves peopled with "sacred scribes," a class of temple priests in Ptolemaic Egypt, suggesting that Chaeremon presented himself as their successor.[212] There is some substance to this self-identification, inasmuch as a significant number of Chaeremon's explanations of hieroglyphs are correct.[213] But his treatment of Egyptian material is heavily colored by Stoic interpretations, which helps explain why authors close to his lifetime call him a Stoic philosopher, rather than a "sacred scribe."[214] Chaeremon linked stories about Isis and Osiris with celestial bodies and the Nile, following the norms of Stoic physics.[215] His work on Egyptian hieroglyphs was even based on the idea that these characters were designed by the "most ancient of the sacred scribes to hide [their] physical doctrine about the gods."[216] This allowed Chaeremon to suggest that there was an allegorical system underlying hieroglyphs, an idea that fits in well with the theories on allegory proposed by his contemporary Cornutus, another Stoic.[217] Chaeremon was evidently working within a Greek philosophical tradition and allowing this to color his interpretation of the sacred Egyptian script.

Chaeremon's link to the Stoic tradition was likely of more significance than his Egyptian expertise when he interacted with the imperial household. The evidence on this point is limited, but some weight can be placed on the wording of the *Suda* passage that identifies Chaeremon as a teacher for the imperial family: "Alexander of Aeageus, a Peripatetic philosopher and teacher of the emperor Nero, together with Chaeremon the philosopher."[218] Stoic philosophy was evidently what mattered here, hinting that Chaeremon was likely the predecessor of Seneca, another Stoic charged with teaching Nero.[219] Chaeremon was surely helped in gaining this position by his previous appointment as head of the Alexandrian libraries, a distinguished title that made him the successor of many prestigious intellectuals who held this role.[220] With the evidence so limited, it is difficult to parse how Chaeremon was received by the imperial family and what would have made him an appealing person to teach Nero. Many Romans in the first century were fascinated with Egypt, but such fascination leaves little trace in our evidence about Chaeremon from the first and second centuries CE.[221] The balance of probability therefore suggests that Chaeremon's credentials in Greek intellectual culture were a more significant factor than his expertise in Egyptian subjects, which only began to be emphasized by readers in the time of Porphyry and later.

Ti. Claudius Balbillus, the last of the ambassadors to concern me, likewise offered to the imperial household a blend of expertise drawn from the Greek and barbarian worlds. As with Chaeremon, there are only small scraps of evidence to work with for Balbillus. But these nonetheless suggest that Balbillus benefited from a family tradition of Greek classical scholarship, while at the same time presenting himself as a master of the barbarian art of astrology. These were the defining features of Balbillus's likely father, Thrasyllus, who is known to us from a collection of fragmentary evidence attesting to his relationship with Tiberius and his career as an astrologer and editor of classical Greek texts.[222] Some basic details about Thrasyllus are uncertain, despite a series of famous anecdotes about his sometimes difficult relationship with Tiberius, which lasted for more than three decades.[223] His native city is unknown, with both Alexandria and Rhodes seeming reasonable possibilities.[224] Thrasyllus's place of birth, though, was basically irrelevant to his career. Even if he was from an obscure town, he most likely would have linked himself with a place like Rhodes or Alexandria, following the same pattern discernible in the careers of Theodorus, Posidonius, and Apion. Connections to one of these cities would have served as a way to link himself with its intellectual traditions and *eugeneia*.

This was a fundamental aspect of Thrasyllus's career, underlying his relationship with Tiberius as an intellectual with major credentials in Greek philosophy, and not simply in astrology. Some sign of Thrasyllus's background in philosophy comes from how he was received by later authors. In the fourth century, Julian and Themistius both cite the pairing of Tiberius and Thrasyllus as representative of the ideal relationship between an emperor and a philosopher, with no emphasis on astrology.[225] Thrasyllus's philosophical labors are best known now from the editorial work he conducted on the corpora of two philosophers who had gained the status of classics, Plato and Democritus.[226] Both philosophers were linked in Thrasyllus's time because of their excellent style, even being regarded by Dionysius of Halicarnassus as two of the best three philosophical authors, along with Aristotle.[227] Thrasyllus's work on Plato and Democritus was therefore a way of establishing his classical credentials, especially given the scope of his project. Diogenes Laertius describes succinctly what Thrasyllus achieved: "He made an ordered catalogue of Democritus's works, as he did also for Plato's, arranging them into tetralogies."[228] He likewise wrote *Prolegomena* for both authors, which evidently included biographical material and assigned second titles to Plato's dialogues to indicate the subject matter that they treated.[229] Thrasyllus thereby offered to readers of the two classic philosophers a guide that was key to his own arrangement of their works. In short, Thrasyllus's works represented a major effort of classical and philosophical scholarship, and something that surely was significant for the place he held in the imperial household.

The other side of Thrasyllus's career was based on astrology, an area where he presented himself as someone sharing the ancient wisdom of the barbarian world with Greeks and Romans. Astrological expertise fits in with the encyclopedic interests displayed in the fragments of Thrasyllus's works, which feature coverage of a diverse range of subjects, including harmonics, animals, and epistemology.[230] Astrology gave Thrasyllus the opportunity to suggest that his areas of expertise extended to the non-Greek world, drawing on the close associations that astrology had in the minds of Greek and Roman observers with regions to the east, particularly Chaldea and Egypt.[231] An extant epitome of one of Thrasyllus's astrological works shows that he exploited these connections. The epitome contains references to three key figures associated with astrology: Hermes Trismegistus, Nechepso, and Petosiris.[232] The reference to Hermes Trismegistus, purportedly an ancient Egyptian king who authored works of mystical content, is one of the earliest extant.[233] The reference to Nechepso and Petosiris, meanwhile, is the earliest extant mention in Greek of these astrological writers, who were identified, respectively, as an ancient Egyptian king and his court sage.[234] Recent discoveries show that these figures were based on a somewhat distorted memory of the Egyptian pharaoh Necho II and the sage Petesis, both active in the seventh century BCE.[235] Thrasyllus may have played a role in the dissemination of the works linked with Nechepso and Petosiris to the Greco-Roman world. One indication of this comes from the Pliny the Elder, who identifies Thrasyllus alongside Nechepso and Petosiris as sources for the second book of his *Natural History*, which treated topics relating to cosmology.[236] Thrasyllus's position in the imperial household surely would have helped him to publicize authors and works of literature, including the editions he produced of Plato and Democritus.[237] His claims to expertise with ancient Egyptian texts on astrology were another component of his self-presentation as an intellectual, demonstrating that he was a master of both Greek and barbarian material.[238]

This was an example that Thrasyllus passed to his likely son Balbillus, who likewise claimed expertise in both Greek and barbarian traditions as part of a successful intellectual career. Many basic points about Balbillus are uncertain, but his credentials as a Greek intellectual are demonstrated by the Younger Seneca's remark that he was an "exceptionally accomplished man in every type of literature."[239] This reputation for learning was likely a factor in his selection as an ambassador to Rome alongside other learned Alexandrians. It may even help explain why the people of Ephesus celebrated games in his honor, with the permission of Vespasian.[240] Like Thrasyllus, though, Balbillus also demonstrated expertise in the ostensibly barbarian subject of astrology. The remaining scraps of his astrological work include two of the earliest extant horoscopes in Greek, dating from the first century BCE.[241] These may be linked to the later history of Balbillus's family. His daughter Claudia Capitolina married C. Julius Antiochus Epiphanes, the son of the last king of Commagene, Antiochus IV.[242] His predecessor Antiochus I commemorated himself in a tomb including an astronomical relief featuring his horoscope, one of the earliest to survive in Greek.[243] Balbillus may consequently have gained access to ancient astrological data from Commagene, helping to spread knowledge of the subject to the Greco-Roman world, just as Thrasyllus seems to have done.[244] This work in barbarian subjects went along with his learning in Greek culture and the marriage connections of his descendants to the distinguished family of the Euryclids in Sparta.[245] Thanks in part to these connections, Balbillus's grandson became one of Greece's first senators, and even served as suffect consul in 109.[246] Family connections and claims to expertise in both Greek and barbarian traditions provided the basis for the privileged position that Balbillus and his descendants gained in the Greco-Roman partnership.

The successes of Balbillus and his descendants stand in contrast to the lives of contemporary Jewish intellectuals, who seem to have faced a choice of either gaining admission to the Greco-Roman partnership or maintaining loyalty to Jewish traditions. An examination of Philo and other members of his family makes this choice clear. Philo himself emphasized that he remained faithful to Jewish traditions when met with a hostile reception by Caligula. This same attitude appears in his other works, which display concern about the likely outcome of marriages between Jews and non-Jews.[247] As Philo says, in a discussion of Jewish laws, "Do not agree to a partnership of marriage with someone of a foreign people, lest you some day be conquered by hostile customs."[248] Children resulting from such a union were likely to be "deceived by spurious customs in place of the genuine," resulting in the end of a family tradition.[249] This was a real concern for Philo thanks to circumstances in his own family. His nephew Tiberius Julius Alexander enjoyed a successful Roman career, becoming prefect of Judea and later of Egypt, in which capacity he was involved in military operations against the Jewish rebellion during the late 60s.[250] Though Alexander may have earlier accompanied Philo as part of the Jewish embassy to Rome, abandoning Jewish traditions seems to have been a necessary step for him to enjoy this career.[251] Josephus makes this point explicitly, noting that Alexander "did not abide by his ancestral customs."[252] The same impression comes through in Alexander's appearance in two of Philo's works, both of which take dialogue form.[253] Alexander and his uncle Philo agree on little in these works. Alexander's departure from ancestral customs is clear when he identifies oysters and hares as acceptable food, contrary to Jewish dietary restrictions.[254] This may not have been as significant as eating pork, but it still functions as a sign that Alexander was more willing to compromise than his uncle. His participation in the Greco-Roman partnership led him to abandon some Jewish customs.

A fuller perspective on the challenges facing intellectuals regarded as non-Greeks is offered by Alexander's younger contemporary Josephus, whose works reveal the expectations and prejudices that shaped his interactions with the imperial household and his life in Rome.[255] The impact of these expectations comes through in the story of how Josephus gained his initial connection with Vespasian, soon after being taken prisoner during the ongoing Jewish rebellion. Josephus predicted that Vespasian would become emperor and thereby presented himself as someone with prophetic knowledge of the future.[256] Josephus emphasizes this skill in his works, connecting it explicitly to his identity as a "priest and the descendant of priests."[257] He was consequently able to interpret dreams and "was not ignorant of the prophecies in the holy books."[258] Josephus's self-presentation on these points suggested to Roman observers that he was like Nechepso, Petosiris, and other figures from the ancient barbarian past, sharing their skill in predicting the future.[259] To use Heidi Wendt's terminology, Josephus presented himself as an expert in "ethnically coded wisdom," demonstrating his foreignness to Greek and Roman observers.[260] The significance of this self-presentation is apparent from the great silences surrounding Josephus on the part of Greek and Roman observers in the next century and a half, except for the story of his prediction about Vespasian. Both Suetonius and Cassius Dio mention the prediction, the former describing Josephus simply as "one of the high-born captives" (*unus ex nobilibus captivis*) and the latter identifying him only as a "Judean man" (ἀνὴρ Ἰουδαῖος).[261] From this perspective, Josephus was no intellectual or philosopher, but simply a foreign prisoner who made an accurate prediction about Vespasian's future. The prediction attracted attention, and Josephus did make himself useful to Vespasian and Titus as they continued to fight the rebellion. But his usefulness was limited to serving as a translator and intermediary during the siege of Jerusalem.[262] This was hardly a foundation for a distinguished career as an intellectual at the emperor's side.

A similar pattern continued in Rome, where Josephus's self-presentation as a foreigner made him a marginal figure, despite his claims otherwise. Josephus is our only real source for his time in Rome, which extended from the early 70s until the mid-90s, at least.[263] He emphasizes his closeness to the imperial household and the privileges he received from them: Roman citizenship; a stipend; land in Judea, together with a tax exemption on it; punishment for some of his many enemies; and the right to stay in the house where Vespasian lived before he became emperor.[264] Josephus describes the tax exemption (ἀτέλειαν) as "the greatest honor for the person receiving it" (μεγίστη τιμὴ τῷ λαβόντι), which is a surprising claim.[265] Tax exemptions were a desirable thing to have but hardly deserved to be called "the greatest honor." By the time that Josephus received this exemption, the three members of the new Flavian dynasty had been offering much greater rewards to provincials who had supported their successful attempt to usurp the throne, making an unprecedented number of them Roman senators.[266] What Josephus received from the Flavians, by contrast, amounted to minor privileges, appropriate for someone of little significance to the imperial household.[267] Josephus provides his readers no hints of this, just as he neglects to mention that his stay in Vespasian's former home must have been only for the short term. We know from other sources that this house was transformed into a temple for the *gens Flavia* by Domitian.[268] Josephus was, at best, an afterthought for the Flavians in Rome.

A major reason why is that Josephus was insufficiently Greek to fit in with the norms of elite intellectual culture in Rome. This was an inevitable consequence of the prevailing mood of Hellenocentrism in the city, and something that Josephus himself identified, referring to the existence of "people who put no faith in barbarian records, and who are willing only to trust Greeks."[269] Josephus made this comment as part of his attempt to demonstrate the great antiquity of the Jewish people, a point that tended to be ignored or dismissed, in keeping with the sorts of attitudes toward the barbarian past apparent in the works of Diodorus and others (as noted previously). This was why Josephus went out of his way to offer proofs of Jewish antiquity from Greek sources, rather than works that would have been dismissed as "barbarian records." Josephus consequently had to read widely in Greek, which was not his native tongue. This is something that he reveals in scattered comments throughout his works, such as when he notes that he wrote the first version of his *Jewish War* in his "ancestral" (πατρίῳ) language, Aramaic, before translating it into Greek.[270] He adds elsewhere that he even made use of some "assistants in the Greek language" (τισι πρὸς τὴν Ἑλληνίδα φωνὴν συνεργοῖς) for this translation.[271] This remark should not be taken as a sign that Josephus had no ability in Greek before coming to Rome, in spite of his comment that he pronounced the language with insufficient "precision" (ἀκρίβειαν).[272] Instead, Josephus's use of assistants is a likely sign that he was unable to imitate on his own the style of classical Greek authors that had long been obligatory for elite Greeks and Romans.[273] Josephus recognized the importance of lending a Thucydidean style to his history, and consequently he needed to turn for help to Greek experts. Josephus emerges as someone who was insufficiently Greek to thrive in Roman intellectual culture, despite his efforts to make up for this lack.

Unlike some intellectuals, however, Josephus was unwilling to deny his roots in a non-Greek civilization, even going out of his way to emphasize these in his works. He depicts himself as different from Greeks and Romans and links this difference as an issue related to ancestry and *eugeneia*. This is an absolutely fundamental point at the beginning of Josephus's *Life*, which opens with a comment about his ancestry: "My family is not insignificant but descends from priests from the beginning."[274] Josephus then frames for his readers the basis for his family's status, connecting it explicitly to *eugeneia*. He explains that "among each [people] there is a different basis for good birth (*eugeneias*)" and adds that "among us a connection with the priesthood is a sign of a distinguished family."[275] These comments provide a likely sign that Josephus had absorbed the same sort of lessons that the emperor Claudius had about how to offer an encomium, in this case to himself and his family. At the same time, though, Josephus offered his own revised definition of *eugeneia*, basing it not on antiquity and autochthony, as Aristotle had, but on a connection to a priestly family. Antiquity still mattered, as did distinguished ancestors—a point that Josephus emphasizes with his claim to royal blood on his mother's side.[276] But Josephus nonetheless emphasized that he possessed a different type of *eugeneia* than the Greeks did.[277] This reveals a fundamental point about Josephus and his place in Rome. With his comments on different types of *eugeneia*, Josephus labeled himself explicitly as a foreigner, and as someone who would not try to deny this. With this admission, Josephus guaranteed that he would be regarded as a barbarian intellectual and limited to a marginal place in Roman intellectual culture.

Josephus's example therefore reveals the challenges facing intellectuals who were regarded as foreign, and thus as barbarians. He was unwilling to call himself Greek, as some other intellectuals with origins in non-Greek regions of the world had done. But Josephus, like the Jewish ambassadors of Alexandria, still wanted to receive the privileges that came with the label of Greek from Roman authorities. These privileges were jealously guarded by those who were successful in identifying themselves as Greeks, even if they also claimed some mastery of ancient barbarian literature and culture, as Apion and others did. Making a convincing claim to be Greek was a basic ingredient of intellectual success in Rome. By contrast, Josephus and Philo, who identified themselves as Jews, were restricted to marginal status in Rome.

Conclusion

The patterns that emerged in the first century CE persisted into the second, when *eugeneia* became the basis for a new league of Greek cities within the Roman Empire. This league, the Panhellenion, was founded by Hadrian in 131/32 and had its membership limited to cities that could claim to possess good birth.[278] Hadrian himself emphasized *eugeneia* in a letter addressed to the people of Cyrene, using the word in a reference to the good birth of the city's ancient founders, who were from Thera, which was itself a colony of Sparta.[279] He even granted to Cyrene additional privileges relative to the neighboring community of Ptolemais-Barca, which he regarded as having a more remote connection to Greek antiquity because of its refoundation in the Hellenistic period under the Ptolemies.[280] The power and functions of the Panhellenion may not have been that significant, but cities were still eager to gain membership in it and to quarrel with rival communities about the privileges that they would receive, as Cyrene and Ptolemais-Barca did. It is consequently no surprise to see that cities manufactured stories that would make them into colonies of Athens or Sparta, and thus potential members of the league.[281] Cities that seemed too Hellenistic in their foundation, or simply even barbarian, were excluded.[282] The Panhellenion therefore stands as a powerful sign of the continuing emphasis on *eugeneia* and a fixation on the ancient Greek past to the exclusion of all others.

Hadrian's Panhellenion, and the intellectual culture that supported its creation, provides key background for the careers of Christian intellectuals in the second century. Mostly thanks to Eusebius, we begin to have our first traces of Christians engaging with the emperor and the intellectual culture surrounding him during the reign of Hadrian.[283] The evidence for their activities is limited, but the nature of the challenges they faced is clear. With limited connections to the Greek past, and the reputation of representing a new movement lacking an ancient past, Christian intellectuals had no reason to expect any success in their encounters with the emperor and the elite intellectuals who associated with him. Faced with these barriers to success, Christian intellectuals needed to decide how to present themselves and how to make clear what exactly their relationship was to the Greek past and its classical literature. They likewise needed to decide how much they could claim to be Greek and what it would mean if they wished to emphasize some links to the barbarian past, especially in relation to Judaism. How Christian intellectuals tried to address these questions and challenges is the concern of the following chapters.

CHAPTER 2

JUSTIN MARTYR
A Would-Be Public Intellectual

At the start of Justin Martyr's *Dialogue with Trypho*, two men meet, walking through the colonnades of a Mediterranean port city, sometime probably in the 130s CE.[1] One man calls out to the other, "Hail, philosopher!" and explains that he had been taught "never to dismiss or despise people looking like this."[2] So begins a conversation between the speaker, a Jew named Trypho, and the man who looked like a philosopher, Justin. As the two talk, Justin describes his early philosophical education, and his encounters with teachers of the Stoic, Peripatetic, Pythagorean, and Platonist schools.[3] Eventually, though, as Justin explains, he met another teacher who led him to believe that Christianity was the only "safe and profitable" (ἀσφαλῆ τε καὶ σύμφορον) philosophy.[4] Based on this characterization of Christianity as a philosophy, Justin had every reason to continue dressing and acting like a philosopher, even after he had switched his loyalties from Platonism to what he would have called the Christian school of philosophy.[5]

Justin also portrays himself as a philosopher in his other extant works, written between roughly 150 and his death by execution, which happened at some point between 163 and 167.[6] He addresses the emperors Antoninus Pius, Marcus Aurelius, and Lucius Verus in his *First Apology* as if he were their philosophical peer, urging them to act toward Christians as if they really were "pious and philosophers and guardians of righteousness and lovers of culture."[7] And he explains to the emperors, in his *Second Apology*, how he had debated and vanquished a representative of the rival Cynic school in Rome, proving him to be "no philosopher" (οὐ φιλόσοφος).[8] Based on this consistent self-presentation across all three of his extant works, Justin made real efforts to cast himself as a philosopher and intellectual, seeking to break into the exclusive Greco-Roman partnership described in chapter 1.

Justin's engagement with the non-Christian intellectual culture of his time, however, has left many scholars with an uneasy feeling. Scholars have, on the one hand, been interested in exploring how Justin's thought may have been informed by prevailing philosophical ideas, in particular probing his engagement with Platonism.[9] But this interest has rarely extended to examinations of how Justin may have fit into the world of his non-Christian intellectual contemporaries and counterparts.[10] In most cases, scholars have been content to offer confident statements about how much, how little, or how well Justin may have actually engaged with non-Christian intellectuals in Rome or elsewhere, with little discussion or evidence to support these claims.[11] This tendency seems linked with a desire to minimize the extent to which Justin was a philosopher. As Runar M. Thorsteinsson suggests, the standard assumption is to view Justin in an "either-or" perspective, making him either a Christian teacher or a philosopher, as if the two were mutually exclusive categories.[12] In short, the assumption prevails that Justin, as a Christian, distanced himself from the non-Christian intellectual world, despite many hints otherwise.

A major reason for this assumption seems to be some untested ideas about persecution, and the belief that this was a phenomenon exclusive to Christianity.[13] As a Christian, Justin is often viewed as being fundamentally different from his intellectual counterparts, who are presumed to have been safer and more secure because they were non-Christian. By this reasoning, Justin would have been obliged to keep to himself and not seek out any attention from the emperor, because "Christians were tried and convicted simply for being Christians."[14] The lurking assumption here is that Justin knew better than to risk his life by acknowledging publicly that he was a Christian. Thus there is a presupposition that Justin's engagement with non-Christian intellectual culture must have been limited by the simple fact that he was a Christian. Even more so, there is an assumption that being a Christian was the defining factor in Justin's life and career and that this is how he would have been regarded by non-Christian intellectuals and by imperial authorities. No other considerations evidently mattered, even if Justin continued to represent himself as a philosopher after he became a Christian.

My concern in this chapter is to show that Justin still saw himself as part of the non-Christian intellectual world following his conversion. In particular, I aim to show that the threat of persecution, which has seemed so significant in the minds of many modern scholars, did little to separate Justin from non-Christian intellectuals. If anything, the threat of persecution was something that Justin and many non-Christian intellectuals shared in common and was a fundamental factor in their identity as intellectuals.

In the first section of this chapter, I argue that persecution was something that any intellectual with ambitions was likely to face when he came to Rome. Persecution might come at the hands of rivals, who were eager to destroy the reputation of anyone who challenged their own standing. It also might come from the emperor or other imperial authorities, who held the power of life and death over intellectuals, even if they were disinclined to pay that much attention to the constant squabbling that characterized Roman intellectual culture. Ambitious intellectuals thus had to work that much harder to capture imperial attention and the possible benefits that came with it. I show in the chapter's second section that Justin should be considered an ambitious intellectual, working with the goal, shared by so many of his counterparts, of being noticed by the imperial household. Justin, however, seems to have struggled to gain any attention from non-Christian intellectuals because of some basic gaps in his education that would have branded him as an amateur in the eyes of the city's elite intellectuals. Justin's struggles to attract attention, I show in the chapter's third and final section, led him to consider a more extreme way to capture attention: risking death. Other philosophers and intellectuals in Justin's lifetime took similar risks when they interacted with the emperor and other imperial authorities. This led to a larger controversy in the first and second centuries about intellectuals—and not just Christians—who were executed by imperial authorities. Persecution and debates about imperial executions were therefore common phenomena in Roman intellectual culture and not something unique to Christianity or Christian intellectuals. Justin's career accordingly needs to be approached from a wider angle than Christianity. His ambitions suggest that he needs to be considered not simply as a Christian, or even simply as a Christian heavily influenced by philosophical thought. He should, rather, be approached as an intellectual and as someone who belongs to the larger context of Roman intellectual culture in the second century. Justin's career provides us with our earliest detailed evidence of a Christian intellectual engaging with the competitive world of Roman intellectual culture.

Public Intellectuals and Persecution

Intellectuals who came to Rome in the second century, as Justin and so many others did, likely had some interest in catching the attention of the emperor, or other imperial authorities, such as the city prefect. Emperors and their representatives could provide valuable privileges and exemptions, whether for the intellectual himself or for the community he may have been representing (see chapter 1). Some intellectuals also hoped to gain a place in the imperial household, as a teacher, physician, administrator, or in some other specialized role. But the privileges and positions that emperors could bestow were jealously sought after by many intellectuals, which meant that Rome had a uniquely competitive intellectual culture. Ambitious intellectuals consequently realized that they needed to stand out from the crowd of their peers and rivals to capture imperial attention. To do this, they needed to gain a reputation of being the best in their particular field, an accomplishment that required frequent competition with rivals. Building such a reputation might also involve becoming known for *parrhēsia*, or frank outspokenness, a trait that would help an intellectual be noticed, though it might not win him many friends.[15] Building a reputation and becoming a public intellectual was therefore a competitive process, filled with controversy and much negative attention from rivals. Rumors and allegations abounded, and some intellectuals even seem to have faced acts of violence. Intellectuals in Rome therefore might expect to face what amounted to persecution at the hands of their rivals. And if they were among the lucky few to attract the notice of the emperor or another imperial authority, the attention they received might be negative, involving exile or death. But even negative attention might serve to enhance an intellectual's reputation, cementing his status as a public figure worthy of capturing an emperor's attention. Thus there was a close link between intellectual fame and the threat of persecution, both of which were omnipresent in Roman intellectual culture during the second century.

These two features of Roman intellectual culture are especially apparent in the works of two figures of this period: the physician Galen of Pergamum (ca. 129–216) and the orator and satirist Lucian of Samosata (ca. 120–180).[16] Any reader of Galen's works will recognize immediately how much emphasis he placed on his own fame and accomplishments, nearly all of which he achieved during his long residence in Rome, which extended, with some interludes of travel, from the early 160s to the time of his death.[17] Though during his own lifetime Galen lacked the fame he was to acquire in later periods, he still makes some appearances in the works of his contemporaries and near contemporaries.[18] These appearances, combined with his status as an imperial physician, connected successively to Marcus Aurelius, Commodus, and the Severan dynasty, confirm that he qualified as a public intellectual, with a big reputation.[19] Galen's works therefore provide evidence for his own successful quest to become a famous intellectual who gained a place in the imperial household.

Lucian, meanwhile, is a different story. Seemingly autobiographical material is scattered throughout his oeuvre, some of which suggests extensive travels throughout the empire, including to Rome, and links to the imperial household and other administrators.[20] Still, it is rarely clear when we are being told about the author's real life versus the backstory of a satirical persona he has adopted.[21] Lucian therefore is an elusive figure, moving in and out of the more and less fictional works that he wrote.[22] The works of his contemporaries and near contemporaries, from which he is almost entirely absent, offer little help in identifying Lucian. Though he may have attained a minor position as an imperial official in Egypt, it seems unlikely that he ever qualified as a public intellectual during his lifetime.[23]

Lucian's works nonetheless have much to say about the desire of intellectuals in his time to become famous. Many figures from second-century intellectual culture are named explicitly by Lucian, and others are hinted at, more or less obliquely.[24] His works offer a satirical and critical perspective on the aspirations of these intellectuals, by and large. Thus what Lucian says can be linked with what Galen and other sources reveal about the desire to become famous. Lucian was evidently eager to expose the pretensions of intellectuals, revealing that they were less knowledgeable, and less virtuous, than they claimed to be. Unsurprisingly, then, some of the best-known intellectuals of his time were among his targets.

As it happens, one of the most famous intellectuals of the second century was a target of Lucian's satire. This was the Cynic philosopher Peregrinus, called Proteus, who famously immolated himself shortly after the Olympic Games of 165.[25] Lucian's work *The Death of Peregrinus* is the major source for the life of this philosopher, but a score of references in other contemporary and near-contemporary authors help establish just how famous he became.[26] From Aulus Gellius and Philostratus, we learn that Peregrinus was a well-known figure in Athens, welcoming visitors to the hut where he lived just outside the city.[27] Menander Rhetor, in the third century, mentions a speech Peregrinus gave in praise of poverty.[28] There is, moreover, a likely allusion to his suicide in Pausanias, and there are definite references to it in the works of the three Christian authors Athenagoras, Tatian, and Tertullian.[29] Athenagoras even reports that after Peregrinus's death, a statue was erected in his memory in his native city of Parium, where it was believed by locals to give oracles.[30] References to Peregrinus in Christian authors are significant because Peregrinus was, for a time, a Christian himself, as Lucian reports.[31] But the three Christian authors who mention him seem unaware of this and only know him because of his famous suicide. On these grounds, Peregrinus's fame seems to have been well established in the second century. Some additional confirmation of this comes from Galen, who says nothing about Peregrinus himself, but who does include a story about the death of one of his pupils, Theagenes, whose "reputation" (δόξαν), he says, made him known to many people in

Rome.[32] By all of these measures, then, Peregrinus was a public intellectual, known to many more than just the philosophers of his school.

Lucian's treatment of Peregrinus, placed in dialogue with information from other sources, helps reveal the basic components of how he became famous. Peregrinus, it seems, went beyond the accepted levels of competition for intellectuals, attracting attention to himself by any means possible, in keeping with the reputation of philosophers of the Cynic school.[33] Hostility to Peregrinus's excessive competitiveness is indicated by the suggestion that he resorted to abuse (λοιδορία) rather than acceptable forms of debate.[34] As Lucian reports, discussing Peregrinus's voyage to Rome, he "sailed to Italy and immediately began abusing (ἐλοιδορεῖτο) everyone."[35] A similar accusation appears in Tatian's attack on Peregrinus, which addresses the dead philosopher directly: "You make a great noise in public (δημοσίᾳ) arguing your own case with plausibility, and if you do not get anything you turn to abuse (λοιδορεῖς) and your philosophic art becomes a way for obtaining money."[36] The charge here about seeking money is stock; it also appears many times in Lucian's account of Peregrinus and in other critiques of Cynics.[37] But the same point is still emphasized—that Peregrinus was simply abusing everyone, rather than engaging more selectively and appropriately with his intellectual peers and rivals, as other intellectuals were careful to emphasize about their own lives and careers.[38] Philostratus says much the same thing about Peregrinus, describing how the sophist Herodes Atticus had to deal with the "abuse" (λοιδορίας) of Peregrinus.[39] Everyone was evidently the potential target of Peregrinus's abuse. His indiscriminately abusive behavior fits in with the larger portrait offered of him in Lucian's work, one section of which suggests that the philosopher was known, during one stage of his career, to whip himself and masturbate in public.[40] Peregrinus seems, based on these reports, to have been violating normal standards of decorum for intellectuals, all in the quest to make himself famous.

Peregrinus's behavior upon his arrival in Rome, however, seems to have been fairly typical for intellectuals. Galen implies that he acted in a similar way when he first came to the city. Galen recalls, looking back at an earlier stage of his career, that "at that time the custom had somehow sprung up of speaking in public each day on any questions that were put forward."[41] Like Peregrinus, Galen and other physicians felt a need to draw attention to themselves, and the best way to do this was to speak in public. A hostile observer may well have suggested that they were simply abusing each other, as Lucian and Tatian remarked about Peregrinus. But Galen would have strenuously objected to this characterization, as Jason König has argued, noting the physician's steadfast insistence that he avoided being excessively competitive.[42] This insistence seems disingenuous, though, given the extent and nature of evidence we have for Galen engaging in public and highly competitive contests with rival physicians.[43] As Galen himself records, he was known to begin vivisecting an ape, severing its veins, and then inviting his rivals to repair the damage.[44] Defining acceptable levels of competition therefore seems to have been a highly relative and subjective matter. It is interesting, in this sense, that Galen offered a neutral characterization of the behavior of Peregrinus's pupil Theagenes, with no hint that he was being abusive or behaving inappropriately. According to Galen, Theagenes built up a reputation in the city because he "spoke publicly (δημοσίᾳ) every day in the gymnasium of Trajan."[45] Tatian's critique of Peregrinus used the same vocabulary of public speech, employing a key word (δημοσίᾳ) that also appears frequently in discussions of sophistic behavior.[46] Speaking in public and arguing with—and, perhaps, abusing—peers and rivals were basic ways that intellectuals built a reputation for themselves when they came to Rome. To some observers, Peregrinus and other Cynics may have been behaving inappropriately, but their desire to build their reputation by speaking in public was completely unexceptional.

Peregrinus's behavior upon his arrival to Rome and the critical responses to it from other authors help reveal the city's exceptionally hostile and competitive climate for intellectuals. According to Galen, intellectual culture in Rome was different than it was anywhere else in the empire. He discovered this soon after his initial arrival, when his unmatched talent as a prognosticator of illnesses made him an unpopular figure among the city's most reputable doctors. This is the starting point for Galen's work *On Prognosis*, which records how the young and naïve doctor was shunned by his medical peers, who soon became implacable rivals. The work is filled with Galen's typical expressions of self-importance and hyperbole,[47] but its content about his first experiences in Rome still helps reveal what the city was like for intellectuals in the second century. Galen notes that his youthful naïveté soon disappeared, thanks in part to the advice of his patron Eudemus, a Peripatetic philosopher and, like Galen, a native of Pergamum.[48] Eudemus apparently told Galen this: "Don't think that good men turn bad in this city. No, those who are already bad, once they find an abundance of opportunities, make much greater profits here than in provincial cities."[49] Their actions, Eudemus explained, inspired other bad men to try to outdo them, and the city's great size granted them an anonymity that they could use to repeat the same behavior.[50] On the larger stage of Rome, intellectuals could be expected to behave differently than they did anywhere else in the empire.

Galen's portrait of the city demonstrates the impact that damaging stories could have on the reputation of intellectuals who sought out public status. An extended anecdote reveals just how widely stories of this sort could spread. It concerns an unnamed young physician from Pergamum who had his reputation destroyed after his arrival in Rome. This young man sought to help a wealthy Roman woman conceive, drawing on his training from an Alexandrian doctor named Metrodorus and on his familiarity with the Hippocratic corpus.[51] Following the advice of his teacher, the young physician instructed the woman to eat large quantities of "extremely hot and half-cooked" flesh of an octopus (πωλύπια) of some sort, as a Hippocratic text instructed.[52] The woman tried her best to eat the unevenly cooked flesh but vomited after her second bite. Word of this incident spread, both because the young doctor was, as Galen says, "a well-known man" and because of the fee that he had charged the woman for this remedy. Galen explains what happened to the young man: "His disgrace was such that when he appeared in the streets, all inhabitants of the city began to wink at each other and pointed him out to each other with much sneering and laughter. They gave him a nickname that has stuck with him to this day, which is derived from the name of that many-legged animal and from the term for his skewering it on spits. Things went so far that he became famous for stupidity and no one trusted him to treat patients."[53] The young physician may well have deserved this reputation, though Galen emphasizes that his teacher Metrodorus was the one who really should have been blamed.[54] Regardless, the anecdote provides an illustration of how much an intellectual's reputation could be damaged by stories spread about him. Galen may be exaggerating in his suggestion that everyone in Rome knew about the incident, but there is still the clear implication here that intellectuals, even young physicians, could be public figures in the city and, consequently, vulnerable to the spread of negative stories about them.

The spread of rumors could even amount to persecution, as Galen describes. Galen himself evidently received such treatment upon his first arrival in Rome, when his jealous rivals attempted to destroy his burgeoning reputation as a skilled prognosticator of illnesses. Galen's predictions, we are told, were so uncannily accurate that his rivals accused him of being a sorcerer.[55] This is an entirely plausible thing to have happened. Many similar charges are apparent in the second century, including those against which Apuleius defended himself in his *Apology* and those made by Irenaeus of Lyons against Marcus "the Magician."[56] But, as Galen reports, the rumors made against a physician in Rome could escalate well beyond common accusations of sorcery. A talented prognosticator might even have this happen to him, Galen claims: "Finally he stirs up such envy against himself that they [sc. his rivals] conspire against him, first by plotting poisoning, second by the trap in which they caught Quintus, the best physician of his generation, who was expelled from Rome on a charge of murdering his patients."[57] Galen suggests here that a talented doctor required real courage in the face of all this negative attention and the spread of rumors by his rivals. A doctor might persist in the face of envious attacks, but this might lead to worse consequences, including poisoning at the hands of his rivals. How seriously we should take this suggestion is unclear, though Galen does report the story of another doctor who was poisoned, together with two servants, at some point in the 150s after he demonstrated his medical skill.[58] These suggestions about poison recall the common charges made about the deeds of emperors and imperial women, so familiar from the works of Suetonius, among others.[59] Galen's claims about the threat of poison should probably be treated with the same amount of skepticism. Poisoning aside, Galen's story raises the possibility of exile, illustrated with the example of Quintus. This doctor is attested only in a few scattered comments by Galen.[60] According to these stories, Quintus, because of his talent—and, perhaps, his attested tendency to be impatient and a little too clever—was driven out of Rome by his rivals during the reign of Hadrian.[61] No source tells us more about this story, so there is no way of establishing with any certainty what happened, but we can still reach one conclusion about it. Extreme competition in Rome could lead an intellectual to leave the city and a rumor-filled climate that amounted to persecution.

One consequence—and perhaps even the point—of all this intellectual controversy was that it attracted the attention of imperial officials. Intellectuals in the Roman Empire, much more so than today, could hope to become real celebrities, known even to the most powerful people in the empire.[62] If we turn back briefly to the first century CE, we find a nice demonstration of this in the career of Thessalus of Tralles, a notorious doctor credited as the founder of the Methodist school of medicine.[63] Pliny the Elder presented Thessalus as an entertainer: "No pantomime actor, no driver of a three-horse chariot had a larger retinue than he when he went out in public."[64] This large entourage certainly fit in with Thessalus's goals to cultivate wealthy people at Rome, and to gain imperial patronage. We have fragments, quoted disparagingly by Galen, of his letter to the emperor Nero that boasted of the new medical school he had founded. According to Galen, Thessalus dismissed the achievements of all other doctors in his letter: "I have established a new sect and the only one that is true, as all the earlier doctors failed to pass along anything useful for the preservation of health or the relief of diseases."[65] Galen himself, though, was guilty of similar boasting; he is always eager in his works to identify the famous and powerful people who came to watch his medical demonstrations: "I became known in Rome to other outstanding men, and thereupon to all the rulers, from the deeds of my art, not from sophistic words."[66] This statement falls completely in line with Galen's care in reporting how his reputation in Rome grew as famous and powerful men came to see him speak and then spread word to their friends. One particularly contentious incident resulted in Galen abandoning an anatomical demonstration midstream after the Peripatetic philosopher Alexander of Damascus interrupted him with an impertinent question.[67] In the aftermath, Galen says that the incident became known "to all the intellectuals in the city of Rome" (τοῖς φιλολόγοις ἅπασιν, ὅσοι κατὰ τὴν τῶν Ῥωμαίων πόλιν), together with a former consul, a future prefect of the city, and a man who was the uncle of Marcus Aurelius's co-emperor Lucius Verus.[68] Eventually, Galen's patron Boethus even spread word of Galen's achievements to Marcus Aurelius himself, helping him to secure a position as imperial physician.[69] As Galen proudly reports, Marcus Aurelius used to say that he was "first among physicians and unique among philosophers" (τῶν μὲν ἰατρῶν πρῶτον εἶναι, τῶν δὲ φιλοσόφων μόνον).[70] Becoming known to an emperor was the pinnacle for ambitious intellectuals and the reason many of them came to Rome in the first place.[71]

For some intellectuals, it mattered little if the attention received from the emperor and other imperial officials was positive. The Cynic Peregrinus provides a telling example of this situation in his behavior upon his arrival in Rome, which happened sometime during the reign of Antoninus Pius. As Lucian reports, Peregrinus "sailed to Italy and immediately began abusing everyone, especially the emperor, knowing that he was extremely mild and gentle, so that he was daring safely."[72] The passage illustrates the fixation on the emperor that many intellectuals who came to Rome seem to have had. It simultaneously suggests that even an extremely abusive intellectual such as Peregrinus might have some difficulty attracting any imperial attention. Antoninus Pius, as it happens, had devised new policies designed to limit the number of ambassadors who sought an audience with him.[73] Still, as Lucian reports, Peregrinus's behavior was helping him to become famous: "But the reputation of this man was still growing from these events, at least among laypeople, and he was a celebrity for his recklessness, until the wise man overseeing the city [the city prefect] sent him away for enjoying this too much, saying that the city had no need for such a philosopher."[74] The involvement of the city prefect is significant here. This official, who might be identified as Q. Lollius Urbicus, prefect from 146 to 160, likely had some involvement in Rome's intellectual culture.[75] As Vivian Nutton has suggested, the city prefect may have been the official who was responsible for determining which intellectuals who came to Rome received the exemptions from liturgies that so many of them seem to have sought.[76] The procedure for granting these exemptions is unknown, but papyrological evidence from Egypt suggests that in making such a determination the official would gauge the prevailing mood in the area toward the intellectual under examination.[77] This is consonant with the importance of rumors and the attitudes of other intellectuals as illustrated in Galen's works. Peregrinus's behavior attracted the attention of the "laypeople," but evidently also that of his intellectual rivals, and eventually gained the notice of the city prefect.

As it happened, being exiled from the city was just what Peregrinus needed to cement his status as a public intellectual. Exile was a common punishment for many famous intellectuals in the decades before Peregrinus's time, and it was a factor that helped them to build their reputations.[78] Lucian's narrator explained what resulted from Peregrinus's expulsion, picking up immediately after the quotation cited in the previous paragraph: "But he was famous for this, too, and on the lips of everyone as the philosopher who was driven out for his frank speech (παρρησίαν) and excessive freedom, and in this respect he approached Musonius [Rufus], Dio [Chrysostom], Epictetus, and any other person who ended up in a similar situation."[79] The three philosophers named here were among the most famous of the recent past. Their exiles were a major part of their fame, to judge by the attention devoted to this aspect of their careers in their own works and those of others who discussed them.[80] In the case of Musonius Rufus, Tacitus even suggests that his exile by Nero was a consequence of the "renown of his name" (claritudo nominis).[81] The brightest philosophical stars were the ones to be exiled, and this, in turn, confirmed their fame. As Lucian's narrator suggests, the same thing happened to Peregrinus, though he was far from being a real philosopher. Peregrinus nonetheless gained the fame and status of a particularly distinguished philosopher, simply by being expelled from Rome. Any imperial attention was good for building an intellectual's reputation, even if it came from a city prefect, rather than the emperor himself.

Interest in gaining fame and imperial attention seems to have been common among intellectuals in the second century. This is clear from Galen's self-presentation and from his discussions of the ambitions of his rivals. It is even clear from the career of the more elusive Lucian, notably in his work *The Death of Peregrinus*. This work contains a dose of satire directed not simply at its target but also at the narrator of the work, who displays an unhealthy degree of fascination with Peregrinus. The work implies that the narrator should be identified with an unnamed speaker who steps up in the text to challenge a speech given in praise of Peregrinus by his pupil Theagenes.[82] The narrator reveals, moreover, that he had traveled on a sea voyage with Peregrinus on an earlier occasion.[83] Why he had done this is left unsaid, but this incidental remark seems almost to imply that the narrator had devoted a good portion of his life simply to following Peregrinus around and observing his behavior.[84] The work therefore offers, as Dana Fields suggests, a commentary on the culture of "agonistic self-promotion" that prevailed among intellectuals in the second century.[85] We should hesitate to assume, however, that the behavior of the work's narrator provides us with biographical information about Lucian, even though he names himself in the opening of the work, which is framed as a letter to a philosopher named Cronius.[86] Yet, in this respect, it is certainly worth noting Galen's story, recorded in an Arabic translation of a work no longer extant in Greek, about a man who may well be our Lucian.[87] As Galen explains, this Lucian "fabricated a book made up of obscure statements that did not have any meaning at all, attributed it to Heraclitus and passed it on to some people."[88] The spurious work was then passed along to a philosopher with a big reputation. His attempts to treat the book seriously and to offer interpretations of it subjected him to ridicule, Galen explains. This Lucian apparently subjected some grammarians to the same treatment, allowing them to offer interpretations of some meaningless oracles he had composed himself.[89] Lucian suggests that he did a similar thing in one of his own works, reporting that he submitted difficult or ridiculous questions to the holy man Alexander of Abonoteichus in an attempt to discredit his authority as a prophet.[90] In effect, then, we may have signs here that Lucian devoted a large part of his life to exposing the pretensions of his intellectual rivals, much as the narrator of *The Death of Peregrinus* seems to have done. Therefore this work may demonstrate that Lucian was displaying some self-awareness of how the competitive culture of intellectual life implicated everyone, including himself. Intellectuals competed against one another to gain the attention of others, with an eye toward attracting notice from the emperor himself. The most famous and successful intellectuals, in turn, were those who were most likely to face persecution—first from their rivals and then perhaps also from the emperor or another imperial official. These rivalries and relationships, and their consequences, shaped intellectual culture in the second century.

Justin's Ambitions

There are many signs that Justin, too, saw himself as taking part in this intellectual world. Like Galen and many other intellectuals of this period, he spent extended periods of time in Rome, dying there around the same time that Peregrinus jumped into the flames at Olympia, and not long after Galen first came to Rome. Like Peregrinus, he seems to have captured the attention, eventually, of a city prefect, Junius Rusticus, who oversaw the death of Justin and his pupils, according to the *Acta* of his martyrdom.[91] And, like Peregrinus, Galen, and so many others, Justin seems to have wanted to gain the attention of the imperial household, as his two apologetic works signal. The second of these works will receive the bulk of my attention in this section of the chapter. Justin wrote his *Second Apology*, as he explains, following the trial of an unnamed Christian woman in Rome that seems to have attracted attention to the city's Christian communities.[92] This incident does seem like a crisis of sorts for Justin and the city's other Christians. But it also functioned as an opportunity for Justin, who seems to have realized that this recent event might give him a better chance to be noticed by the imperial household and his intellectual peers and rivals in the city. More than his other works, the *Second Apology* displays Justin's ambitions to become a public intellectual. It also hints at some of the issues that he seems to have had in gaining the attention of other intellectuals, not to mention the imperial household. Though Justin shared many things in common with his non-Christian intellectual counterparts, he must have had a difficult time getting them to take him seriously, and even to regard him as a peer. Justin may have presented himself as a philosopher and sought to gain a public reputation, but most other intellectuals would have regarded him, at best, as a poorly educated representative of a second-rate school of philosophy.

The very form of the *Second Apology* reveals Justin's desire to attract attention to himself. It was a petition (βιβλίδιον/*libellus*) addressed to the emperors, following the pattern familiar from many other surviving examples of petitions from this period.[93] The *Second Apology*, moreover, was separate from the *First Apology*, and not an appendix to it, as Thorsteinsson has recently argued, noting that it is of a recognizably different style, and much more like a letter addressed to the emperors.[94] Justin offers many hints that he wanted this work to be read by the emperor. In the first place, he provides two examples demonstrating that other Christians in his period were addressing similar petitions to the emperor. One example comes from the story of the unnamed Christian woman reported at the start of the *Second Apology*, who submitted a petition to Antoninus Pius after her husband accused her of being a Christian.[95] The other is of an Alexandrian youth who submitted a petition to the governor of Egypt, seeking exemption from a law that forbade doctors from performing castrations.[96] Thus there is little reason to doubt that Justin, too, may have submitted his own petition to the emperors, asking the emperor to "subscribe" (ὑπογράψαντας) it, as he requests at the start of the *Second Apology*, using the standard vocabulary associated with petitions.[97] This was exactly how other residents of the empire behaved, especially in the second century, which seems to have been a litigious age, based on patterns discernible from the survival of petitions on papyri in Egypt.[98] It was normal, moreover, for people to ask for exemptions and exceptions to previous judgments and laws, just as the Christian youth seeking permission to be castrated did.[99] Justin's behavior, then, fits in with larger trends in the empire and the desire of many people to have their grievances or requests heard by the emperor.

Justin's petition to the emperor even provides signs of his larger ambitions as an intellectual seeking to capture imperial attention. Justin goes out of his way to mention a debate he claims to have had with a Cynic philosopher named Crescens.[100] This Crescens is introduced in a way that recalls what Lucian has to say about Peregrinus's behavior in Rome: "For the man is unworthy of being called a philosopher, who bears witness against us publicly (δημοσίᾳ) concerning matters he fails to understand, [saying] that Christians are godless and impious, and doing this for the goodwill and enjoyment of the misled mob."[101] Like Peregrinus, Crescens was "a lover of noise and boasting" (φιλοψόφου καὶ φιλοκόμπου), and his behavior was designed to please the city's uneducated masses, Justin claims.[102] Justin even uses the key word δημοσίᾳ to emphasize Crescens's public speech, in keeping with the pattern already apparent from Tatian, Galen, and other intellectuals of the second century. As in Lucian's denunciation of Peregrinus, Justin also emphasizes that Crescens was no philosopher, despite what some people in the city may have thought. In short, Justin's method of introducing Crescens fits in completely with the norms of second-century intellectual culture, as apparent from the works of Galen and Lucian.

Justin's report of his encounter with Crescens even contains the same concern displayed by Galen that important people in Rome know about what he has done. This concern emerges as a major reason, it seems, why Justin mentioned the debate in the first place. He says, addressing himself to the emperors, "I would have you know that when I had been asked to solve problems put to me I in turn asked [Crescens] certain questions and so discovered and demonstrated that in truth he knows nothing. And to show that I speak the truth, in the event that these exchanges have not been reported back to you, I am prepared to exchange questions with him again, even in your presence."[103] What Justin presents us with here is similar to when Galen and other physicians convened in public to answer questions that were put to them. The same conceit that the emperor and his household kept themselves informed of the endless series of intellectual debates going on in the city is also apparent in Galen's works. Justin even considers the possibility that his questions and Crescens's answers had already "been made known" (ἐγνώσθησαν) to the emperors.[104] How exactly this might have happened is unclear; Justin's use of the passive verb offers no hints. We are thus left in the same territory apparent in Galen's *On Prognosis*, where we are informed again and again about the growth of the author's reputation in Rome, reaching eventually to the imperial household. Justin even seems to suggest that a repeat of his debate with Crescens might warrant imperial attention, much like what Galen has to say about the excitement caused after his spat with Alexander of Damascus. Both intellectuals seem to take for granted that their actions were being noticed by important people in Rome.

Like Galen, Justin displays awareness of the importance of rumor in building or destroying the reputation of intellectuals. His attempt to damage Crescens's reputation is obvious, and it even includes the suggestion that the emperors themselves would recognize immediately how little this Cynic philosopher knew about Christianity. As Justin says, if the emperors had already heard about his encounter with Crescens, they would already know that he is "no philosopher but rather a lover of glory" (οὐ φιλόσοφος ἀλλὰ φιλόδοξος).[105] This desire to spread stories about Crescens's qualifications as a philosopher sits somewhat uneasily with Justin's own discussion of the impact that rumors have had on the treatment of Christians by the Roman Empire. According to Justin, "evil rumor" (φήμην πονηρὰν) has led Christians to be punished on a variety of false charges, including atheism, immorality, and disloyalty to the emperors.[106] It is therefore odd to see Justin claim ignorance about the behaviors of Christians he deemed heretical in his discussion of Simon Magus, Menander, and Marcion.[107] "Whether," Justin says, "they do the wicked things related in stories—turning over lamps, shameless intercourse, and meals of human flesh—we do not know."[108] These were the same stories being told about what Christians did when the lights went out, as it were.[109] But Justin implies, first, that Christians he deemed heretical might actually be doing these things and, second, that they should receive imperial punishment for their behavior: "But that they are not being persecuted or killed by you [sc. the emperors], at least for their beliefs, this we do know."[110] In effect, Justin is suggesting here that imperial authorities should intervene in Christian disputes, based on the rumors that he is spreading—or at least not denying—about his rivals. He even offers to let the emperors read another of his works, now lost, that contained his attacks "against all the heresies that have risen up" (κατὰ πασῶν τῶν γεγενημένων αἱρέσεων), spreading this campaign of rumors even further.[111] Like the rivals of Galen and Apuleius, moreover, Justin indulges in stock charges about magic, alleging that Simon and Menander were both magicians.[112] Whether discussing Crescens or other Christians he deemed heretical, Justin shows himself willing to deal in rumors, all for the sake of damaging the reputations of his rivals.[113] This is quite in keeping with the picture of intellectual culture offered by Galen and Lucian.

Justin evidently wanted to be part of this culture, but there are many hints that he struggled to gain the attention that he might have liked. In this regard, it seems significant that Justin has so much to say about his encounter with Crescens, and basically nothing else to say about other debates or conversations with rival intellectuals, apart from the Jewish philosopher Trypho. Justin does suggest that he talked to other people, but he provides strikingly few details about these conversations. At best, Justin places some words in the mouth of Trypho, making him suggest that Justin's skill at answering questions derived from experience of "much debate with many people" (πολλῆς προστρίψεως . . . πρὸς πολλοὺς).[114] But few of these people were likely intellectuals of the sort who appear in the works of Galen and Lucian. Justin surely would have mentioned his encounters with men of this type, especially if he could claim to have bested them in a debate, as he did in his report of his encounter with Crescens. Justin's debate with Crescens therefore seems to have been a rare occasion when a non-Christian, non-Jewish intellectual actually was willing to speak with him.

Ironically, Justin's debate with Crescens may simply have been a consequence of simple Cynic abusiveness. As is clear from the example of Peregrinus, Cynics were more inclined than most intellectuals to be indiscriminate in conversing and debating with others.[115] Crescens, then, like Peregrinus, may well have simply been "abusing everyone," a situation that led him to engage in a debate with Justin. Justin may therefore simply have been an incidental target of Crescens's ongoing attempt to build a reputation for himself. I am consequently disinclined to accept Thorsteinsson's suggestion that Crescens was a Stoic philosopher and that Justin was offering a slanderous charge by calling him a Cynic.[116] At best, Justin's charge may have been pointing to a basic overlap between the behavior of some Stoics and Cynics that is well attested in sources from the second century.[117] Crescens, behaving like a stereotypical Cynic, seems to have been the rare intellectual who did Justin the favor of debating him in public.

As it happens, Rome's intellectual elite would have taken little notice of the encounter between Justin and Crescens, dismissing both of them as poorly educated philosophers representing second-rate schools of philosophy. This dismissive attitude fits in with a broader tendency for intellectuals in the second century to group Christians and Cynics together and to criticize them in similar ways.[118] Justin hints at this, suggesting that Crescens's attack on Christianity may have been motivated by his wish "not to be suspected of being a Christian himself."[119] Crescens may well have had reason to fear this. Lucian seems to regard Cynicism and Christianity as similarly illegitimate philosophies, both practiced by the great fraud Peregrinus. A similar critique appears also in an oration by Aelius Aristides, which compares some unnamed philosophers who behave very much like Cynics to "the impious people in Palestine" (τοῖς ἐν τῇ Παλαιστίνῃ δυσσεβέσι), noting that both were inclined "to be abusive" (λοιδορεῖν).[120] These people in Palestine may be Jews, rather than Christians, but Aristides's reference to them is vague enough to apply to either or both.[121] Christians and Jews were often grouped together by outside observers, in any case. We therefore have definite hints from multiple sources about a basic similarity between Christians, Cynics, and Jews, and disapproval of it.

Clearer signs of this attitude are in Galen, who subjects Christians, Cynics, and Jews to the same criticisms, focusing on their lack of interest in logical training. This lack is a fundamental part of how Galen describes Christians and Jews, whom he regarded as bad philosophers.[122] In one passage, Galen casually mentions the "school of Moses and Christ" (Μωϋσοῦ καὶ Χριστοῦ διατριβὴν), using the word διατριβή, which connotes a philosophical school.[123] But Galen's other references to Christians help show that his characterization of them as philosophers is less positive than it might at first seem. Christians were, in Galen's view, like the most dogmatic doctors and philosophers, who operated in the realm of "indemonstrable laws" (νόμων ἀναποδείκτων) and demanded faithful adherence to their doctrines without providing proof.[124] Galen was, in this sense, disrespecting rival philosophers and doctors by likening them to Christians, rather than respecting Christians by likening them to philosophers. Cynics were clearly among these philosophers who received Galen's disrespect. In Galen's view, Cynicism, like Christianity, depended on dogma rather than logical proof: "All the Cynics, in fact, whom I have seen in my life, together with some people who claim to be philosophers, admit that they avoid training in logic."[125] This sort of criticism of philosophers is relatively common in Galen's works, but Cynics were evidently in a different category than representatives of other schools. As Galen says, he still did spend time conversing and debating with philosophers who were "enslaved to a philosophical school" (δουλευόντων αἱρέσει τινὶ τῶν κατὰ φιλοσοφίαν).[126] But these philosophers were limited to representatives of the Platonic, Epicurean, Stoic, Peripatetic, and Skeptical schools.[127] Cynics were unwelcome at these gatherings, as were Christians. Justin and Crescens thus would have seemed to Galen to be similar types of bad philosophers who depended more on dogma than logic.

Somewhat surprisingly, Justin even suggests that he was the sort of badly educated philosopher that Galen critiqued. This suggestion comes in Justin's account of his education at the start of his *Dialogue with Trypho*, which forms part of his story about how he came to be a Christian philosopher. As Justin claims, he sought to receive an education from a succession of teachers representing different philosophical schools: Stoic, Peripatetic, Pythagorean, Platonic, and finally Christian.[128] Along the way, though, Justin says that he was rejected as a pupil by the Pythagorean teacher on the grounds that he lacked the necessary preliminary training in "music, astronomy, and geometry" (μουσικῇ καὶ ἀστρονομίᾳ καὶ γεωμετρίᾳ).[129] At first sight, this is a surprising admission by Justin of major gaps in his education. As Peter Lampe notes, this admission is out of keeping with the larger genre of biographical stories about a philosopher's education to which Justin's account belongs.[130] Many scholars have wished to deny any reality to Justin's account on the grounds of this generic affiliation, according to which a philosopher progresses from one school to the next as part of his training.[131] Justin's admission of an inadequate education in his story is therefore a likely sign that it was grounded somewhat in reality, providing a guide to how he would have been regarded by other intellectuals with better educations.

Justin's better-educated counterparts would have been just as dismissive of him as the Pythagorean teacher in his story was. The three fields of music, astronomy, and geometry were regarded as essential preparatory training by many intellectuals in the second century.[132] There even developed a tradition that Plato's Academy contained an inscription above its entrance forbidding admission to anyone lacking this training: "Let no one ignorant of geometry enter" (ἀγεωμέτρητος μηδεὶς εἰσίτω).[133] The earliest-known references to this inscription date from the fourth century CE, but traces of this attitude are apparent among Platonic philosophers in Justin's lifetime.[134] The philosopher Calvenus Taurus, who was active around the middle of the second century, offered a critique of poorly trained philosophical students who came to him "ignorant of geometry" (ἀγεωμέτρητοι).[135] These students came with unreasonable demands about how they would like to be taught, Taurus charges: "One says, 'Teach me this first,' and another likewise says, 'I wish to learn this, not that.'"[136] The scenario here evokes what Justin says about his own education and his decision to forgo the preliminary studies recommended by the Pythagorean teacher: "When I thought about the time that I would be expending on these studies (τὰ μαθήματα), I could not bear waiting that long."[137] In his story, Justin was hoping that he could dictate the pace and topics of his education, much like the students mentioned by Taurus. In effect, Justin is characterizing himself as one of the poorly trained philosophical students critiqued by Taurus. Justin therefore emerges from the story about his early life as someone who would have fit in poorly with Taurus and other distinguished philosophers of his time.

Justin seems, instead, to fit in better with the crowds of would-be intellectuals who are mentioned in the works of Galen and Lucian. Both authors suggest that there were many people in their lifetime seeking to become intellectuals, despite their poor preliminary educations. Galen has much to say on this subject in relation to the Methodist school of medicine, founded by the hypercompetitive Thessalus of Tralles, who announced his new school in a letter to Nero (see chapter 1).[138] According to Galen, Thessalus claimed that doctors could be trained in a mere six months, without requiring any training in "geometry, astronomy, dialectic, music, or any of the noble arts."[139] As a result, Galen claimed that "shoemakers, carpenters, dyers, and bronze-workers have abandoned their trades and plunge into medicine."[140] Lucian makes a similar suggestion, referring to "shoemakers and carpenters" (σκυτοτόμων ἢ τεκτόνων) abandoning their trades and taking up instead the cloak (τριβώνιον) of a philosopher, filling the city up with men who looked the part but lacked the requisite training.[141] Justin may match up poorly with some aspects of this caricature, but his choice to dress as a philosopher, despite his evident lack of training in music, astronomy, and geometry, surely would have opened him up to the sort of charges made by Galen and Lucian.

Other features in Justin's works, moreover, suggest that he lacked the training enjoyed by the more privileged intellectuals of his time. Justin's style is best described as pedagogical, lacking the artificial and polished language of his sophistic contemporaries.[142] As Mark Edwards shows, Justin does seem to have studied some of Plato's works at first hand, which implies a certain amount of philosophical education.[143] But his works are sparing in their use of classical references and quotations—an absence that stands out when he is compared to Christian intellectuals of slightly later periods, including his own pupil Tatian, not to mention the learned Clement of Alexandria.[144] In short, Justin's report of his early education in the *Dialogue with Trypho* seems to present a basically accurate picture, at least in terms of the gaps in his training. These gaps link him with the caricatured would-be philosophers mentioned by Galen and Lucian and reveal how difficult it surely was for him to be taken seriously by other intellectuals in Rome.

Justin therefore represents a different sort of intellectual in second-century Rome. He evidently did share some things in common with Galen, as is clear from the ambition displayed in his *Second Apology*. His debate with the Cynic Crescens, moreover, brings him into contact with Lucian's portrait of the abusive Peregrinus and the agonistic struggles of intellectuals in his time. But the account he offers of his own education brands him as an outsider of sorts, similar to the unnamed doctors and philosophers mentioned by Galen and Lucian who sought to become intellectuals, despite their lack of training. The *Second Apology*, though, shows no signs of hesitation on Justin's part. He implies that the emperors should already know about his debate with Crescens, and he presents himself as a willing participant in future debates with his vanquished foe, or, it seems, anyone else who might try to attack the Christian philosophical school that he represented. It is nonetheless hard to imagine that Justin, with his poor education and nonexistent standing as a philosopher, would have gained much attention, whether from the imperial household or other intellectuals. The *Second Apology* provides no further information about how it would have been received or who in Justin's time may have read it. It stands for us now, therefore, as a petition without a response. Justin does, however, include some speculation in it about what might happen to him in the future. I turn to this speculation in the chapter's final section.

Justin and Voluntary Martyrdom

Justin, it emerges from the *Second Apology*, expected to face persecution and death: "I expect that I will be plotted against and impaled on a stake by one of these mentioned, or at least by Crescens, that lover of noise and of empty praise."[145] Some issues in the text of the work make it unclear who the unnamed people "mentioned" are, but it is most likely that they are the demons who are often identified by Justin as the cause of hatred against Christians.[146] This point aside, this passage, like others, shows how Justin's self-presentation is similar to that of his intellectual contemporaries, including Galen, who had so much to say about the persecution—and even death—that talented doctors could face in Rome (as noted previously). Justin and Galen were both evidently concerned to establish that they might face persecution at the hands of their rivals. This comparison with Galen is a welcome reminder that Christians were not the only people in Justin's time who could claim to be persecuted and who wanted to advertise this state of affairs.

There was, however, controversy in Justin's time about how willingly someone should risk persecution and death by confronting imperial authorities. Debates on this point are familiar to scholars of early Christianity, who have had much to say about the attitudes of the early church toward what has been termed "voluntary martyrdom."[147] But, even in the recent surge of interest in this topic, little attention has been paid to the larger controversy taking place among non-Christians about the proper attitude to take when confronting an emperor. A large body of literature from the first and second centuries, besides Christian acts of martyrdom, demonstrates that the encounter between an intellectual and an emperor was something that resonated for people in Justin's time.[148] This literature, and the debate about intellectual-imperial confrontations, provide a larger context for Justin's behavior and for the contemporaneous controversy among Christian intellectuals about voluntary martyrdom. Justin's remarks in the *Second Apology* about death and persecution functioned as a way for him to link himself to a larger culture of intellectual behavior and to other, more famous intellectuals who were persecuted and killed. Justin suggests that legitimate philosophers were almost inevitably persecuted and exe-cuted—a claim that allows him to legitimate the deaths by execution of previous Christians. This strategy of self-presentation again shows Justin's efforts to fit in with the norms of contemporary intellectual culture. But, like his other efforts to fit in, this strategy was likely not well received by his elite intellectual contemporaries. Intellectuals who experienced per-secution and death may often have been revered and remembered within their own communities, but the responses to them by outsiders tended to be less positive. Seeking out persecution and death was an action critiqued by outsiders and rivals, though it served for Justin as a way to prove the legitimacy of himself and other Christians as philosophers.

Justin's attempt to cast himself as a persecuted intellectual is apparent throughout the *Second Apology*, notably in his attempt to liken himself to some famous philosophers of the past. This strategy fits in with Justin's larger goal of presenting himself as a philosopher. But it also forms part of his surprising argument that some philosophers of the past were basically Christians, even though they lived before the time of Christ. This claim comes out especially in how Justin treats Socrates.[149] Justin suggests that Socrates was a Christian avant la lettre, in keeping with his argument that Jesus, as the Logos of God, was the "entire rational principle" (τὸ λογικὸν τὸ ὅλον) behind the real wisdom of every system of philosophy.[150] In effect, then, Justin could claim that Christ, as the Logos, had shaped the develop-ment of philosophy even before he was made flesh in the relatively recent past.[151] Justin's suggestion therefore allowed him to claim whomever he wanted as a Christian, based on the surprising rationale that "whatsoever has been well said by anyone belongs to us Christians."[152] Socrates con-sequently qualified as a virtuous proto-Christian, simply because Justin agreed with some aspects of what he said. Christianity, by this argument, was really the true philosophy, and all other philosophical schools could be judged by how closely they adhered to its doctrines.

The proto-Christian philosophers identified by Justin inevitably faced persecution, suggesting that all representatives of true philosophy would experience this treatment from earthly authorities. Socrates was a perfect illustration of this point for Justin. The agents driving Socrates's persecution, Justin claims, were not the accusers who brought charges against him but rather demons, who were concerned that the Athenian philosopher's use of "true reason" (λόγῳ ἀληθεῖ) would prevent people from worshipping them as gods.[153] The same thing was now happening to Justin and other Christians: Socrates, Justin says, "was accused of the same things as we are."[154] The emphasis here is significant. Justin is not suggesting that he is a persecuted philosopher, and therefore like Socrates. Rather, he is suggesting that Socrates was basically a persecuted Christian, even if this identification only became clear once Jesus came to earth. Still, for Justin's purposes there were evidently some advantages to making these comparisons between himself and Socrates. He claims that both of them were representatives of "true wisdom" on earth and were persecuted for it because of the actions of demons and evil men. Persecution was therefore a fundamental part of the identity of a philosopher, and a likely sign that he was speaking on behalf of the truth.

Dying for the truth was even better. Justin argues that this act provided extra confirmation of a philosopher's virtue, even for some philosophers whose executions seem to have belonged completely to his imagination. The example of Socrates and his famous death, of course, was one that Justin could emphasize, in keeping with the continuing veneration of this philosopher in the second century.[155] But Justin also attempted to make similar claims for other philosophers whose deaths were substantially less famous. He accordingly suggests that the philosophers Heraclitus and Musonius Rufus were "hated and put to death" (μεμισῆσθαι καὶ πεφονεῦσθαι).[156] Justin's claim here fits in with his larger strategy of claiming some philosophers as Christians. He does this explicitly for Heraclitus, linking him with Socrates and others "similar to them" as proto-Christian philosophers.[157] He may have attempted to do the same for Musonius Rufus, referring to him with a phrase that might mean "from amongst our own" (ἐν τοῖς καθ' ἡμᾶς), though this philosopher lived only decades before Justin's time and therefore would not qualify as a proto-Christian philosopher.[158] This point aside, it does seem to have mattered that these philosophers, whether they were (proto-) Christians or not, had been executed, like Socrates. The complicating factor here is that neither Heraclitus nor Musonius Rufus seems to have been put to death. In the case of Heraclitus, there were several stories about his death, most of which revolved around the disease of dropsy (edema) and an attempted remedy for it that involved cow dung.[159] Marcus Aurelius was familiar with these stories, which would have made Justin's unattested claim about Heraclitus seem odd to him, if not entirely unbelievable.[160] There is likewise no sign that Musonius Rufus was put to death. From evidence now available to us, the cause of Rufus's death is unclear.[161] But the authors who mention Musonius emphasize his exile from Rome during the reign of Nero, meaning that they surely would have mentioned that he had received even harsher treatment from a subsequent emperor.[162] Thus Justin's claim would have again surprised Marcus Aurelius, whose *Meditations* make clear his veneration for the philosopher Epictetus, a pupil of Musonius Rufus.[163] In short, Justin's *Second Apology* displays a surprising insistence that good philosophers tended to be put to death, even in cases where members of the ostensible audience of the work would have known this was not the case. According to Justin's arguments, being put to death was just something that happened to good philosophers.

It was inevitable, therefore, that Christians were put to death more than any other philosophers, in keeping with Justin's claim that Christianity was the only "safe and profitable" school of philosophy. This is a point that Justin makes by offering a contrast between Christ and Socrates, saying, "No one was persuaded by Socrates to die for this teaching."[164] But this was not the case for Christ. Thanks to him, Justin claims, "not only philosophers and scholars were persuaded [to die], but also manual laborers and those entirely unskilled, who came to look down on honor, fear, and death."[165] Even ordinary uneducated Christians became philosophers, according to Justin's argument. And they demonstrated this by their scorn for death—something that Justin claims had a major impact on his own choice to become a Christian. When he was still a Platonist, Justin explains, he heard "Christians being slandered and saw them fearless towards death and all the other things judged to be frightening."[166] This display on the part of Christians proved to Justin that it was "impossible for them to be caught up in evil and hedonism."[167] In effect, the Christian willingness to die proved that they were true philosophers, like Socrates, Heraclitus, and Musonius Rufus. The display was all the more impressive because the Christians put to death lacked the education of these other philosophers. By Justin's telling, Christianity was confirmed as unique among all other philosophical schools, in large part because of the impact that it could have on a broader cross section of the population.

This emphasis on philosophy and death underlies Justin's account of the recent persecutions in Rome with which the *Second Apology* begins. As Justin explains, this situation escalated when the husband of an unnamed Christian woman at Rome had her teacher, a man named Ptolemy, arrested.¹⁶⁸ Ptolemy is identified explicitly as a "teacher of Christian doctrines" (διδάσκαλον . . . τῶν Χριστιανῶν μαθημάτων), a label that makes him into a philosopher.¹⁶⁹ A similar impression is given when Ptolemy is taken to be tried in front of the urban prefect Lollius Urbicus, the same man who likely exiled Peregrinus from Rome. Ptolemy told Urbicus about the "school of divine virtue" (τὸ διδασκαλεῖον τῆς θείας ἀρετῆς) that he represented, portraying Christianity again as a philosophical school.¹⁷⁰ During this trial, two more Christians spoke up to identify themselves, proving themselves to be not simply Christians but also philosophers. One of these Christians is left unnamed, but Justin draws out the story of the other, whose name was Lucius.¹⁷¹ Lucius objected to Urbicus's judgment to have Ptolemy put to death, claiming that it "was not befitting a pious emperor [sc. Antoninus Pius], nor his son, the philosopher Caesar [sc. Marcus Aurelius]."¹⁷² Lucius's speech to Urbicus embodies the outspokenness (*parrhēsia*) of a true philosopher, questioning the authority of the urban prefect and of the senior and junior emperors, who portrayed themselves as pious and philosophical men. This encounter, as depicted by Justin, may not have been dissimilar to the occasions when urban prefects met with philosophers, as happened in the case of Peregrinus. In Justin's view, Ptolemy, Lucius, and the unnamed Christians proved themselves to be true philosophers when they confronted Urbicus. The sentence of death that they received confirmed this status, whereas Peregrinus was merely exiled. True philosophers, and true Christians, demonstrated their virtue by being persecuted and executed.

It is tempting at this point to begin discussing Justin's perspective on death, persecution, and philosophy in relation to the responses that Christianity generated from outside observers in his lifetime, including Galen, Lucian, and Marcus Aurelius. Christian attitudes to death certainly were a major feature emphasized in outside reports of them in Justin's lifetime, as Judith Perkins notes.¹⁷³ But framing this issue solely in terms of Christianity, and treating it as the key factor in Justin's identity, risk obscuring a larger context for his perspective and the responses that it may have generated. Many people outside of the Christian community were likewise interested in the meeting between a petitioner or ambassador and imperial authorities, especially if an emperor was involved.¹⁷⁴ Encounters of this sort dramatized the threat of "arbitrary violence" that characterized the Roman Empire, providing moments when people might be faced with death or punishment at the hands of the emperor or might receive the rewards that could come with gaining imperial favor.¹⁷⁵ These encounters were also controversial, raising the question of how an intellectual should behave when faced with an authority who could have him put to death. Justin suggests that accepting death, and perhaps even seeking it out, would serve as a demonstration of a philosopher's virtue. But this view was not universally held, by any means.

Some people in the second century did regard death by persecution as an act worthy of celebration, in keeping with views about the proper way to respond to tyrannical rulers. An entire genre of literature in Latin was devoted to commemorating people who had been killed by earlier Roman emperors.[176] Pliny the Younger is our major source for this genre, which he links especially with his friend Titinius Capito, who had been granted imperial permission, evidently by Nerva, to set up a statue in the Roman Forum for a man executed by Nero: Lucius Silanus.[177] Pliny also mentions attending a public reading given by Capito, which was to come from the work he was writing "on the deaths of famous men" (*exitus inlustrium virorum*).[178] Another of Pliny's friends, Gaius Fannius, had been composing a similar work before his own death, focusing on the "deaths of people killed or exiled by Nero."[179] All of these works seem motivated by an impulse, familiar also from the works of Pliny's friend Tacitus, that Rome's fortunes had improved after the death of Domitian and the end of the Flavian dynasty.[180] These celebrations of men killed by earlier emperors fit in with the official view of a new age.

The Latin works mentioned by Pliny also fit in with a body of literature in Greek that celebrated the encounters of ambassadors with the emperor and that shows signs of similarity to Justin's work. These Greek works have sometimes been called the "Acts of the Pagan Martyrs," based on the controversial proposition that they provided some inspiration for Christian acts of martyrdom.[181] Both bodies of literature celebrated the deaths of people who were speaking on behalf of a larger community, whether this was Christianity or one of a number of cities in the Eastern part of the empire. Works of this sort were written in Antioch and Athens, but our knowledge of this genre comes almost entirely from the survival, on papyri, of works celebrating representatives from Alexandria, hence the name *Acta Alexandrinorum*.[182] The situations described in the texts are not entirely historical, but they feature real emperors, ranging chronologically from Augustus to Caracalla.[183] Recent work on these documents rejects the old tendency to see them as signs of resistance against Rome.[184] Rather, they were linked with Egyptian and Greek identity, celebrating the resolve of local men who spoke to the emperor on behalf of their communities.[185] In this respect, they are similar to Justin's discussion of Christian martyrs, who represented Christianity as a whole when they spoke to imperial authorities. One set of documents called the *Acta Appiani* shows the title character speaking to Commodus and attacking his credentials. Appian says: "It was fitting (ἔπρεπε) for your father, the divine Antoninus [sc. Marcus Aurelius] to be emperor. Listen [to me]: first, he was a philosopher. Second, he was not greedy for money. Third, he loved goodness. But the opposites of these traits are present in you: tyrannical rule, dishonesty, and a lack of education."[186] This recalls what the Christian Lucius is supposed to have said to the urban prefect, objecting that the judgment against Ptolemy "was not befitting" (πρέποντα) the piety and philosophical natures of Antoninus Pius and Marcus Aurelius.[187] Justin and the *Acta Appiani* both celebrate the outspokenness of the men commemorated, demonstrating that they were true to their identities. Lucius emerges from the text as a true Christian and therefore a true philosopher. Appian, meanwhile, is presented as a true representative of Alexandrian "good birth" (εὐγενείᾳ), as the text emphasizes when he is on his way to be executed.[188] A meeting with the emperor provided an opportunity for people to prove who they really were, especially if death resulted.

There were negative responses, however, to this veneration for people who died confronting the emperor and consequently became famous. Critics put the emphasis not on the need to die when confronting a tyrant but rather on the virtues that would allow someone to survive the encounter. This is the perspective taken especially by Tacitus, who argues that "great men can exist even under bad rulers."[189] To head off criticism that these men must have been sycophants or cowards, Tacitus notes that they had to have "compliance and modesty" (*obsequiumque ac modestiam*) mixed with "purposefulness and energy" (*industria ac vigor*).[190] His father-in-law, Agricola, possessed these virtues, Tacitus claimed, which meant that he had no need to seek glory by means of a "showy death" (*ambitiosa morte*) that offered "no advantage to the republic" (*nullum rei publicae usum*).[191] The same point is made in an epigram by Tacitus's younger contemporary Martial, which rejects the tendency of people to seek fame by dying: "I do not want the man who purchases fame easily with blood. I prefer the man who can be praised without death."[192] Similar claims show up in a range of Greek philosophical authors of the period, many of whom were opposed to deaths that might have been avoided and therefore may as well have been outright suicides.[193] This comes close to the critique offered in Lucian's treatment of Peregrinus, which has much to say about how this philosopher attempted to stage-manage and publicize his death.[194] Peregrinus's example perhaps even appears in a legal context with the jurist Ulpian, who mentions philosophers who chose to die as a way of "showing off" (*iactatione*).[195] Choosing to die in a confrontation with the emperor or other imperial authorities was not always something celebrated. It seemed to some observers that these willing deaths were more the result of a love of glory than a love of wisdom.

The more challenging and valuable thing was to confront an emperor and survive, as Tacitus emphasized. The same point is made in Philostratus's *Lives of the Sophists*, which often discusses moments when a sophist survived a difficult encounter with an emperor.[196] As Philostratus notes, this was fundamental to the self-presentation of Favorinus of Arles, who clashed with the emperor Hadrian and lived.[197] An intellectual's education protected him when he met with the emperor, who had been raised to appreciate the same elite values associated with learning.[198] Surviving an encounter with an emperor might even serve to demonstrate, contrary to Justin's claim, that someone was a true philosopher. One sign of this attitude comes out in Philostratus's biography of Apollonius of Tyana, which suggests in absolute terms that "tyrannies are the best touchstone of philosophers."[199] This proves to be true for Apollonius, who proves himself truly philosophical in his interactions with a series of Roman emperors, ultimately outliving the tyrant Domitian.[200] A similar motif also appears in a text of the late second century that tells of the meeting between the philosopher Secundus and Hadrian.[201] Secundus had taken a vow of silence, and this helped him attract the attention of Hadrian while he was visiting Athens. "Nothing that was good," the text explains, "escaped the notice" of Hadrian.[202] Hadrian wished to speak with Secundus, which caused obvious problems. Secundus continued to keep his vow of silence, even when he was being threatened with death by Hadrian and members of his entourage. Finally, Hadrian ordered that Secundus should be taken off and executed. But he gave the executioner special instructions: "When you are about to take away the philosopher, speak to him on the road and encourage him to talk. And if you persuade him to answer, cut off his head. But if he doesn't answer, bring him back here unharmed."[203] The executioner followed these instructions and did his best to make Secundus speak to him. But the philosopher refused, and his life was accordingly saved. He survived to write down his responses to a series of philosophical questions posed to him by Hadrian. The text concludes by explaining that Hadrian had Secundus's written responses deposited in a "sacred library" (ἱερατικῇ βιβλιοθήκῃ), thus demonstrating the respect that the philosopher gained from this encounter.[204] Secundus's story, fictional though it likely is, resonates when read alongside Justin's account of the trials of Ptolemy, Lucius, and the unnamed third Christian.[205] Like Secundus, these Christians persisted in their own vows, as it were, refusing to deny that they were Christians. But they were executed for this, while Secundus was able to earn the respect of the emperor. The *Life* of Secundus therefore presents an ideal situation. An intellectual angers an emperor but comes out of the encounter unscathed. Secundus confirmed his credentials as a philosopher by not speaking, and Hadrian recognized this, letting him live. True philosophers need not die when they met an emperor, despite what Justin suggested.

The foregoing discussion shows that Justin's presentation of martyrdom was taking part in a larger debate about persecution and death. Within this debate, which extended far beyond Christianity, there are some signs of praise for the Christian scorn of death. Some observers might have been able to interpret this attitude as confirming Stoic views and larger Roman ideologies about courage in the face of death.[206] We may even see traces of this interpretation, perhaps, in a passage by Galen about Christians that suggests that the "strong desire for justice" makes some Christians "not fall short of the real philosophers."[207] This may qualify as a watered-down version of what Justin had to say about his response to the death of Christians, though Galen's other references to Christians reveal that he thought them to be bad philosophers (as discussed previously). But the positive view of Christian death must be balanced with signs of impatience with, if not disgust at, people who seemed to seek out death. The example of Peregrinus is again significant in this respect. Lucian explains that Peregrinus, during his time as a Christian, was arrested and consequently risked death. But the response he got was not what he wanted. "Peregrinus," Lucian explains, "was released by the man then ruling Syria, who was fond of philosophy."[208] Though Lucian omits this governor's name, he can plausibly be identified with Sergius Paullus, subsequently a city prefect of Rome and someone identified by Galen as a student of Aristotelian philosophy.[209] As Lucian notes, Paullus recognized Peregrinus's desire for fame and set him free without punishment.[210] In effect, then, this passage shows one philosopher rejecting the credentials of someone else who claimed to be a philosopher. Peregrinus wished to die for the wrong reasons, so the philosophical Paullus set him free. Paullus evidently shared the opinion of Tacitus and Martial, who were tired of people making themselves into martyrs. And these were not isolated responses, either. A similar story appears in Tertullian's *Ad Scapulam*, which mentions the actions of a proconsul of Asia named Arrius Antonius, who was active in the reign of Commodus.[211] Faced with a crowd of Christians, Antonius ordered a few of them to be executed and then said to the others: "Wretches! If you want to die, you have precipices or nooses!"[212] Antonius linked martyrdom with an urge for suicide and the consequent attention that came with it. He and other Roman observers evidently saw nothing philosophical or virtuous in the willingness of some Christians to be executed.

This was an attitude shared by one of the ostensible addressees of Justin's work, the philosophical emperor Marcus Aurelius. From his own writings, it emerges that Marcus would have rejected Justin's claim that a willingness to die proved the truth of Christianity and the status of Christians as philosophers: "A soul is ready, if it needs to be freed from the body immediately, to disappear or be dispersed or keep together. But this readiness must come from someone's own decision and not be the result of simple opposition, as is the case with the Christians, but [must be done] with reflection and dignity and, so others may be persuaded, without histrionics."[213] This is a controversial passage. The phrase "as is the case with the Christians" has been dismissed as a gloss added by a later scribe.[214] But, gloss or not, Marcus's comments here still apply to the larger controversy surrounding the veneration of people who were executed by imperial authorities. It is worth noting, in this respect, that elsewhere in his *Meditations*, Marcus does praise the philosophers Thrasea Paetus, Helvidius Priscus, Cato the Younger, Dio of Syracuse, and M. Junius Brutus, all of whom committed suicide or were executed as a result of conflicts with monarchs he would have considered tyrants.[215] Their deaths demonstrated for Marcus a dedication to philosophy and serve to show his own desire not to seem a tyrant.[216] But he found nothing praiseworthy in the choice of others to die out of "simple opposition" to authority. This type of death, accompanied with "histrionics," fits the behavior of Peregrinus and the response of the governor Sergius Paullus to this philosopher when he seemed ready to be put to death.[217] Marcus's comments would apply equally well to the recorded behavior of some Christians, like Ptolemy and Lucius, who were steadfast in their answer and self-identification when they were faced with the city prefect. The critique he offers effectively rejects the claim of anyone who died in a showy way to be a philosopher, implying that this act would have been without "reflection and dignity." By his view, people who made this choice were acting in an unphilosophical way. For Marcus, therefore, Christians proved themselves to be anything but philosophers when they were put to death.

Justin's arguments, and his own death by martyrdom, would consequently have done nothing to convince Marcus Aurelius and those who shared his perspective that he was a real philosopher. The *Acta* of Justin's martyrdom reveal that the city prefect who oversaw the proceedings was a man known well to Marcus, as it happens.[218] This prefect, Junius Rusticus, appears in the early acknowledgments of Marcus's *Meditations*, where he is thanked for having introduced the emperor to the works of the philosopher Epictetus.[219] The shared interest of the two men in Epictetus suggests that they were both likely familiar with this philosopher's comment about

Christians, whom he calls Galileans. These Galileans, Epictetus says, had been trained "by habit" (ὑπὸ ἔθους) not to fear a tyrant or his guardsmen, thus making them like a child or a madman, who places no value on his own life.[220] This was additional proof, if Marcus or Rusticus needed any more convincing, that the Christians being put to death were no philosophers. From their perspective, instead, Justin was more like a madman or a child, and perhaps even with histrionic impulses, like Peregrinus. Though Marcus and Rusticus both respected some philosophers who had been put to death by tyrants, including Rusticus's own grandfather Q. Junius Arulenus Rusticus, they were both surely adamant that Justin and the other Christians were unphilosophical and acting out of "habit" rather than "reflection and dignity."[221] Just as Christians rejected as illegitimate the martyrdom of other Christians they deemed heretical, so too would Marcus and Rusticus have rejected the claims of Justin and other Christians to be dying in a philosophical way.[222] If Justin and the other Christians put to death were really philosophers, then Marcus and Rusticus would have become tyrants, rather than the philosophers that they believed themselves to be. Thus, despite his best efforts and his argumentative ingenuity about the significance of persecution and death, Justin would have convinced few people by his behavior that he was a real philosopher. His definition of a philosopher was simply incompatible with the definitions used by Marcus and a host of others.

Conclusion

Justin's self-presentation in his works engages closely with the realities of intellectual culture as they appear in the works of his contemporaries who also lived in Rome. Justin was a Christian, but he emphasizes again and again that he was a philosopher, and a better one than representatives of any other philosophical school besides Christianity. His works therefore manifest the competitive spirit of Roman intellectual culture in the second century. They seem especially similar in this respect to the works of Galen, who explains in them how he came to be a public intellectual in Rome, with connections to the imperial household. But despite these similarities, Justin often looks more like a Cynic philosopher, such as Peregrinus and Crescens, who were less concerned than Galen about following the norms of intellectual culture and more interested in being outspoken, if not abusive. Justin, too, celebrated the outspokenness of Christian martyrs like Ptolemy and Lucius, suggesting that their behavior, combined with their contempt for death, proved them to be real philosophers. But it is hard to imagine that Justin's claims would have gained him much attention. Like the Cynics, Justin mostly would have been dismissed as an abusive man with a poor education, and thus as a sham philosopher. Increased attention may have come his way when he was arrested and tried, following a slight gain in publicity for Christians in Rome, as he describes at the start of his *Second Apology*. But Justin's death, which was supposed to prove him a real philosopher, would have been dismissed as an empty act by most non-Christian onlookers, especially those who considered themselves philosophers, including the urban prefect who had him executed. Despite his best efforts, Justin remained a would-be public intellectual during his career in Rome, and this is how Galen and other non-Christians would have regarded him.

Justin's coreligionists, however, viewed him in a much more positive light. Though Justin seems only to have been an independent teacher and philosopher rather than a cleric, he gained a large reputation after his martyrdom.[223] As Sara Parvis argues, Justin's apologetic works served as a basic model for subsequent Christians who offered defenses to Roman authorities.[224] Justin's self-presentation as a philosopher likewise provided a template for Christian intellectuals who sought to define themselves as experts. This is especially clear in the case of Athenagoras, a learned Christian and self-styled philosopher who offered his own work of apology to Marcus Aurelius in the late 170s.[225] Athenagoras makes obvious his familiarity with Justin's apologetic works and follows Justin in representing himself as a petitioner to the imperial household.[226] Athenagoras even goes further than Justin, presenting himself explicitly as an ambassador speaking on behalf of the Christian philosophical school.[227] This serves as an important sign of Justin's significance for later Christian intellectuals. Justin provided a model that later Christians followed when they presented themselves as intellectuals and when they addressed Roman imperial authorities. But later Christian intellectuals soon began to move beyond the template provided by Justin. This process was already under way in the case of one of Justin's pupils, to whom I now turn.

CHAPTER 3

TATIAN VERSUS THE GREEKS
Diversity in Christian Intellectual Culture

The *Ecclesiastical History* of Eusebius of Caesarea presents a complicated portrait of Justin Martyr's pupil Tatian.[1] Eusebius's initial mention of Tatian emphasizes that he was "a man who in the first part of his life trained as a sophist in the learning of the Greeks, and gained a not inconsiderable reputation in it, having left behind many memorials of himself in writing."[2] A few chapters later, Eusebius adds that Tatian's most famous work was his *Against the Greeks* (or simply *To the Greeks*), which was "quoted by many" (παρὰ πολλοῖς μνημονεύεται) and "seems to be the finest and most useful of all his works."[3] In Eusebius's judgment, Tatian put his training in Greek learning to good use, applying it in an influential attack on the Greeks. But this is only one part of the portrait of Tatian. Eusebius records the tradition that Tatian became a heretic who blasphemed against the church following the death of his teacher Justin.[4] During this heretical phase, Tatian also composed a work, traditionally called the *Diatessaron*, that was a "combination and collection of the gospels" (συνάφειάν τινα καὶ συναγωγὴν . . . τῶν εὐαγγελίων).[5] Eusebius likewise suggested that Tatian "dared to paraphrase the words of the apostle [Paul], as if he were correcting their style."[6] Though Eusebius makes this point only implicitly, Tatian evidently applied his Greek learning in an attempt to correct the text of the New Testament.[7] For Eusebius, therefore, Tatian inspired contradictory responses. He was the pupil of the heroic martyr Justin, and he put his Greek learning to use in defense of Christianity, composing his work *Against the Greeks*. But this "most useful" work itself raised further issues. Eusebius cited *Against the Greeks* for the story of how Justin was martyred.[8] This implies that Eusebius judged the work to have been written after Justin's death, when Tatian had become a heretic. Eusebius tacitly overlooks this point and the problems that it would cause for him and other readers bothered by the idea of drawing too much from a heretic.

Similar problems persist for readers of Tatian today. Scholarship on *Against the Greeks*, his only work extant in the original Greek, is often still based on the tradition that Tatian became a heretic after Justin's death. Attempts to confirm or deny details from this tradition continue to play a major part in discussions of Tatian and his works.[9] There have also been many questions about the genre and purpose of *Against the Greeks*. The work has often been grouped with the apologetic literature written by Justin and others.[10] But this label of apology seems inadequate. Tatian is not so much defending Christianity as he is attacking Greek culture. And even Eusebius's description of the work mentions only the final section, in which Tatian set out to prove that Greek civilization was a relatively recent development in the history of the world.[11] But there is much else besides this in *Against the Greeks*, which switches back and forth between topics quickly and almost chaotically.[12] Like Eusebius, later scholars have been uncertain about what to do with Tatian. Basic details about him and his work remain open questions, despite much recent scholarly attention.[13]

This chapter offers a new solution to the problem of what to do with Tatian. It takes inspiration from a trajectory in recent scholarship on Tatian that approaches him and his work more in terms of the broader intellectual context of the second century.[14] This is a helpful approach, but it has not yet been exploited fully. To do this, I seriously consider Eusebius's suggestion that Tatian "trained as a sophist in the learning of the Greeks," which seems to be borne out by the content of *Against the Greeks*. For my approach, I also take a cue from the work itself, which has little at all to say about Christianity and includes no explicit references to Jesus.[15] *Against the Greeks* is clearly a work composed by a Christian, but it has been easy for readers to get caught up in this fact and to regard Christianity as the key to its interpretation. Instead, I suggest that the key themes of the work itself require further investigation, particularly the opposition that Tatian creates between Greek culture and the rest of the world. Tatian portrays himself throughout the work as a barbarian and emphasizes that he has rejected Greek culture. *Against the Greeks* makes more sense if it is approached in terms of this Greek/barbarian dichotomy, rather than through the distorting lens of orthodoxy and heresy found in the later biographical tradition of Tatian.

Using this approach, I characterize *Against the Greeks* as an act of cultural criticism that questions the value and meaning of the concepts "Greek" and "barbarian." Tatian acts in this work like he is Greek, but he makes abundantly clear that he is a barbarian. In the process, he destabilizes

the Greek/barbarian dichotomy and suggests that many features believed
to be Greek in the second century were really of barbarian origin. He
even suggests that Greek culture was holding people back from achieving
their full potential as human beings, leading them to worship demons
whom they wrongly believed to be gods. In *Against the Greeks*, Tatian uses
his encyclopedic command of Greek culture to point out its flaws and
to explain why he eventually came to reject it. I advance the first part of
this argument in the first section of this chapter, which argues that *Against
the Greeks* presents itself implicitly as a miscellany, while simultaneously
rejecting that it should be characterized as one. Tatian thereby exploits the
familiarity of his contemporaries with the Greek genre of the miscellany,
even as he claims to reject Greek culture. In the second section, I show that
Tatian's arguments offer an audacious recharacterization of Greek views
on religion and medicine, engaging in detail with second-century debates
about astrology and health. In the process, Tatian suggests that Greeks are
unhealthy in body and mind because they have been deceived by demons.
Then, in the third section, I contextualize Tatian's perspective on the Greek
language with the increased second-century interest in the Attic dialect and
the ancient history of Athens. Tatian emerges from this section as someone
who claims to reject Atticism while still taking for granted some of the
basic assumptions of extreme Atticists about the pure roots of the dialect
in Athens's distant past. The fourth section continues this line of argu-
mentation, demonstrating that even Tatian's interest in the ancient past of
the barbarian world was shaped by the desire of many intellectuals in his
time to gain access to unadulterated sources of ancient wisdom, Greek or
otherwise. Tatian was distinguished from his Greek contemporaries only by
his desire to redefine what was typically associated with the words "Greek"
and "barbarian" and by his willingness to apply the latter word to himself.
Finally, in the last section, I focus on how Tatian was received by later
Christian authors and argue that his attitude toward Greek culture played a
significant role in the reputation he gained as a heretic. Though Tatian and
his fellow Christians shared many things in common, he and they often had
different attitudes about the relative value of Greek and barbarian culture.
Some Christians, including his teacher Justin, were much less eager than
Tatian was to describe themselves as barbarians.

Greek culture therefore emerges as key to interpreting Tatian and
explaining how he was received by other Christians in the second century. Tatian helps reveal the increasing diversity of Christian intellectual
culture. In the 160s and 170s, after the death of Justin, a more complicated
world for Christian intellectuals was developing, mirroring the complexi-
ties of intellectual culture in the Roman Empire. Tatian's work shows this

new complexity, demonstrating that it was no longer enough for Christian intellectuals to present themselves as philosophers, as Justin did. Instead, Tatian and subsequent Christian intellectuals had to demonstrate that they were fully fledged men of culture, with mastery over the many subjects that were engaging their non-Christian intellectual counterparts. These circumstances underlie the escalating accusations of heresy within Christianity, including those directed at Tatian himself. And the same Christians who dismissed Tatian as a heretic emerge as figures similar to the "Greek men" addressed throughout *Against the Greeks*.

Against the Greeks as a Miscellany

Tatian's *Against the Greeks* resists easy characterization. Despite many attempts, no satisfactory label or explanation for the work has been advanced.[16] There has even been much debate about the date of its composition, with estimates ranging from the early 150s to the late 170s.[17] But a new consensus of sorts has been emerging. This holds that the work was the product of the early 170s, when Tatian assembled a disparate collection of speeches that he had delivered earlier in his career.[18] The suggestion about dating is likely to be basically right.[19] I am less convinced, however, that *Against the Greeks* can be divided up so neatly into different pieces and that this division provides any real insight into the work.[20] As an alternative, I will suggest in this section that the seeming disorganization of *Against the Greeks* was an intentional feature meant to evoke the genre of the miscellany.[21] This genre fits with the breadth of topics covered in the work, which are similar to those treated in other works of the second and third centuries with encyclopedic pretensions, including a desire to display polymathic knowledge.[22] The genre was likewise a popular choice for intellectuals who might qualify as outsiders to the restrictive norms of elite intellectual culture in the second century. As Tatian was a self-identified outsider, his engagement with this genre was meant to evoke his Greek learning, even as he went out of his way to reject the label of a miscellany. This is a fundamental pose for his self-presentation in *Against the Greeks* and a basic point to keep in mind for the interpretation of the work. Tatian depicts himself as an outsider and a barbarian, but one with great expertise ine Greek culture.[23]

Tatian's wide-ranging critique of Greek culture is tied together by his ethnographic gaze, through which as a self-proclaimed foreigner he analyzes and diagnoses the flaws of the Greeks.[24] Tatian presents himself as a traveler familiar with Greek culture and therefore qualified to critique it. He claims considerable expertise and experience throughout *Against the*

Greeks, emphasizing again and again what he has himself seen and done.[25] Toward the end of the work, Tatian says to his Greek addressees, "What I expound I have not learned from someone else. Instead, I have covered much of the earth, occupying myself as a sophist with your teachings, and encountering many arts and ideas."[26] This comment locates Tatian in the world of his Greek addressees. But, as he explains, he experienced a change of heart about the merits of Greek wisdom after he read some "barbarian writings" (γραφαῖς τισιν . . . βαρβαρικαῖς), which a few hints reveal were surely the Hebrew scriptures.[27] Tatian's encounter with these writings led him to renounce Greek culture and the pursuit of its "many arts and ideas."[28] Instead, as Tatian emphasizes repeatedly, his life came to revolve around what he presents as the unitary wisdom of the barbarian world, rather than the Greek multiplicity that he had observed in his travels.[29]

This emphasis on multiplicity functions as a key marker in Tatian's engagement with the genre of the miscellany. Tatian suggests implicitly that this was a necessary form to offer a critique of all the many things that he saw on his tour of the Greek world. His targets for attack include many topics that were significant in second-century intellectual culture, and themselves the subject of debates among Greek intellectuals. *Against the Greeks* moves quickly to and fro in this diverse intellectual world. It offers attacks on philosophy, mythology, astrology, magic, medicine, and entertainment culture. These are combined with stories about Tatian's own life and experiences and with a substantial argument about the antiquity of Greek civilization to conclude the work, oddly interrupted midstream by a discussion of Greek art.[30] The breadth of subjects covered gives the work encyclopedic pretensions, despite its brevity. Tatian even emphasizes periodically that he has written, or intends to write, more substantial treatments of the subjects he discusses.[31] Readers are left with the impression that Tatian could well have written a longer work on all the different subjects that *Against the Greeks* covers. The work therefore seems like an encyclopedia in miniature, with the varied subjects and contrived disorganization of a miscellany.

Tatian adds to this impression with his strategic use of vocabulary that evokes the genre of the miscellany while simultaneously rejecting this label for his work. The key word in this strategy is *poikilia* (variety), a concept that was linked to literature's ability to entertain readers with varied contents and style.[32] Authors of miscellanies used the word *poikilia* as a defining feature of their genre and as a sign that they were being deliberately unsystematic in how they organized their works. The word's status as a marker of the genre is apparent from Tatian's younger contemporary Aelian, who closes his *On the Nature of Animals* with a straightforward comment about its lack of organization: "I mixed up even the varied contents (*poikila*) in a varied manner (*poikilōs*)."[33] Tatian's use of the word *poikilia* therefore suggests that *Against the Greeks* would have been interpreted as a miscellany by some readers in the second century.[34] In *Against the Greeks*, the word *poikilia* twice serves to mark a transition between subjects, as Tatian shifts abruptly from making an argument about chronology to a defense of Christian virtue, and then from his critique of Greek art back to the argument about chronology.[35] In both cases, *poikilia* has a contradictory force. The first passage suggests that Christians have no need for it: "With us there is no longing for empty praise, and we do not make use of varieties (*poikiliais*) of doctrines."[36] The second passage, likewise, associates the word with the shameful people depicted in Greek art. It comes at the end of a long list of statues that Tatian claims to have seen: "Finally I spent time in the city of the Romans and observed the varieties (*poikilias*) of statues that they brought back from you [sc. Greeks]."[37] Both passages make clear that *poikilia* is something that is foreign to Tatian. He rejects the variety of doctrines taught by the Greeks and has no use for their statues. But the use of the word *poikilia* in transitional passages in a work with varied contents still points readers in the direction of a miscellany, however much Tatian rejects the label.

Even Tatian's objection to the idea of *poikilia* helps situate him in the non-Christian intellectual culture of the second century. Though Aelian and other authors might forthrightly use the word to define the methods of their works, they also were aware that *poikilia* might be associated with effeminacy and a superficial attainment of culture.[38] The emptiness associated with *poikilia* is even hinted at by Aelian himself, who praises farmers for their simple wisdom, noting that it is "unembellished" (*ou pepoikilmenē*).[39] Even the sophist and grammarian Julius Pollux suggested that the adjective *poikilos* (wily) might be applied in a negative sense to sophists, who also might be described as "shifty, untrustworthy, and underhanded."[40] Tatian's use of the word *poikilia* therefore joins him to this world, where authors might simultaneously seek to entertain readers with varied contents, even as they sometimes distanced themselves from this technique. Tatian, at least, may be somewhat more consistent in presenting *poikilia* in a bad light. The word invariably has a negative sense in *Against the Greeks*.[41] Variety is something always to be avoided, despite the implicit similarities of *Against the Greeks* to the genre and literary techniques associated with the word *poikilia*.

For Tatian, the theme of *poikilia* is closely linked to his self-presentation and identity, as it was for other authors of miscellanies in the second century. As Katerina Oikonomopoulou shows, the genre was popular with

intellectuals who had hybrid identities that challenged assumptions linking culture with masculinity and Greek ancestry.[42] For these intellectuals,
the miscellany provided a way to establish their learning and cultural credentials, even though they failed to measure up in some respects to the
restrictive norms of elite, male intellectual culture in the second century.
The genre was therefore a good fit for Favorinus, a native of Gaul born
with no testicles who nonetheless became a leading intellectual and orator,
despite his effeminate voice and appearance and his non-Greek ancestry.[43]
It also provided a vehicle for a woman of the mid-first century CE to
demonstrate her learning in an intellectual culture dominated by men. This
was Pamphila, who made no attempt in her miscellany to hide that she was
a woman and that the miscellaneous information she had collected came
from things she "learned from her husband," from the learned men who
visited him, and from books that she read.[44] A woman was not expected
to be so learned, and neither was a barbarian, but both Pamphila and
Favorinus demonstrated their learning by means of the miscellanies they
authored. The same was true for Tatian, a self-identified barbarian, though
he claimed to reject the Greek idea of *poikilia*. The miscellany thus was an
appealing genre for intellectuals who challenged prevailing norms about
gender and identity.

   In sum, engagement with the genre of the miscellany is key for interpreting *Against the Greeks*. There are definite seams within the work, which
give it the appearance of disorganization. But Tatian's use of the word
poikilia suggests that the seams and abrupt transitions were intentional
and designed to be noticed by readers familiar with the genre of the miscellany. Even Tatian's multiple rejections of *poikilia* locate him within the
discourse of the genre and the ambivalent prevailing attitude toward too
much variety in literature. In short, *poikilia* is a fundamental part of *Against
the Greeks*. It was also likely a part of his lost work *Problems* (Προβλήματα),
the title of which was popular for works of miscellany in the second century.[45] Tatian's engagement with the genre of the miscellany hints that he is
simultaneously an insider and a hostile outside observer of Greek culture.
In effect, Tatian's pose as an ethnographer of the Greek world makes him
something like a heresiologist describing with encyclopedic detail the great
diversity of Greek errors.[46]

Demons, Health, and Medicine

The same pose characterizes Tatian's critique of how his Greek addressees view the world and their inability to achieve their full potential as
human beings. He portrays himself as a hostile but well-informed critic

of Greek perspectives on the nature of humanity and the differences that distinguish people from the categories of the animal and the divine. This self-presentation comes out especially in Tatian's views on demons, semi-divine beings that were a topic of great interest for many intellectuals of his time.[47] Tatian's perspective on demons is key to the arguments in *Against the Greeks* and has been the subject of increased scholarly attention recently.[48] This research has clarified some aspects of Tatian's complicated views on demons, but without giving sufficient attention to how his demonology led him to engage with several different areas of second-century intellectual culture, including prevailing interests in astrology, medicine, and zoology.[49] In Tatian's totalizing demonology, demons were closely tied up with all of these fields. This was a result of Tatian's view that the Greek gods were actually demons and the source of all the evils in the world. According to Tatian, these demons had invented astrology, and likewise tricked humanity into believing that they had healing powers. Their goal in doing this, Tatian alleges, was to keep people at the level of animals, and prevent them from achieving their true potential to become like gods themselves. This argument about a massive demonic conspiracy serves as the basis for how Tatian attempts to distinguish Christians from Greeks. He claims that Christians were immune from the influence of demons and astrological fate, with the result that they had excellent mental and physical health, something that Tatian presents as their first step to becoming like divine beings. The end result of Tatian's argument is an odd mix of ideas drawn from the Greek world that often shows surprising agreement with Greek perspectives that he claims to be attacking. But Tatian presents his argument within a larger frame that suggests Greek views on the world are fundamentally wrong. Tatian's demonology serves as the basis for his recharacterization of Greek religion and culture and his claim that Greeks are unhealthy in both body and mind, making them more like the demons they worshipped rather than humans seeking to become divine.

Tatian's treatment of demons engages with an ongoing Greek debate about what these beings were and how divine they might be. Intellectuals in Tatian's time could turn for guidance to the discussions of demons in classical Greek authors, above all Homer, Hesiod, and Plato.[50] A key passage from Plato suggested that "the demonic is between divine and mortal," and that demons served as intermediaries between gods and humanity.[51] But this left much middle ground to explore about the status of demons. Plutarch's works take up this question, showing a group of intellectuals debating whether some demons might be less than good.[52] One of the speakers, a certain Cleombrotus of Sparta, offers the opinion that some rites and sacrifices are performed "not for any god, but for the averting of bad demons."⁵³ Plutarch is generally more positive about demons in his other works, citing a passage from Hesiod to support the idea that some demons are "attentive of men" (ἀνθρώπων ἐπιμελεῖς) and help them to attain virtue.⁵⁴ Plutarch also drew from Plato the idea that all people were assigned a personal demon, which would offer them divine advice and guidance throughout their lives.⁵⁵ Demons, much like people, had something of the mortal and the divine to them. But there was no unanimous perspective about demons among Tatian's contemporaries.

Faced with this debate, Tatian offered an audacious claim, insisting that Greek gods were demons and drawing on ancient Greek authorities to support his argument, just as his non-Christian contemporaries did. In the process, Tatian entered into another debate, this time about how literally the descriptions of gods in Homer and other early poets should be taken.⁵⁶ He rejected completely the tendency among some Greek intellectuals to treat Homer's stories about the gods as allegory.⁵⁷ Tatian critiques one prominent allegorist, Metrodorus of Lampsacus, suggesting that he spoke "in a completely ridiculous way" (λίαν εὐήθως).⁵⁸ Directing himself to his Greek addressees, Tatian says: "Don't allegorize your stories or your gods."⁵⁹ The stories Homer told about the gods were better for Tatian's arguments if they were true and if the gods themselves were real. The gods' immoral behavior, though, demonstrated that they were demons, and far removed from Tatian's conception of divinity. Tatian even went so far as to identify these gods/demons with the same angels who rebelled against God, led by the firstborn among them.⁶⁰ Tatian therefore brought together Greek and Christian mythology, insisting on the literal reality of both. His knowledge as a Christian and an informed observer of Greek culture allowed him to see the gods for what they really were and to recognize that the stories told about them by Homer were true.

Tatian's recharacterization of the gods as demons provided him the means to mount a challenge to astrological determinism, showing his familiarity with another controversial subject for intellectuals in the second century.⁶¹ From this period, major attacks on astrology survive from Favorinus (as reported by Aulus Gellius) and the philosopher Sextus Empiricus.⁶² There were defenses offered of astrology, too, by Tatian's younger contemporaries Ptolemy and Vettius Valens.⁶³ The debates have a stock character to them.⁶⁴ Attackers and defenders tended to focus on the same key issues, such as why twins might have substantially different lives, though they were born at almost the same time.⁶⁵ There clearly was an ongoing conversation about astrology, even if the extant works show few signs of direct responses between defenders and attackers. In this sense, it is unsurprising that Tatian shows no knowledge of Ptolemy or Vettius Valens, though there are hints that he may have been familiar with the latter's work, or something similar to it. He likewise makes no acknowledgment that his basic objections against astrology were shared by other critics. But it is still manifestly clear that he was taking part in the same conversation about astrology.

As it happens, Tatian is in surprising agreement with Vettius Valens on several points, particularly on the topic of the involvement of demons in astrology.[66] This agreement seems to be the result of Tatian's engagement with astrological literature and its distinctive terminology. Tatian signals his familiarity with a derisive reference—"as they say" (ὥς φασιν)—to the use of the term τὸ ἐπικρατῆσαν by astrologers for the "starting point" of calculations relating to the length of someone's life.[67] The word makes frequent appearances in the works of both Ptolemy and Vettius Valens.[68] More striking, though, is the emphasis that Tatian and Vettius Valens place on demons. Valens says, "I write out these things exalting in the knowledge poured down on me from heaven by the demon."[69] His expertise in astrology came, evidently, from one of the good types of demons, who was serving as a personal guide to him.[70] As it happens, Tatian also suggests that astrology came from demons. But he presents this in a negative light, suggesting that demons "displayed to [humanity] a chart of the constellations (ἀστροθεσίας) and introduced the exceedingly unjust [idea] of fate, playing just like people with dice."[71] Tatian's use of the word ἀστροθεσία here is another technical astrological term, and one that appears in Valens's work.[72] Tatian seems to be aware of the arguments and idioms of astrological authors, whether or not this includes familiarity with Valens's work in particular. Tatian attempts to turn the claims of astrologists back on them, suggesting that the demons so prominently involved in astrology were evil, rather than good. Tatian may even have found some support for his claims in the works of astrologers. Much in keeping with Tatian's view, Valens acknowledges the potential influence of evil demons on people. Some young men, Valens notes, "do not honor the gods or fear death but are led by a demon."[73] This sort of admission was exactly what Tatian wanted to emphasize about astrology, though he extended the point much further than Valens did. Demonology therefore proved to be an area where Tatian had more in common with astrologers than one would expect.

Tatian's basic objections to astrology were likewise similar to those of other critics. A fundamental objection to astrology was its deterministic claims.[74] Favorinus illustrates this critique, charging that astrologers presented people as if they were "some type of laughable and ridiculous puppets" (*ludicra et ridenda quaedam neurospasta*) governed by the movements of the planets.[75] Sextus Empiricus notes that this was a standard point of astrological critics, who charged that "unless everything happens according to fate (εἱμαρμένην), which is the claim of astrology, there is no astrology."[76] This is Tatian's criticism, too. He equates his evil demons with the planets and claims that they are the ones who "defined fate" (τὴν εἱμαρμένην ὥρισαν).[77] The fate that they created was "extremely unjust" (λίαν ἄδικον), and "every nativity [cast] provided delight to them, as in a theatre."[78] The demons, Tatian charges, watched the actions of mortals on earth and derived entertainment from them. Tatian even includes a Homeric quotation—"Unquenchable laughter arose among the blessed gods"—to illustrate his claim about the demons acting as spectators in a theater.[79] This is much the same image used by Favorinus in his analogy of humanity as puppets, governed by the movements of the "wandering stars" (errantium siderum).[80] Tatian rejected completely the authority of these demonic astral bodies and the fate that they created: "We are above fate, and instead of wandering demons we have recognized an unwandering master. We are not led by fate, and we have rejected its lawgivers."[81] The Greeks' gods were inconstant in their heavenly movements, while Tatian's God was like one of the nonwandering stars, constant in its movements.[82] The irregular movements of the planets, moreover, were likened by some to the inconsistent behavior of people who lacked a firm moral compass. According to Plutarch, who offers an extended metaphor on this point, such people were "at one point gaining control and turning to the right, and at another being turned by the passions and dragged along by their errors."[83] The Greeks' gods were therefore revealed to be less than divine by their irregular movements in the skies. Demons of this sort had no authority over Tatian, who joined Favorinus and others in rejecting what they portrayed as the deterministic claims of astrologers.

Tatian's discussion of demons and astrology has much relevance in his treatment of health and medicine, two subjects of great interest for intellectuals in the second century. With his choice to treat these subjects, Tatian was entering a competitive medical marketplace, filled with intellectuals of many different specialties, including philosophers, athletic trainers, and religious specialists of all sorts, in addition to physicians.[84] Clearly, in Tatian's time, medicine and health were not areas reserved for the select group of people we might now recognize as physicians. This has been an elusive point in studies of Tatian's views on medicine, which have attempted to challenge suggestions that he rejected completely the types of medicine associated with Galen and other physicians of the second century.[85] These studies have nuanced understanding of Tatian's views on medicine, but they have often depended on a problematic attempt to segregate medicine from religion. This attitude is apparent in Owsei

Temkin's suggestion that Tatian "is concerned with theology, not with medicine."[86] Temkin and others have argued that Tatian objected only to select aspects of medicine as it was practiced in his time. They suggest that Tatian reserved his critiques for pharmacology, a field that he associated with the malicious influence of demons on humanity.[87] Because of this emphasis on demons, the assumption emerges that Tatian confined himself to the field of religion ("theology") and had no objections to the physicians of his time and their ideas about health. This is wrong. Tatian's views on medicine amount to a major challenge to Greek views on health, bringing together his larger objections to Greek ideas about humanity's place in the world.[88]

Tatian's critique of medicine is based on the idea that Greeks are confused about how to achieve mental and physical health and thereby to become divine. Demons are at the root of this confusion. Tatian says, appealing to the theme of *poikilia* again: "Demons in their malevolence rage against people, and with varied (*poikilais*) and false devices they divert [humanity's] thoughts."[89] Variety, again, equals falsehood, and the Greeks are consequently distracted by the many ideas presented to them by demons and thus are not able to reach their potential as real humans. This demonic conspiracy against humanity is focused especially on areas relating to health. Demons present themselves as "helpers" (βοηθούς) to humanity, Tatian alleges.[90] They offer ways for people to be healthy, but the cures they provide are illusory. This leads Tatian into a discussion of the spells and remedies that were associated in his time with the word "pharmacy" (φαρμακεία).[91] This area of medicine, Tatian claims, is rooted in the trickery of demons, again in keeping with his insistence on the varied and false tricks developed by them. According to him, "The varieties (*poikiliai*) of roots and the applications of sinews and bones are not effective on their own but are the elements of the demons' wickedness."[92] Demonic variety leads the Greeks astray, making them think that the remedies they seem to provide are effective. In fact, as Tatian explains, this is simply another demonic trick. The demons "determine what each of [the remedies] should be able to do" and thus make slaves of the people who believe they have been cured.[93] Demons offered the illusion of health and thereby made themselves seem like gods to the people they had deceived.

Tatian extends his critique to the Greeks taken in by the tricks of the demons. He directs a major part of his attack at people who praise the gods for their healing abilities and thereby spread the false and varied wisdom sown by demons in the world. Tatian's argument on this point comes in an extended analogy borrowed from his teacher Justin, who likened demons to bandits (λησταῖς) who "kidnap men, then return them to

their families for a ransom."[94] Demons do much the same thing in matters
of health and sickness. As Tatian explains, "These supposed gods visit the
bodies of men, then leave them the impression of their presence through
dreams, and order them to come forward in public (δημοσίᾳ) with everyone
watching them."[95] What Tatian describes here is the familiar scene in the
second century of an orator or sophist about to declaim publicly for an
attentive audience. Even the demons form part of this audience, listening
to the speeches offered in praise of their abilities as healers. "When," Tatian
explains, "[the demons] have derived enjoyment from the praise, they fly
away from the sick, remove the sickness that they have contrived, and
return the men to their previous [condition]."[96] Demons therefore only have
an illusory ability to heal. Like kidnappers, the only problems they solve
are ones that they themselves created. Tatian's claims on this point demonstrate close engagement with a real phenomenon of his time. He may well
have been familiar with the hymns to the god Asclepius offered by his contemporary Aelius Aristides, who was one of the most famous intellectuals
of the period.[97] Whether or not he was familiar with Aristides, Tatian offers
little sympathy to anyone who might praise Asclepius. Though Tatian likened them to victims of extortion and kidnapping, people who praised
Asclepius were still perpetuating the false idea that demons had healing
powers. And this was a point that Tatian denied firmly: "The demons do
not heal but take men prisoner with their cunning."[98] Demons required no
help from people in spreading their deceptions further.

The same charge appears in Tatian's attack on physicians, who were
also complicit in the great demonic conspiracy about human health.
Tatian objects in a straightforward way to the status that physicians have
gained. In the most explicit reference to physicians in *Against the Greeks*,
Tatian asks, "Why are you called a benefactor (εὐεργέτης) for healing your
neighbor?"[99] The language here evokes the common Greek suggestion
that health was a great benefaction to humanity.[100] It also helps demonstrate a link between the categories of religion and medicine. Tatian, in
effect, is attacking the claims of someone like Aristides, who praised the
sons of Asclepius—popularly identified as the first physicians—for offering "benefactions (εὐεργεσιῶν) to the Greeks . . . and all humanity."[101] But
Tatian's critique also applied to the physician Galen, who emphasized that
physicians in training needed to be concerned with "benefaction for men"
(εὐεργεσίας ἀνθρώπων).[102] The idea of a physician as a benefactor seems
to be linked with Galen's great respect for the god Asclepius, whom he
identified as the founding father of the Greek medical tradition, just as
Aristides did.[103] Galen even depicts himself as someone who had gained a
godlike reputation for his healing, suggesting that "great was the name of

Galen" (μέγα ἦν τοὔνομα Γαληνοῦ) in Rome, a phrase that echoes a common shout offered up by worshippers of Asclepius: "Great is Asclepius" (μέγας ὁ Ἀσκληπιὸς).¹⁰⁴ In Galen's view, physicians and divinities both deserved praise for the benefactions they provided to humanity. And this was not a point with which Tatian could agree. A physician like Galen and a worshipper of Asclepius like Aristides were both to be rejected.

According to Tatian, Christians simply had no need for the sort of healing that Greek physicians and others misled by demons might provide. Part of the reason for this was Tatian's claim that physicians might do more harm than good to their patients. *Against the Greeks* shows only one example of Greek medicine at work, and this led to the death of the patient. This episode comes as part of Tatian's attack on philosophy and focuses on the early philosopher Heraclitus (see chapter 2). "The death of this man," Tatian claims, "helps to prove his ignorance."¹⁰⁵ As Tatian explains, Heraclitus "was afflicted with dropsy and practiced medicine as he did philosophy, smearing himself with cow dung. When the filth hardened, it caused cramps over his entire body, and he died in convulsions."¹⁰⁶ Tatian says nothing about the point of this treatment, which another source suggests was supposed to dry out Heraclitus's dropsy with the "heat of the cow-dung" (τῇ τῶν βολίτων ἀλέᾳ).¹⁰⁷ This detail was evidently irrelevant to Tatian. What mattered, instead, was the great failure of Heraclitus to cure himself and the disgusting circumstances that led to his death. In Tatian's view, Christians need not subject themselves to Greek physicians, and the deadly remedies that they might offer, misled as they were by demons.

Physicians and others who claimed expertise in health might even offer a more serious threat, tied to the negative influence of demons on humanity. They might distract people from what Tatian sees as humanity's potential to become more like divine beings themselves. Tatian expresses this concern directly when he discusses how demons use tricks to divert humanity's "thoughts, [which are] already inclined to lower regions, so that people are quite unable to rise up on their journey to the heavens."¹⁰⁸ Demons thereby became key agents in the process by which "the world drags us down," causing the human soul to lose the wings it once possessed, and bringing it down to earth.¹⁰⁹ The demons' tricks were aided by physicians, whose use of remedies derived from animals and plants helped keep the thoughts of people focused on the earth rather than on God. In Tatian's view, demons "divert people from the worship of God with their cunning and contrive that they are won over by herbs and roots."¹¹⁰ Tatian does grant that some of the treatments offered by physicians might prove to be effective. But he argues that gratitude to physicians was out of place: "Even if you are healed by drugs (I yield [this point] to you as

an excuse), you still ought to offer witness to God."[111] Tatian alleges that
the sort of healing offered by physicians was akin to the self-medication
of animals and was beneath the dignity of humans. To make this point,
he asks his Greek addressees a question: "For what reason do you not
draw near to the more powerful master but rather heal yourself just as
a dog does with grass, a deer with a snake, a hog with river crabs, or a
lion with monkeys?"[112] These examples of self-healing came directly from
collections of Greek animal lore, where they often were deployed in arguments to demonstrate the intelligence of animals.[113] Tatian redeploys these
examples, taking for granted that animals lacked rationality. He uses these
stories of animal self-medication to suggest that human use of medicine
was exactly what demons wanted. Physicians were aiding demons and
thereby keeping people's thoughts focused on the earth below them, as if
they were animals.

   According to Tatian, human health depended on people escaping
the influence of demons and acting more like divine beings than animals.
Tatian's claim was based on his insistence that there was a fundamental
difference between animals and humans, contrary to the claims of some
contemporary philosophers, who were debating the point with rivals,
led by the Stoic school of philosophy.[114] Tatian wrote a separate treatise
on this point, now lost, called *On Animals*, which he mentions in *Against
the Greeks*.[115] This work engaged with a popular definition of humanity,
challenging the suggestion that a human was a "rational animal capable
of thought and knowledge" (ζῷον λογικὸν νοῦ καὶ ἐπιστήμης δεκτικόν).[116]
According to Tatian, this definition opened up the possibility that even
"irrational animals" (τὰ ἄλογα) might be "capable of thought and knowledge" (νοῦ καὶ ἐπιστήμης δεκτικά).[117] This was a point that Tatian rejected
strongly. He justified his perspective simply by citing a paraphrase of a
verse from Genesis, suggesting that "humanity alone is 'the image and
likeness of God.'"[118] The key point at stake for Tatian is that there are
different types of people, some of whom "have progressed far beyond
humanity towards God himself," while others are content to "do the same
things as animals."[119] Achieving this human potentiality was the first step in
escaping from demons, whose claims to make people healthy were really
making them act like animals.

   The negative influence of demons on humanity was a consequence of
their poor mental and physical health. This is an odd claim, at first glance,
and something that one might not expect from demons, who were substantially different from humans. Tatian acknowledges as much, observing
that "all demons lack any piece of flesh."[120] They were consequently all
but immortal: demons "do not die easily, because they lack flesh."[121] But,

in Tatian's view, demons were quite unhealthy creatures in spite of their near immortality and lack of flesh. As Tatian explains, as part of an attack on the behavior of Homer's gods, the demons were "ruled by the same passions (*pathesin*) that also rule men."[122] The key word here for Tatian is *pathos* (pl. *pathē*), a concept linked to extreme emotions, but also to disease.[123] If demons were ruled by *pathē*, as the evidence of Homer suggests, then they surely lacked good mental and physical health. Tatian makes exactly this point, charging that the Greeks' demons "were found to be far from [being in] good condition (*eutaxias*)."[124] Tatian's use of the word *eutaxia* here tends to be interpreted as if it relates to ordered behavior on the part of the demons.[125] This is one possible meaning, but it misses the medical connotations that the word had in Tatian's time.[126] *Eutaxia* might refer to moderate eating, as a passage from the doxographer Pseudo-Plutarch demonstrates, citing the opinion of the Hellenistic physician Erasistratus: "Erasistratus [says] that diseases [result] because of an abundance of food, and because of indigestion and emaciation, but that health is moderation in diet (*eutaxian*) and self-sufficiency (*autarkeian*)."[127] Galen, meanwhile, linked the word *eutaxia* to the sexual abstinence of some athletes, suggesting that this lifestyle had a noticeable impact on their genitals: "The athlete's penis is shriveled and collapsed from sexual abstinence (*eutaxias*)."[128] Tatian's demons that lacked *eutaxia* were consequently creatures that were immoderate in their appetites for food and sex. This may clash with modern ideas on the nature of demons. But it was normal in antiquity for people to believe that demons fed on the smoke and blood associated with animal sacrifices.[129] Tatian also offered some comments about the prodigious sexual appetites of Zeus, whom he presented without hesitation as a demon.[130] These sorts of habits meant that demons were hardly to be regarded as benefactors providing good health to their worshippers. Demons themselves lacked the good health that they pretended to offer.

It is no surprise, therefore, to encounter Tatian's suggestion that his Greek addressees were quite unhealthy, both physically and mentally. Like the demons they worshipped, Greeks were ruled by the passions, and consequently were little more than animals. This comes out clearly in Tatian's critique of Greek philosophers, who appear as gluttons only interested in their own pleasures.[131] Some of the philosophers receive special attention for their animalistic behavior, above all the Cynics who explicitly identified themselves with dogs, revealing that they had "no knowledge of God and [had] sunk to imitating irrational creatures."[132] Other philosophers devoted little care to grooming and personal hygiene, meaning that they had unclipped nails like those of "wild animals" (θηρίων).[133] Amid this group, Tatian tells the story of Diogenes the Cynic, who "prided himself on his self-sufficiency (*autarkeian*)."[134] This is the same word that Pseudo-Plutarch, via Erasistratus, associated closely with health. But the story of Diogenes's death proved for Tatian just how unhealthy he really was: after "eating raw octopus, he was afflicted with suffering (*pathei*) and died from an intestinal blockage because of his lack of control."[135] Emotional distress was another common issue for Greeks, according to Tatian. He cites as an example of this tendency Alexander the Great's response after killing his friend Cleitus in a drunken rage.[136] Alexander "cried and starved himself to death from grief (*lupēs*), so that he might not be hated by his friends."[137] The word *lupē* shows up frequently in Galen's discussions of his patients, at times referring to grief, as in Tatian's discussion of Alexander, but also sometimes describing a condition that seems more akin to chronic anxiety.[138] Tatian displays a decided lack of sympathy for those suffering from *lupē*, ridiculing a hypothetical Greek for being "distressed" (*lupeitai*) because he missed a gladiatorial bout.[139] This Greek's distress exemplified the poor mental and physical health that Tatian diagnosed as chronic conditions among the Greeks.

The poor health of Greeks provides the backdrop for Tatian's views on the health of Christians and the negative influence of demons on humanity. According to Tatian, the excellent mental and physical health of Christians was a direct result of their escaping the influence of demons. Christians enjoy their good health because they are "protected by the spirit of God," something that also allows them to see easily the bodies of demons, unlike the Greeks, who are deceived by them.[140] In short, Tatian and other Christians have progressed upward on their paths toward divinity, rising above the influence of demons.[141] This is a key point of emphasis for Tatian, drawing from the influential claim in Plato's *Phaedrus* that the human soul once possessed wings that kept it above earthly concerns.[142] Tatian, in effect, suggests that his soul has regained its wings, causing him to rise "above" (*anōteroi*) the astrological fate devised by demons.[143] A similar motif appears in his discussion of *pathē*: "If you are above (*anōteros*) the passions (*pathōn*), you will despise everything in the world. Do not reject us for being like this, but reject the demons and obey the only God."[144] Christians had risen above the passions because of their rejection of demons. Using similar language, Tatian even claims that he is immune to the diseases and *lupē* that afflict so many Greeks: "I rise above (*anōteros*) every type of disease, grief (*lupē*) does not destroy my soul."[145] This is a preview of sorts for what Christians can expect when they die. Tatian promises that there are "better worlds above this one that have no change of seasons, through which various (*poikilai*) diseases come into being."[146] *Poikilia* again has negative connotations. With this word, Tatian all but suggests that the varied knowledge of Greeks and their demonic overlords are responsible for the diseases that strike humanity. *Poikilia* aside, Tatian fits in here with standard Greek ideas about the spread of disease, reflected in the Hippocratic corpus, and in the works of his contemporary Galen, who explained that the "unevenness of climate" (*kraseōs*) is what makes autumn "especially unhealthy" (μάλιστα νοσῶδες).[147] Tatian's claims about heaven spoke exactly to his point. Heaven has a "completely well-balanced climate" (*pasēs . . . eukrasias*), which means that no one gets sick there.[148] This comment provides final emphasis to Tatian's claim that those who reject the authority and influence of demons can rise up above earthly concerns and gain excellent health.

Tatian's demonology, in sum, shows off his ambivalent attitude toward Greek culture of the second century. *Against the Greeks* is committed to the idea that Greeks were seriously wrong in their views of the world. But Tatian still is heavily concerned with contemporary debates about demons, health, medicine, and the nature of humanity. He draws from Greek ideas about all these topics to explain why Greeks were subject to the influence of astrological fate and the mental and physical ailments sent to them by demons. Tatian's attack on the Greek worldview therefore contains many signs that it comes from his deep engagement with Greek intellectual culture. Though Tatian presents himself as a complete outsider to the Greek world, rejecting all of its errors, all that separated him was his insistence that the beings identified as gods by the Greeks were demons. This simple difference in terminology provided the basis for Tatian's insider attack on Greek culture and his suggestion that he and other Christians had surpassed the Greeks in achieving their full potential as human beings.

Antiquity, Atticism, and *Paideia*

Tatian's attack continues in his comments about Greek views of their own past, and of what they called *paideia* ("culture" or "education"). The Greeks Tatian was addressing turned to the past for how they understood themselves, seeking to recapture features of Greek antiquity that they believed had been lost or corrupted over time, with a particular focus on Athenian history (see chapter 1). Their interest in Athens was reflected in their use of the Attic dialect, which served as a way for intellectuals in the second century to claim for themselves some piece of the classical Athenian past. Tatian engages with this same tendency, displaying an attitude toward Atticism that is not entirely consistent. He critiques the tendency of people to affect Atticism and claims that he is no longer part of this group. But he still makes use of some characteristically Attic features in his Greek.[149] Previous studies of Tatian's complicated perspective on Atticism have reached few conclusions, offering little more than biographical criticisms about his pos- sible struggles in his youth to master Attic and his fierce resentment of the dialect when he was older.[150] I offer a different approach to this question, probing further into the reasons why intellectuals of Tatian's time sought to Atticize. Their motivations emerge as focused on an elusive purity of language and a desire to rid the Greek they spoke of foreign words, trying to get back to what they believed was the pure essence of the Attic dialect spoken centuries before in Athens. Tatian seems to reject this justification for Atticism, challenging the idea that there is such a thing as Greek purity with his argument that Greece was a young civilization that owed much to the barbarian world. Despite this argument, though, Tatian still reveals himself as a believer in the concept of Attic purity, taking this concept for granted in his treatment of early Athenian history. The end result is a complicated attitude that shows how closely Tatian was tied to prevailing Greek ideas about history, language, and *paideia*.

Tatian's engagement with Greek views on language reflects an older desire to revive ancient forms of spoken Greek. This was a continuation of the project of Dionysius of Halicarnassus, and his aim to revive the style of oratory that existed in Athens during the fifth and fourth centuries BCE (see chapter 1). But, in the second century, fascination with Athenian litera- ture of this period grew, with increased focus on imitating features of Attic morphology and vocabulary.[151] Though not all intellectuals shared this fas- cination equally (see the later discussion about this), many of them now sought to replicate the Attic speech of educated Athenians from centuries before, a difficult task that was only accessible to elite men with consider- able time and money on their hands. At its core, this interest in the Attic dialect was the result of a continuing fascination with the classical Greek past and a desire to recapture the lost essence of this period.

All of this interest in Atticism comes out especially in the works of lexicographers, who sought to define an acceptable standard for Greek, basing this on use by classical Athenian authors.[152] The central figure for my concerns is Phrynichus, who also happens to be the lexicographer we know the most about. He was active in the 160s and 170s and a resident of Rome—two factors that he shared in common with Tatian.[153] Unlike Tatian, though, Phrynichus was a well-connected figure in Roman intellectual culture, dedicating the *Sophistic Preparation* to the emperor Commodus and the *Excerpts* to Cornelianus, the official who was in charge of the emperor's correspondence (*ab epistulis graecis*).[154] Phrynichus was also the most rigorous of the Attic lexicographers, offering proscriptive advice about the minutiae of language and how to speak like the best Athenian authors some five centuries earlier.[155] His linguistic concerns are clear from a programmatic statement at the start of his *Excerpts*: "Whoever wishes to speak in an ancient and approved fashion, these are [the words] to be guarded against."[156] As this suggests, the work is simply a list of words that Phrynichus rejected, together with alternative words, spellings, or pronunciations that he approved. The entries are often filled with telling remarks about how much it mattered to speak like an ancient author. One notable entry concerns two different variants of a word meaning "fruit-seller": "*Opōropōlēs*. Vulgar people say this, but educated (*pepaideumenoi*) people say *opōrōnēs*, as Demosthenes did."[157] According to Phrynichus, the difference of one syllable, and the substitution of an *l* for an *n* could distinguish an educated person from a vulgar one. Speaking in the way that Demosthenes did was necessary to demonstrate one's mastery over *paideia* and thus to qualify as a Greek.

Phrynichus's views were based on the idea that there was a pure essence to Attic speech. This comes out in the emphasis that he placed on antiquity, something that shows up especially in his frequent references to how "the ancients" (οἱ παλαιοί) spoke Greek.[158] Phrynichus never quite offers a full rationale as to why it was so important to speak like people from Athens's ancient past. But a few comments show that this was related to the idea of purity. Phrynichus was clearly familiar with older ideas about the autochthonous origins of the Athenian people, which implied that the city's first inhabitants developed on their own, free from any foreign influences. Signs of this emphasis on purity are scattered throughout his work, including the suggestion that his dedicatee Cornelianus was a "pure and ancient orator" (καθαρὸς καὶ ἀρχαῖος ὢν ῥήτωρ).[159] In Phrynichus's mind, this meant that Cornelianus spoke Greek in the same way that the ancient inhabitants of Athens did, before the city's dialect was corrupted in later periods. Some insight into how Phrynichus envisioned this corruption comes from his largely critical comments against the comic playwright Menander, whose life in Athens spanned the late classical and early Hellenistic periods, and thus the period when corruption set in, according to standard ideas (see chapter 1). Phrynichus mostly rejects Menander as an approved author, and he even charges him with "gathering up such a trash heap of words, dishonoring the ancestral speech."[160] By the third century BCE, therefore, Phrynichus noted a change in Attic and a departure from the pure ways in which the city's founders spoke the dialect—hence his accusation that Menander was corrupting "ancestral speech." Clearly, for Phrynichus's ideas to work, there needed to be a time when Attic was pure, and this was located in the most distant past of Athens's history. Atticizers in his time needed to restore this purity, based on Phrynichus's claim that

"Atticism does not accept foreign speech" (οὐ προσίεται ὁ Ἀττικισμός . . . τὴν ἀλλοδαπὴν διάλεξιν). Atticism, he argues, "wishes to remain pure and undefiled" (ἀνεπίμικτος καὶ ἄχραντος βούλεται μένειν) and would hardly "accept unapproved and half-barbarous speech" (ἀδόκιμον καὶ μιξοβάρβαρον προσεῖτο φωνήν).[161] Phrynichus's desire to restore the lost purity of Attic was closely tied up with his views on the ancient history of Athens.

This idea was not unique to Phrynichus. The most influential exploration of the connection between ancient purity and Atticism comes from Aelius Aristides, whose orations Phrynichus knew and admired.[162] Aristides explored this link in his most famous and popular work, the *Panathenaic Oration*, which was likely known to Phrynichus and perhaps even to Tatian, too.[163] In this work, Aristides provided a full justification for the superiority of Attic over all other forms of speech. Much of his argument rests on remarkable suggestions about the great antiquity of Athens.[164] Aristides claims that Athens's origins made it as old as the Assyrian Empire.[165] This was already a surprising claim, but Aristides pushes it further, arguing that Athens was "the oldest city on record" and that "its origins reach back further than is clear or easily grasped."[166] The city was even "the first [place] that brought forth humanity and its first homeland."[167] Athens was likewise exceptional because its location had kept it free from the influence of barbarians. The rest of Greece acted as a buffer, protecting Athens from corruption. The end result was that Athens "alone bears the nobility of the Greeks purely and is as different from the barbarians as it is possible to be."[168] Athenians were also the only people in the world who could "boast of pure good birth and citizenship" (καθαρὰν εὐγένειάν τε καὶ πολιτείαν αὐχῆσαι) because of their ancestors' autochthonous origins in the city.[169] Antiquity and autochthony therefore explained why the Attic dialect itself was "pure" (καθαρὰν).[170] By Aristides's claims, then, Attic was not only the world's first language but also one that had resisted the corrupting influence of foreign speech. Both suggestions were outlandish, and surely everyone who encountered the speech was familiar with contrary claims.[171] But the influence of the *Panathenaic Oration* still speaks to how seriously some people in the second century might take the superiority of Attic over other languages, imagining a fantastic history for the dialect and its status as an ur-language.

The attitudes of Aristides and Phrynichus provide the background for Tatian's argument about the great antiquity of the barbarian world, which he used to undercut claims about the purity of Greek language and culture. This argument is made in most detail at the end of *Against the Greeks*, but the basic claim frames the work as a whole. *Against the Greeks* begins with comments chiding Greeks on their youth and dismissing their culture and achievements as derivative products from barbarians. Tatian says: "Don't treat the barbarians with such hostility, Greek men, nor begrudge their beliefs. For which habit of yours does not take its origins from the barbarians?"[172] Tatian then offers a long list of inventions that came from the barbarian world, including the suggestion that it was the Phoenicians who invented "*paideia* through the letters of the alphabet (διὰ γραμμάτων)."[173] This claim was certainly familiar to Greeks, including any reader of Herodotus, but it might still be an uncomfortable point for some.[174] Aristides ignored Herodotus's story completely in his *Panathenaic Oration*, presenting Greek *paideia* and the Greek alphabet as Athenian inventions.[175] This stands in contrast to Tatian's views on the subject: "We shall discover not only that our teachings are prior to Greek culture (*paideias*), and even the invention of writing."[176] According to Tatian, Greek culture was young and of barbarian origins and therefore lacked the purity attributed to it by Aristides, Phrynichus, and other extreme Atticists.

Oddly, though, some of Tatian's critiques of Atticism take for granted basic assumptions used by extreme Atticists. These assumptions relate to the key idea of Attic purity, a concept that Tatian actually seems to consider is a real possibility. Tatian's engagement with this concept comes in his story about how he rejected Greek culture. As Tatian explains, he eventually noticed that Greek speech failed to live up to the extreme standards of purity defended by Aristides, Phrynichus, and others like them. He expresses this point directly to his Greek addressees: "You honor words that are not kin to yours and make your language confused by sometimes using barbarian terms."[177] This realization, Tatian claims, was what led him to "abandon the [Greek] type of wisdom, though [he] was quite distinguished in it."[178] Tatian basically depicts his past self as someone like Aristides or Phrynichus, thoroughly caught up with their concerns about Attic purity. When he realized that Greek was less pure than he thought, this evidently destroyed his desire to be Greek and to indulge in Atticism.

Tatian's charge about the impurity of Greek shows that he still took for granted some basic points about the early history of Athens. He does accuse his Greek addressees of hypocrisy in using barbarian words, but this is based on an inconsistency in his argument and his views on Athenian history. *Against the Greeks* devotes much time to suggesting that the idea of Greek purity is nonsense, given the many contributions made by barbarian civilizations to the earliest development of Greek *paideia*. Tatian even rejects the tendency of some of his Greek contemporaries to focus on their "good birth" (*eugeneia*) as a way of linking themselves directly to the early roots of the Greek essence (see chapter 1). "I do not boast of good birth (*eugeneian*)," says Tatian, separating himself from his peers who linked this concept with Greek purity.[179] But Tatian's accusation about Greeks admitting foreign words into their language implies that there might be such a thing as a pure core to the Greek language. This seems to be a consequence of some intellectual laziness on his part, combined with his relatively lax discussion of early Athenian history. In this discussion, which comes as part of his attempt to prove the greater antiquity of the barbarian world, Tatian never challenges the idea that the first inhabitants of Athens were autochthonous. Instead, he simply notes that the records of Athenian kings were nearly as ancient as Argos, which serves for him as the oldest Greek city.[180] His brief discussion of early Athenian history is uncritical, accepting that the king Cecrops was really "of double-form" (διφυής), half man and half snake, and therefore a symbol of the city's autochthonous origins.[181] Tatian's rejection of allegory meant that he could not dismiss this claim and take it to mean something else, such as the suggestion recorded by Plutarch that the "double-form" of Cecrops referred to his transition from being a "fierce and snake-like tyrant" (ἄγριον καὶ δρακοντώδη . . . τύραννον) to a good king.[182] This was something of a missed opportunity for Tatian, who could certainly have followed the story reported by Diodorus of Sicily that Cecrops was of Egyptian ancestry and thus a mix of Greek and barbarian—hence the label "double-form."[183] This would have provided yet more fodder for Tatian's charge that the Greek world had barbarian roots. But Tatian's aversion to allegory and his simple goal of proving the greater antiquity of the barbarian world led him to accept stories about Athenian autochthony. This approach to Athenian history leads Tatian to indulge in something like Greek essentialism, following the examples of Aristides and Phrynichus.

Tatian's perspective on Atticism, in short, is strange and contradictory, revealing his closeness to the very Greeks he was critiquing. His claim that Greek *paideia* had roots in the barbarian world provided him the means to challenge the idea of a pure essence to the Greek language, even as he suggested that Christianity had access to the pure wisdom of the ancient barbarian past. Instead, Tatian simply repeated back the claims of Athenians about the ancient history of their city, accepting the autochthonous origins of its first inhabitants, and the existence of a being that was half man, half snake. Challenging these stories was evidently extraneous to what Tatian saw as his key arguments to make. One wonders, though, how much Tatian may have viewed Atticism in the same way that he did the genre of the miscellany and the key concept of *poikilia*. Tatian claimed to have rejected both Atticism and *poikilia*, though his own work suggests otherwise. This contradictory persona and self-presentation shows how close Tatian remained to the very Greeks he was ostensibly critiquing, including extreme Atticists like Aristides and Phrynichus. Though Tatian claims that he was undercutting prevailing Greek ideas about *paideia*, his methods show that he remained part of the Greek world.

Greek Perspectives on the Barbarian Past

Tatian's self-presentation seems to link him to other intellectuals of his period from the Near Eastern provinces of the Roman Empire, who had their own issues with Atticism and the restrictive views on Greek identity and *paideia* championed by extreme Atticists. There has been some exploration of these links, especially with his contemporary Lucian of Samosata, who demonstrated a mastery of Atticism even as he ridiculed the fixation on the dialect of many of his contemporaries.[184] Comparisons of this sort between Tatian and Lucian have become almost obligatory and play into the idea that there was a characteristically Syrian or even Near Eastern response to the prevailing norms of Greek intellectual culture in the second century.[185] But focusing only on Tatian and Lucian leads to a partial view about how intellectuals from the Near East responded to Greek culture. Consideration of a larger group of intellectuals shows that there was a range of different responses to Atticism and that others from the Near East were much more willing to focus on the ancient past of Athens rather than on the places where they were born. Tatian also needs to be studied alongside broader tendencies in second-century intellectual culture. Viewed from this perspective, Tatian's interests in the ancient past of the barbarian world form part of a much larger trend and not something that was limited to him, Lucian, and other intellectuals from the Near East. Many of his contemporaries displayed similar interests in the ancient literature of the barbarian world, seeking to claim its authority as their own. Tatian does the same thing, offering his own version of barbarian antiquity and rejecting how others who self-identified as Greeks tried to appropriate some aspects of the barbarian past. There is consequently little that is characteristically Near Eastern or Syrian, much less Christian, in how Tatian approached the barbarian past. At best, Tatian is distinguished from many of his contemporaries by his willingness to call himself a barbarian. Even with this self-identification, though, Tatian is still joined to a larger group of intellectuals who sought to challenge restrictive views on *paideia*, seeking to defend their own credentials as men of culture.

Tatian's claims about the great antiquity of barbarian civilization place him squarely within Greek intellectual culture of his time.[186] Tatian's views on this subject are part of an older conversation, represented in Greek literature from the time of Herodotus and Plato, and gaining more significance

in the Hellenistic period (see chapter 1). Debates about the relative antiquity of Greece and other civilizations were an old and contentious thing,
and this persisted in the second century.[187] Tatian is forthright about his
participation in this conversation and his engagement with an older Greek
tradition on this point. This comes out early in the work, when he critiques
his addressees for "praising yourselves, procuring as advocates people from
your own household."[188] Tatian is here alleging that his addressees have
only cited other Greeks in their claims about the Greek origins of many
significant inventions. Toward the end of *Against the Greeks*, he claims that
he will not be guilty of doing the same thing in the proofs that he offers of
the youth of Greek civilization: "I shall not take as witnesses people from
our own household but rather fully exploit Greek assistants."[189] Tatian's
ostensible goal here is to suggest that his discussion of the issue will be
unbiased. But his method also situates him within the Greek tradition and
its explorations of the early history of Greece.

   Tatian's links to Greek culture are obvious even when he discusses the
chronology of barbarian civilizations, for which he depends exclusively on
Greek sources. The goal of his treatment here is demonstrating that Moses
was more ancient than Homer, a task that leads him to cite Chaldean,
Phoenician, and Egyptian sources as evidence.[190] But a quick glance at
the sources Tatian cites reveals that he mostly depended on Greek works
for these subjects. Tatian does mention the Babylonian priest Berossus,
but he seems to have learned about this author via citations in a work
called *On Assyrians* by Juba II of Mauretania.[191] He likewise cites ancient
Egyptian chronological records via the translation of them by a priest of
the Hellenistic period named Ptolemy of Mendes.[192] Even this reference to
Ptolemy comes from the later writer Apion of Alexandria (see chapter 1),
meaning that Tatian is citing Egyptian sources at multiple removes from
the original.[193] A similar situation is true for his information from Phoenician history. One of the sources he names for this is a Greek author,
Menander of Pergamum (or Ephesus).[194] The other is a Greek translation
by someone named Laetus of three earlier Phoenician histories by Theodotus, Hypsicrates, and Mochus.[195] Even Tatian's comment about this
translation raises some questions, inasmuch as the names Theodotus and
Hypsicrates are Greek.[196] How much actual translation Laetus may have
done from Phoenician to Greek is unclear. This uncertainty adds yet more
doubts concerning Tatian's engagement with barbarian literature produced
in Chaldea, Phoenicia, or Egypt. His treatment of barbarian history and
chronology actually seems quite Greek in character.

   Tatian's approach to the barbarian past fits in with growing interest in the ancient barbarian world among Greek intellectuals, especially

philosophers.[197] One sign of this trend is evident in Tatian's reference to Laetus. Besides his interest in Phoenician history, this Laetus also "wrote carefully about the lives of philosophers," Tatian says.[198] This comment, combined with the rarity of the name Laetus (Λαῖτος) in Greek, helps identify this author with a philosopher of the late first century CE named Ofellius Laetus.[199] A small collection of evidence reveals that Ofellius Laetus had an interest in the ancient pasts of both the Greek and the barbarian worlds. From two inscriptions, one Athenian and the other Ephesian, we learn that Laetus was a Platonist and a theologian (Θεολόγου) who wrote a "heavenly hymn" (μετάρσιον ὕμνον).[200] The two inscriptions conclude with nearly identical lines, pointing out Laetus's interests in Pythagoreanism: "If according to Pythagoras the soul crosses over into another [person], / in you, Laetus, Plato appears to live again."[201] What this reveals is an intellectual who venerated Plato, but who was also part of a revival of interest in Pythagoras during the early imperial period.[202] One more piece of information comes from Plutarch, who twice cites Laetus in his *Natural Questions*, referring to this philosopher's discussions of natural science.[203] All of this information fits in well with the brief portrait offered of Laetus by Tatian. The "heavenly hymn" in the inscription matches with Laetus's translation of the Phoenician Mochus, whose work included a discussion of the creation of the world.[204] A Phoenician perspective on the world's early history therefore provided more fodder for Laetus's interests in cosmology and natural science. His interests in Plato and Pythagoras, together with his works of philosophical biography mentioned by Tatian, likewise suggest his familiarity with traditions that associated both philosophers with the ancient wisdom of the Near East.[205] All of this is indicative of Laetus's interests in both Greek and barbarian antiquity, something that he shared with Tatian.

Tatian and Laetus are also linked by the emphasis that both placed on their encounters with ancient books, which they used to legitimate themselves as authority figures. This was evidently a basic feature in how Laetus presented his work of Phoenician history and why he may have misrepresented how much actual translation was involved on his part. The same theme is likewise present in Tatian's discussion of his conversion from Greek to barbarian wisdom. Tatian claims that he was disillusioned with Greek wisdom and that he was seeking other ways to "discover the truth" (τἀληθὲς ἐξευρεῖν).[206] This moment of uncertainty soon came to an end, though, as Tatian explains: "When I was contemplating serious matters it happened that I encountered some barbarian writings. They were more ancient than the doctrines of the Greeks and more divine than their error."[207] Tatian explains that the "barbarian writings"—the Hebrew

Bible—appealed so much to him because they contained "an easily understood [account] of the creation of the universe."[208] Tatian's emphasis on
the creation story of Genesis links him again to the philosopher Laetus,
who was likewise interested in ancient Phoenician stories on this subject.
Tatian, like Laetus, sought to intrigue and convince his readers by pointing
out to them what might be learned by consulting ancient, barbarian books.
Both authors evidently sought to gain authority by claiming direct access
to ancient sources of wisdom.

Tatian's use of this motif suggests that he was engaging with a broader
interest in the discovery of ancient books among intellectuals of his time.
This was a popular theme in literature of the second century, extending well
beyond the examples of Laetus and Tatian.[209] It was especially popular in
a few fields that Tatian critiqued, including astrology and magic, which is
also suggestive of his familiarity with the theme. Within astrology, the focus
tended to be on access to ancient books from the barbarian world, with a
special focus on Egyptian literature.[210] The same motif appears in other
fields, too, including in a work by Philo of Byblus, a learned intellectual of
the second century CE who claimed to offer a translation of an ancient Phoenician work written by a certain Sanchuniathon.[211] So many people claimed
to be discovering or translating ancient books that the theme became a topic
for parody. Novelistic works of the period employ the theme, using it as a
way to authenticate the fantastic or fictitious claims they made.[212] One such
work is Antonius Diogenes's *Marvels Beyond Thule*, which claims to be based
on a document discovered in the grave of the novel's (fictional) protago-
nist.[213] Another is Dictys of Crete's *Journal of the Trojan War*, which presents
itself as a translation from Phoenician to Greek of an alternative history of
the Trojan War written by an eyewitness.[214] Such use of the discovery motif
had clearly become a trope, to the point where its appearance in literature
might serve as a warning that the information to follow was inauthentic.[215]
The frequency with which the theme appears in second-century literature
suggests that Tatian was familiar with it, beyond his unambiguous knowledge of it in the case of the philosopher Laetus.

Tatian's use of this theme provided a way for him to redefine barbarian antiquity and its literature, challenging contemporary Greek views on
this point. In much of Greek literature, the ancient barbarian books had a
tendency to be surprisingly focused on Greek history. This is apparent in
Dictys of Crete's *Journal of the Trojan War*, which contained only information about the Trojan War, though it was supposed to have been written
in Phoenician.[216] The sophist Dio Chrysostom exploited a similar motif,
claiming that the alternative information he had about the Trojan War was
based on conversations with an Egyptian priest who had read inscriptions

on ancient temples and columns in that country.[217] Other ancient books, meanwhile, that appear in Greek literature tend to be about subjects that Tatian dismissed as errors developed by demons and taken up by Greeks. This was obviously the case in astrological literature, including the work of Vettius Valens, who claimed to have visited Egypt himself and who often cited the astrological works of the ancient Egyptian pharaoh Nechepso and his sage Petosiris, using their barbarian wisdom to authenticate his own authority and expertise (see chapter 1).[218] Tatian, by contrast, was seeking to offer a different version of barbarian antiquity, rejecting the associations it had with astrology and magic for many Greeks of his time. His presentation of barbarian antiquity is much more comparable with the goals of Philo of Byblus, whose *Phoenician History* emphasized the great antiquity of the Phoenician people, while criticizing Greek authors for offering "inconsistent" (διάφωνος) accounts of ancient history, drawing from the accounts of more ancient peoples.[219] Both Philo and Tatian sought to offer different perspectives on barbarian history, emphasizing its great antiquity and challenging how Greeks attempted to claim distorted aspects of it for their own purposes.[220]

Though there is a pattern in terms of how Philo and Tatian approached the barbarian past, this was by no means the only way in which intellectuals from the Near East thought about themselves and their relationship to Greek and barbarian antiquity. Put in different terms, categorizing Tatian's response to Greek culture as characteristically Near Eastern risks oversimplification.[221] Tatian's preference for identifying himself with the ancient past of the barbarian world was something that he shared with Philo of Byblus, but not with other intellectuals from the Near East. Two additional examples can help illustrate the range of ways in which Near Eastern intellectuals approached the ancient pasts of the Greek and barbarian worlds.

One example comes from the sophist Ulpian of Tyre, an Atticist who resisted stereotypes that he should be more interested in the ancient history and literature of his native Phoenicia than of Athens. Ulpian appears among the guests in Athenaeus's *Sophists at Dinner*, a work of the late second century.[222] He was likely an older relative of the homonymous jurist (see chapter 4).[223] Despite his origins in Phoenicia, Ulpian appears in Athenaeus's work as an especially pedantic Atticist who had earned the nickname "Attested or Not Attested" (*Keitoukeitos*) because he was constantly asking people if the words for food served to him were "attested or not" (*keitai ē ou keitai*) in ancient authors.[224] Ulpian's companions at dinner, though, often teased him about his origins in Tyre, calling him a "Syro-Atticist" and implying that his origins in the Near East should have disqualified him from being such an Atticizer.[225] His chief antagonist, a Cynic philosopher with the nickname Cynculus (Cynic Master), even attacks Ulpian directly, using what seems to be a genuine Syriac word for a type of honey cake: "Fill yourself up, Ulpian, on your ancestral *chthōrodlapsos*, a word written in none of the ancient authors, by Demeter, except perhaps in the *Phoenician Histories* composed by Sanchuniathon and Mochus, your fellow-citizens."[226] Cynculus offers a stereotype of Phoenicians here, implying that Ulpian should be interested in the ancient works of Phoenician history written by the authors identified as his fellow citizens. Both authors, of course, had been translated into Greek, Sanchuniathon by Philo of Byblus, and Mochus by Laetus—hence Cynculus's awareness of them. Ulpian, Cynculus charges, should have been prouder of his Phoenician origins, with Sanchuniathon and Mochus categorized among his personal list of ancient and approved authors. In effect, Cynculus suggests that Ulpian should have been more like Philo, or even Tatian, and less interested in Atticism. Clearly, though, Ulpian defined himself by his fascination with the Attic dialect and his fixation on the idea of linguistic purism, even accusing Cynculus of "barbarizing" (βαρβαρίζοντες) when he used a Latin word.[227] The stereotypes of his dining companions suggested that Ulpian should have been interested in ancient barbarian wisdom, but his example shows that an intellectual from the Near East might choose to be more interested in classical Athenian literature.

Another Atticist from the Near East was Hadrian of Tyre, who shared with Tatian a sometimes contradictory attitude about the relationship between the Greek and barbarian worlds in antiquity. Hadrian was from Phoenicia, but he nevertheless became an extreme Atticist, and even the imperial chair of rhetoric in Athens sometime in the early 170s.[228] In this capacity, Hadrian was still willing to acknowledge his Phoenician roots, using this as a theme in his inaugural address, which he began with the phrase "Again letters [have come] from Phoenicia."[229] This was a clever beginning to what Philostratus says was an unusually arrogant speech, which offered allusions to Athens's cultural dependence on Phoenicia and engaged directly with the Phoenician origins of the Greek alphabet, contrary to the example of Aristides.[230] These aspects of Hadrian's speech were things that even Tatian might appreciate. But Hadrian was still a proponent of linguistic purism. We learn this from Lucian, who explains that Hadrian critiqued him for being "barbarous in [his] speech" (βάρβαρον εἶναί με τὴν φωνὴν) after the Syrian sophist had used a word that Hadrian judged was "not native and autochthonous to Attica" (οὐκ οἰκείαν καὶ αὐτόχθονα τῆς Ἀττικῆς).[231] Thanks to Lucian's report of this incident, Hadrian emerges as someone with other similarities to Tatian. Both intellectuals emphasized the cultural dependence of Greece on the barbarian world, something that should have challenged the concept of the linguistic purity of Attic. But Tatian and Hadrian nonetheless still acted as if there were such a thing as pure Attic and critiqued others for failing to live up to this impossible and imaginary standard. Hadrian and Tatian had this much in common, but their paired examples, together with the rigorous Atticism of the sophist Ulpian, suggest that there was no consistent response of Near Eastern intellectuals to Atticism.

Instead, Tatian's response qualifies simply as one of many different critiques in his time of Atticism offered by people from all over the Mediterranean world.[232] Like Nicolaus of Damascus centuries earlier (see chapter 1), Tatian chose to emphasize where he was from and objected to the efforts of many intellectuals of his time to link themselves with Athens. This comes out in his critique of Atticism: "If you Atticize without being an Athenian, tell me the reason why you do not Doricize? How does one seem to you more barbarous, and the other more pleasing for conversation?"[233] Tatian's questions are comparable to the objections that his contemporary Galen had to Atticism.[234] Like Tatian, Galen objected to the idea that the Attic dialect somehow had qualities that other dialects or languages lacked. He claimed that he was writing for people who believed that Attic "was no more honorable by nature than the speech of other peoples."[235] Tatian and Galen likewise shared the perspective that the mastery of Atticism was basically useless and arbitrary. Tatian asks the incredulous question "What benefit can come from Attic diction?" and makes it clear that the answer is nothing.[236] According to Tatian, attempting to master Attic, and insisting that other people adhere to it, was "the work of someone who makes laws from his own opinions."[237] Galen, meanwhile, claims that Atticizers "practice no useful skill in life" and dismisses the fascination with Atticism as "pseudo-education" (*pseudopaideian*).[238] Both authors suggested that Atticism was a waste of time, and no marker of true education, though they disagreed in many other areas, including Tatian's deep objections to Greek medicine. This is a clear sign of the critiques that Atticism inspired, even among people who might otherwise get along poorly.

What unites Tatian with other critics of Atticism's outsized influence is his claim that perceptions of Greek identity should not be based so much on Athens. He has a seemingly surprising ally on this point: a lexicographer of the early second century traditionally called the Antiatticist.[239] His views on the Greek language were challenged by Phrynichus.[240] Unlike Phrynichus, the Antiatticist was much more open-minded about which Greek authors and dialects could qualify as acceptable Greek. He evidently made a point of citing classic authors who wrote in dialects besides Attic, such as Herodotus, who wrote in Ionic.[241] Tatian makes a similar point, though he pushes it in a different direction, pointing to the great disparity in how Greek is spoken: "The speech of the Dorians is not the same as that of the people from Attica. The Aeolians don't sound the same as the Ionians. There is so much disagreement, which should not exist, that I'm at a loss whom to call a Greek."[242] This comment shows awareness of the debates apparent in the works of lexicographers about which dialect qualified as most Greek. Whereas the Antiatticist would have suggested that all of these different dialects were Greek, Phrynichus insisted that Attic needed to remain uncorrupted even from the "rest of Greece," which he added included "the Aeolians, Dorians, and Ionians."[243] Tatian exploits this assumption, which seemed to imply that a significant portion of people who spoke Greek failed to qualify as real Greeks. One might even wonder if Tatian was familiar with the type of categorization employed by another contemporary lexicographer, Moeris, who contrasted "Attics" (Ἀττικοί) with "Greeks" ("Ελληνες) in his work, almost seeming to imply that those who used the Attic dialect were excluded from being Greeks, and vice versa.[244] Tatian's comment makes exactly this point, emphasizing the disagreements among his contemporaries about how best to speak Greek. He was evidently not alone in objecting to the fixation on Athens on the part of some of his contemporaries.

Tatian therefore was linked with a wider circle of intellectuals seeking to offer their own different—and typically more expansive—definitions of *paideia*, which was a basic component of Greek identity in the second century. A large group of intellectuals were engaging in this project, including Galen, the Antiatticist, and Philo of Byblus. They wished to ensure that their places of birth, educational credentials, and the ways they spoke or wrote Greek were no barrier to their being recognized as educated. In this sense, their attitudes reflected a combination of different professional or local identities that existed around the Mediterranean world, resisting the prevailing fixation on Athens and a select body of classical Athenian literature.[245] Everyone evidently faced some pressure to Atticize and to emphasize connections to classical Athens. But this existed alongside the desire of people to say that there were other ways to be educated and prove oneself as Greek.

Tatian was part of this same effort, defending his barbarian identity and offering his own reconception of *paideia* and Greek history, emphasizing the roots of both in the barbarian world. This is a fundamental part of *Against the Greeks*, which explicitly identifies the "Greek men" (ἄνδρες "Ελληνες) who are its addressees as *pepaideumenoi* (men of culture/education).[246] This was a word used by intellectuals of many different specialties to define themselves, and one closely bound up with ideas of Greekness.[247]

Tatian's arguments that made Greek *paideia* a derivative product of the barbarian world were a key part of his effort to redefine it. In place of it, he refers to something that he calls "our *paideia*," which he claims is "higher (*anōterō*) than worldly apprehension," and thus above the negative impact of demons.[248] Tatian therefore insists that barbarians have their own *paideia* and that it is uncorrupted by the negative impact of demons, much as Aristides and Phrynichus claimed that there was a pure essence to the Attic dialect. In effect, then, Tatian recasts the terms of this interest in maintaining the purity of a culture. He depicts the *pepaideumenoi*, the same "Greek men" he addresses throughout the work, as corrupting influences, making people around the world turn away from their native cultures and ways of speaking. In Tatian's view, the same people who have taken up the Attic dialect also "cling to [Athenian] *paideia*," thus exposing themselves to the distorted form of culture perpetuated by demons and their Greek supporters on the world.[249] Against this negative force, Tatian envisions a day when Atticism and its advocates would lose their power. As he says, speaking to the Greek *pepaideumenoi*, "If each city would take its own diction back from you, your sophisms will lose their force."[250] Tatian therefore challenges the narrative of Atticism spreading around the world, leading people to define *paideia* through Athens. Instead, Tatian celebrates his own superior form of ancient *paideia*, telling his Greek addressees that their views of themselves and their own history are wrong.

The end result of all this is a strategy and perspective that is clearly the product of Tatian's deep engagement with second-century culture and its views on Greek and barbarian antiquity. Besides demonstrating familiarity with prevailing views on astrology, demons, and health, Tatian also shows his knowledge of contemporary views on Atticism and its significance for perceptions of *paideia* and Greek identity. Tatian does attack these narrow views on Greekness, but he still reveals himself to be part of the same world as his addressees. Like them, he was fascinated by the idea of ancient wisdom and the possibility of gaining unadulterated access to it via ancient books. He also shared their same concerns with purity, both in his critique of Greeks for using barbarian words and in his emphasis on the uncorrupted form of barbarian *paideia* that he had mastered. Even Tatian's critique of his addressees and their restrictive views on language and *paideia* shows that he was part of the mainstream of second-century culture, linking him with the efforts of many other intellectuals eager to defend a local or more inclusive perspective on Greek identity. In short, Tatian emerges from *Against the Greeks* as someone who claimed mastery over both Greek and barbarian forms of *paideia*. But the form and content of the work still draw largely on the same Greek world that he claimed to have rejected, making Tatian into someone who self-identified as a barbarian, while acting more like the Greek men he was critiquing.[251] It is fitting, therefore, to see Tatian conclude his work by suggesting that he "offers [himself] ready for an examination of [his] doctrines" by his Greek addressees.[252] For someone who claimed to have rejected the Greek world completely, this comment serves as a reminder that he was still a part of it, even as a self-proclaimed barbarian.[253]

Receptions of Tatian

Tatian's self-identification as a barbarian who had mastered Greek culture, at first glance, seems to have been a minor consideration in how later Christian authors received him and his work.[254] Much more significant in the minds of later Christians was the simple claim that Tatian had become a heretic after the death of his teacher Justin. My aim in this section is to probe the early development of this claim and to consider how much Tatian's views on Greek culture and his self-designation as a barbarian may have played into the developing consensus that he was a heretic. The approach I take places emphasis on how Tatian's attitude toward Greek culture differed from that of his teacher Justin, suggesting that this difference played a factor in why Tatian was mostly rejected by later Christian authors. Traces of a similar approach appear in earlier scholarship on Tatian, emphasizing that some of his reputation as a heretic was the result of a division between Eastern and Western varieties of Christianity.[255] My aim here is to develop this argument further and to express it more in terms of differing attitudes on Greek culture, treating the Christians who condemned Tatian as little more than Greek ethnographers describing the strange practices of foreign peoples.[256] An irony emerges from this perspective on the condemnations of Tatian as foreign. Some of the same people who dismissed Tatian as a heretic shared much in common with him, at least in terms of the depth of their engagement with Greek culture. Like Tatian, later Christians had advanced beyond the comparatively simple self-presentation that Justin offered in his works as a Christian philosopher.[257] Tatian, meanwhile, was dismissed as a heretic, even though he was a better model than Justin was for later Christian intellectuals, offering to them examples of how to engage in more sophisticated ways with Greek culture, history, and literature. In short, little distinguished Tatian from his later critics except for the words "heretic" and "barbarian." Tatian's critics assigned the label of heretic to him themselves, and they did have some rationale for this in issues of Christian dogma and practice.[258] Social and cultural factors nonetheless seem to have played a role in how

Tatian's critics portrayed him, as is common in issues of religious rivalry.[259] The same people who called Tatian a heretic seem to have shared some significant features in common with the "Greek men" addressed throughout *Against the Greeks*. Though Tatian presented himself as something like a heresiologist of Greek culture, offering an encyclopedic treatment of its diverse errors, his critical perspective on Greek culture seems to have played a role in his being labeled as a heretic by Christian heresiologists working with a similar methodology.

A major part of the story for the mostly negative reception of Tatian comes from the different attitude he had about the virtues of barbarians and barbarian culture when compared to his teacher Justin.[260] Tatian was unequivocal about being a "philosopher among the barbarians, born in the land of the Assyrians."[261] Being a barbarian was a good thing to Tatian, as part of his attempt to recharacterize this word. For Justin, on the other hand, the concept of barbarian was decidedly less positive.[262] Justin did say that he was of the Samaritan race (ἀπὸ τοῦ γένους τοῦ ἐμοῦ), but he stopped short of calling himself a barbarian.[263] The same tendency is clear in how the two authors dealt with the issue of the greater antiquity of the barbarian world. Justin and Tatian are in basic agreement on this point, but they express it in different terms. Tatian calls the Hebrew Bible "barbarian writings" (γραφαῖς . . . βαρβαρικαῖς).[264] Justin, meanwhile, simply said that Moses was "more ancient than all of the writers among the Greeks."[265] This implies that Moses was a barbarian but refrains from giving the same emphasis on this point that Tatian did. Justin does seem to accord the Jewish people a special status among barbarian peoples, suggesting that what Socrates brought to the Greeks "by reason" (*hupo logou*) was equivalent to what was brought to the barbarians "by the Word himself" (*hup' autou tou Logou*).[266] This hints at the idea that Justin could have envisaged a world that was made up of four categories of peoples, much as the earlier Christian Aristides of Athens pointed to the world's four races: barbarians, Greeks, Jews, and Christians.[267] Still, even if Justin had viewed the world in this way, he was much less eager than Tatian to link Christians with barbarians. As Justin says, Christians "are not a contemptible people, nor a barbarian tribe, nor some nation like the Carians or Phrygians."[268] The emphasis here on Carians and Phrygians follows the same tendency in the classicizing work of Dionysius of Halicarnassus and his objections to the influence of Asianism (see chapter 1). With his comment, Justin suggests that Christians were more like an uncorrupted type of Greek, and not Asiatic, much less barbarian. Justin does acknowledge that there were barbarian members of the Christian philosophical school, but his reference to them is somewhat dismissive, implying that one would not normally expect barbarians to be educated: "Among us, therefore, it is possible to hear and to learn these things [sc. doctrines of Christian philosophy] from people who are ignorant of the shapes of the alphabet, being untrained and barbaric in speech but wise and faithful in their mind."[269] Barbarians stand in here for the simple believers in Christianity, as befits its status as a more democratic school of philosophy (see chapter 2). Justin is accepting enough of these unlearned Christians but is still paternalistic in his characterization of them. This was exactly the sort of attitude that Tatian objected to throughout *Against the Greeks*.[270] Justin seems to be claiming barbarian wisdom as his own, while denying that he and Christians as a whole were barbarians.

A similar attitude about the Greek/barbarian dichotomy appears in the work of a crucial figure in the later reception of Tatian. This was the heresiologist Irenaeus, a longtime resident of Lyons in Gaul, but originally a native of western Asia Minor, perhaps the city of Smyrna.[271] Irenaeus's journey from Asia Minor to Gaul certainly brought him to Rome for a stay of an uncertain length of time, most likely in the 150s or 160s, the same period when Justin and Tatian were active in the city.[272] Irenaeus is silent on whether he knew Justin and Tatian personally, but he offers several hints indicative of his familiarity with Justin, at least, whose lost work of heresiology was a source for his own.[273] Justin was a key model and source for Irenaeus, whereas Tatian was not.

Irenaeus shares with Justin a similar perspective about Greeks and barbarians and even displays signs of linguistic purism and Greek chauvinism. He offers a comment about the spread of Christianity among illiterate barbarian peoples that echoes almost exactly what Justin had to say on this subject: "Those who believed in this faith without writings, as much as they are barbarians in their speech, are nonetheless extremely wise and pleasing to God on account of faith because of their doctrine, habits, and behavior."[274] Though this part of Irenaeus's work survives only in a Latin translation, there are still some clear signs of Justin's language, and a similarly paternalistic attitude about Christians who were ignorant of Greek. Irenaeus has more to say on this subject, revealing that his long residence in Gaul required him to speak in a language besides Greek. He explains these circumstances to his unnamed dedicatee in the opening preface to his work: "You will not seek from us, residing as we are in the Celtic provinces and busy most of the time with a barbarian language (*barbaron dialekton*), the art of eloquence."[275] The preface continues with a long list of other qualities that Irenaeus claims to lack, demonstrating its formulaic character and hinting that we should not take its contents too seriously. Still, Irenaeus's comment about a *barbaron dialekton* is striking.

I have argued elsewhere that this likely refers to Latin, rather than Celtic, given the urban character of Christianity in Gaul.[276] Whichever language he means, Irenaeus reveals that he shares some features in common with the linguistic purists of the second century, including the sophist Ulpian, who claimed that a rival was "barbarizing" by using a Latin word (see the previous discussion). Irenaeus displays similar tendencies in his choice of geographical vocabulary, preferring to use old-fashioned Greek terms, as if he were writing for an audience unfamiliar with the geography of the Western regions of the Roman Empire.[277] Like the lexicographer Phrynichus, Irenaeus seems to have had a preference for ancient and approved vocabulary, at least in matters relating to geographical terminology. Viewed from this perspective, Irenaeus emerges as someone who fits in with many of the same attitudes displayed by his sophistic contemporaries, which is entirely fitting for someone who may have grown up in Smyrna. Like many of his Greek peers, Irenaeus viewed the concept of barbarian in a negative light.

Irenaeus's perspective on Tatian was therefore predisposed to be negative, thanks to the contrasting views that the two had about the Greek/barbarian dichotomy. This gives a cultural underpinning to Irenaeus's comments on Tatian, though these are frustratingly brief, especially if the two did know each other. Cultural objections come out in how Tatian is introduced. Characteristically, Irenaeus associates Tatian with other heretics that he has already treated, condemning him by creating a succession of heretics. In Tatian's case, Irenaeus links him with "those called the Encratites" (οἱ καλούμενοι ἐγκρατεῖς), who practiced both sexual abstinence and vegetarianism.[278] One of the founders of the Encratites was Saturninus, and Irenaeus notes that he was from Antioch in Syria.[279] All of this underlies Irenaeus's brief discussion of how Tatian came to be a heretic: "He was a pupil of Justin, and as long as he was with him, he exhibited nothing of this. But after Justin's martyrdom he withdrew from the church, and, puffed up and deluded by the self-conceit of [being] a teacher, as if he were different from everyone else, he developed his own type of doctrine."[280] The biographical vignette here is brief, which is typical for Irenaeus. There is no comment even that Tatian was a native of Syria. But regional differences between Irenaeus and Tatian still stand out. When Irenaeus attacks Tatian for holding negative views about marriage, he was effectively attacking some basic features of Christianity in Syria, which placed great emphasis on sexual abstinence for its members.[281] Even Irenaeus's objections to the vegetarianism of the Encratites seem to echo the comments of Greeks discussing the dietary restrictions of people from Syria, including their well-known disinclination to eat fish.[282] The end result of all this is a basic cultural difference between Irenaeus and Tatian, who took with them different perspectives on what was normal behavior for Christians when they left their homes.

From Tatian's perspective, the critique that Irenaeus offered of him might well have classified the heresiologist among the "Greek men" that he addressed throughout his work. Irenaeus's dismissive comments about barbarians, combined with his upbringing in Asia Minor, help link him somewhat with Greek sophists of his time, including his contemporary Aelius Aristides, whose long residence in Smyrna meant that he and Irenaeus could have crossed paths.[283] Irenaeus was certainly less erudite than Aristides, not to mention Tatian himself, but his attitudes on language and culture still contain traces of Hellenocentrism, if not the excessive fixation on Athens of some of his sophistic contemporaries. At the very least, Irenaeus's charge that Tatian was innovating a new way of teaching is something that is anticipated in *Against the Greeks*. A critic, he says, might suggest that "Tatian inaugurates new doctrines of the barbarians, surpassing the Greeks and the countless multitude of philosophers!"[284] In effect, this is what Irenaeus says about Tatian, even if he is less explicit about the barbarous nature of the heretic's new doctrines. Though Irenaeus apparently did write a work, no longer extant, called *On Knowledge* (Περὶ ἐπιστήμης), that was directed "against the Greeks" (πρὸς Ἕλληνας), this work must have been of a substantially different character from Tatian's *Against the Greeks*.[285] Irenaeus consequently emerges as someone who was closer to the "men of Greece" of *Against the Greeks* than the self-proclaimed barbarian Tatian.

A more ambivalent response to Tatian comes from Clement of Alexandria, who shows some respect for the Syrian's learning, while still disagreeing with him on several points. Clement was likely familiar with Irenaeus's story of Tatian's descent into heresy, but he still seems to have found some value in his works.[286] Indeed, Clement engages more with Tatian's work than any other extant Christian author, showing definite familiarity with *Against the Greeks*, the lost *On Perfection According to the Savior*, and probably other works.[287] The two references to *Against the Greeks* are to its section on Greek and barbarian chronography. Clement praises Tatian for "carefully" (ἀκριβῶς) demonstrating the great age of Moses and even cites him again for the detail that the Athenian king Cecrops was of "double-form" (διφυοῦς).[288] The chronological section of *Against the Greeks* was evidently helpful to Clement, just as it was to later readers, including Eusebius.[289] Clement was less complimentary, however, about some of Tatian's other views, critiquing his claims about marriage and sexuality and his interpretation of the key biblical phrase "Let there be light."[290]

In the process, Tatian appears in the company of others whose doctrines Clement rejected, including the person he identifies as the "founder of docetism" (ὁ τῆς δοκήσεως ἐξάρχων).[291] Clement never explicitly calls Tatian a heretic, but the sum total of his references leans in this direction.

As with Irenaeus, there is a cultural component in Clement's response, making him seem something like one of Tatian's addressees in *Against the Greeks*. This is a complicated response to assess, though, in large part because even basic biographical details about Clement are uncertain.[292] The outline of Clement's biography comes from his own brief story about his education and the travels associated with it, including encounters with a series of teachers, culminating in his decision to "rest" after "having hunted down [a teacher] concealed in Egypt."[293] The story implies that Clement was not originally from Egypt, but it gives no firm answer to the question of his place of birth, besides revealing that he met the first teacher in Greece. From Epiphanius, we learn that "some people call him an Alexandrian, but others an Athenian," which is often taken to mean that Clement was born in Athens.[294] This may be true, but another possibility needs to be considered. The label of Athenian may have attached itself to Clement because of his fondness for Attic dialect and style and his evident interest in the city.[295] One of his works, *The Instructor*, is dotted with comments about Attic usage, including etymological speculation and learned citations of the comic poets Menander and Philemon.[296] Three of Clement's observations on Attic usage find exact parallels in the lexicons of Moeris, Phrynichus, and Pollux.[297] These similarities serve to demonstrate the emptiness of Clement's claim elsewhere in his corpus that he has not "studied to speak correct Greek" (ἐπιτηδεύειν ἑλληνίζειν).[298] Whether or not he was from Athens, Clement shared some of the fascination with the city that characterized Tatian's addressees.

This self-identification with Athens colors Clement's treatment of Tatian, making the author of *Against the Greeks* seem something like a barbarian being discussed in a Greek work of ethnography. The key element lending this ethnographic character is Clement's choice to identify Tatian as a "Syrian" (Σύρον), something that was not mentioned by Irenaeus.[299] "Syria" and "Syrian" were words that had different connotations for Clement, depending on the context. Clement does mention the story that the alphabet came to Greece from Phoenicia, noting that "the Phoenicians and Syrians were the first to invent letters," according to prevailing opinions.[300] Syria might therefore connote antiquity, in keeping with the praise Clement offers Tatian for his careful demonstration of Greek youth compared to the barbarian world. Clement, however, also reveals another side of his perspective on Syrians in a long and erudite discussion of foreign peoples who worshipped animals. This concludes with a reference to "the Syrian inhabitants of Phoenicia, some of whom worship doves, and others of whom worship fishes."[301] Clement's familiarity with this stereotype gives another association to the word "Syrian," making him seem something like the rivals of Ulpian in Athenaeus's *Sophists at Dinner*, who charged that he had "robbed [them] of fish because of the ancestral customs of the Syrians."[302] As a Syrian, therefore, Tatian might be expected to practice similarly foreign customs. His understanding of Greek might likewise be imperfect, a charge that Clement levels explicitly at Tatian, alleging that he had misidentified the verb form *genēthētō* (let there be) as optative, rather than an imperative.[303] The optative mood, of course, was being kept artificially alive by Atticists in the second century and had long since begun to disappear from common Greek.[304] Clement therefore implies that Tatian was unable to understand the ancient and autochthonous form of Greek. There is consequently a note of condescension in this critique of Tatian, whose origins in Syria evidently mattered to Clement.

Even Clement's use of the adjective "Syrian" to apply to Tatian seems like a form of disrespect, rejecting the label of "Assyrian" that appears in *Against the Greeks*. "Syrian" and "Assyrian" were sometimes treated as synonyms, but the latter form was what Tatian evidently preferred, in keeping with the usages of his archaizing contemporaries.[305] "Assyria" connoted the extreme antiquity of the Assyrian Empire—something that even Aelius Aristides recognized.[306] Clement himself was familiar with this connotation, using the word "Assyrian" in most contexts relating to the ancient past of the region, even suggesting to the Greeks that "the Assyrians have taught you much."[307] Tatian and Clement were in agreement on this point, but Clement nonetheless denied Tatian his preferred nomenclature. This choice on Clement's part resonates because of his reference elsewhere to one of his teachers who was, he says, "from [the land] of the Assyrians."[308] Clement evidently recognized that the term "Assyrian" was preferential and conferred more respect because of the antiquity associated with it. But he nonetheless called Tatian a Syrian, a choice that makes Clement look like a Greek ethnographer discussing the customs of a foreign people.

Ultimately, what distinguished Clement from Tatian was their different perspectives on Greek culture and its significance in the history of the world. Though the two were in basic agreement that the barbarian world was more ancient than Greek civilization, they still expressed this claim with different emphases. The difference comes out clearly in how Clement words his critique of Greek culture and his suggestion about the changes that had resulted after the Logos had come to earth. Now that this had happened, Clement says, "we should no longer go to human

teaching, seeking eagerly Athens and the rest of Greece, or even Ionia."[309]
Tatian could have had few objections to this comment, which matches
his own suggestion that he had rejected "the nonsense of the Athenians"
(τῇ Ἀθηναίων ψυχρολογίᾳ) after he became a Christian.[310] But Clement's
subsequent remark reveals how much he and Tatian differed. Though
Clement does suggest that everyone should now seek out the teaching of
the Logos instead of going to Athens, he expresses this idea by claiming
that "the entire world has now become an Athens and a Greece through
the Word."[311] This remark is ostensibly directed to the Greek addressees of
Clement's work, which surely does explain some of the reason why it is
presented in such conciliatory terms. Tatian, however, displayed nothing of
this attitude in *Against the Greeks*, denying Athens and Greece the status of
cultural center that Clement granted them. For Tatian, Greek culture was a
derivative product from the barbarian world, distorted by the demons that
the Greeks wrongly believed to be gods. It was not something deserving
of the respect that Clement granted it. On this point, there was simply no
potential for agreement between Tatian and Clement. And this difference
in perspective was something that likely contributed to Clement's dismissal
of Tatian as a heretic.

Ironically, though, Tatian's growing reputation as a heretic obscures
the extent to which his profile as an intellectual anticipated new directions
in Christian intellectual culture. Several of Tatian's critics were prominent
members in this new generation of Christian intellectuals, better able than
their forebears to engage in detail with all aspects of Greek *paideia*. Clement
is chief among this group, but he is joined also by Tertullian, Pseudo-Hippolytus, and Origen, all of whom offered their own critiques of Tatian.[312]
Tertullian seems to have been familiar with *Against the Greeks* and draws from
some of its content in his own works, though without acknowledging a debt
to Tatian.[313] Clement and Origen are more explicit about Tatian's status as
a new type of Christian intellectual, both of them showing respect for the
learning displayed in his argument concerning the great antiquity of barbarian civilization.[314] Origen even says that Tatian demonstrated his claim "with
great learning" (πολυμαθέστατα).[315] This is high praise from someone who set
new standards for erudition among Christian intellectuals. Tatian's learning
was something that Christians who deemed him a heretic could recognize,
even if they might not acknowledge it explicitly.[316]

But if we move beyond this sporadic praise, other signs emerge of
how much Tatian's later critics followed his lead. One example comes from
the popularity of Tatian's argument about the link between demons and
astrology among Christian intellectuals.[317] Like Tatian, later Christians
also found reason to engage with Greek ideas about these subjects, which

continued to be influential.[318] Medicine and health were likewise subjects
that intrigued the next generation of Christian intellectuals, who again
followed Tatian's example in offering real engagement with prevailing
ideas on these subjects.[319] Tertullian cited the works of the second-century
doctor Soranus, Pseudo-Hippolytus was familiar with the conventions
associated with public medical demonstrations, and Origen seems to show
some awareness of his older contemporary Galen.[320] Tatian's successors
and critics followed up on similar topics and made their engagement with
Greek culture increasingly obvious.

Such engagement even shows up in the choice of some Christians
to write works in the form of miscellanies, following but also modifying
the example of Tatian. Tatian, of course, had only played with this genre,
signaling this with his strategic use of the word *poikilia*, while denying
that the varieties of Greek wisdom held any interest for someone who had
mastered the unitary wisdom of the barbarian world. But two of Tatian's
critics were less coy about their use of this genre. Both Clement and Origen
wrote works called *Stromateis*, a title that literally meant "bedspread," referring to the patchwork that normally went into such coverings.[321] This was
a popular choice of title for miscellanists, and Clement may well have
known of earlier examples, including a work attributed to Plutarch.[322] The
great length and lack of organization of Clement's *Stromateis* reveal to any
reader that it is a miscellany, and passages scattered throughout show his
familiarity with the conventions of the genre. These include Clement's use
of the word *poikilia*, including in one key spot at the end of the seventh
book where he likens his readers to fishes looking through his work for
something that catches their attention: "For many and various (*poikila*)
are the baits for different types of fish."[323] *Poikilia* here is a virtue of Clement's work, rather than something that he was claiming to reject, as Tatian
did. The value that Clement attributes to *poikilia* comes out with additional clarity earlier in the *Stromateis*, when he suggests that "the paths of
wisdom that lead directly to the path of truth are various (*poikilai*)."[324] This
statement encapsulates the basic difference between Tatian and Clement.
Tatian insisted on the unitary nature of wisdom and rejected the possibility that there might be multiple "paths of wisdom," claiming that truth
was to be found only in the ancient barbarian world. Clement, contrarily,
demonstrated more willingness to accept different forms of wisdom and to
acknowledge a variety of different paths to the truth. Both authors engaged
with the genre of the miscellany and the key concept of *poikilia*, but only
Clement was willing to embrace this genre.

The differing attitudes of Clement and Tatian concerning *poikilia*
and miscellanies embody the key points that separated them and helped

cement Tatian's reputation as a heretic. Though the issue of Tatian's heresy is typically framed simply in terms of the doctrines he supported, cultural differences also played a significant factor. This shows up in the tendency of later Greek heresiologists to identify Tatian as a "Syrian," while authors working in Syriac labeled him as a "Greek," speaking to the complicated hybridity his work embodies.[325] In keeping with this tendency, Tatian's Greek critics almost invariably reveal themselves to be more similar to the "Greek men" addressed throughout *Against the Greeks* than to its author. Both Irenaeus and Clement demonstrate concerns with linguistic purity while at the same time displaying a paternalistic attitude toward barbarians, following the example of Justin. Though Tatian's own engagement with Greek culture anticipated subsequent developments in Christian intellectual culture, this easily gets lost amid the accusations of heresy leveled against him. His views may have differed from those of Irenaeus and his other critics, but what distinguished him most was simply the frankness with which he called himself a barbarian. Even in an age when there was increasing interest in barbarian wisdom, few of Tatian's contemporaries writing in Greek were willing to do the same. This raises one final question. When Tatian "offer[ed] [himself] ready for an examination of [his] doctrines" at the end of *Against the Greeks*, was this an offer directed in part at other Christians, especially Irenaeus, who may well have already dismissed him as a heretic by this point? Put in different terms, Tatian's seeming attack on the non-Christian culture of his time may have also functioned as a rejoinder to Christians who had dismissed him as a barbarian and a heretic.

Conclusion

Against the Greeks is clearly the product of its author's sustained engagement with the diverse intellectual culture of the second century. The perspective that it offers on this period is idiosyncratic, but not as distinct or critical as Tatian suggests. Throughout the work, Tatian demonstrates awareness of a great variety of literature and intellectual activity, ranging from astrology, demons, and medicine to ongoing conversations about language and the histories of the Greek and barbarian worlds. Tatian's claim to reject all this variety is key to his strategy to define himself as a barbarian, but also as someone who had nonetheless mastered Greek *paideia*. This hybrid identity that Tatian claims for himself points to his effort to redefine the words "Greek" and "barbarian" and to claim back the latter word from Greeks who wished to bolster their own authority with the great antiquity of the barbarian world. In sum, Tatian presents himself as a barbarian, but little distinguished him from people who claimed to be Greek.

Tatian's idiosyncratic views on Greek culture, moreover, cannot be described as characteristically Christian. Some of his claims were common enough among later Christian intellectuals, including his insistence that the Greek gods were demons and the detailed proof he offered of the greater antiquity of the barbarian world relative to Greece. Though Tatian's critics Irenaeus and Clement accepted these points, he was still marked off from them by his willingness to label himself a barbarian. When Irenaeus and Clement wrote about Tatian, they seem like Greek ethnographers writing about the strange customs of a foreign people. Cultural differences between Tatian and his critics therefore played a role in their decision to label him as a heretic. Seen in this light, it is clearly wrong to say that "Christianity instills in Tatian a new appreciation for his barbarian origin."[326] Rather, the pride that Tatian displayed in his barbarian identity was something that distinguished him from some other Christians of his time, who seem similar to the "Greek men" addressed throughout *Against the Greeks*.

Tatian nonetheless led the way forward for later Christian intellectuals in terms of his engagement with Greek intellectual culture. His flirting with the genre of the miscellany was taken up without hesitation by Clement and by other later Christians. They likewise display similar levels of familiarity with Greek culture in all its variety. Tatian still may present himself sometimes as a philosopher, following the example of his teacher Justin. But he also emerges from *Against the Greeks* as someone like the same *pepaideumenoi* he critiqued, who defined themselves by their wide-ranging mastery of Greek *paideia*. Tatian therefore provides a preview of Christian intellectual culture in the coming decades, when fully fledged Christian *pepaideumenoi* would finally begin to gain the attention that Justin had tried but failed to attract.

CHAPTER 4

CHRISTIAN INTELLECTUALS AND CULTURAL CHANGE IN THE THIRD CENTURY

An entry in the *Chronography* of Georgius Syncellus summarizes the career of Julius Africanus and his connections to the emperor Severus Alexander (r. 222–35): "Emmaus, the village in Palestine which is mentioned in the holy gospels, was honored by being called Nicopolis by the emperor Alexander, with Africanus, who composed a history in five books, serving as an ambassador. Africanus dedicated to this Alexander a work in nine books called the *Cesti*, which concerns the properties of medical, natural, agricultural, and alchemical substances."[1] This is a good outline of Africanus's career and some of his most significant achievements. It is silent, though, on the fact that Africanus was a Christian and arguably the first Christian intellectual to gain such a close connection to the imperial household. Syncellus evidently expected his readers to know this. Not much later in his *Chronography*, Syncellus even identifies Africanus as one of "the holy and blessed fathers" (ἱερῶν καὶ μακαρίων πατέρων) active in the early third century.[2] Syncellus's silence on this point earlier in his discussion of Africanus still seems notable, though. It was evidently difficult to present Africanus's actions in an especially Christian light, inasmuch as he was representing a village in Palestine as an ambassador, rather than the Christian church, like Justin and other earlier apologists. Even more so, Syncellus would have struggled to explain how the *Cesti*, a miscellany treating a range of scientific topics, might have qualified as a Christian work. From Syncellus's account, then, Christianity played no obvious role in Africanus's relationship with Severus Alexander.

Syncellus's treatment of Africanus raises questions about how important Christianity was for his career as an intellectual and how visible it was in his literary output, especially the *Cesti*. The extant fragments of this work show no signs of Christian influence whatsoever, going well beyond

even a work like Tatian's *Against the Greeks*, which contained no references
to Christ but was demonstrably written by a Christian (see chapter 3).[3]
Indeed, all indications suggest that the *Cesti* seemed almost un-Christian
in its contents. One later reader who was familiar with the complete work
described some of the advice and recipes that Africanus offered, including
the following: "From the dung and urine of copulating cattle [Africanus]
makes a man defecate and a woman urinate whenever he wishes, and to
laugh uproariously."[4] This sort of content led some readers of the work,
both ancient and modern, to deny that it could have been written by a
Christian. One Byzantine author insisted that the *Cesti* had to have been
written by another man named Africanus, and not the "blessed and holy"
father who wrote works that were obviously Christian.[5] More recently, the
author of a substantial monograph on Africanus has made a similar suggestion, insisting that the *Cesti* must have been written before Africanus
became a Christian.[6] This suggestion is impossible for chronological reasons: the *Cesti* clearly postdates Africanus's *Chronographies*, the "history
in five books" mentioned by Syncellus, which is obviously written by a
Christian.[7] Simply put, objections that the *Cesti* could not have been written by a Christian are baseless. This unusual work of miscellany lacking
any explicit signs of Christianity was nonetheless dedicated to a Roman
emperor by a Christian intellectual.

The non-Christian work that Africanus dedicated to Severus Alexander presents problems for narratives that identify newfound imperial
sympathy to Christianity under the Severan dynasty. This period does
seem to have marked a breakthrough of sorts for Christianity, with unprecedented evidence for Christians serving in the imperial household.[8] We
also have evidence for two other Christian intellectuals, Origen and
Hippolytus, gaining connections with members of the Severan dynasty.[9]
Explanations for the new prominence of Christian intellectuals in this
period are sometimes based on claims that members of the imperial family
were interested in Christianity and were perhaps even Christians themselves.[10] Evidence for the Christian sympathy of the imperial household,
however, derives from late sources of questionable reliability (as will be
explored later). This point notwithstanding, it is often taken for granted
that the interest of the imperial household in Christian intellectuals was
a reflection of a larger religious policy that tends to be described with
the words "syncretic," "henotheistic," or "universalizing."[11] Arguments on
these points have moved beyond older, simplistic suggestions about the
Eastern origins of the Severan dynasty and a consequent interest in religions of the East.[12] But much is still taken for granted about the growing
prominence of Christianity and Christian intellectuals in the early third

century. Though this was a period when the number of Christians in the Roman Empire seems to have expanded considerably,[13] caution is still necessary in assuming that such expansion was linked to a more sympathetic attitude from the imperial household.

My aim here is to challenge the idea that changes in attitude toward Christianity led to the growing prominence of Christians under the Severan dynasty. The starting point for this argument is Africanus, and the many hints that Christianity was not the defining factor in his relationship with Severus Alexander and the imperial household. Africanus's example, in turn, suggests that a larger context is needed to explain new developments of the Severan period, rather than simply focusing on Christianity. The first section of this chapter begins to provide this context, emphasizing changes in the empire as a result of the end of the Antonine dynasty and the transition to the Severan. As members of a new dynasty, the Severans proved themselves more open than their Antonine predecessors to seeking out new clients and allies from regions of the empire that were once treated as marginal, including the Near Eastern provinces. Greater emphasis on this region contributed to the rise to prominence of jurists, legal experts whose interests and expertise extended beyond the Greek world. The second section of this chapter shows that Africanus and Origen were able to take advantage of these circumstances, rather than any particular sympathy for Christians that the Severan dynasty may have had. Both Africanus and Origen successfully conformed to the standard roles that intellectuals had held for centuries before. Their successes are less a breakthrough for Christianity than a sign that some Christian intellectuals were now able to fit in better with the elitist norms of intellectual culture in the Roman Empire. This culture was evolving, however, and the third section of this chapter explores how the Hellenocentrism of earlier periods was beginning to decay in the third century. Intellectuals and their patrons now became more open to non-Greek forms of culture and wisdom, despite a rearguard effort of Hellenocentrists. This greater openness benefited not only Christians, but also other intellectuals who could claim some expertise in the ancient wisdom of the barbarian world.

The third century consequently represented a period of major changes for Roman intellectual culture. These changes had a noticeable impact on Christian intellectuals, but they were not directly related to new imperial attitudes toward Christianity. Rather, new opportunities for Christian intellectuals were an incidental by-product of a larger transformation taking place within the Severan Empire. Amid this transformation, Greek culture still remained basic to the careers of intellectuals in the Severan period. But the balance had nonetheless shifted, with the result that non-Greek forms of culture and expertise carried more weight in intellectual culture than they had previously.

Severan Intellectual Transformations: The Rise of Jurists

The Severan era was a period of transition for the Roman Empire, nestled between the relative stability of the Antonine dynasty and the uncertainties that characterized the decades following the death of Severus Alexander in 235.[14] Many aspects of this transition have received much attention. The senate was remade in the wake of the Antonine plague and the accession of Septimius Severus, with many more of its members coming from the empire's Greek-speaking provinces, including those in the Near East.[15] Imperial interest in these regions increased overall, and it is likely that the personal connections of Septimius Severus and other members of his family played a significant role in this.[16] The growing significance of these regions of the empire forms part of the background for changes in Severan intellectual culture—a topic that has received somewhat less attention amid the empire's other transformations in the third century.[17] Much of the attention on intellectual developments has focused on the influence of jurists, legal experts who enjoyed a short-lived prominence during the Severan period.[18] There has been some acknowledgment, notably in the work of the late Fergus Millar, that the rise of jurists signals a new development in intellectual culture, especially because the work they conducted was in Latin, rather than Greek, though many of them came from Greek-speaking regions of the empire.[19] This is an important point, and one that I shall explore. But the increased importance of jurists and their use of Latin represent only one aspect of a larger trend in the empire, whereby classical Greek culture and literature came to lose some of their dominance over Roman intellectual life. Other cultures and literatures began to emerge as more significant for intellectual culture under the rule of the Severans.

A key figure illustrating these transformations is the jurist Ulpian of Tyre, whose career highlights the link between legal expertise and political power under the Severans. Ulpian is significant because we know much more about his life and career than we do for any other of the jurists, whose extant writings offer little by way of personal information.[20] What we do know about other jurists, though, tends to match the broad outlines of Ulpian's career, which allows us to speak of general patterns for jurists in this period. One such pattern is the tendency of successful jurists to hold administrative positions in charge of the emperor's correspondence and petitions.[21] From these offices, which themselves tended to be treated as political appointments, some jurists advanced to higher positions.[22] One jurist, M. Cn. Licinius Rufinus, held a series of administrative positions before becoming a senator.[23] Three jurists gained the title of praetorian prefect, an office that Ulpian held from 222 until his death in 224.[24] This sort of political power was linked to the intellectual activities of jurists and the connections they gained to the imperial household while holding administrative posts. Ulpian's career, in particular, was surely bolstered by his massive productivity as an intellectual. The roughly three hundred thousand words extant from his works in the *Digest* represent only a small fraction of what he seems to have written.[25] Ulpian was therefore part of what Jason König and Greg Woolf describe as the Roman Empire's culture of "bibliographical proliferation," deriving authority from the sheer quantity of his written output.[26] This demonstration of intellectual expertise was the foundation for his political career under the Severans, just as it was for other jurists in this period.

Ulpian's career was furthered by the later Severans, but his successes owed something to the policies taken by Septimius Severus in the Near Eastern provinces of the empire. The key factor aiding Ulpian was the foundation by Severus of many colonies in this region.[27] Previous emperors had founded four colonies here, the oldest of which was Berytus (modern Beirut), dating to the reign of Augustus.[28] Severus expanded the number of colonies considerably, offering colonial status as a reward to cities that supported him in the civil war against Pescennius Niger from 193 to 196.[29] Ulpian himself is a key source for this policy, offering a list of colonies founded by Severus. One of these was Heliopolis, "which received the status of an Italian colony from the divine Severus on the occasion of a civil war."[30] Other cities in the region received colonial status under similar circumstances, including Ulpian's home of Tyre. Ulpian elaborates on why the city was rewarded, suggesting that Tyre was "most steadfast in the alliance it made with the Romans."[31] He adds that "the divine Severus and our emperor [sc. Caracalla] gave [Tyre] Italian right because of its exceptional and conspicuous loyalty to the Roman state and empire."[32] The "Italian right" that it was granted gave the city exemption from some forms of taxation, in addition to other privileges.[33] Ulpian was no doubt already in his twenties by the time that Tyre was made a colony, but he was nonetheless likely to have benefited from the increased imperial attention to the region.[34] Too little is known about the origins of other jurists to suggest that there was an imperial policy of favoring natives of Syria in this role.[35] At best, we have the example of Ulpian, and possibly of another successful jurist, Papinian, who may have been from Syria.[36] The growth in the number of senators from the province of Syria, however, suggests that the Severans looked favorably on people of this region.[37] Ulpian's career surely owed something to the increased significance of Tyre and Syria in the Roman Empire under the Severans.[38]

Ulpian's career depended on his mastery of Roman law and Latin, despite his origins in the East. There is a definite pattern at work here, even if we are uncertain of the origins of nearly all of the other jurists of Ulpian's time. Some of these jurists, though, must have been from Greek-speaking regions of the empire and not native speakers of Latin. This much is clear from the existence of bilingual teaching materials that seem designed for the use of Greeks seeking to learn the language of Roman law.[39] Such material would have been useful in the schools of the colony of Berytus, a major center for the teaching of Roman law.[40] Learning Latin was evidently a struggle for some of the students who came here. We have as a witness for this Gregory, later called by Christians the Wonderworker, who traveled to Bertyus with the initial goal of learning law.[41] Other factors, including his encounter with Origen, led Gregory in a different direction, but he does note that the Latin language proved to be "burdensome" (φορτική) for him to master.[42] The prospect of gaining legal expertise, however, made learning Latin a worthwhile endeavor for some native speakers of Greek.[43] It was a necessary step in accessing the opportunities that might come with being a successful jurist.

Making so much use of Latin, however, was a sign that jurists of Ulpian's time were less fixated on Greek culture than many intellectuals who came to Rome in earlier periods. Ulpian is our best witness for this phenomenon, thanks to what we know of the man who may have been his father, or at least another member of his family. This is the pedantic Atticist Ulpian, who makes a notable appearance in Athenaeus's *Sophists at Dinner*, where his interlocutors label him as a Syro-Atticist and tease him about his origins in Phoenicia (see chapter 3). In keeping with his extreme Atticism, the elder Ulpian charged his rival Cynculus with "barbarizing" (βαρβαρίζοντες) when he used a Latin word.[44] This is a sign of extreme Atticism, heavily tied up with the idea of the purity of the Greek language. The younger Ulpian, by contrast, had no objections to writing at great length in Latin and to mixing Greek words and phrases into his prose frequently.[45] His writings consequently display no concern with linguistic purity. The same is true of Ulpian's pupil Herennius Modestinus, who made the unusual choice of writing a book on Roman law in Greek.[46] A prefatory comment to this work shows that Modestinus recognized the difficulty inherent in such a task.[47] And the work's extant fragments reveal that Modestinus often dealt with this issue simply by transliterating Latin words into Greek.[48] This is exactly the sort of thing to which the elder Ulpian had objected and a sign of a much more relaxed attitude about linguistic purity on the part of Modestinus.

Though it is unclear what Modestinus's native language may have been, and where he was from, his laxity with respect to Greek was something unthinkable to anyone concerned with the idea of linguistic purity.[49] This was a step back from the rigorous Atticism and Hellenocentric attitudes of many intellectuals in earlier periods.

In the case of Ulpian, at least, this attitude may have been related to his origins in Tyre and his pride in the ancient and non-Greek history of this city. Evidence on this point is limited, and there is little basis to suggest major similarities between Ulpian and other intellectuals who emphasized the great antiquity of Near Eastern civilizations, such as Tatian and Philo of Byblus (see chapter 3). But some sense of a similar attitude comes through in Ulpian's one extant remark about Tyre, which he describes as "the most splendid colony of the Tyrians, which is my place of birth, outstanding in its territories, most ancient in the succession of generations (*serie saeculorum antiquissima*)."[50] The final clause is unusual, and Alan Watson simply translates it as "of very ancient foundation."[51] This is a very free rendering of the words *serie saeculorum*, both of which can connote the idea of ancestry, especially in terms of a family tree traced back generation by generation.[52] The pairing of the two words suggests that Ulpian was referring not simply to the antiquity of Tyre's foundation but also to the family links of people in his time to the city's ancient founders. Ulpian may be connecting himself more directly to the ancient past of Tyre, just as many Greeks emphasized their direct descent from heroic or divine figures from the ancient Greek past (see chapter 1). Little else can be said about Ulpian's connections to Tyre. Efforts to find traces of Semitisms in his Latin have been fruitless, and the common suggestion that he knew Aramaic lacks any evidence to confirm it.[53] The absence of evidence makes it difficult to draw a conclusion, but there is nonetheless a strong hint that the younger Ulpian emphasized his origins in Tyre much more than the elder. He evidently saw no need to hide or disown his origins in a region associated with the barbarian world, unlike other intellectuals from Syria in earlier periods.

The Severans may have provided some license for Ulpian to emphasize his origins in Tyre, thanks to the dynasty's own connections to the empire's Near Eastern provinces. These connections were present for Septimius Severus through his origins in the Roman colony of Lepcis Magna, which possessed ancient links to Phoenicia via Carthage.[54] Both Tyre and Lepcis Magna found reason to emphasize their link in the second and third centuries. Lepcis had erected in Tyre a statue identifying the Phoenician city as its founder, and Tyre returned the favor by erecting a statue in Lepcis of Septimius Severus's son Geta, calling itself a mother-city.[55] Ulpian consequently had some reason to be proud of his origins in Tyre, which

Septimius Severus may well have regarded as the ancestral home of his own forebears. The Syrian origins of Severus's wife Julia Domna would have only provided more encouragement for Ulpian and others from the region, including the aforementioned influx of senators from Syria in the early third century.[56] An intellectual from the ancient metropolis of Tyre, which had recently become a Roman colony thanks to its loyalty to Severus, certainly had good reason to advertise his origins there.

There is some reason overall to believe that influence from the imperial household was a significant factor in the career of Ulpian and in the larger rise to prominence of jurists. Besides the Severans' close connections to the provinces of the Near East, we also have evidence to suggest that Septimius Severus took special interest in legal affairs. This comes from the eyewitness account of Cassius Dio, who reports that Severus "used to allow sufficient water [i.e., time] to the pleaders and gave us, his co-judges, much freedom to speak."[57] Severus's investment in court activities may well have provided another boost to the careers of jurists and the political roles that several of them subsequently gained during the reigns of his successors. We have definite hints, therefore, that imperial influence was working to reshape the empire's intellectual culture and granting jurists additional standing that they had previously lacked.

This boost to the prestige of jurists was a concern for intellectual culture, and not just relevant for legal and political affairs. There are many indications that the jurists presented themselves as intellectuals.[58] Though they wrote almost exclusively in Latin, the jurists sometimes demonstrated their familiarity with a range of classical authors.[59] In one notable instance, extended quotations from Demosthenes and Homer served to bolster and illustrate the claims of the jurist Claudius Saturninus regarding the factors that should be considered when determining a punishment for a crime.[60] These sorts of citations were a natural outcome of the jurists' educations, but they also served as signs that they were engaging with the broader intellectual culture of the Roman Empire. Such engagement is especially clear in an excerpt from Ulpian that comes at the very beginning of Justinian's *Digest*. In this passage, which tackles the question of defining justice and law, Ulpian suggests that the latter is the "art of goodness and equality" (*ars boni et aequi*) and that jurists are the "priests" (*sacerdotes*) of this art.[61] Ulpian is here moving into the contentious territory of which fields of study deserved to be described as an art (*technē/ars*). His older contemporary Galen did grant law this status, but only at the end of a long list of other fields.[62] Ulpian, by contrast, elevates the status of law, suggesting that it is concerned at a basic level with "distinguishing just from unjust, separating lawful from unlawful, and seeking to make men good not only from fear of punishments but also by the inducement of rewards."[63] This description of law leads Ulpian to an obvious conclusion. The field that he and other jurists study is a "true philosophy, not counterfeit."[64] This is a strong claim, bringing Ulpian into the competitive world of his contemporary intellectuals, so many of whom claimed to offer the true version of philosophy (see chapter 2).[65] The imperial household's influence no doubt gave additional prominence to Ulpian and other jurists when they sought to present themselves as intellectuals. Becoming a jurist might bring with it the possibility for a successful career as an intellectual, but also the chance to claim to be a true philosopher.

The influence of the imperial household was consequently a factor in the rise of jurists and in the beginnings of a transformation of Roman intellectual culture. Severan interest in the provinces of the Near East surely helped the career of Ulpian and other jurists from the region, while at the same time making the study of Roman law a more fashionable option for intellectuals. Severan jurists continued to demonstrate their knowledge of Greek and of Greek classical literature, but their interest in both was different from the interests of Atticists like the elder Ulpian. The rise of jurists therefore represents a blow to the Hellenocentrism that had once characterized so much of the empire's intellectual culture. Ulpian's career may seem to have little bearing on Christianity and Christian intellectuals, though we do know that he collected a set of imperial rescripts illustrating how Roman governors should deal with Christians under their rule.[66] But his relationship with the imperial household, together with his interest in non-Greek subjects, can nonetheless help explain the interactions of Christian intellectuals with members of the Severan dynasty.

Christian Intellectuals and the Imperial Household

Like Ulpian, Christian intellectuals were able to benefit from the increased attention that the Severans devoted to the empire's Near Eastern provinces and from the dynasty's greater openness to intellectual activity revolving around subjects besides the classical period of Greece. Certainly, the Severans were less Hellenocentric than earlier emperors like Tiberius, and this was important for Christian intellectuals of their period who tended to share Tatian's views about the relative insignificance of Greek culture and history. But there are complicating factors at work amid this shift away from a fixation on Greece. These factors resulted from the actions of Elagabalus, the fourth member of the Severan dynasty, who had a short and controversial reign as emperor.[67] He received the nickname "Assyrian" for his foreign habits, which included a refusal to eat pork, an unwillingness to wear Greek or Roman clothing, and the heavy-handed introduction to Rome of the worship of his god.[68] This created a challenge for his successor Severus Alexander and his mother, Julia Mamaea, both of whom are key figures in the relationship of the Severan dynasty to Christian intellectuals. Julia sought to establish that her young son live up to Greek and Roman standards of education and that he not seem like a foreigner in Rome, as Elagabalus did.[69] This mission to fit in with Greco-Roman culture provides crucial background for the encounters that Julius Africanus and Origen had with the imperial household during Alexander's reign. Both intellectuals possessed expertise in non-Greek culture and history, and this was of some relevance for their interactions with the imperial household. But Africanus and Origen also demonstrated substantial expertise in Greek culture, together with the ability to serve the imperial household in ways that intellectuals had been doing for centuries. The Greek learning of Africanus and Origen helps establish that Christianity was of little relevance for the connections that they gained to the imperial household. Both men seemed little different from the types of public intellectuals who tended to catch the attention of the imperial household. Africanus and Origen were likewise able to pass as sufficiently Greek to fit in with the goals of Alexander and Julia, who were in no position to be seen embracing the foreign cult of Christianity in Rome.

Julius Africanus

Africanus's success in gaining the attention of the imperial household depended on his connections to Roman colonies in the Near East, much like his contemporary Ulpian. As Africanus himself reports, his "homeland" was "Colonia Aelia Capitolina of Palestine."[70] This was the former city of Jerusalem, renamed and resettled in the second century CE, and one of the four Roman colonies established in the Near East before the Severan dynasty.[71] Africanus seems to have been from a leading family there, and he was perhaps a member of the equestrian class, like Ulpian and the other jurists.[72] This background fits in with his status as a Roman citizen, demonstrated by his *tria nomina*, Sextus Julius Africanus.[73] These names likewise show that he or someone in his family was granted citizenship before 212, when citizenship was extended to all free people in the empire by Caracalla's decree.[74] Roman citizenship and possible membership in the equestrian class went along with Africanus's obvious learning, which suggests that he received an excellent and expensive education. All of these features made him a good candidate to serve as an ambassador to the imperial court on behalf of the Palestinian village of Emmaus.[75] The successful outcome of this embassy fit in completely with Severan interest in the region. Africanus's participation in it likewise provided him with an excellent entrée to Rome, securing him a connection with the new emperor, Alexander.[76] Severan emphasis on the Near East was of obvious significance for establishing the career of Africanus close to the imperial household.

Africanus was able to present himself as something of an expert in the Near East, which was likely another factor in the connections he gained with Alexander. Before he came to Rome, he had already visited Alexandria and the Dead Sea and spent time at the court of King Abgar the Great (177–212 CE) in Edessa.[77] The report of this visit in the *Cesti* provided Africanus an opportunity to show off his literary skills and to demonstrate his expertise in military and scientific matters. He offered a memorable example of ekphrasis from his own experiences, describing how the talented archer Bardesanes (Bardaisan) was able to create a portrait of a handsome youth with his arrows, shooting them at a shield held up by his subject.[78] Africanus likewise described his observation of a strange experiment designed to demonstrate how far an arrow might travel in the course of an entire day if it could stay aloft that long.[79] These descriptions of life in Edessa accompanied Africanus's other journeys, including his search for the place where Noah's ark had landed.[80] During his travels, Africanus undertook archival research and acquired rare books that he came across, such as a copy of the *Sacred Book* of Pharaoh Suphis in Alexandria.[81] Septimius Severus had done much the same when he visited Egypt, seeking out ancient books in Alexandria.[82] Africanus's expertise and experience in the Near East surely did help him gain the attention and interest of the Severans.

But Africanus's service for Alexander in Rome seems to have been confined to areas that allowed him to demonstrate his learning in Greek and Roman subjects. The main activity that we know about was Africanus's role in the development and likely even the construction of a new imperial library. The evidence for Africanus's involvement with this new library comes only from a single passage of his *Cesti*.[83] The reference to the library is preserved on a papyrus found at Oxyrhynchus, and it comes in the midst of an odd discussion concerning what Africanus claimed to be the original incantation used by Odysseus to summon the spirits of the dead in *Odyssey* 11.[84] Africanus refers to the places where a reader might find copies of the incantation, one of which was "in Rome near the baths of Alexander in the beautiful library in the Pantheon, which I myself designed for the emperor (ἣν αὐτὸς ἠρχιτεκτόνησα τῷ Σεβαστῷ)."[85] The context of the passage has not inspired complete confidence in Africanus's claims about a library in the Pantheon.[86] This library is unattested in any other literary sources, and no material remains of it have been found. But, as Christopher Siwicki argues, what Africanus called the "Pantheon" likely referred to a larger complex of buildings extending beyond the extant structure still associated with this name.[87] Africanus's involvement in the development of the new library's collection is generally granted, on the grounds of his obvious experience with books.[88] But serious doubts have been cast on Africanus's claim to have constructed the library.

Despite these doubts, there is good reason to believe that Africanus possessed the training and learning associated with architects, a profession that placed emphasis on command of an encyclopedic range of material. Architects were supposed to be masters of many different fields of study, according to Vitruvius, who suggests that an architect "should be lettered, experienced with drawing, and skilled in geometry. He should know much of history and diligently listen to philosophers. He should understand music and be not ignorant of medicine. He should know the answers of jurists and be familiar with astronomy and its calculations."[89] The list of fields mentioned matches well with Africanus's self-presentation of his own expertise, hinting that he could have possessed the skills of an architect.[90] There is also a suggestion in the twelfth-century *Chronicle* of Michael the Syrian that Africanus "presided over the construction" of the colony of Nicopolis, which was the new name of Emmaus, the village he had represented on his embassy to Rome.[91] This evidence reconciles easily with what else we know of Africanus's life. He could well have gone back to Emmaus/ Nicopolis after the embassy and then returned to Rome at a later date to take up his place at the court of Alexander.[92] Africanus's learning and expertise as an architect were evidently beneficial to his career in Rome.

Africanus seems to have put these skills to use to decorate the new library. This library was "beautiful," Africanus says, which suggests that he was referring to the room or building where the books were kept and not simply the books themselves.[93] The beauty of Africanus's library was instead likely to have derived from other elements in the structure, including its cupboards (*armaria*) used for the storage of scrolls, which were often made from ivory and valuable types of wood.[94] Statues and a sculptural program would also have contributed to the beauty of the space. Such features were ubiquitous, so much so that a bust or statue of an author almost necessarily accompanied his works in imperial libraries.[95] If Africanus did design the library of the Pantheon for Alexander, then he surely had a hand in the design and placement of its furniture and sculptural program, in addition to the development of its collection of scrolls.

Africanus's involvement in the new library for Alexander speaks to his closeness to the emperor and to his finding roles for himself at the imperial court that had been held before him by many non-Christian intellectuals. The new library, located so prominently in or around the complex of the Pantheon, surely formed part of the larger project to demonstrate that Alexander fit in with Greek and Roman norms of education. Alexander and his advisers no doubt provided considerable input on the design and contents of the new library, which would have meant working closely with Africanus. All of this is clear from evidence relating to other imperial libraries, which functioned as politicized spaces that were used for the reception of embassies.[96] Emperors before Alexander had also exerted personal control over the collections and sculptural program of imperial libraries, sometimes simply for reasons of personal taste. Tiberius had ensured that the works and *imagines* of three erudite and difficult Hellenistic poets were placed in the libraries of Rome; Caligula also apparently contemplated removing the works and *imagines* of Livy and Vergil from Roman libraries.[97] Alexander may well have been less demanding than these earlier emperors, but Africanus would still have had to liaise with him and to translate his demands and desires for the library into reality. Such tasks would have linked Africanus to a larger group of imperial librarians and architects, who likewise had worked closely with other emperors.[98] Previous imperial librarians included a number of extremely learned intellectuals, including Varro, Hyginus, and Suetonius.[99] Imperial architects are less well-attested as individuals, but their closeness to the emperor cannot be doubted to judge from comments about their presence in the imperial entourage.[100] We also have the specific example of Apollodorus of Damascus, who was famous for the projects he undertook and for his interactions with Trajan and Hadrian.[101] Africanus's place close to Alexander joined with him a distinguished company of non-Christian intellectuals.

Africanus's work for Alexander as a librarian and likely architect suggests that Christianity had little bearing on his connections to the imperial household. Fragments of his *Cesti*, which he dedicated to Alexander in 231, confirm this impression. The lack of any references to Christianity in the work's extant fragments is surely significant, as is its odd collection of recipes, veterinary advice, and a bewildering range of other contents. Of greater significance, though, is one clear passage where Africanus missed an obvious opportunity to mention Christianity. This comes in his reference to life at the court of King Abgar and the talented archer Bardesanes he met there. Bardesanes also happened to be a distinguished Christian intellectual and someone of great significance for the development of Syriac Christianity.[102] But Africanus made no mention of this, a subject that might seem to have been relevant to his dedicatee Alexander. Instead,

Africanus simply called Bardesanes a Parthian.[103] This silence about Bardesanes is suggestive that Christianity had no real place in the *Cesti* and that Africanus's own Christianity had no relevance for the position that he held at the court of Alexander.

Africanus consequently provides no support for the popular claim that Alexander was sympathetic to Christianity. Despite its popularity, this claim is based on limited evidence, much of it coming from Alexander's biography in the *Historia Augusta*, a work written late in the fourth century by a single author, rather than a group of authors active in the time of Constantine, as it presents itself.[104] The imperial biographies contained in the *Historia Augusta* turn mostly into fantasy by the time that it reaches the reign of Septimius Severus.[105] Alexander's biography fits into this trend, offering what amounts to a historical romance of this emperor's reign.[106] This includes the famous story that Alexander had a shrine containing statues of Christ, Apollonius of Tyana, Abraham, and Orpheus, among others.[107] References to this shrine inevitably appear in discussions of Alexander's sympathy for Christianity, and sometimes also in speculative treatments of the books contained in the library that Africanus developed for this emperor.[108] But, if we discount the stories of the *Historia Augusta* about Alexander's supposed interest in Christianity, we come away with a meager set of evidence, most of this deriving from Eusebius's hyperbolic claim that the emperor's household "contained many of the faithful."[109] Africanus's connection to Alexander might seem to bolster this claim and to support the fictions of the *Historia Augusta* regarding the emperor's interest in Christians. But if Africanus's link to Alexander had nothing to do with Christianity, much of the justification for this assumption disappears. There is consequently little basis to say anything about Alexander's supposed interest in Christianity.

Overall, Africanus's career at Rome provides no support to the claim that Alexander had any great sympathy for Christianity. Africanus found a place for himself at the court of Alexander that differed little from the places held by earlier, non-Christian intellectuals. He also fit in well with contemporary intellectual trends and the emperor's attempt to demonstrate his Greco-Roman credentials. Africanus's range and skill as an intellectual provide some confirmation for Eusebius's claim that he was "a learned man known to those inclined toward secular learning" (τοῖς ἀπὸ τῆς ἔξωθεν παιδείας ὁρμωμένοις).[110] His career at Rome serves as a demonstration not of any new Severan interest in Christianity but rather of his ability as a Christian intellectual to conform to established expectations for intellectual behavior.

Origen

Africanus's associate Origen presents a more complicated case. His interactions with the imperial household were much less extended than those of Africanus. Origen met only relatively briefly in 231–32 with Julia Mamaea, Alexander's mother.[111] And this meeting was more explicitly religious in character than the interactions that Africanus had with Alexander at Rome. Origen may well have had much to say about Christianity to Mamaea, perhaps even demonstrating to her his command of Hebrew and the ancient literature of the Near East.[112] But Origen still seems to have carried himself in his meetings with Mamaea in a way that would have been familiar to her from her interactions with non-Christian intellectuals. Origen fits well within the world of his non-Christian contemporaries. Though Africanus may also have some claim to this title, Origen emerges as the earliest Christian to qualify as a public intellectual, famous enough to be sought out by a member of the imperial household.

Origen's fame is clear from multiple sources that emphasize his great learning and productivity as a writer. This is true regardless of the position one takes in the controversy surrounding the possibility that there were two different intellectuals named Origen active at basically the same time, one a non-Christian Platonist philosopher and the other the prolific Christian intellectual who also happened to be quite interested in the works of Plato.[113] No end to this controversy seems likely, thanks to ambiguous and potentially contradictory evidence.[114] Suffice it to say, I follow the argument that there was only one Origen.[115] Regardless of the position one takes in this controversy, Origen's learning is not in doubt. His father, martyred when Origen was young, likely possessed the training of a grammarian, and he may well also have been a Roman citizen, to judge from Eusebius's suggestion that he was beheaded.[116] After his father's death in 202/3, Origen's education continued thanks to the generosity of an unnamed wealthy woman in Alexandria.[117] Origen's father and this woman ensured that he received an excellent general education along with special training as a grammarian.[118] Origen put all of this education to use in his later career as a teacher. We know from multiple sources that he instructed his students in the same group of preparatory subjects that Justin had earlier lacked (see chapter 2): geometry, music, grammar, rhetoric, and astronomy.[119] Origen received additional patronage in his later career from Ambrose, a man of immense wealth who, in Jerome's words, "furnished him with parchment (*chartas*), funds, and copyists" and thus allowed his client to produce his "innumerable books."[120] Origen was consequently well-equipped to become a public intellectual and to gain attention from the imperial household.

We learn about this imperial attention from a brief report in Eusebius, which leaves much unsaid about the nature of the meeting between Origen and Julia Mamaea.[121] Eusebius's report is characterized by a certain amount of defensiveness that the meeting even took place. This defensiveness came from Origen himself, whose own account of the meeting in a now-lost autobiographical letter was the source of Eusebius's information, according to the arguments of Pierre Nautin.[122] The report emphasized that the meeting was primarily of a religious character. Mamaea is described as "an exceptionally religious woman" (θεοσεβεστάτη γυνή), and she wished to test Origen's "knowledge of divine things" (τὰ θεῖα συνέσεως αὐτοῦ).[123] Origen "revealed to her many things relating to the glory of the lord and the excellence of divine teaching" before he "hurried back to his normal pursuits."[124] The letter also emphasized that he was summoned to Antioch by Mamaea and accompanied by a military escort.[125] The same factor was mentioned in the report concerning Origen's earlier meeting with the Roman governor of Arabia: "A certain soldier arrived bearing letters to Demetrius the bishop of the region and to the current prefect of Egypt from the governor of Arabia, [asking] that they send Origen with all haste to converse with him."[126] As the son of a martyr and the teacher of many pupils who had been martyred, Origen was careful to make clear that his encounters with the imperial household and a Roman governor were not the result of his own choice. Origen was evidently less eager than Africanus to cultivate imperial connections.

But other sources suggest that Origen's behavior in Antioch would have corresponded closely to what Mamaea would have expected from any sufficiently distinguished non-Christian intellectual. We gain insight into Origen's demeanor especially from a letter he wrote concerning his actions during what may have been the same visit to Antioch.[127] The relevant portion of the letter is extant only in a Latin translation by Rufinus.[128] Even in its translated form, the story reported would not be out of place in any work describing the lives and actions of Origen's contemporary intellectuals, such as Philostratus's *Lives of the Sophists*, or any number of works by Galen. Origen described his encounter with a "certain heretic" (*quidam haereticus*) in Ephesus and how this man had later forged a work that he claimed to be the record of a debate between himself and Origen, though such a debate had never taken place. The heretic then distributed the document widely, as Origen explains: "I indeed know that he sent it to those who were at Rome, but I do not doubt that he sent it to others in different places."[129] Origen confronted the heretic at Antioch, where he claimed to have "refuted him in front of many onlookers" (*multis eum praesentibus argui*).[130] In their public confrontation, the heretic was unwilling to produce the debate that he had forged, so that the audience would have the opportunity to recognize Origen's style. The heretic was thus "found guilty by everyone and convicted of falsehood" (conuictus ab omnibus et confutatus est falsitatis).[131]

The free movement and communication between Ephesus, Antioch, and Rome evoke the wide-ranging travels of Philostratus's sophists, as does the dramatic public debate between Origen and the heretic.[132] A comparable example comes from the rivalry between Herodes Atticus and Philagrus of Cilicia in the second century and the memorable occasion when Herodes's pupils were able to prove that Philagrus was guilty of repeating the same declamations that he pretended were improvised on the spot. Herodes's pupils acquired a copy of a declamation that Philagrus had already given in Asia and then asked him at Athens to declaim on the same theme. When Philagrus began to speak, Herodes's pupils read his previous composition alongside him, which resulted in "laughter and a great din" and the verdict from the assembled audience that he stood convicted of the charge leveled against him.[133] Origen's request that the audience authenticate his treatise also recalls the famous story told by Galen of an encounter he witnessed in a Roman bookshop: after reading only the first two lines, a grammarian dismissed as a forgery a treatise for sale that was represented as a work by "Galen the doctor."[134] Origen's handling of this controversy is suggestive of a confident and even slightly histrionic attitude in his public demeanor. His time in Antioch in 231–32 with Mamaea likely also involved continued work on his massive commentary on the Gospel of John, which he had set aside when he left Alexandria.[135] Such an effort would have been a demonstration to Mamaea that her summons would not keep him away from his work, and it was in keeping with the attitude of a philosopher trying to demonstrate that imperial attention had no real impact on him.[136] Behavior of this sort would have been completely familiar to Mamaea; she would no doubt even have been surprised if Origen had acted any differently.

Origen's encounter with Mamaea also gave him an opportunity to demonstrate his skill as an extemporaneous speaker, another area where he conformed to prevailing expectations for intellectual behavior. Origen's skills as an extemporaneous speaker were emphasized by his later defenders, such as Pamphilus, who suggested that he spoke off the cuff on an almost daily basis in church (paene cotidie in Ecclesia . . . ex tempore).[137] Small pieces of his extemporaneous output survive in the form of homilies, which were copied down by shorthand writers.[138] Most of these homilies are extant only in Latin translations made by Rufinus and Jerome, but the small collection of Greek homilies has recently been expanded with twenty-nine new works, thanks to the discovery in 2012 of a manuscript in Munich that had previously been misidentified.[139] Three of these new homilies are explicitly identified in the manuscript as being extemporaneous productions.[140] These new pieces of evidence join a few other explicit signs in the older body of homilies that clearly identify them as unrehearsed works. One telling example is Origen's fifth homily on First Samuel: the selection read from scripture was sufficiently long for him to ask that the bishop present should "propose" (προτεινάτω) an aspect from it that he should discuss.[141] The situation outlined here may not correspond exactly to the familiar motif in the works of Philostratus and Galen, where a speaker would offer an extemporaneous speech on a subject proposed by an audience member.[142] The verb for proposing used by Origen was προτείνω rather than προβάλλω, which we might have expected to see instead.[143] Origen was nonetheless completely able to replicate this characteristic behavior of sophists and iatro-sophists, even if he did so in a slightly different setting. Once again, Mamaea would have expected as much, and Origen no doubt demonstrated to her that he was up to the challenge of extemporaneous speech.

Compared to Africanus, Origen had a substantially different experience in his interactions with the imperial household. He had only a brief encounter with Mamaea, and he met her in Antioch rather than Rome. His meeting with Mamaea, however, was a consequence of his education and the reputation that he had gained as an intellectual. This encounter with Mamaea gave Origen an opportunity to display his skills as an extemporaneous speaker and to establish that he was not overly impressed to be summoned by a member of the imperial household. Origen, however, was never a good candidate to take up a more permanent role at the imperial court. He lacked the elite background that Africanus had, and he was little inclined to forget that his father and many of his pupils had been martyred in an earlier persecution. But Origen still was able to conduct himself like his contemporary sophists, and he no doubt proved that this was the case in his brief interactions with Mamaea.

In sum, the paired examples of Origen and Africanus offer little support to suggestions that Christianity itself experienced a major breakthrough with the Severan dynasty. Rather, we simply have some evidence to suggest that two Christian intellectuals gained connections of varying degrees of closeness with members of the imperial household. Origen's link with Julia Mamaea may well have involved some discussion of Christian doctrine. But Origen's behavior, and his overall self-presentation, still belong to the broader intellectual culture of the Roman Empire in the third century. He and Africanus seem simply to be the first Christian intellectuals to gain wider recognition of their skills and learning among non-Christian circles. This was a significant development attesting to the increasing intellectual respectability of Christianity. But it should not be interpreted as if

Christianity were the defining factor in the relationships of Africanus and Origen with members of the imperial household.

Cultural Conflict in the Third Century

Christianity should likewise not be granted too much status in discussions of the broader intellectual culture of the third century. A broad consensus holds that this period was characterized by "intense intercultural competition" and "cultural debate."[144] This is surely correct, but there has been much uncertainty regarding the nature of this conflict and the relevance of Christianity to it. My aim here is to suggest that Christianity played only an incidental role in the cultural conflict of the third century, which revolved around the status and significance of Greek civilization and culture in the broader history of the world. Once marginal views regarding the youth of Greece of the sort defended by Tatian became more prevalent in the third century. Christian intellectuals of this period took up Tatian's argument, but it has been too little appreciated how many of their non-Christian contemporaries were now willing to admit this same point.[145] Awareness of this shift among non-Christian intellectuals helps reveal the outlines of a broader cultural conflict. The Hellenocentrism that characterized so much of the Roman Empire's intellectual culture in earlier periods was now facing more serious dissent than it had before. Alongside this dissent, we possess many signs suggestive of a larger defense of Greek culture mounted by people committed to the idea that Greece was the source of philosophy and all the world's wisdom. Africanus, Origen, and other Christian intellectuals participated in this cultural conflict and benefited from the greater interest devoted to the ancient history of non-Greek civilizations. But Christianity was not a central factor in the cultural conflict of the third century, however much Christians ultimately benefited from the weakening of Hellenocentric assumptions in Roman intellectual culture.

A key figure who brings out the terms of the third-century debate is Diogenes Laertius, an obscure individual who wrote a collection of philosophical biographies. Diogenes says little in the text about himself, and there is little external information to date or locate him in a particular context. But there is no reason to accept the older view that he was a marginal, bookish figure who lived "outside of his time."[146] Contrary to this suggestion, two passages of Diogenes's work help establish his engagement with the intellectual world of the third century. One of them is an address to the work's dedicatee, a woman who had a strong interest in Plato.[147] Her identity is not known, but her evident familiarity with Platonism speaks to her education and elite background.[148] Diogenes's connection to this

CHRISTIAN INTELLECTUALS AND CULTURAL CHANGE   139

woman confirms that he had a life outside of the library and hints also that he may have worked in a major center of political and intellectual activity, rather than a backwater town.[149] The second key passage from Diogenes's work is a list of Skeptical philosophers that concludes with Sextus Empiricus and his pupil Saturninus.[150] The significance of this reference to Sextus Empiricus is the subject of some controversy because he, much like Diogenes himself, is a poorly attested figure.[151] But he and his pupil Saturninus can still be dated to the first half of the third century, suggesting that Diogenes was active not much later.[152] The references to Sextus Empiricus and Saturninus provide the best sign that Diogenes was familiar with contemporary and near-contemporary intellectuals and their written output. We still know little about Diogenes's life. But the great silence surrounding him should not be taken literally. We should instead grant that Diogenes was selective in what he told us about himself and the world in which he lived, just as he was selective in his presentation of philosophical history.[153] Wherever and whenever exactly he lived, Diogenes was still in tune with the realities of intellectual culture in the third century.

Diogenes's significance for the cultural conflict of the third century comes from the strident Hellenocentrism displayed in the opening section of his work. "Some say," Diogenes suggests, "that the discipline of philosophy had its beginning from the barbarians."[154] He subsequently proceeds to list a range of people who might qualify as barbarian philosophers, including the Magi of Persia, among others, citing as his sources for this Aristotle and Sotion, who wrote a work in the Hellenistic period on the successions of philosophers.[155] After mentioning the suggestions of these authors, however, Diogenes offers a firm rejoinder: "They forget that the achievements that they bestow on the barbarians belong to the Greeks, with whom not only philosophy, but even the human race began."[156] He buttresses this claim further with an argument based on language: "And thus philosophy took its beginning from the Greeks. Its very name rejects a barbarian appellation."[157] This claim suggests that philosophy's true essence was Greek. Perhaps Diogenes knew that this Greek word was transliterated directly into Latin—a point that would provide some support to his argument. At a more basic level, however, Diogenes was countering any suggestion that would make Greece subordinate to other civilizations. As he insists, Greece was not simply responsible for the birth of philosophy but also for the very first humans on earth. Diogenes consequently displays a total unwillingness to concede that Greece was secondary in any respect when compared to other civilizations.

Contextualizing Diogenes's Hellenocentric attitude has proven to be difficult, with scholars offering a range of assessments, most of these

emphasizing how unusual his perspective was. There has been basic disagreement on whether Diogenes's attitude belongs to a third-century
context, in keeping with suggestions that he lived "outside of his time."
One extremely literal reading of the opening sections of Diogenes's work
has suggested that he was simply responding to the Hellenistic authors he
named as sources, rather than engaging in a contemporary debate.[158] By contrast, other scholars have suggested that Diogenes was responding directly
to the claims of contemporary Christian intellectuals, perhaps Clement of
Alexandria.[159] But amid this debate, there has been general agreement that
Diogenes was odd and perhaps even unique in holding such an extreme
view of Hellenocentrism. His perspective has thus been identified as "far
outside the mainstream of both his genre and his own time" and "firmly
against the tide of contemporary opinion."[160] Though the quoted suggestions derive from a serious effort to contextualize Diogenes, the end result
is the conclusion that he was a poor fit for the context of the third century.

Further probing, however, suggests that Diogenes was responding to
an increasingly prominent group of intellectuals who challenged the Hellenocentric view of the world that he championed. Though he nowhere
makes this explicit, Diogenes may well have been familiar with Christian
intellectuals, including Africanus and Origen, who emphasized that Greece
was young when compared to the ancient civilizations of the Near East.[161]
But the key point to recognize is that there were non-Christian intellectuals in the third century who operated with similar assumptions. One
obvious example is Ulpian and his emphasis on the pre-Greek past of the
Roman colony of Tyre (as noted previously). Ulpian was joined by other
intellectuals with similar perspectives, extending well beyond the jurists
who may have been from Syria. It is hard to quantify the increasing numbers of prominent intellectuals from the provinces of the Near East, but
many notable figures stand out. Among sophists, Callinicus of Petra is a
significant example; he was joined also by a host of other third-century
sophists from Phoenicia, Syria, and Arabia.[162] There were many significant philosophers from these same regions, as is clear from the school of
Plotinus, who numbered among his hearers Porphyry of Tyre and other
intellectuals from Arabia and Syria.[163] Simply being from these regions
was no guarantee that an intellectual would be proud of his native land
and its past. Many intellectuals from the Near Eastern provinces spent a
significant part of their careers away from home.[164] But intellectuals from
the Near East nonetheless might be proud of their native regions, even if
they pursued careers abroad and dedicated themselves to the mastery of
Greek or Latin literature, as the jurist Ulpian did. Diogenes consequently
had many possible targets for his polemic among his contemporaries.

Diogenes may still seem to be out of tune with his context, inasmuch as challenges to the antiquity and originality of Greece seem to have become increasingly common. The commonness of this view is evident from a comparison of Tatian's aggressive attacks on Hellenocentrism and the restrained attitude of Africanus when he notes the youth of Greece as an unquestioned fact.[165] A similar attitude appears even in Porphyry, a critic of Christianity who nonetheless presented in his works a major challenge to Hellenocentric perspectives, even if he was himself fully invested in the Hellenic tradition.[166] Porphyry took for granted that Greece was late to encounter some branches of learning, presenting this belief incidentally as an unquestioned fact: "It is agreed that the forms of knowledge came late to the Greeks, such as geometry, arithmetic, and astronomy. But they were nevertheless things that could be known, even if the Greeks did not know them."[167] Porphyry's comment on the lateness of Greeks to learn geometry and other fields helps establish how commonplace challenges to Hellenocentrism had become in the third century, and not just among Christian intellectuals. Diogenes's polemic in defense of his Hellenocentric worldview should thus be read in light of the increasingly influential challenges made to it, not simply by Christians but also by intellectuals like Ulpian and Porphyry.

And Diogenes was not alone in his response. In spite of suggestions that Diogenes was unusual or even unique, other intellectuals also took a dim view of any suggestion that Greek culture was somehow derivative, or of secondary importance.[168] This attitude extends back into earlier periods of history, but it was kept alive in the third century. Signs of this perspective are apparent in the attempts of Greek intellectuals in the late Hellenistic period to deflate claims about how ancient barbarian civilizations were (see chapter 1). In the second century, Aelius Aristides displayed much the same perspective when he suggested that Athens was just as ancient as Assyria (see chapter 3). This is perhaps not quite the same as Diogenes's claim, but it still demonstrates an effort to portray Greece as no younger than any barbarian civilization.

Signs of a similar viewpoint come out in philosophical literature of the second century. Diogenes had an ally of sorts in Plutarch, despite the interest some of his works display in Egyptian culture and history.[169] A Hellenocentric attitude is apparent especially in his essay *On the Malice of Herodotus*. In this work, Plutarch rejected out of hand the historian's claims that some early Greek heroes were of barbarian birth. It was impossible, in Plutarch's view, that Perseus and Hercules could have been descended from Assyrians, as Herodotus had suggested.[170] Plutarch was similarly bothered that Herodotus "represents Thales as a Phoenician by birth, barbarian by origin."[171] This claim about Thales's origins was evidently outlandish enough that Plutarch felt no need to refute it. In Plutarch's view, philosophy was a Greek development and something that Greeks were supposed to teach to barbarians—not the other way around.[172] This perspective anticipates Diogenes, who cites Herodotus among a list of authors who claimed Thales as a Phoenician.[173] Though he includes this suggestion, Diogenes ultimately offered a contrary opinion: "Most say that [Thales] was a true-born native of Milesia, and from an illustrious family."[174] Like Plutarch, Diogenes rejected a claim that made an early philosopher of great significance into a barbarian.

A few decades after Plutarch's time, the Platonist philosopher Atticus offered a similar defense of philosophy's Greek origins. Atticus is another obscure figure, though we can date him roughly via Eusebius's suggestion that he flourished in the late 170s.[175] Apart from this date, we can surmise from his name that Atticus had a connection to Athens, and perhaps even to the millionaire sophist Herodes Atticus.[176] Fragments of his works suggest that he emphasized the Greek and Athenian origins of philosophy. Atticus presented Plato's philosophy as something new, unifying and systematizing what came before. As Atticus says, Plato was the "first to bring together all the parts of philosophy into one."[177] Atticus does mention a few of Plato's predecessors, listing some of the pre-Socratics, plus statesmen such as Solon who applied their philosophical knowledge to politics.[178] But this list contains a significant absence, listing no philosophers from the barbarian world. Instead, Atticus simply emphasizes how great and innovative Plato was as a philosopher: "He was better than others, newly initiated, as if he were truly sent by the gods, so that all of philosophy might be seen through him."[179] Atticus's emphasis on Plato as a divine, nearly miraculous figure forging philosophy into something completely new was not accidental. Another section of Atticus's work excerpted by Eusebius places Plato squarely within a Greek tradition: "We trust in what he reasoned for us with clear and distinct speech as a Greek to Greeks."[180] Atticus here implies that there was philosophical continuity within the Greek tradition, linking himself with it as Plato's heir. His perspective on the development of a Platonist tradition makes philosophy a Greek property. Like Diogenes, he was uninterested in suggestions that would find barbarian origins for Greek philosophy.

This emphasis on philosophy as Greek is tied to a larger interest in origins, reflecting Greek fascination with ancestral connections to the classical and heroic past (see chapter 1). Diogenes displays an interest in genealogies of this sort amid his defense of philosophy's Greek origins. He refers to the Eumolpidae, a family that claimed exclusive access over ancestral priesthoods in Athens.[181] This is a significant point because we know from other sources that the Eumolpidae were still active in the third century.[182] One of their number, the sophist Apollonius, was even mentioned by Philostratus as a near contemporary.[183] The continuing existence of this family has some bearing on how Diogenes attempted to justify his claim of the Greek origins of philosophy. To do so, he referred to Musaeus, the legendary disciple of Orpheus. This Musaeus was an Athenian, Diogenes believed.[184] Musaeus's civic origin certainly mattered to Diogenes, but one additional detail about his biography was also of great significance. Musaeus's father was named Eumolpus, and it was from this Eumolpus, Diogenes added, "that the Eumolpidae at Athens take their name."[185] There is no evidence to connect Diogenes to any of the Eumolpidae who still lived at Athens when he was writing in the third century, but his reference to them would no doubt have resonated with contemporary readers. Diogenes was claiming not only that philosophy had Greek origins but that one of its founding fathers still had living descendants in Athens. These were claims that mattered not just to historians of philosophy but also to members of elite families who were proud of their distinguished Greek ancestors. Barbarian influence and barbarian ancestors were consequently excluded from his view on the origins and development of Greek philosophy.

Something similar to Diogenes's perspective seems to have been taught in rhetorical schools of the third century. This comes out in one of the works attributed to Menander Rhetor, a younger contemporary of Diogenes who produced substantial manuals on how to tailor a speech to any possible occasion.[186] Students using Menander's work would have encountered an attitude of implicit Hellenocentrism in its discussion of how to praise a city. Menander here suggests that all cities belong to one of three categories: ancient, middle, and recent, which included cities founded under Roman rule.[187] The most ancient category was reserved for a "city or country that we say was founded before or with the stars, or before or after the flood."[188] Menander illustrates this category with the examples of Athens, Arcadia, and Delphi, accepting the exaggerated claims to antiquity of these places.[189] These cities were all older than the places mentioned in the middle category, which was when "Greece flourished," and the time of the "power of the Persians, Assyrians, and Medes."[190] Menander adds that "most of the [cities] of Greece and barbarian lands" were founded during the middle period.[191] This is not quite a suggestion that Greece was older than all other peoples, as in Diogenes's claim. Menander leaves open the possibility that some barbarian cities and regions may have belonged to his "most ancient" (παλαιοτάτων) category. But Menander's choice of examples is nonetheless telling, emphasizing only the claims of Greek cities and regions to be extremely ancient.

There is consequently a hint here that Menander and those who followed his instructions were taking for granted the great antiquity of Greek civilization and dating it to the earliest beginnings of the human race.

The Hellenocentric attitude underlying such views seems sometimes to have been accompanied by hostility to anyone who would question Greece's great antiquity and significance in the history of the world. Diogenes's opening polemic demonstrates how poorly one Hellocentrist responded to contrary views. There are other signs of similar responses in a range of Greek texts from the second and third centuries, providing more context for the views defended by Diogenes. One example comes from the traveler Pausanias, who describes an unfriendly encounter he had with an unnamed man from the Phoenician city of Sidon.[192] The Sidonian, Pausanias explains, claimed that "the Phoenicians have better ideas about the divine than the Greeks," offering as an example the Phoenician belief that Asclepius, the god of healing, was nothing more than the air.[193] Pausanias's response to the Sidonian reveals a basic disagreement between the two men. Pausanias reports, "I told him that I approved of what he said, but I said that his claim was no more Phoenician than it was Greek."[194] Though the two men were in basic agreement about Asclepius and even willing to accept that the Phoenician god Eshmun was identical with the Greek Asclepius, they were divided about the origins of their shared belief and whether it was Greek or Phoenician.[195] This conversation hints at the potential for basic disagreements between Hellenocentrists and intellectuals who identified with the ancient civilizations of the Near East.

We have many more signs of such disagreements, particularly in the form of hostile portrayals of Near Eastern intellectuals in Greek literature of the late second and third centuries. Some of these examples are already familiar, including the consistently negative portrayal of the Severan emperor Elagabalus (noted previously). The Syro-Atticist Ulpian of Tyre provides a similar case. He is identified repeatedly as a "Syrian" or a "Phoenician" by his fellow diners, with these labels being used interchangeably.[196] Two more such figures show up in the works of Philostratus. One is Damis of Nineveh, a character likely invented by Philostratus, who is repeatedly called an "Assyrian."[197] There is also the "Phoenician," a fictional native of the "region around Tyre and Sidon" who participates in the *Heroicus*.[198] These ethnic labels may have an element of playfulness and banter associated with them, but they were nonetheless used to define and label the figures to whom they were assigned. In Athenaeus, there is a common implication that Ulpian should behave in the way that the ancient Phoenicians or Assyrians did (see chapter 3). Damis, meanwhile, has only a mediocre command of Greek because he "had been educated among the barbarians" (παιδευθεὶς ἐν βαρβάροις).[199] And the Phoenician of the *Heroicus* is defined completely by his national and ethnic origin; he is unnamed throughout the work, and we learn only that he practiced the stereotypically Phoenician profession of merchant.[200] Collectively, these three characters reveal the negative treatment that intellectuals associated with the Near East might expect to receive in the third century. Though intellectuals from these regions did gain increased standing throughout the empire in this period, they could still expect to be treated with a certain amount of hostility by intellectuals who were proud of, and not a little defensive about, their own intellectual and familial pedigrees as Greeks.

Viewed from this broader perspective, Diogenes Laertius fits well into the context of the third century. His Hellenocentrism emerges as a more explicit statement of an attitude still common among other Greek intellectuals of the third century. This was a time when more and more intellectuals from the Near Eastern provinces came to prominence, helped along by the increased status of this region in the empire. Intellectuals from the Near East often challenged assumptions that insisted on the centrality of Greece to intellectual culture and discussions of the history of the world. There were Christians among this group, but they were far from its only members. They had as allies Ulpian and Porphyry, who might otherwise be regarded as enemies of Christianity. What emerges, therefore, is a more complicated picture of the third century and its cultural conflict. There was more impacting intellectual culture in the third century than simply the growth of Christianity.

Conclusion

In sum, a broader focus on intellectual culture in the third century helps reveal problems with teleological views regarding the growth of Christianity in the Roman Empire. It has long been tempting for scholars to anticipate the reign of Constantine, especially when considering all of the seeming hints regarding the Severan dynasty's greater interest in Christianity. But the limitations of teleology are obvious when other factors in the third century are considered. The rise of jurists like Ulpian, combined with the increased prominence of intellectuals from the empire's Near East, demonstrates that there were other changes taking place alongside the growing numbers of Christians. Hellenocentric attitudes were challenged as a result of these changes, threatening the central status that classical Greek culture had throughout the Roman Empire. This led to a cultural debate in the third century that had an impact on Christianity, but without revolving around it, despite many assumptions to the contrary.

Though challenges were leveled against Hellenocentric attitudes, the mastery of Greek culture was still a significant factor in the careers of Christian intellectuals under the Severans. Origen and especially Julius Africanus continued to display the characteristics and skills of intellectuals who had gained connections to the imperial household in earlier periods of history. There was, in this sense, little real change when these two Christian intellectuals managed to capture the attention of the imperial household. Africanus and Origen were fulfilling the goals of earlier Christian intellectuals like Justin Martyr who had failed to attract positive attention from the imperial household. They likewise followed the example of Tatian in demonstrating their expertise in an encyclopedic range of Greek subjects, while nonetheless suggesting that barbarian civilization and culture had existed before Greece. Africanus and Origen consequently represent a breakthrough for Christian intellectuals, who seem never to have gained such close connections to the imperial household in earlier periods. But the imperial connections that they gained had little to do with changing attitudes toward Christianity. Any suggestion to the contrary is based on an anachronistic and narrow interpretation of intellectual culture in the third century.

CONCLUSION

Even as Christian intellectuals were making themselves known to a larger public, and taking advantage of changing circumstances in the empire, Christianity itself was becoming increasingly institutionalized. In the 250s, we know from a letter written by Cornelius, the bishop of Rome, that his community included "46 presbyters, 7 deacons, 7 subdeacons, 42 acolytes, 52 exorcists, readers, and doorkeepers, and more than 1,500 widows and distressed people."[1] Cornelius's evidence fits the broader picture of growing hierarchies and organization within third-century Christianity.[2] This represents a significant change from earlier periods, and the independence that characterized the careers of many Christian intellectuals in the second century. Justin and Tatian were teachers rather than clerics. Julius Africanus likewise seems not to have held any church office. But Origen's career and his conflicts with Demetrius, the bishop of Alexandria, demonstrate that Christian intellectuals were now struggling to maintain the independence that they had previously enjoyed.[3] There was a different climate now, with the title of bishop carrying more weight than the types of authority and expertise claimed by independent Christian intellectuals.[4]

Institutionalization had a major impact on how Christianity was viewed by Roman emperors during the middle decades of the third century. We have little evidence from this period for the relationship of emperors with Christian intellectuals, apart from our knowledge that Origen wrote letters to the emperor Philip the Arab and his wife Otacilia Severa.[5] Instead, most of our evidence focuses on imperial recognition of Christianity as a hierarchical organization that owned considerable properties throughout the empire. This type of recognition comes especially from the emperor Gallienus (r. 260–68), who issued a decree in 260 that seems to have made Christian organizations legal in the empire.[6] Quoted by Eusebius, the decree was directed toward a group of "bishops" (ἐπισκόποις), ordering that people who had evidently occupied Christian "places of worship" (τόπων τῶν θρησκευσίμων) should depart from them.[7] The bishops addressed are thereby identified as responsible for Christian community properties, with no acknowledgment of whatever credentials they may have had as intellectuals, even if these may be taken for granted. There is similar emphasis in another of Gallienus's decrees, mentioned but not quoted by Eusebius, that was addressed "to other bishops, permitting them to recover the places of the so-called cemeteries."[8] The focus here is on the administrative, organizational side of the Christian community, with attention directed toward land and property. Gallienus's decrees suggest that intellectual matters were a secondary concern, at best, for his policies relating to Christianity, though this emperor and his wife did have some interest in contemporary intellectual culture, including connections to the school of the philosopher Plotinus in Rome.[9] Christians, by contrast, seem to have mattered to Gallienus only inasmuch as they were part of an organization of some significance in the empire and were a group of people that he wanted to keep on his side while he engaged in conflicts with both internal and external enemies.[10] Christians consequently gained some of the recognition and support that they had long sought. But, at first glance, this was in response to Christianity's increasingly institutionalized character rather than the sorts of arguments and petitions that Justin and other intellectuals had directed in earlier periods toward the imperial household.

A growing number of Christian intellectuals in the third century, however, had achieved a real measure of intellectual respectability, much more so than in earlier periods. Africanus and Origen are chief among this group, though it is by no means clear that the former intellectual self-identified as a Christian in his interactions with the Severan dynasty. This doubt aside, we have clear evidence that some later Christian intellectuals were being regarded as philosophers, fulfilling the unmet goal of Justin Martyr roughly a century before. Our evidence for this comes from the school of Plotinus in Rome. Porphyry's biography of Plotinus refers to the existence of "many types of Christians, including sectarians who based their teachings on the ancient philosophy."[11] Plotinus and his pupils had many issues with these Christians, but they still deemed them worth engaging with at some length. Porphyry describes the ancient books that the Christian philosophers possessed, including writings that they attributed to the prophet Zoroaster.[12] Porphyry was in basic agreement with the Christians that ancient books of this sort were of great value, but he and other members of Plotinus's school had doubts regarding the authenticity of the writings. Porphyry tells us that he wrote "multiple refutations of the book of Zoroaster," joining the efforts of other members of his school to demonstrate that the ancient writings of the Christians were "entirely spurious and recent" (ὅλως νόθον τε καὶ νέον).[13] What we have here is another sign of congruence between Christian and non-Christian intellectuals in the third century thanks to a common emphasis on the importance of ancient wisdom. Though Porphyry and others of his school sought to discredit the "ancient" books of the Christians, they nonetheless granted to them the status of peers. In effect, Plotinus and his school were admitting that the Christians they sought to refute qualified as philosophers and representatives of a real philosophical school, however misguided they were in what they taught. This was a significant step forward for Christian intellectuals and the sort of attention that Justin and Tatian wanted but failed to receive. Alongside the growing institutionalization of Christianity, Christian intellectuals had finally arrived in the Roman Empire.

Justin, Tatian, Africanus, and Origen all contributed to this development, providing a basis of intellectual respectability for Christianity's emergence as an institution worth the notice of an emperor. Justin demonstrated that a Christian intellectual could address himself to the imperial household and ask for the respect befitting a serious philosophical school. Not much later, Tatian showed that Christians could present themselves not simply as philosophers but also as masters of the wide-ranging intellectual culture of the Roman Empire, while at the same time engaging with the key question of Greek culture's status and significance in the history of the world. Justin and Tatian, teacher and pupil, set out the basic agenda for later Christian intellectuals and officials, staking out ambitious places for themselves within the changing context of the Roman Empire in the late second and early third centuries. Africanus looks something like a hybrid of Justin and Tatian, introducing himself to the imperial household as a petitioner and dedicating to the emperor a work of miscellany, demonstrating the great range of learning that a Christian intellectual might possess. Together with Origen, Africanus shows that Christian intellectuals in the early part of the third century could simply blend into the intellectual culture of the Roman Empire, perhaps not even being singled out or recognized as Christians, depending on the context. It was only the growing institutionalization that gave new recognition to Christians as Christians, though they were identified by Gallienus as bishops rather than philosophers or any other title claimed by intellectuals. Still, it was the efforts of independent Christian intellectuals and teachers like Justin and Tatian that allowed for the institutional recognition that later Christian officials were to gain.

Before Christianity achieved this recognition, however, independent Christian intellectuals engaged deeply with the intellectual culture of the Roman Empire. This engagement, in turn, helps reveal some of the ways in which Christianity was unexceptional and a product of the empire in which it developed, rather than a wholly new phenomenon. The phrase "I am a Christian" and thousands of years of Christian exceptionalism have predisposed scholars and the general public to believe otherwise. But we still have definite signs, particularly in some of the works authored by Justin, Tatian, Africanus, and Origen, of the direct and sustained engagement of Christian intellectuals with the imperial household and the broader intellectual culture of the Roman Empire. These works should not be segregated or exceptionalized from the contexts in which they were written. Rather, they should be approached as part of a broader and more inclusive intellectual history of the Roman Empire, which this book has attempted to provide.

NOTES

Introduction

1. Eusebius, *Hist. eccl.* 5.21.1: ὅτε καὶ ὁ σωτήριος λόγος ἐκ παντὸς γένου ἀνθρώπων πᾶσαν ὑπήγετο ψυχὴν ἐπὶ τὴν εὐσεβῆ τοῦ τῶν ὅλων θεοῦ θρησκείαν, ὡς ἤδη καὶ τῶν ἐπὶ Ῥώμης εὖ μάλα πλούτῳ καὶ γένει διαφανῶν πλείους ἐπὶ τὴν σφῶν ὁμόσε χωρεῖν πανοικεί τε καὶ παγγενεῖ σωτηρίαν.

2. Eusebius, *Hist. eccl.* 5.21.2, 4.

3. See Eusebius, *Hist. eccl.* 5.21.4.

4. On this work, see the discussion of Musurillo (1972, xxiii–xxv), who notes that the extant text has only a tenuous relationship to the documents mentioned by Eusebius (*Hist. eccl.* 5.21.5) relating to the trial of Apollonius. Lampe (2003, 321–29) is more eager to suggest that there may be some historical basis for the text, but without offering any substantial support for this view.

5. *The Martyrdom of Apollonius* 2 (ed. Musurillo 1972).

6. For one example, note *Passion of the Scillitan Martyrs* 9. See Barnes 2010 for discussion of the authenticity of early accounts of martyrdom.

7. See Rebillard 2012, 92–95.

8. See Stanton 1973, 364; Snyder 2000; Lauwers 2013, 331–34.

9. See König and Whitmarsh 2007b; König and Woolf 2013a; König, Oikonomopoulou, and Woolf 2013; König and Woolf 2017.

10. For an emphasis on high-level literacy, see Rawson 1985, vii, with Capponi 2017, 11. Toner (2017, 168–71) emphasizes that intellectual activity in the Roman Empire need not have involved books or other written material. This point is well taken, but outside the scope of this book, which focuses on intellectuals who were highly literate.

11. Markschies 2006, 239. See also Fürst 2007, 10.

12. See Morgan 1998, 50–52.

13. On astrology, see Barton 1994, 27–94; on dream interpretation, see Harris-McCoy 2013.

14. Signs of this complicated relationship come from the existence of separate Greek lexica for Christian and non-Christian literature. On the history of this division, see Riedweg 2018, 13–14.

15. See Wilken 2003, xviii.

16. Note the comments of Whitmarsh (2005, 9) suggesting that the "hysteria surrounding the historiography of the early Church" had mostly vanished, opening up new possibilities for considering Christians as participants in the intellectual culture of the Roman Empire. Despite this suggestion, Christians still tend to be absent in much work on Greek imperial literature, though there have been some promising steps to challenge this tendency, notably in König 2009, 2012; Eshleman 2012; and LaValle Norman 2019.

17. Treatment of Christian authors is either absent (König, Oikonomopoulou, and Woolf 2013; König and Woolf 2017) or limited to coverage of the late antique, medieval, and Byzantine periods (König and Whitmarsh 2007b; König and Woolf 2013a).

18. See Marx-Wolf 2016; Wendt 2016.

19. See Lampe 2003; Green 2010.

20. See Ferrary 1988; Kaplan 1990; Swain 1996; Hidber 2011. Noy (2000, 85–127) offers discussion of the various motivations people had for moving to Rome.

21. See Dupont and Valette-Cagnac 2005.

22. See Noy 2000, 173–74. On Aelian, see Smith 2014.

23. See Millar 1992, 491–506.

24. The apologetic works of Marcianus Aristides and Quadratus (Eusebius, *Hist. eccl.* 4.3.1–3) are earlier, but the extant portions of

them are brief in the case of Quadratus (see
Foster 2007), and only vaguely addressed to
the emperor in the case of Aristides (see Parvis
2007, 119–20, with the discussions of editorial
interventions on the *Apology* in Pouderon and
Pierre 2003 and Simpson 2017).

25. Note that I have excluded Tertullian
because his extant works are only in Latin,
and his connections to the city of Rome are
uncertain. See Barnes 1985, 243–45. I have
likewise excluded the literature associated
with the name Hippolytus, including
the *Refutation of All Heresies*, because of
uncertainties about authorship and dating.
See Cerrato 2002; Cosentino 2018.

26. One of several such fragmentary figures
is Hegesippus, whose floruit is somewhat
uncertain, but likely not as early as implied by
Eusebius, *Hist. eccl.* 4.8.1–2. See DeVore 2019
for details.

27. Contrast the methods of Lampe (2003)
for Rome and Fürst (2007) for Alexandria.

28. See Stead 1994; Dillon 1996, 384–89;
Thorsteinsson 2010; Karamanolis 2013.

29. See Staden 1982, 96–100; Le Boulluec
1985, 1:39–64; Eshleman 2012, 213–58, against
Smith 2015, 15.

30. See König and Whitmarsh 2007a, 21 and
26.

31. E.g., Brent 2006; Nasrallah 2010.

32. See Eshleman 2012, 125–48.

33. See Richter and Johnson 2017, a
handbook on the Second Sophistic that treats
a diverse collection of subjects, including
Latin authors and late antiquity.

34. For a useful guide, see Whitmarsh 2005.

35. See Whitmarsh 2013.

36. E.g., Ferguson 2009 (on baptism);
Nicolotti 2011 (on exorcism).

37. See de Labriolle 1948; Wilken 2003;
Levieils 2007.

38. E.g., Rankin 2006.

Chapter 1

1. Tacitus, *Ann.* 12.61: *Argivos vel Coeum
Latonae parentem vetustissimos insulae cultores;
mox adventu Aesculapii Artem medendi inlatam
maximeque inter posteros eius celebrem fuisse.*

2. Tacitus, *Ann.* 12.61: *Xenophontem, cuius
scientia ipse uteretur, eadem familia ortum,
precibusque eius dandum, ut omni tributo vacui
in posterum Coi sacram et tantum dei ministram
insulam colerent.*

3. See LSJ, s.v. εὐγένεια.

4. Aristotle, *Rhetoric* 1.5.5 (1360b30–33):
εὐγένεια μὲν οὖν ἐστιν ἔθνει μὲν καὶ πόλει τὸ
αὐτόχθονας ἢ ἀρχαίους εἶναι, καὶ ἡγεμόνας
τοὺς πρώτους ἐπιφανεῖς, καὶ πολλοὺς ἐπιφανεῖς
γεγονέναι ἐξ αὐτῶν ἐπὶ τοῖς ζηλουμένοις.

5. See Levick 1990, 17–20.

6. Kennedy (2003) translates the four
major works of *progymnasmata*. For reviews
of these works, and discussion of their
significance in education, see, respectively,
Heath 2003, 129–41, and Penella 2011, 89–90.

7. Aelius Theon, *Progymnasmata* 9
(110.12–13 Spengel). Heath (2003, 141–58)
challenges the conventional suggestion, based
on Quintilian, *Inst.* 9.3.76, that Aelius Theon
should be dated to the first century CE.

8. See Kaplan 1990, 348–51; Buraselis
2000, 66–110.

9. See Segre 1993, vol. 1, EV 224, with
Buraselis 2000, 83–84, 92.

10. See Hall 2002, xvii; Gruen 2013, 20.

11. Galen, *On the Preservation of Health*
1.10 (6.51 Kühn): Ἕλλησι καὶ ὅσοι τῷ γένει μὲν
ἔφυσαν βάρβαροι, ζηλοῦσι δὲ τὰ τῶν Ἑλλήνων
ἐπιτηδεύματα.

12. Galen, *AA* 2.1 (2.280 Kühn): τοῖς μὲν
γὰρ περιττὸν ἦν αὐτοῖς ἢ ἑτέροις ὑπομνήματα
γράφεσθαι παρὰ τοῖς γονεῦσιν ἐκ παίδων
ἀσκουμένοις.

13. Galen, *AA* 2.1 (2.281 Kühn): ἐκπεσοῦσα
τοίνυν ἔξω τοῦ γένους τῶν Ἀσκληπιαδῶν ἡ τέχνη,
κἄπειτα διαδοχαῖς πολλαῖς ἀεὶ χείρων γιγνομένη.

14. See *IG* XII.9 4 = Curty 1995, 65–67, with
Hall 2002, 223 n. 224.

15. See Jones 1999, 135–36.

16. See Quass 1993, 68–70; Heller 2011.

17. See Tacitus, *Ann.* 11.24. The reference to
Athens and Sparta is absent in the preserved
epigraphical copy of Claudius's speech (*CIL*
XIII 1668 = *ILS* 212), but Griffin (1982, 410)
notes that this was "a traditional argument . . .
and could have been mentioned by Claudius."

18. Aelius Theon, *Progymnasmata* 9 (111.16–17
Spengel).

19. See Ker and Pieper 2014, 2–14.

20. See Montana 2015.

21. See Rawson 1985, 3–18.

22. See Plutarch, F 139–41 (Sandbach 1969)
= Stobaeus, *Florilegium* 4.29.21, 22, 51; Philo,
On the Virtues 187–227; Dio Chrysostom,
Or. 15.29–32; Galen, *Exhortation to the Arts* 7
(1.11–15 Kühn); Arius Didymus *apud* Stobaeus,
Eclogae 2.107–8 = *SVF* 3.366.

23. *Suda* Θ 151 = Woerther 2013 F 1:
Θεόδωρος, Γαδαρεύς, σοφιστής, ἀπὸ δούλων,
διδάσκαλος γεγονὼς Τιβερίου Καίσαρος. ἐπεὶ
δὲ συνεκρίθη περὶ σοφιστικῆς ἀγωνισάμενος
Ποτάμωνι καὶ Ἀντιπάτρῳ ἐν αὐτῇ τῇ Ῥώμῃ,
ἐπὶ Ἀδριανοῦ Καίσαρος ὁ υἱὸς αὐτοῦ Ἀντώνιος
συγκλητικὸς ἐγένετο.

24. See Suetonius, *Tiberius* 57.1 = Woerther
2013 T 5.

25. See Woerther 2013, 92–94 and the
bibliographical essay in Graf 2014.

26. Contrast Schepens 1999 in his
commentary on *FGH* 1085 T3, suggesting that
the story "may well be some scholarly yarn."

27. E.g., Suetonius, *Aug.* 89.1.

28. Seneca, *Controversiae* 10.5.22: *Saepe
solebat apud Caesarem cum Timagene confligere,
homine acidae linguae et qui nimis liber erat.* On
Timagenes, see Capponi 2019, 43–62.

29. See Strabo 16.2.29 (C 759), with
discussion in Hadas 1931, 25–30.

30. See Theodorus T 6 (Woerther 2013) =
Quintilian, *Inst.* 3.1.17.

31. Theodorus T 6 = Quintilian, *Inst.* 3.1.17:
Theodorus Gadareus, qui se dici maluit Rhodium.

32. See Isaac 2004, 335–50; Andrade 2013,
48–49.

33. E.g., Diodorus Siculus 5.56.3.

34. See Mygind 1999.

35. See [Plutarch,] *Lives of the Ten Orators*
840d; Philostratus, *VS* 1 (481–84). Dionysius,
Dinarchus 8.3 lists orators of the Rhodian
school.

36. See Woerther 2013, 32–33.

37. See *Suda* Θ 151 = Woerther 2013 F 1 with
Graf's commentary on *BNJ* 850 T 1.

38. See Cichorius 1888, 63; Bowersock 1965,
134; Kaplan 1990, 5. Toher's (2017, 453) doubts
are based only on an argument from silence.
For Nicolaus's life, see Toher, 1–21.

39. Nicolaus of Damascus F 131.2 and 132.2
(ed. Parmentier and Barone 2011).

40. Nicolaus of Damascus F 131.2 and 132.2.

41. Theodorus T 3 = Dio Chrysostom, *Or.*
18.12.

42. Nicolaus of Damascus F 137.5: πόλεως
μὲν οὔποτ' ἀφ' ἑτέρας οἰόμενος δεῖν, ἀλλ'
ἀπὸ τῆς αὐτοῦ προσαγορεύεσθαι· κατεγέλα
δὲ καὶ τῶν καθ' αὑτὸν σοφιστῶν, οἳ μεγάλοις
τιμήμασιν ἐωνοῦντο Ἀθηναῖοι ἢ Ῥόδιοι καλεῖσθαι,
βαρυνόμενοι τὴν ἀδοξίαν τῶν πατρίδων (ἔνιοι
δὲ καὶ συνέγραψαν περὶ τοῦ μὴ εἶναι ἀφ' ἧς
πόλεως ἦσαν, ἀλλ' ἀπό τινος τῶν δι' ὀνόματος
Ἑλληνίδων), ὁμοίους τε ἀπέφαινε τοῖς τοὺς
ἑαυτῶν γονέας βαρυνομένοις.

43. See Parmentier and Barone 2011,
316 n. 43. Vanderpool (1959) suggests that
Theodorus may also have had connections to
Athens, in addition to Rhodes.

44. Apamea: Posidonius T 1a (Edelstein and
Kidd 1989) = *BNJ* 87 T 1 (Dowden 2013) = *Suda*
π 2107–10. Rhodes: Posidonius T 27 = *BNJ* 87
T 6 = Strabo 7.5.8 (D 316).

45. E.g., Posidonius F 62a = *BNJ* 87 F 10 =
Athenaeus 12.527e–f.

46. See Habicht 1994, 231–47.

47. Antipater F 66 (*SVF* 3.257) = Plutarch,
On Stoic Self-Contradictions 1034a: Καὶ μὴν
Ἀντίπατρος ἐν τῷ περὶ τῆς Κλεάνθους καὶ
Χρυσίππου διαφορᾶς ἱστόρηκεν, ὅτι Ζήνων καὶ
Κλεάνθης οὐκ ἠθέλησαν Ἀθηναῖοι γενέσθαι, μὴ
δόξωσι τὰς αὐτῶν πατρίδας ἀδικεῖν. ὅτι μέν, εἰ
καλῶς οὗτοι, Χρύσιππος οὐκ ὀρθῶς ἐποίησεν
ἐγγραφεὶς εἰς τὴν πολιτείαν.

48. Plutarch, *On Stoic Self-Contradictions*
1034a.

49. See *FGH* 4.1085 T 6; Parker 1991, 117–18.

50. See Strabo 13.2.3 (C 617); Bowie 2011,
181–96.

51. See *FGH* 4.1085 T 6.

52. *FGH* 4.1085 T 6c = *IG* XII Suppl. 7. See
Pausanius 3.2.1 and Strabo 13.2.3 (C 582) for
Penthilus's reputation.

53. See Apollodorus T 1 (Woerther 2013) =
Strabo 13.4.3 (C 625); T 2 = Suetonius, *Aug.*
2.89; T 3 = [Lucian,] *Octogenarians* 23.15; T 4
= Eusebius, *Chronica* ad Olymp. 178 (154.4–6
Helm); T 6 = Quintilian, *Inst.* 3.1.17.

54. Apollodorus T 6 = Quintilian, *Inst.*
3.1.18: *Apollodorei ac Theodorei ad morem certas in
philosophia sectas sequendi.*

55. Apollodorus T 7 = Quintilian, *Inst.* 2.11.2.

56. See Theodorei T 1 (Woerther 2013) =
Seneca, *Suasoriae* 3.7, with T 6 = Quintilian,
Inst. 3.1.17.

57. See Rutledge 2008.

58. *Suda* θ 151 = Woerther 2013 F 1.

59. See Bowersock 1965, 35–36.

60. See Allen 2009, 15–23.

61. Nicolaus T 2 = Sophronius, *Narration
of the Miracles of Saints Cyrus and John*
54.3: Δαμασκηνὸς ἦν καὶ τῶν ἐν τέλει
λαμπρῶν Διονύσιος, ἐκ γένους βλαστήσας ἀεὶ
διαλάμψαντος· οὗπερ ἀρχή τε καὶ ῥίζα Νικόλαος
ἦν ὁ φιλόσοφος, ὁ Ἡρώδου παιδευτής,
καὶ παίδων τῶν Ἀντωνίου καὶ Κλεοπάτρας
διδάσκαλος· ἀφ' οὗ καὶ Νικόλαοι δώδεκα κατὰ
διαδοχὴν ἐξανθήσαντες, φιλοσοφίᾳ γαυρούμενοι,
τὸ γένος ἐφαίδρυναν καὶ εἰς μέγα δόξης καὶ
λαμπρότητος ἤγαγον.

62. See Fazzo 2008.

63. See Chaniotis 2004, with Sharples 2005.

64. See Parker 1991, 117–18.

65. *BNJ* 147 T 1 (Tuci 2017) = *Suda* π 2127: Ποτάμωνα Λεσβώνακτος εἴ τις ἀδικεῖν τολμήσοι, σκεψάσθω, εἴ μοι δυνήσεται πολεμεῖν.

66. See Parker 1991, 119, with Price 1984, 56–57.

67. *FGH* 1085 T 6d = *IG* XII 2, 154.

68. See *IG* 656, with discussion in Parker 1991, 119.

69. See Parker 1991, 121–27.

70. *IG* 255, with discussion in Parker 1991, 128.

71. See Dihle 1977, 170–73; Bowersock 1979, 63–65; Dihle 2011; Hintzen 2011. Contrast Wisse 1995, 76.

72. Contrast Bowersock 1969, 58, with Bowie 1982, 54. See also Whitmarsh 2005, 8; Swain 1996, 89.

73. See Dionysius, *Ant. Rom.* 1.7.2 (ed. Fromentin 2002).

74. See Dionysius, *Comp.* 20.23 and 26.17 (ed. Aujac 2002).

75. See [Plutarch,] *Lives of the Ten Orators* 836a; Russell 1981, 160–61.

76. *Suda* δ 1174: πρόγονος τοῦ ἐπὶ Ἀδριανοῦ γεγονότος Ἀττικιστοῦ.

77. See Bru and Filippini 2016, 321–30 for a summary of Aelius Dionysius's life.

78. See Dionysius, *On Thucydides* 1.1, 55.5; *Second Letter to Ammaeus* 1.1, with Bowersock 1965, 130 n. 3. Bru and Filippini (2016, 323 n. 94) suggest that the name Aelius more likely came from Aelius Dionysius's connection to the emperor Hadrian.

79. Dionysius, *Pomp.* 3.16.

80. Dionysius, *Pomp.* 3.16: Ἡρόδοτός τε γὰρ τῆς Ἰάδος ἄριστος κανὼν Θουκυδίδης τε τῆς Ἀτθίδος.

81. Dionysius, *Ant. or.* 1.5.

82. See [Plato,] *Letters* 8.353a; Isocrates, *Evagoras* 20, 47.

83. See Dubuisson 1982, 18–21; Bowersock 1995, 5.

84. See Dionysius, *Comp.* 4.15.

85. Dionysius, *Ant. Rom.* 1.89.4: ὀλίγου χρόνου διελθόντος ἅπαν τὸ Ἑλληνικὸν ἀπέμαθον, ὡς μήτε φωνὴν Ἑλλάδα φθέγγεσθαι μήτε ἐπιτηδεύμασιν Ἑλλήνων χρῆσθαι, μήτε θεοὺς τοὺς αὐτοὺς νομίζειν, μήτε νόμους τοὺς ἐπιεικεῖς, ᾧ μάλιστα διαλλάσσει φύσις Ἕλλὰς βαρβάρου, μήτε τῶν ἄλλων συμβολαίων μηδ᾽ ὁτιοῦν.

86. Solon F 36.11–12: γλῶσσαν οὐκέτ᾽ Ἀττικὴν / ἱέντας, ὡς ἂν πολλαχῇ πλανωμένους.

87. Aelius Dionysius φ 2 (Erbse 1950): οὗτοι [sc. Ἴωνες] γὰρ διὰ τὴν τῶν βαρβάρων παροίκησιν ἐλυμήναντο τῆς διαλέκτου τὸ πάτριον· τὰ μέτρα· τοὺς χρόνους. For the influence of Didymus, see Braswell 2013, 73–74.

88. Dionysius, *Ant. or.* 1.2.

89. Dionysius, *Ant. or.* 1.5.

90. Dionysius, *Ant. or.* 1.7: ἡ δὲ ἔκ τινων βαράθρων τῆς Ἀσίας ἐχθὲς καὶ πρῴην ἀφικομένη, Μυσὴ ἢ Φρυγία τις ἢ Καρικόν τι κακόν.

91. See Cicero, *Brutus* 37–38 and 285–86; *Orator ad M. Brutum* 226.

92. See Spawforth 2012, 22–23.

93. Suetonius, *Aug.* 86.3: *An potius Asiaticorum oratorum inanis sententiis verborum volubilitas in nostrum sermonem transferenda?*

94. Plutarch, *Antonius* 2.8: ἐχρῆτο δὲ τῷ καλουμένῳ μὲν Ἀσιανῷ ζήλῳ τῶν λόγων, ἀνθοῦντι μάλιστα κατ᾽ ἐκεῖνον τὸν χρόνον. See also Cassius Dio 48.30.1.

95. See Seneca, *Controversiae* 10.5.22; and the previous discussion.

96. Dionysius, *Ant. or.* 2.4.

97. Dionysius, *Ant. or.* 3.1: αἰτία δ᾽ οἶμαι καὶ ἀρχὴ τῆς τοσαύτης μεταβολῆς ἐγένετο ἡ πάντων κρατοῦσα Ῥώμη πρὸς ἑαυτὴν ἀναγκάζουσα τὰς ὅλας πόλεις ἀποβλέπειν.

98. Dionysius, *Ant. or.* 3.1: εὐπαίδευτοι πάνυ καὶ γενναῖοι τὰς κρίσεις γενόμενοι, ὑφ᾽ ὧν κοσμούμενον τό τε φρόνιμον τῆς πόλεως μέρος ἔτι μᾶλλον ἐπιδέδωκεν καὶ τὸ ἀνόητον ἠνάγκασται νοῦν ἔχειν.

99. Dionysius, *Ant. or.* 3.2.

100. See Hogg 2013.

101. See Dionysius, *Ant. Rom.* 1.4.2–3, with Marincola 2011.

102. E.g., Plutarch, *Pyrrhus* 16.7, with Mossman 2005.

103. Dionysius, *Ant. Rom.* 1.89.2: τούτων γὰρ ἂν οὐδὲν εὕροι τῶν ἐθνῶν οὔτε ἀρχαιότερον οὔτε Ἑλληνικώτερον.

104. See Stevens 2006; Gitner 2015.

105. See Stevens 2006, 117–18.

106. Dionysius, *Ant. Rom.* 1.90.1: Ῥωμαῖοι δὲ φωνὴν μὲν οὔτ᾽ ἄκρως βάρβαρον οὔτ᾽ ἀπηρτισμένως Ἑλλάδα φθέγγονται, μικτὴν δέ τινα ἐξ ἀμφοῖν, ἧς ἐστιν ἡ πλείων Αἰολίς.

107. Dionysius, *Ant. Rom.* 1.89.3.

108. Dionysius, *Ant. Rom.* 1.90.1, with discussion in Gitner 2015, 39–40.

109. See Stevens 2006, 116–21.

110. Dionysius, *Ant. Rom.* 7.70.2: ἔθη καὶ νόμιμα καὶ ἐπιτηδεύματα παλαιὰ παρεχόμενος

αὐτῶν, ἃ μέχρι τοῦ κατ' ἐμὲ φυλάττουσι χρόνου οἷα παρὰ τῶν προγόνων ἐδέξαντο.

111. Dionysius, *Ant. Rom.* 7.70.2.

112. Dionysius, *Ant. Rom.* 7.70.3: ταῦτα γὰρ ἐπὶ μήκιστον χρόνον διὰ φυλακῆς ἔχει Ἑλλάς τε καὶ βάρβαρος χώρα, καὶ οὐθὲν ἀξιοῖ καινοτομεῖν εἰς αὐτὰ ὑπὸ δείματος κρατουμένη μηνιμάτων δαιμονίων.

113. Dionysius, *Ant. Rom.* 7.70.4: εἰ μή τινες ὑφ' ἑτέρων ἐξουσίᾳ ποτὲ γενόμενοι τὰ τῶν κρατησάντων ἠναγκάσθησαν ἐπιτηδεύματα μεταλαβεῖν.

114. See Heath 1998, 38–39.

115. Dionysius, *Ant. Rom.* 7.72.2–4, with Homer, *Iliad* 23.685; *Odyssey* 18.66–69, 75–76.

116. Dionysius, *Ant. Rom.* 7.72.3–4: τοῦτο δὴ τὸ ἔθος ἀρχαῖον ἐν τοῖς Ἕλλησιν ὂν διαφυλάττοντες μέχρι τοῦδε Ῥωμαῖοι δῆλοί εἰσιν οὐ προσμαθόντες παρ' ἡμῶν ὕστερον, ἀλλ' οὐδὲ μεταθέμενοι σὺν χρόνῳ καθάπερ ἡμεῖς.

117. See Dionysius, *Ant. Rom.* 7.70.4–5.

118. Dionysius, *Ant. Rom.* 7.70.5: καὶ οὐθὲν ἂν ἐκώλυσεν ἅπαν ἐκβεβαρβαρῶσθαι τὸ Ἑλληνικὸν ὑπὸ Ῥωμαίων ἑβδόμην ἤδη κρατούμενον ὑπ' αὐτῶν γενεάν, εἴπερ ἦσαν βάρβαροι. See also *Ant. Rom.* 1.3.5.

119. See Dionysius, *Ant. Rom.* 1.44.3, with Fromentin 2002, 1:223 n. 18.

120. See Dionysius, *Ant. Rom.* 2.6.4, 4.24.4, and 10.17.6; with Wiater 2011, 198–205.

121. Dionysius, *Ant. Rom.* 10.17.6: ἔστηκεν ἔτι τὸ τῆς πόλεως ἀξίωμα καὶ τὸ σώζειν τὴν πρὸς ἐκείνους τοὺς ἄνδρας ὁμοιότητα.

122. See Clarke 1999, 294–336; Cornell 2010.

123. See Nicolet 1991, 29–56.

124. See van Nuffelen 2011, 27–28, building on arguments made by Boys-Stones (2001).

125. See Sacks 1990, 160–61.

126. Diodorus Siculus 1.4.4: πολλὴν ἐμπειρίαν τῆς Ῥωμαίων διαλέκτου περιπεποιημένοι.

127. See Diodorus Siculus 1.44.1, 1.46.7, and 1.83.9.

128. Diodorus Siculus 1.4.3.

129. Diodorus Siculus 40.8. See also 1.5.2.

130. Pompey: Goukowsky 2004, 621; Westall 2018, 118–26. Caesar: Muntz 2017, 8–11.

131. See Sacks 1990, 64–68; Too 2010, esp. 144.

132. Diodorus Siculus 1.9.5: περὶ πρώτων δὲ τῶν βαρβάρων διέξιμεν, οὐκ ἀρχαιοτέρους αὐτοὺς ἡγούμενοι τῶν Ἑλλήνων.

133. Diodorus Siculus 1.9.5: προδιελθεῖν βουλόμενοι τὰ πλεῖστα τῶν περὶ αὐτούς.

134. See Dillery 2015 for both historians.

135. Diodorus Siculus 1.46.8 (Hecataeus); 2.2.2, 2.15.1–2, 2.32.4 (Ctesias).

136. Diodorus Siculus 1.28.1–4.

137. Diodorus Siculus 1.29.5: λέγοντες φιλοτιμότερον ἤπερ ἀληθινώτερον, ὥς γ' ἐμοὶ φαίνεται, τῆς ἀποικίας ταύτης ἀμφισβητοῦσι διὰ τὴν δόξαν τῆς πόλεως.

138. Diodorus Siculus 1.29.6: ὑπὲρ ὧν μήτε ἀποδείξεως φερομένης μηδεμιᾶς ἀκριβοῦς μήτε συγγραφέως ἀξιοπίστου μαρτυροῦντος.

139. See Christesen 2007, 12.

140. Censorinus, *On the Birthday* 21.1–2. The translations are modified from Parker 2007.

141. See Censorinus, *On the Birthday* 21.9.

142. See Christesen 2007, 311–22; Burgess and Kulikowski 2013, 88, 364–65.

143. See *FGH* 250 T 1 = *Suda* κ 469.

144. See *FGH* 250 F 5, with Sacks 1990, 169–72. Mosshammer (1979, 131) and Christesen (2007, 315 n. 21) argue that Diodorus made no use of Castor's work.

145. See Christesen 2007, 315.

146. See *FGH* 250 F 2, with Burgess and Kulikowski 2013, 364–65.

147. See Christesen 2007, 316.

148. See *BNJ* 273 F 1 (Blakely 2016).

149. *Suda* α 1129: οὗτος συνέγραψε βίβλους ἀριθμοῦ κρείττους.

150. See Adler 2011, 226–32.

151. Jewish writers: Adler 2011. Berossus: Breucker 2012.

152. See Schironi 2013, 244–45.

153. See Schironi 2009, 53–73.

154. See Schironi 2009, 52, 132.

155. Schironi 2009, 8. The quotation is from line 16 of fragment 3, ii.

156. Schironi 2009, 138–39.

157. Whitmarsh 2013, 213.

158. See Andrade 2013, 245–47.

159. See Wendt 2016, 76–81.

160. See Harker 2008, 9–47.

161. See Pliny, *Ep.* 10.5–7, 10, with Harker 2008, 5.

162. See Harker 2008, 17–21; Capponi 2017, 97–98. Claudius's letter: Tcherikover and Fuks 1957–64, 2:36–55.

163. Josephus, *AJ* 18.259: Φίλων ὁ προεστὼς τῶν Ἰουδαίων τῆς πρεσβείας, ἀνὴρ τὰ πάντα ἔνδοξος Ἀλεξάνδρου τε τοῦ ἀλαβάρχου ἀδελφὸς ὢν καὶ φιλοσοφίας οὐκ ἄπειρος.

164. See Schwartz 2009, 12–13.

165. Josephus, *AJ* 19.276.

166. See Schwartz 2009, 18; Kamesar 2009a, 66–71.

167. Philo, *On the Preliminary Studies* 44.

168. Philo, *Moses* 1.23.

169. Philo, *Every Good Man Is Free* 140: οἱ τῶν Ἑλλήνων ὀξυδερκέστατοι διάνοιαν Ἀθηναῖοι.

170. Philo, *Leg.* 147: ὁ τὰ ἄμικτα ἔθνη καὶ θηριώδη πάντα ἡμερώσας καὶ ἁρμοσάμενος, ὁ τὴν μὲν Ἑλλάδα Ἑλλάσι πολλαῖς παραυξήσας, τὴν δὲ βάρβαρον ἐν τοῖς ἀναγκαιοτάτοις τμήμασιν ἀφελληνίσας.

171. See Niehoff 2001, 45–72.

172. See Smelik and Hemelrijk 1984, 1916–18.

173. Philo, *Leg.* 163: ἴβεσι καὶ ἰοβόλοις ἀσπίσι ταῖς ἐγχωρίοις καὶ πολλοῖς ἑτέροις τῶν ἐξηγριωμένων αὐτῆς θηρίων.

174. Philo, *Leg.* 165.

175. Philo, *Leg.* 166: κροκοδείλων καὶ ἀσπίδων τῶν ἐγχωρίων ἀναμεμαγμένοι τὸν ἰὸν ὁμοῦ καὶ θυμὸν ἐν ταῖς ψυχαῖς.

176. See Harker 2008, 15–16.

177. *Acta Isidori* (*P.Berol.* 8877, in Musurillo 1961), ll. 25–27: οὔκ εἰσιν Ἀλ[εξανδρεῦσιν] ὁμοιοπαθεῖς, τρόπῳ δὲ Αἰγυπτηίων ......] οὔκ εἰσι ἴσοι τοῖς φόρον τελ[οῦσι;]

178. See *BNJ* 616 T 6 (Keyser 2015) = Josephus, *AJ* 18.257.

179. Josephus, *Ap.* 2.65 = Apion, *BNJ* 616 F 4g: *Quomodo ergo, inquit, si sunt cives, eosdem deos quos Alexandrini non colunt?* See also Josephus, *Ap.* 2.38, with Barclay 2007, 188 n. 124.

180. See Apion, *BNJ* 616 F 4a = Josephus, *Ap.* 2.15–17; and Chaeremon F 1 = *BNJ* 618 F 1 = Josephus, *Ap.* 1.288–92.

181. See Tacitus, *Hist.* 5.5.2, with Stern 1976–89, 2:39–41.

182. See Harker 2008, 14.

183. Philo, *Leg.* 358–59.

184. Philo, *Leg.* 361: διὰ τί χοιρείων κρεῶν ἀπέχεσθε; See also Mendelson 1988, 70–71.

185. *P.Lond.* 6.1912, ll. 82–86, trans. Tcherikover and Fuks 1957–64: διόπερ ἔτι καὶ νῦν διαμαρτύρομαι εἶνα Ἀλεξανδρεῖς μὲν / πραέως καὶ φιλανθρόπως προσφέροντε Ἰουδαίος τοῖς / τὴν αὐτὴν πόλειν ἐκ πολλῶν χρόνων οἰκοῦσι / καὶ μηδὲν τῶν πρὸς θρησκείαν αὐτοῖς νενομισμένων / τοῦ θεοῦ λοιμένωνται.

186. *P.Lond.* 6.1912, ll. 98–100, trans. Tcherikover and Fuks 1957–64: εἰ δὲ μή, πάντα / τρόπον αὐτοὺς ἐπεξελεύσομαι καθάπερ κοινήν / τεινα τῆς οἰκουμένης νόσον ἐξεγείροντας.

187. *P.Lond.* 6.1912, l. 95.

188. See Harker 2008, 19.

189. See Cichorius 1922, 390–98, followed by Kaplan 1990, 49–62; Harker 2008, 19–20.

190. See Suetonius, *Nero* 36.1; Cassius Dio 65.9.2, emending Barbillus to Balbillus.

191. *P.Lond.* 6.1912, l. 105.

192. See Chaeremon T 3 (Horst 1987) = *BNJ* 618 T 2 (Keyser 2014) = *Suda* α 1128.

193. See Harker 2008, 219.

194. Polybius 34.14.5 = Strabo 17.1.12 (C 797): ἐμέμνηντο τοῦ κοινοῦ τῶν Ἑλλήνων ἔθους.

195. See *Suda* ει 190 and π 29. Haupt (1875–76, 235–40) collects Irenaeus's fragments.

196. See *Suda* ει 190: Περὶ τῆς Ἀλεξανδρέων διαλέκτου, ὅτι ἔστιν ἐκ τῆς Ἀτθίδος.

197. See *Suda* π 29.

198. Irenaeus F 13 (Haupt 1875–76) = Socrates, *Ecclesiastical History* 3.7.18.

199. See *Suda* π 29.

200. Apion, *BNJ* 616 T 4a = Josephus, *Ap.* 2.29: γεγενημένος ἐν Ὀάσει τῆς Αἰγύπτου πάντων Αἰγυπτίων πρῶτος ὤν, ὡς ἂν εἴποι τις, τὴν μὲν ἀληθῆ πατρίδα καὶ τὸ γένος ἐξωμόσατο, Ἀλεξανδρεὺς δὲ εἶναι καταψευδόμενος ὁμολογεῖ τὴν μοχθηρίαν τοῦ γένους. For discussion of Apion's place of birth, see Capponi 2017, 70–72.

201. See *BNJ* 616 F 20 = *Etymologicum Magnum*, s.v. Ἀθύρ (26.8 Kallierges), with the commentary of Keyser (2015).

202. See *BNJ* 616 F 4n = Josephus, *Ap.* 2.135, with Delia 1991, 28–29.

203. See *BNJ* 616 F 1 = Josephus, *Ap.* 2.10.

204. See Dillery 2003.

205. See *P.Oxy.* 89.5202.

206. *BNJ* 616 T 13 = Pliny, *HN* praef. 25.

207. See *BNJ* 616 F 25 = Athenaeus 15.680d.

208. *BNJ* 616 T 14b = Aulus Gellius, *NA* 7.8.1.

209. See Rodriguez 2007.

210. Chaeremon is identified as a sacred scribe only by Porphyry and Tzetzes, in T 6 (Horst) = *BNJ* 618 T 6, F 4 = *BNJ* 618 F 5, and F 13 = *BNJ* 618 F 3. All identifications of Chaeremon by authors earlier than Porphyry say that he was a Stoic: T 9 = *BNJ* 618 T 8, T 10 (not in *BNJ*), F 3 = *BNJ* 618 F 8; F 10 = *BNJ* 618 F 6, F 11 = *BNJ* 618 T 9b, F 14 = *BNJ* 618 F 9.

211. See Chaeremon T 1 = *BNJ* 618 T 1 = *Suda* χ 170; T 2 (not in *BNJ* 618) = *Suda* ι 175.

212. See the commentary of Keyser (2014) on *BNJ* 618 T 4.

213. See F 12 = *BNJ* 618 F 2, with the commentary of Keyser (2014).

214. See Keyser 2014 on *BNJ* 618 T 4.

215. See Chaeremon F 5 = *BNJ* 618 T 4 = Porphyry, *Letter to Anebo* 2.12b, with the commentary of Horst (1987).

216. Chaeremon F 12 = *BNJ* 618 F 2 = Tzetzes, *Exegesis on Homer's Iliad* 1.97: βουλόμενοι γὰρ οἱ ἀρχαιότεροι τῶν ἱερογραμματέων τὸν περὶ θεῶν φυσικὸν λόγον κρύπτειν.
217. See Boys-Stones 2003, 210–11.
218. Chaeremon T 3 = *BNJ* 618 T 2 = *Suda* α 1128: Ἀλέξανδρος Αἰγαῖος· φιλόσοφος Περιπατητικός, διδάσκαλος Νέρωνος τοῦ βασιλέως, ἅμα Χαιρήμονι τῷ φιλοσόφῳ.
219. See the biographical essay in Keyser 2014.
220. See Chaeremon T 4 = *BNJ* 618 T 3 = *Suda* δ 1173, with the conflicting discussions of Bowie 2013, 249–50 and Keyser 2014.
221. Contrast Rodriguez 2007, 50.
222. Tarrant (1993, 215–49) collects the testimonia for Thrasyllus.
223. See Tarrant 1993, 7–11.
224. See Tarrant 1993, 7. See Burstein 2010 for dismissal of the possibility that our Thrasyllus was from Mendes.
225. See Julian, *Letter to Themistius* 265b–d (11); Themistius, *Orations* 5.63d, 8.108b, 11.173b, 34.31d–32a.
226. See Tarrant 1993; Mansfeld 1994, 58–107.
227. See Dionysius, *Comp.* 24.5. Erotian, praef. (4.6–20 Nachmanson 1918) also cites Democritus as a classic author.
228. Diogenes Laertius 9.45: Τὰ δὲ βιβλία αὐτοῦ καὶ Θράσυλλος ἀναγέγραφε κατὰ τάξιν οὕτως ὡσπερεὶ καὶ τὰ Πλάτωνος κατὰ τετραλογίαν.
229. See Diogenes Laertius 9.41 and 3.57, with Tarrant 1993, 18.
230. See Tarrant 1993, 215–49. Tarrant's T 12 = *BNJ* 253 F 1 (Williams 2018) should be assigned to a different Thrasyllus.
231. See Barton 1994, 9–10, 23–29.
232. Nechepso and Petosiris: *CCAG* 8.3 (100.19–20). Hermes Trismegistus: *CCAG* 8.3 (101.16–17).
233. See Fowden 1993, 3 n. 11 and 216.
234. See Heilen 2011.
235. See Ryholt 2011.
236. See Pliny, *HN* 2.88; 7.160.
237. See Tarrant 1993, 201–6.
238. For discussion of Thrasyllus as one of several freelance experts to emphasize his knowledge of foreign religion, see Wendt 2016, 81–82.
239. Seneca, *Natural Questions* 4.2.13: *Balbillus . . . perfectusque in omni litterarum genere rarissime.*
240. See Cassius Dio 65.9.2.

241. See *CCAG* 8.4 (236.24–237.10 and 236.8–23) = Neugebauer and Van Hoesen 1959, 76–78.
242. See Kaplan 1990, 62.
243. See Neugebauer and Van Hoesen 1959, 14–16.
244. See Beck 2004, 323–24.
245. See Spawforth 1978, 253–54.
246. This was C. Julius Antiochus Epiphanes Philopappus (Halfmann 1979, no. 36), on whom see Puech 1992, 4870–73.
247. See Mendelson 1988, 71–75.
248. Philo, *On the Special Laws* 3.29: μηδὲ ἀλλοεθνεῖ . . . κοινωνίαν γάμου συντίθεσο, μή ποτε μαχομένοις ἔθεσιν ὑπαχθεὶς.
249. Philo, *On the Special Laws* 3.29: δελεασθέντες νόθοις πρὸ γνησίων ἔθεσι.
250. See Tcherikover and Fuks 1957–64, 2:189–97.
251. See Philo, *On Animals* 54, with Terian 1981, 30–31.
252. Josephus, *AJ* 20.100: οἷς γὰρ πατρίοις οὐκ ἐνέμεινεν οὗτος ἔθεσιν.
253. See Royse 2009, 57–58.
254. Oysters: Philo, *On Animals* 31 (Terian 1981). Hares: Philo, *On Providence* 2.92 (Richter 1830).
255. See Hollander 2014.
256. See Josephus, *BJ* 3.399–402.
257. Josephus, *BJ* 3.352: ἱερεὺς καὶ ἱερέων ἔγγονος.
258. Josephus, *BJ* 3.352: τῶν γε μὴν ἱερῶν βίβλων οὐκ ἠγνόει τὰς προφητείας. See also Josephus, *Life* 208, with Mason 2003, 104 n. 929.
259. See Hollander 2014, 91–105.
260. See Wendt 2016, 92–99.
261. Suetonius, *Vespasian* 5.6; Cassius Dio 65 (66).1.4.
262. E.g., Josephus, *BJ* 5.261, 325, 361; 6.94–97, 129, with Hollander 2014, 155–64.
263. See Jones 2002.
264. See Josephus, *Life* 423–30.
265. Josephus, *Life* 429.
266. See Jones 1993, 170–73.
267. See Mason 2003, 168 n. 1742; with Cotton and Eck 2005; and Hollander 2014, 120–38.
268. See Edmondson 2005, 18.
269. Josephus, *Ap.* 1.161: τῶν ἀπιστούντων μὲν τοῖς βαρβάροις ἀναγραφαῖς μόνοις δὲ τοῖς Ἕλλησι πιστεύειν ἀξιούντων.
270. Josephus, *BJ* 1.3. See also *AJ* 20.263.
271. Josephus, *Ap.* 1.50, with Barclay 2007, 36 n. 202.

272. Josephus, *AJ* 20.263.

273. See Rajak 2004, 61–62.

274. Josephus, *Life* 1: Ἐμοὶ δὲ γένος ἐστὶν οὐκ ἄσημον, ἀλλ' ἐξ ἱερέων ἄνωθεν καταβεβηκός.

275. Josephus, *Life* 1: ὥσπερ δ' ἡ παρ' ἑκάστοις ἄλλη τίς ἐστιν εὐγενείας ὑπόθεσις, οὕτως παρ' ἡμῖν ἡ τῆς ἱερωσύνης μετουσία τεκμήριόν ἐστιν γένους λαμπρότητος.

276. See Josephus, *Life* 2.

277. See Jones 2004, 21.

278. See Spawforth and Walker 1985, 1986; Jones 1996; Spawforth 1999; Romeo 2002.

279. See Jones 1996, 47–53.

280. See Jones 1996, 49–52.

281. For the example of Halicarnassus, see Spawforth and Walker 1986, 95–96, with Bru and Filippini 2016, 324–25.

282. See Spawforth 1999, 349.

283. See Eusebius, *Hist. eccl.* 4.3.1–3. For discussion of Eusebius, and the influence his work has had on historical approaches to early Christianity, see Corke-Webster 2019 and DeVore forthcoming.

Chapter 2

1. See Justin, *Dial.* 1.3 and 9.3 for the dramatic date of the conversation.

2. Justin, *Dial.* 1.2: ὅτι οὐ δεῖ καταφρονεῖν οὐδὲ ἀμελεῖν τῶν περικειμένων τόδε τὸ σχῆμα (ed. Bobichon 2003).

3. Justin, *Dial.* 2.1–6.

4. Justin, *Dial.* 8.1.

5. Philosopher's dress: Justin, *Dial.* 1.1–2, 9.2; Eusebius, *Hist. eccl.* 4.11.8; Jerome, *On Illustrious Men* 23.

6. For dating, though both articles are too confident, see Bagatti 1979; Hamman 1995.

7. Justin, *1 Apol.* 2.2 (ed. Minns and Parvis 2009): εὐσεβεῖς καὶ φιλόσοφοι, καὶ φύλακες δικαιοσύνης καὶ ἐρασταὶ παιδείας. See also Secord forthcoming b for more on Justin's self-presentation as a philosopher.

8. Justin, *2 Apol.* 8.6.

9. See Nahm 1992.

10. See Snyder 2007 for one notable exception to this tendency.

11. See Barnard (1967, 23), apropos of Justin's dialogue with Trypho: "Discussions such as these must have been frequently held, as Christians sought to commend their faith openly." Compare Munier (2006, 14), that Justin's philosophical education allowed him to "dialoguer efficacement avec l'élite

intellectuelle de son temps." Malherbe (1981) doubts that Justin had a face-to-face debate with the Cynic philosopher Crescens.

12. See Thorsteinsson 2012a, 492. See also Lyman 2003; 2007, 163.

13. See Moss 2013, 8–13.

14. Buck 2003, 54.

15. See Brown 1992, 61–70.

16. Galen: Boudon-Millot 2012; Mattern 2013. Lucian: Jones 1986.

17. See Jones 2012 for Galen's travels.

18. See Nutton 1984; Lloyd 2008; Pietrobelli 2019. Nutton (2008) discusses Galen's *Nachleben*.

19. Imperial household: Boudon-Millot 2012, 179–239. Celebrity: Garland 2006, 84–85; Mattern 2013, 160; Pietrobelli 2019, 11–13.

20. See Jones 1986, 6–23.

21. See Whitmarsh 2001, 250–52; Goldhill 2002, 66–67; Richter 2005.

22. E.g., Lucian, *True History* 2.28.

23. See Lucian, *Apology* 12, with Leest 1985; and Jones 1986, 21.

24. See Jones 1972; Baldwin 1973, 21–40.

25. See Jones 1986, 124–25.

26. See Baumbach and Hansen 2005, 112–14.

27. Aulus Gellius, *NA* 12.11; Philostratus, *VS* 2.1 (563–64).

28. See Menander Rhetor 1.2, 346.18–19, with the commentary of Russell and Wilson 1981, 249.

29. Pausanias, 6.8.4; Athenagoras, *Embassy for the Christians* 26.3–4; Tatian, *Ad Gr.* 25.1; Tertullian, *To the Martyrs* 4.5.

30. Athenagoras, *Embassy for the Christians* 26.3–4.

31. See Lucian, *De mort. Peregr.* 11–16 (ed. Pilhofer et al. 2005), with Edwards 1989; Pilhofer 2005; and Bremmer 2007. I am less skeptical of Lucian's account than Edwards is.

32. See Galen, *MM* 13.15 (10.909 Kühn).

33. Competition: König 2011. Cynics: Desmond 2008.

34. For discussion of examples when Philostratus's sophists resorted to λοιδορία, see Bowie 2006, 145.

35. Lucian, *De mort. Peregr.* 18: ἐπὶ Ἰταλίας ἔπλευσεν καὶ ἀποβὰς τῆς νεὼς εὐθὺς ἐλοιδορεῖτο πᾶσι. See also *De mort. Peregr.* 3 for another example of abusive speech.

36. Tatian, *Ad Gr.* 25.1: ὁ δὲ κεκραγὼς δημοσίᾳ μετ' ἀξιοπιστίας ἔκδικος γίνῃ σαυτοῦ, κἂν μὴ λάβῃς, λοιδορεῖς, καὶ γίνεταί σοι τέχνη τοῦ πορίζειν τὸ φιλοσοφεῖν.

37. See Lucian, *De mort. Peregr.* 13–14, 16; and Desmond 2008, 54–56.

38. E.g., Dio Chrysostom, *Or.* 77/78.38, with Malherbe 1970; König 2011, 287.

39. See Philostratus, *VS* 2.1 (33).

40. Lucian, *De mort. Peregr.* 17.

41. Galen, *On Bloodletting against the Erasistrateans at Rome* 1 (11.194 Kühn): συνέβη γάρ πως ἐν ἐκείνῳ τῷ χρόνῳ καθ' ἑκάστην ἡμέραν εἰς τὰ προβαλλόμενα λέγειν ἐν πλήθει.

42. See König 2005, esp. 264–65.

43. See Gleason 2009.

44. See Galen, *On Recognizing the Best Physician* 9.6 (CMG Suppl. Or. IV 104.4–14), with Gleason 2009, 92–96.

45. Galen, *MM* 13.15 (10.909 Kühn): δημοσίᾳ διαλεγομένου κατὰ τὸ τοῦ Τραϊανοῦ γυμνάσιον ἑκάστης ἡμέρας.

46. See Staden 1997, 44–46.

47. See Petit 2018, 213–23 for Galen's self-presentation.

48. See Nutton 1979, 157–58.

49. Galen, *Praen.* 4.6 (14.621 Kühn = CMG V 8.1 90.10–13): μὴ νόμιζε τοὺς ἀγαθοὺς ἄνδρας ἐν ταύτῃ τῇ πόλει γίνεσθαι πονηρούς, ἀλλ' ὅσοι φθάνουσιν εἶναι πονηροί, πραγμάτων ὕλην εὑρόντες ἐνταῦθα καὶ κέρδη πολὺ μείζονα τῶν ἐν ταῖς ἔξω πόλεσιν ἔχουσιν. Translation modified from Nutton 1979.

50. Galen, *Praen.* 4.8–10 (14.621–12 Kühn = CMG V 8.1 90.19–91.1).

51. See Galen, *Hipp. Epid.* 2.6.41 (CMG Suppl. Or. V 2 934–38, ed. Vagelpohl 2016). For Metrodorus, see Irby-Massie 2008, 554.

52. Galen, *Hipp. Epid.* 2.6.41.

53. Galen, *Hipp. Epid.* 2.6.41 (CMG Suppl. Or. V 2 938.6–13), trans. Vagelpohl 2016.

54. Galen, *Hipp. Epid.* 2.6.41 (CMG Suppl. Or. V 2 938.13–14).

55. Galen, *Praen.* 1.8 (14.602 Kühn = CMG V 8.1 70.14).

56. See Apuleius, *Apology*, e.g., 2.2, with Taylor 2011, 149–66; Irenaeus, *Adv. haer.* 1.13, with Secord forthcoming a. On the larger phenomenon, see also Dufault 2019, 51–69.

57. Galen, *Praen.* 1.9 (14.602–3 Kühn = CMG V 8.1 70.20–25), trans. Nutton 1979: τελευταῖον δὲ φθόνον ὑφ' ἑαυτοῦ ἤγειρεν, ὥστ' ἐπιβουλεύεσθαι πρὸς αὐτῶν. πρώτη μέντοι τῆς φαρμακείας ἐνέδρα· δευτέρα δὲ ἡ Κόϊντος ἥλω, βελτίων μὲν ὢν ἰατρὸς τῶν καθ'ἑαυτὸν, ἐκβληθεὶς δὲ τῆς πόλεως, ὡς ἀναιρῶν τοὺς νοσοῦντας.

58. Galen, *Praen.* 4.16 (14.623–24 Kühn = CMG V 8.1 92.21–26).

59. See Kaufman 1932.

60. See Grmek and Gourevitch 1994, 1503–13.

61. E.g., Galen, *On the Preservation of Health* 3.13.1–4 (6.228 Kühn = CMG V 4.2 100.27–101.5), with Grmek and Gourevitch 1994, 1505–7.

62. See Garland 2006, 89–90.

63. See Scarborough 2008.

64. Pliny, *HN* 29.9: *nullius histrionum equorumque trigarii comitatior egressus in publico erat.*

65. Galen, *MM* 1.2 (10.8 Kühn) = Tecusan 2004, F 156: παραδεδωκὼς νέαν αἵρεσιν καὶ ὡς μόνην ἀληθῆ διὰ τὸ τοὺς προγενεστέρους πάντας ἰατροὺς μηδὲν παραδοῦναι συμφέρον πρός τε ὑγείας συντήρησιν καὶ νόσων ἀπαλλαγήν.

66. Galen, *Loc. Aff.* 3.3 (8.144 Kühn): ἀπό τε τῶν ἔργων τῆς τέχνης ἐγνώσθην, οὐκ ἀπὸ λόγων σοφιστικῶν, τοῖς τ' ἄλλοις τῶν ἐν Ῥώμῃ πρώτων ἀνδρῶν καὶ πᾶσιν ἐφεξῆς τοῖς αὐτοκράτορσιν.

67. See Galen, *Praen.* 5.9–15 (14.626–28 Kühn = CMG V 8.1 96.5–98.8). Nutton (1979, 189) considers the possibility that this Peripatetic should be identified with Alexander of Aphrodisias. Hankinson (2008b, 29 n. 48) is more skeptical.

68. See Galen, *Praen.* 5.17 (14.629 Kühn = CMG V 8.1 98.11–13).

69. See Galen, *Praen.* 8.21 (14.647 Kühn = CMG V 8.1 116.21–22).

70. See Galen, *Praen.* 11.8 (14.660 Kühn = CMG V 8.1 128.28).

71. See Flinterman 2004, 373, 376.

72. Lucian, *De mort. Peregr.* 18: ἐπὶ Ἰταλίας ἔπλευσεν καὶ ἀποβὰς τῆς νεὼς εὐθὺς ἐλοιδορεῖτο πᾶσι, καὶ μάλιστα τῷ βασιλεῖ, πρᾳότατον αὐτὸν καὶ ἡμερώτατον εἰδώς, ὥστε ἀσφαλῶς ἐτόλμα.

73. See Williams 1967; Rémy 2005, 189–90; with Oliver 1989, no. 124.

74. Lucian, *De mort. Peregr.* 18: τούτῳ δὲ καὶ ἀπὸ τούτων τὰ τῆς δόξης ηὐξάνετο, καὶ περίβλεπτος ἦν ἐπὶ τῇ ἀπονοίᾳ, μέχρι δὴ ὁ τὴν πόλιν ἐπιτετραμμένος ἀνὴρ σοφὸς ἀπέπεμψεν αὐτὸν ἀμέτρως ἐντρυφῶντα τῷ πράγματι, εἰπὼν μὴ δεῖσθαι τὴν πόλιν τοιούτου φιλοσόφου.

75. See Jones 1986, 124.

76. See Nutton 1971, 63.

77. See Lewis 1965, 87–92; Nutton 1971, 62–63; Israelowich 2015, 35–43.

78. See Whitmarsh 2001, 133–80.

79. Lucian, *De mort. Peregr.* 18: πλὴν ἀλλὰ καὶ τοῦτο κλεινὸν αὐτοῦ καὶ διὰ στόματος ἦν ἅπασιν, ὁ φιλόσοφος διὰ τὴν παρρησίαν καὶ τὴν ἄγαν ἐλευθερίαν ἐξελαθείς, καὶ προσήλαυνε κατὰ τοῦτο

τῷ Μουσωνίῳ καὶ Δίωνι καὶ Ἐπικτήτῳ καὶ εἴ τις ἄλλος ἐν περιστάσει τοιαύτῃ ἐγένετο.

80. Musonius: Lutz 1947, 14–18. Dio Chrysostom: Jones 1978, 45–51. Epictetus: Long 2002, 34–35. See also Kemezis 2014, 191–92; Tacoma 2016, 94–95.

81. Tacitus, *Ann.* 15.71.

82. See Lucian, *De mort. Peregr.* 7.

83. See Lucian, *De mort. Peregr.* 43.

84. See König 2006, 244.

85. Fields 2013, 215. Compare König 2006, 229.

86. On the rare occasions when Lucian names himself, see Lucian, *De mort. Peregr.* 1, with Goldhill 2002, 63–65.

87. See Galen, *Hipp. Epid.* 2.6.41 (CMG Suppl. Or. V 2 940–42). For discussion, see Strohmaier 1976; MacLeod 1979; Hall 1981, 4–6; Jones 1986, 19, 41. Richter (2005, 93) rejects the consensus view of identifying this Lucian with the satirist.

88. Galen, *Hipp. Epid.* 2.6.41 (CMG Suppl. Or. V 2 940–42), trans. Vagelpohl 2016.

89. Galen, *Hipp. Epid.* 2.6.41 (CMG Suppl. Or. V 2 942). For the argument that the passage should be emended to refer to Christians and Jews, rather than grammarians, see Strohmaier 2012.

90. See Lucian, *Alexander* 53–54, with discussion in Branham 1989, 181–210.

91. See *The Acts of Justin and Companions* 1 (ed. Musurillo 1972).

92. See Justin, *2 Apol.* 1–2, with Grant 1985; Buck 2002; Lampe 2003, 237–40.

93. Justin, *2 Apol.* 14.1; with Minns and Parvis 2009, 24–25; and Lans 2019, 124–30. Note that I differ from Minns and Parvis and still regard the cited passage as part of Justin's *Second Apology*, rather than the dislocated conclusion of the *First Apology*.

94. See Thorsteinsson 2012b.

95. See Justin, *2 Apol.* 2.8.

96. Justin, *1 Apol.* 29.2.

97. Justin, *2 Apol.* 14.1.

98. See Bryen 2013, 37.

99. See Rives 2009, 125.

100. See Justin, *2 Apol.* 8(3).1–7; Tatian, *Ad Gr.* 19.2.

101. Justin, *2 Apol.* 8.2: οὐ γὰρ φιλόσοφον εἰπεῖν ἄξιον τὸν ἄνδρα, ὃς γε περὶ ὧν μὴ ἐπίσταται δημοσίᾳ καταμαρτυρεῖ, ὡς ἀθέων καὶ ἀσεβῶν Χριστιανῶν ὄντων, πρὸς χάριν καὶ ἡδονὴν τῶν πολλῶν τῶν πεπλανημένων ταῦτα πράττων.

102. Justin, *2 Apol.* 8.1.

103. Justin, *2 Apol.* 8.4–5, trans. Minns and Parvis 2009: Καὶ γὰρ προταθέντα με καὶ ἐρωτήσαντα αὐτὸν ἐρωτήσεις τινὰς τοιαύτας καὶ μαθεῖν καὶ ἐλέγξαι ὅτι ἀληθῶς μηδὲν ἐπίσταται, εἰδέναι ὑμᾶς βούλομαι. καὶ ὅτι ἀληθῆ λέγω, εἰ μὴ ἀνηνέχθησαν ὑμῖν αἱ κοινωνίαι τῶν λόγων, ἕτοιμος καὶ ἐφ᾽ ὑμῶν κοινωνεῖν τῶν ἐρωτήσεων πάλιν.

104. Justin, *2 Apol.* 8.6.

105. Justin, *2 Apol.* 8.6.

106. Justin, *1 Apol.* 3.1. See also Justin, *1 Apol.* 29; *Dial.* 10.1.

107. Simon Magus and Menander: Ferreiro 2005. Justin and Marcion: Hayes 2017.

108. Justin, *1 Apol.* 26.7: εἰ δὲ καὶ τὰ δύσφημα ἐκεῖνα μυθολογούμενα ἔργα πράττουσι, λυχνίας μὲν ἀνατροπὴν καὶ τὰς ἀνέδην μίξεις καὶ ἀνθρωπείων σαρκῶν βοράς, οὐ γινώσκομεν.

109. See Minns and Parvis 2009, 151 n. 9.

110. Justin, *1 Apol.* 26.7: ἀλλ᾽ ὅτι μὴ διώκονται μηδὲ φονεύονται ὑφ᾽ ὑμῶν—κἂν διὰ τὰ δόγματα—ἐπιστάμεθα.

111. Justin, *1 Apol.* 26.8. For a convincing refutation of Smith's (2015, 70–71) argument that Justin was not the author of this work, see Dulk 2018b. For another example of an intellectual sending copies of his work to members of the imperial household, compare Aristides, *Or.* 19.1.

112. See Justin, *1 Apol.* 26.2, 4; 56.1; *Dial.* 120.6.

113. For discussion of Justin's interest to attack the doctrines of rival Christians in *1 Apol.*, see Dulk 2018a, 13–26.

114. Justin, *Dial.* 50.1. Compare *Dial.* 64.2, where Justin expresses his willingness to speak to anyone who seeks his advice. For the suggestion that Justin may have traveled around the empire debating rival Christians, see also Slusser 2007, 20.

115. Compare Minucius Felix, *Octavius* 31.6, suggesting that non-Christians "either blush or dread to hear us [sc. Christians] in public" (*audire nos publice aut erubescitis aut timetis*).

116. See Thorsteinsson 2013, esp. 476–77.

117. See Dudley 1998, 187–99.

118. See Goulet-Cazé 1990, 2788–800; Downing 1998; Moles 2006; Goulet-Cazé 2014.

119. Justin, *2 Apol.* 8(3).3, trans. Minns and Parvis 2009: πρὸς τὸ μὴ ὑποπτευθῆναι τοιοῦτος.

120. Aristides, *Or.* 46 309 Jebb = 3.670–71 Behr 1981–86.

121. For suggestions that Aristides was referring to Christians, see de Labriolle 1948,

83; Behr 1981–86, 477 n. 745; Levieils 2007, 132–34. Contrast Stern 1976–89, 2:217–18.

122. See Walzer 1949 for Galen's references to Jews and Christians. Compare Flemming 2017; Secord 2017a.

123. Galen, *Differences of Pulses* 2.4 (8.579 Kühn), with Walzer 1949, 43–44.

124. Galen, *Differences of Pulses* 2.4 (8.579 Kühn).

125. Galen, *Pecc. Dig.* 3.13 (5.71 Kühn = CMG V 4.1.1 49.7–10): ὥσπερ οὖν οἱ Κυνικοὶ πάντες, οὕς γε δὴ τεθέαμαι κατὰ τὸν ἐμαυτοῦ βίον, οὕτω καὶ τῶν φιλοσοφεῖν ἐπαγγελλομένων ἔνιοι φεύγειν ὁμολογοῦσι τὴν ἐν τῇ λογικῇ θεωρίᾳ γυμνασίαν.

126. Galen, *Pecc. Dig.* 5.31 (5.93 Kühn = CMG V 4.1.1 62.17–18).

127. See Galen, *Pecc. Dig.* 5.30 (5.92 Kühn = CMG V 4.1.1 62.2–6).

128. See Justin, *Dial.* 2–7.

129. Justin, *Dial.* 2.4.

130. See Lampe 2003, 258 n. 4.

131. See Hyldahl 1966, 154–58; Girgenti 1990.

132. See Lampe 2003, 258 n. 4, with additional references in Secord 2017b, 215 n. 10.

133. See Saffrey 1968.

134. See Saffrey 1968, 72–73.

135. Aulus Gellius, *NA* 1.9.8. For Taurus's life, see Dillon 1996, 237–47.

136. Aulus Gellius, *NA* 1.9.9: *Alius ait "hoc me primum doce," item alius "hoc volo," inquit, "discere, istud nolo."*

137. Justin, *Dial.* 2.5: πάλιν τε τὸν χρόνον σκοπῶν, ὃν ἔμελλον ἐκτρίβειν περὶ ἐκεῖνα τὰ μαθήματα, οὐκ ἠνειχόμην εἰς μακρὰν ἀποτιθέμενος.

138. See Nutton 2013, 191–206.

139. Galen, *MM* 1.1 (10.5 Kühn): οὔτε γεωμετρίας οὔτε ἀστρονομίας οὔτε διαλεκτικῆς οὔτε μουσικῆς οὔτε ἄλλου τινὸς μαθήματος τῶν καλῶν.

140. Galen, *MM* 1.1 (10.5 Kühn): σκυτοτόμοι καὶ τέκτονες καὶ βαφεῖς καὶ χαλκεῖς ἐπιπηδῶσιν ἤδη τοῖς ἔργοις τῆς ἰατρικῆς, τὰς ἀρχαίας αὐτῶν ἀπολιπόντες τέχνας.

141. Lucian, *Twice Accused* 6.

142. See Stander 1985/86; Bobichon 2005, esp. 46–47.

143. See Edwards 1991, 17–21.

144. See Zeegers-Vander Vorst 1972, 86, 302–3.

145. Justin, *2 Apol.* 8(3).1, trans. Minns and Parvis 2009: Κἀγὼ οὖν προσδοκῶ ὑπό τινος τῶν ὠνομασμένων ἐπιβουλευ θῆναι καὶ ξύλῳ

ἐμπαγῆναι, ἢ κἂν ὑπὸ Κρίσκεντος τοῦ φιλοψόφου καὶ φιλοκόμπου.

146. See Justin, *2 Apol.* 7.3, with Minns and Parvis 2009, 299 n. 6.

147. See Moss 2012; Middleton 2013; Tite 2015. Contrast Birley 2006.

148. See Harker 2008, 141–73.

149. See Fédou 1998, 51–66.

150. See also Justin, *2 Apol.* 10.1–3 (quotation is from 10.1); *1 Apol.* 46.3.

151. See Justin, *1 Apol.* 46.1.

152. Justin, *2 Apol.* 13.4: ὅσα οὖν παρὰ πᾶσι καλῶς εἴρηται ἡμῶν τῶν Χριστιανῶν ἐστι.

153. Justin, *1 Apol.* 5.3.

154. Justin, *1 Apol.* 10.5: τὰ αὐτὰ ἡμῖν ἐνεκλήθη. See also *1 Apol.* 5.3.

155. See Justin, *1 Apol.* 5.3. See also Döring 1979, 129–61; Hunter 2012, 10–24, 130–42, 142–50.

156. Justin, *2 Apol.* 7(8).1.

157. Justin, *1 Apol.* 46.3.

158. Justin, *2 Apol.* 7(8).1. Minns and Parvis (2009, 297 n. 8) suggest that the phrase means "within our own times."

159. See Diogenes Laertius 9.3–5; Tatian, *Ad Gr.* 3.2, with discussion in chapter 3. Note also Tertullian, *To the Martyrs* 4.5.

160. See Marcus Aurelius, *Med.* 3.3.

161. See Lutz 1947, 18, with reference to Pliny, *Ep.* 3.11.

162. See Cassius Dio 66.13.2; Favorinus, *On Exile* 2.1; 23.1; Lucian, *De mort. Peregr.* 18; Philostratus, *VA* 7.16. The suggestion that Rufus was put to death in *Suda* μ 1305 (Adler) is late, and it may well derive from Justin's claim.

163. See Marcus Aurelius, *Med.* 1.7; Rutherford 1989, 225–58.

164. Justin, *2 Apol.* 10.8: Σωκράτει μὲν γὰρ οὐδεὶς ἐπείσθη ὑπὲρ τούτου τοῦ δόγματος ἀποθνήσκειν.

165. Justin, *2 Apol.* 10.8: οὐ φιλόσοφοι οὐδὲ φιλόλογοι μόνον ἐπείσθησαν, ἀλλὰ καὶ χειροτέχναι καὶ παντελῶς ἰδιῶται, καὶ δόξης καὶ φόβου καὶ θανάτου καταφρονήσαντες.

166. Justin, *2 Apol.* 12.1: διαβαλλομένους ἀκούων Χριστιανοὺς ὁρῶν δὲ ἀφόβους πρὸς θάνατον καὶ πάντα τὰ ἄλλα νομιζόμενα φοβερά.

167. Justin, *2 Apol.* 12.1: ἀδύνατον εἶναι ἐν κακίᾳ καὶ φιληδονίᾳ ὑπάρχειν αὐτούς.

168. Justin, *2 Apol.* 2.9–10. On the identity of this Ptolemy, see Lampe 2003, 237–40; Dunderberg 2008, 77–94.

169. Justin, *2 Apol.* 2.9.

170. Justin, *2 Apol.* 2.13.

171. Justin, *2 Apol.* 2.15–20.

172. Justin, *2 Apol.* 2.16: Οὐ πρέποντα εὐσεβεῖ αὐτοκράτορι οὐδὲ φιλοσόφῳ Καίσαρι παιδί.

173. See Perkins 1995, 18–20.

174. See Bryen 2014, 243–45; Kemezis 2014, 183.

175. See Brown 1992, 50.

176. See Ronconi 1996.

177. On the date of the letter, see Pliny, *Ep.* 1.17; with Tacitus, *Ann.* 16.7–9; Sherwin-White 1966, 125.

178. Pliny, *Ep.* 8.12.4.

179. Pliny, *Ep.* 5.5.3: *Scribebat . . . exitus occisorum aut relegatorum a Nerone.*

180. See especially Tacitus, *Agr.* 3.1–3, together with *Hist.* 1.1.

181. See Harker 2008. Contrast the problematic treatment in Musurillo 1954, esp. 236–46.

182. See Harker 2008, 127–30.

183. See Harker 2008, 1.

184. Harker 2008, 118–19.

185. See Harker 2008, 175.

186. Musurillo 1961, 11b, col. 2, ll. 7–13 = *P.Oxy.* 2.33: τῷ γὰρ θεῷ Ἀντωνείνῳ [τ]ῷ π[ατ]ρί σου ἔπρεπε αὐτοκρατορεύειν. ἄκουε, τὸ μὲν πρῶτον ἦ[ν] φιλόσοφος, τὸ δεύτερον ἀφιλάργυρος, τ[ὸ] τρίτον φιλάγαθος· σοὶ τούτων τὰ ἐναντία ἔνκειται, τυραννία ἀφιλοκαγαθία ἀπαιδία.

187. Justin, *2 Apol.* 2.16.

188. Musurillo 1961, 11b, col. 3, l. 2.

189. Tacitus, *Agr.* 42.4: *Posse etiam sub malis principibus magnos viros esse.*

190. Tacitus, *Agr.* 42.4.

191. Tacitus, *Agr.* 42.4.

192. Martial, *Epigrams* 1.8.5–6: *Nolo virum facili redemit qui sanguine famam; / hunc volo, laudari qui sine morte potest.*

193. E.g., Arrian, *Discourses of Epictetus* 1.1.26–27; for Hooff 1990, 181–97; Cooper 1999, 537–41.

194. See Lucian, *De mort. Peregr.* 41.

195. *Dig.* 28.3.6.7, cited by Brunt 1979, 490. See also Hooff 1990, 129–30.

196. See Kemezis 2014, 214–25; Jażdżewska 2019, 160–77.

197. See Philostratus, *VS* 1.8 (489). Compare *VS* 1.15 (500) and 2.24 (607) on intellectuals who unwisely provoked kings or emperors.

198. See Brown 1992, 52–59.

199. Philostratus, *VA* 7.1: τὰς τυραννίδας, ὡς ἔστιν ἀρίστη βάσανος ἀνδρῶν φιλοσοφούντων.

200. See Philostratus, *VA* 8.26.1–2. For Apollonius's interactions with Roman emperors, see Flintermann 1995, 165–70.

201. See Perry 1964, 1, 12–14.

202. *Life of Secundus* (Perry 1964, 70.17–18): οὔτε γάρ τι τῶν καλῶν αὐτὸν ἐλάνθανεν.

203. *Life of Secundus* (Perry 1964, 72.16–19): ἡνίκα τὸν φιλόσοφον μέλλεις ἐπάγειν, κατὰ τὴν ὁδὸν λάλησον αὐτῷ καὶ παραμύθησαι τοῦ λαλῆσαι. καὶ ἐὰν μὲν ἀποκριθῆναι αὐτὸν πείσῃς, ἀποκεφάλισον αὐτόν, ἐὰν δὲ οὐκ ἀποκριθῇ, σῷον πάλιν αὐτὸν ἐνταῦθα ἄγαγε.

204. *Opinions of Secundus* 20 (Perry 1964, 90.14).

205. For a sophist named Secundus, see Perry 1964, 2–3; Philostratus, *VS* 1.26 (544–45).

206. See Straw 2002, 39–50; Denzey 2010, 188–92.

207. Galen, *On Plato's Republic*, trans. Engberg et al. 2014, 235.

208. Lucian, *De mort. Peregr.* 14: Πλὴν ἀλλ' ὁ Περεγρῖνος ἀφείθη ὑπὸ τοῦ τότε τῆς Συρίας ἄρχοντος, ἀνδρὸς φιλοσοφίᾳ χαίροντος.

209. See Galen, *Praen.* 2.24 (14.612 Kühn = CMG V 8.1 80.15–19); with Eck 2014; and Eck and Pangerl 2014, 258–59, on Sergius Paullus.

210. Lucian, *De mort. Peregr.* 14.

211. See SHA *Commodus* 7.1 for Antonius.

212. Tertullian, *To Scapula* 5: δειλοί, εἰ θέλετε ἀποθνήσκειν, κρημνοὺς ἢ βρόχους ἔχετε.

213. Marcus Aurelius, *Med.* 11.3: Οἵα ἐστὶν ἡ ψυχὴ ἡ ἕτοιμος, ἐὰν ἤδη ἀπολυθῆναι δέῃ τοῦ σώματος, [καὶ] ἤτοι σβεσθῆναι ἢ σκεδασθῆναι ἢ συμμεῖναι. τὸ δὲ ἕτοιμον τοῦτο ἵνα ἀπὸ ἰδικῆς κρίσεως ἔρχηται, μὴ κατὰ ψιλὴν παράταξιν ὡς οἱ Χριστιανοί, ἀλλὰ λελογισμένως καὶ σεμνῶς καὶ ὥστε καὶ ἄλλον πεῖσαι, ἀτραγῴδως. See Brunt 1979, 484–94 for discussion of the passage.

214. See Brunt 1979, 498.

215. Marcus Aurelius, *Med.* 1.14.2, with Gill 2013, 67–69.

216. See Gill 2013, 69.

217. For Marcus Aurelius's likely familiarity with stories of Peregrinus's death, see Brunt 1979, 490–91.

218. See *Acts of Justin and Companions* 1.

219. See Marcus Aurelius, *Med.* 1.7, with Gill 2013, 57–60.

220. See Arrian, *Discourses of Epictetus* 4.7.1–6 (quotation from 4.7.6).

221. See Cassius Dio 67.13.2; Pliny, *Ep.* 3.11.2; Plutarch, *On Being a Busybody* 522d–e; Suetonius, *Domitian* 10.3; Tacitus, *Agr.* 2.1, with Gill 2013, 59.

222. See Dunderberg 2013 for Christian debates about martyrdom.

223. On Justin as an independent teacher, see Lampe 2003, 377; Thomassen 2004, 242.

224. See Parvis 2007, 119–20.

225. See Pouderon 1989, 35–62, 203–61.

226. See Pouderon 1989, 347–50.

227. See Pouderon 1989, 57–62.

Chapter 3

1. For Tatian's relationship with Justin, see Trelenberg 2012, 195–203. For Eusebius's reception of Tatian, see Ritter 2016, 294.

2. Eusebius, *Hist. eccl.* 4.16.7: Τατιανός, ἀνὴρ τὸν πρῶτον αὐτοῦ βίον σοφιστεύσας ἐν τοῖς Ἑλλήνων μαθήμασι καὶ δόξαν οὐ σμικρὰν ἐν αὐτοῖς ἀπενηνεγμένος πλεῖστά τε ἐν συγγράμμασιν αὐτοῦ καταλιπὼν μνημεῖα.

3. Eusebius, *Hist. eccl.* 4.29.7: ὃς δὴ καὶ δοκεῖ τῶν συγγραμμάτων ἁπάντων αὐτοῦ κάλλιστός τε καὶ ὠφελιμώτατος ὑπάρχειν.

4. Eusebius, *Hist. eccl.* 4.29.3, quoting from Irenaeus, *Adv. haer.* 1.28.1. See the later discussion of this passage.

5. Eusebius, *Hist. eccl.* 4.29.6. For discussion of the *Diatessaron*, see Crawford 2013; Schmid 2013. Following Schmid (2013, 115 n. 5), I take that this work was originally written in Greek, rather than Syriac, as Petersen (1994, 428) suggests.

6. Eusebius, *Hist. eccl.* 4.29.6: τοῦ δ᾽ ἀποστόλου φασὶ τολμῆσαί τινας αὐτὸν μεταφράσαι φωνάς, ὡς ἐπιδιορθούμενον αὐτῶν τὴν τῆς φράσεως σύνταξιν.

7. See Crawford 2015.

8. See Eusebius, *Hist. eccl.* 4.16.7–9.

9. See Trelenberg 2012, 204–19. See also Hunt (2003, 20–51), who responds to older suggestions that linked Tatian with Valentinianism (e.g., Grant 1954; Barnard 1968). Koltun-Fromm (2008, 15 n. 29) provides a critique of Gaca's (2003, 221–46) problematic attempt to find traces in *Against the Greeks* of the radical asceticism imputed to Tatian by heresiologists.

10. E.g., Hunt (2003, 2) straightforwardly calls *Against the Greeks* "an apologetic work," together with Trelenberg (2012, 238–40). For the history of the modern concept of early Christian apologetic literature, see Parvis 2007, 115–16; Nasrallah 2010, 23–28.

11. See Eusebius, *Hist. eccl.* 4.29.7.

12. See Whittaker 1982, xx; Trelenberg 2012, 25–29; Nesselrath 2016, 9–14.

13. E.g., Trelenberg 2012; Aragione 2015; Nesselrath 2016; Crawford 2016.

14. E.g., Norelli 1998, 109–13; Nasrallah 2010, 65–70 and 236–48; Aragione 2015, 14–16; Crawford 2015.

15. See Trelenberg 2012, 58, 219–24.

16. See Trelenberg 2012, 230–40; Nesselrath 2016, 17–19. Contrast Grant 1988, 115–17; McGehee 1993.

17. See Lössl 2016.

18. See Karadimas 2003, 9–24; Trelenberg 2012, 15; Lössl 2016, 46–47.

19. See Lössl 2016, 50; Prostmeier 2016, 193–201; Nesselrath 2016, 14–17.

20. See Crawford 2016, 565–66.

21. On this genre, see König and Whitmarsh 2007a, 31–34; Smith 2014, 47–60; Oikonomopoulou 2017, 447–62.

22. Encyclopedic writing: König and Woolf 2013b. Polymathy: Oikonomopoulou 2017, 452–55.

23. See Gemeinhardt 2016, 265.

24. See Nasrallah 2010, 68.

25. See Trelenberg 2012, 237.

26. Tatian, *Ad Gr.* 35.1 (ed. Nesselrath 2016): Ταῦτα μὲν οὖν οὐ παρ᾽ ἄλλου μαθὼν ἐξεθέμην, πολλὴν δὲ ἐπιφοιτήσας γῆν καὶ τοῦτο μὲν σοφιστεύσας τὰ ὑμέτερα, τοῦτο δὲ τέχναις καὶ ἐπινοίαις ἐγκυρήσας πολλαῖς. Translations from Tatian are my own, but they often take inspiration from Whittaker 1982.

27. Tatian, *Ad Gr.* 29.2 and 30.3, with the latter passage citing the Temple of Babel story.

28. See *Ad Gr.* 1.5, 24.2, 26.7, 35.2.

29. See Elze 1960, 34–40.

30. *Ad Gr.* 31–42, with the intrusion of the critique on Greek art from 32–35.

31. See Tatian, *Ad Gr.* 15.3, 16.2, 40.3; and the fragments in Whittaker 1982, 78–83.

32. See Smith 2014, 54–60.

33. Aelian, *On the Nature of Animals* ep.: ἀνέμειξα δὲ καὶ τὰ ποικίλα ποικίλως. On this passage, see Smith 2014, 51–52.

34. See Oikonomopoulou 2017, 449 on the implied readership of miscellanies in the second century.

35. Tatian, *Ad Gr.* 32.1, 35.1.

36. Tatian, *Ad Gr.* 32.1: παρ᾽ ἡμῖν δὲ τῆς μὲν κενοδοξίας ὁ ἵμερος οὐκ ἔστιν, δογμάτων δὲ ποικιλίαις οὐ καταχρώμεθα.

37. Tatian, *Ad Gr.* 35.1: ἔσχατον δὲ τῇ Ῥωμαίων ἐνδιατρίψας πόλει καὶ τὰς ἀφ᾽ ὑμῶν ὡς αὐτοὺς ἀνακομισθείσας ἀνδριάντων ποικιλίας

καταμαθών. On the list of statues, see Thorsen 2012.

38. See Smith 2014, 57, citing Philostratus, *VS* 486.

39. Aelian, *Letters* 20. See also Smith 2014, 58 n. 36.

40. Pollux, *Onom.* 4.47: ποικίλος, πολύτροπος, παλίμβολος, ἐγκρυφίας.

41. See Tatian, *Ad Gr.* 16.3, 17.4, 20.4; with further discussion of these passages later in this chapter.

42. See Oikonomopoulou 2017, 455–58.

43. See Gleason 1995; and the fragments of Favorinus's miscellanies in Amato 2010, 175–351.

44. See Photius, *Bibl.* 175.

45. See Eusebius, *Hist. eccl.* 5.13.8 (= Whittaker 1982, F 4), with Aulus Gellius, *NA* praef. 7 on the title of *Problems*.

46. For this as a characteristic feature of Christian heresiology, see Berzon 2016, 170–79.

47. See Brenk 1986; Martin 2004, 98–108; Timotin 2012; Greenbaum 2016.

48. See Smith 2008, 490–92; Trelenberg 2012, 45–49; Timotin 2016; Crosignani 2017; Crawford forthcoming.

49. For some contextualization of Tatian's demonology, see Timotin 2016, 274–86.

50. See Brenk 1986, 2071–86; Greenbaum 2016, 4–5.

51. Plato, *Symposium* 202e: τὸ δαιμόνιον μεταξύ ἐστι θεοῦ τε καὶ θνητοῦ. For discussion, see Timotin 2012, 42–46.

52. See Martin 2004, 98–108; Greenbaum 2016, 17–33.

53. Plutarch, *The Obsolescence of Oracles* 417c: θεῶν μὲν οὐδενὶ δαιμόνων δὲ φαύλων ἀποτροπῆς ἕνεκα. Cleombrotus: Puech 1992, 4843; Timotin 2012, 194–98.

54. Plutarch, *De gen.* 593d–e, citing Hesiod, *Works and Days* 122.

55. See Plutarch, *De gen.* 592c, with Plato, *Timaeus* 90a.

56. See Herren 2017, 109–45.

57. See Lamberton 1986, 44–82.

58. Tatian, *Ad Gr.* 21.6. On Metrodorus, see Califf 2003.

59. Tatian, *Ad Gr.* 21.5: μηδὲ τοὺς μύθους μηδὲ τοὺς θεοὺς ὑμῶν ἀλληγορήσητε.

60. See Tatian, *Ad Gr.* 7.1–5, with Martin 2010, 676.

61. See Barton 1994; Beck 2007; Hegedus 2007.

62. See Aulus Gellius, *NA* 14.1.1–36; Sextus Empiricus, *Math.* 5.1–106. For Sextus Empiricus, see discussion in chapter 4.

63. See Ptolemy, *Tetr.* 1.2–3, with Feke 2018. For Vettius Valens, see Riley 1996; Komorowska 2004.

64. See Long 1982.

65. Twins: Ptolemy, *Tetr.* 3.7; Vettius Valens 3.7.14–15; 6.2.17–19; 8.3.6, 8.4.9–10 (ed. Pingree 1986); Aulus Gellius, *NA* 14.1.26; Sextus Empiricus, *Math.* 5.88–89.

66. See Greenbaum 2016 for astrological demonology, and Crawford forthcoming for Tatian's views on demons and astrology.

67. Tatian, *Ad Gr.* 9.2, with Hegedus 2007, 125.

68. E.g., Vettius Valens 3.1.3; Ptolemy, *Tetr.* 3.5.11. Compare Sextus Empiricus, *Math.* 5.32.

69. Vettius Valens 6.pr.7: Προέγραψα μὲν οὖν ταῦτα καὶ αὐτὸς σεμνυνόμενος ἐπὶ τῇ περιχυθείσῃ μοι ὑπὸ τοῦ δαίμονος οὐρανίᾳ θεωρίᾳ.

70. See Greenbaum 2016, 33–45.

71. Tatian, *Ad Gr.* 8.1: διάγραμμα γὰρ αὐτοῖς ἀστροθεσίας ἀναδείξαντες ὥσπερ οἱ τοῖς κύβοις παίζοντες, τὴν εἱμαρμένην εἰσηγήσαντο λίαν ἄδικον.

72. See Vettius Valens 3.13.13, 9.9.13, and 9.12.31.

73. Vettius Valens 6.9: θεούς τε μὴ τιμῶντες τὸν θάνατον οὐ φοβοῦνται, ἄγονται δὲ ὑπὸ τοῦ δαίμονος.

74. For a defense of ancient astrology from these sorts of critiques, see Greenbaum 2016, 391–93.

75. Aulus Gellius, *NA* 14.1.23, with Long 1982, 184–85.

76. Sextus Empiricus, *Math.* 5.45: εἰ γὰρ μὴ πάντα γίνεται κατὰ εἱμαρμένην, οὐκ ἔστι Χαλδαϊκὴ ἢ τοῦτο ἀξιοῦσα.

77. Tatian, *Ad Gr.* 9.1.

78. Tatian, *Ad Gr.* 8.1: πᾶσά τε γένεσις ὥσπερ ἐν θεάτρῳ τερπωλὴν παρέσχε τούτοις.

79. Tatian, *Ad Gr.* 8.1: ἄσβεστος δ᾽ ἄρ᾽ ἐνῶρτο γέλως μακάρεσσι θεοῖσιν, citing Homer, *Iliad* 1.599 and *Odyssey* 8.326.

80. Aulus Gellius, *NA* 14.1.23.

81. Tatian, *Ad Gr.* 9.3: ἡμεῖς δὲ καὶ εἱμαρμένης ἐσμὲν ἀνώτεροι καὶ ἀντὶ πλανητῶν δαιμόνων ἕνα τὸν ἀπλανῆ δεσπότην μεμαθήκαμεν καὶ οὐ καθ᾽ εἱμαρμένην ἀγόμενοι τοὺς ταύτης νομοθέτας παρῃτήμεθα.

82. See Hegedus 2007, 165–66.

83. Plutarch, *De gen.* 592b: πῇ μὲν κρατοῦντας καὶ περιάγοντας ἐπὶ δεξιάν, πῇ δὲ καμπτομένους ὑπὸ τῶν παθῶν καὶ

συνεφελκομένους τοῖς ἁμαρτήμασιν. See also
Hegedus 2007, 176 n. 59 for the metaphor.

84. See Nutton 2013, 205–6, 297–98; Secord
2018, 467.

85. See Temkin 1991, 119–25; Amundsen
1995; Ferngren 2009, 52.

86. Temkin 1991, 122.

87. See Temkin 1991, 122; Amundsen 1995,
379; Ferngren 2009, 141. Contrast Crosignani
2017, 188–89 and Crawford forthcoming.

88. See Secord forthcoming b for an
expanded treatment of Tatian's views on
medicine and humanity.

89. Tatian, Ad Gr. 16.3: δαίμονες γὰρ τῇ
σφῶν κακοηθείᾳ τοῖς ἀνθρώποις ἐμβακχεύοντες,
ποικίλαις καὶ ἐψευσμέναις δραματουργίαις τὰς
γνώμας αὐτῶν παρατρέπουσι.

90. Tatian, Ad Gr. 17.3.

91. Tatian, Ad Gr. 18.1.

92. Tatian, Ad Gr. 17.4: καὶ τῶν ῥιζῶν αἱ
ποικιλίαι νεύρων τε καὶ ὀστέων παραλήψεις
οὐκ αὐταὶ καθ' ἑαυτὰς δραστικαί τινές εἰσι,
στοιχείωσις δέ ἐστι τῆς τῶν δαιμόνων μοχθηρίας.

93. Tatian, Ad Gr. 17.4: οἳ πρὸς ἅπερ ἑκάστας
αὐτῶν ἰσχύειν ὡρίκασιν.

94. Tatian, Ad Gr. 18.6: ζωγρεῖν τινας, εἶτα
τοὺς αὐτοὺς μισθοῦ τοῖς οἰκείοις ἀποκαθιστᾶν.
Wejenborg (1972, 374) links the metaphor to
Justin, 2 Apol. 5.5–6, but this is implausible.

95. Tatian, Ad Gr. 18.6: οἱ νομιζόμενοι θεοὶ
τοῖς τινων ἐπιφοιτῶντες μέλεσιν, ἔπειτα δι'
ὀνείρων τὴν εἰς αὐτοὺς πραγματευόμενοι δόξαν
δημοσίᾳ τε τοὺς τοιούτους προϊέναι κελεύσαντες
πάντων ὁρώντων.

96. Tatian, Ad Gr. 18.6: ἐπειδὰν τῶν ἐγκωμίων
ἀπολαύσωσιν, ἀποπτάμενοι τῶν καμνόντων, ἣν
ἐπραγματεύσαντο νόσον περιγράφοντες, τοὺς
ἀνθρώπους εἰς τὸ ἀρχαῖον ἀποκαθιστῶσιν.

97. On Aristides's fame, see Behr 1968;
with Jones 2008, 253–62; Robert 2009. For
Aristides's hymns, see Goeken 2012; Russell,
Trapp, and Nesselrath 2016.

98. Tatian, Ad Gr. 18.5: οὐ θεραπεύουσιν
οἱ δαίμονες, τέχνῃ δὲ τοὺς ἀνθρώπους
αἰχμαλωτεύουσι.

99. Tatian, Ad Gr. 18.5: τί δὲ θεραπεύων τὸν
πλησίον εὐεργέτης ἀποκαλῇ;

100. See Samama 2003, index s.vv. εὐεργεσία,
εὐεργετέω, εὐεργέτημα, and εὐεργέτης.

101. Aristides, Or. 38.14: εἰς τοὺς Ἕλληνας
εὐεργεσιῶν . . . καὶ εἰς ἅπαντας.

102. Galen, The Best Doctor Is Also a Philosopher
2 (1.57 Kühn).

103. See Galen, AA 2.1 (2.280–81 Kühn), with
the dossier of passages in Tieleman 2016. For

Galen and Aristides, see Boudon-Millot 2016;
Brockmann 2016.

104. Galen, Praen. 5.4 (CMG V 8.1 94.15 =
14.625 Kühn). For praise of Asclepius, see
Aristides, Or. 48.7 and 21, with Brockmann
2016, 122–23.

105. Tatian, Ad Gr. 3.2: τούτου μὲν οὖν τὴν
ἀμαθίαν ὁ θάνατος συνήλεγξεν.

106. Tatian, Ad Gr. 3.2: ὕδρωπι γὰρ συσχεθεὶς
καὶ τὴν ἰατρικὴν ὡς φιλοσοφίαν ἐπιτηδεύσας
βολβίτοις τε περιπλάσας ἑαυτὸν τῆς κόπρου
κρατυνθείσης συνολκάς τε τοῦ παντὸς
ἀπεργασαμένης σώματος σπασθεὶς ἐτελεύτησεν.

107. See Diogenes Laertius 9.4.

108. Tatian, Ad Gr. 16.3: τὰς γνώμας
αὐτῶν παρατρέπουσι κάτω νενευκυίας, ὅπως
μεταρσιοῦσθαι πρὸς τὴν ἐν οὐρανοῖς πορείαν
ἐξαδυνατῶσιν.

109. Tatian, Ad Gr. 20.1: κόσμος γὰρ ἡμᾶς ἔτι
καθέλκει.

110. Tatian, Ad Gr. 17.5: τέχνη γὰρ τῆς
θεοσεβείας τοὺς ἀνθρώπους παρατρέπουσι, πόαις
αὐτοὺς καὶ ῥίζαις πείθεσθαι παρασκευάζοντες.

111. Tatian, Ad Gr. 20.1: Κἂν θεραπεύησθε
φαρμάκοις (κατὰ συγγνώμην ἐπιτρέπω σοι), τὴν
μαρτυρίαν προσάπτειν σε δεῖ τῷ θεῷ.

112. Tatian, Ad Gr. 18.4: τίνος δὲ χάριν οὐ τῷ
δυνατωτέρῳ προσέρχῃ δεσπότῃ, θεραπεύεις δὲ
μᾶλλον αὐτὸν ὥσπερ ὁ μὲν κύων διὰ πόας, ὁ δὲ
ἔλαφος δι'ἐχίδνης, ὁ δὲ σῦς διὰ τῶν ἐν ποταμοῖς
καρκίνων, ὁ δὲ λέων διὰ τῶν πιθήκων;

113. For an identical list, see Nepualius, On
Antipathy and Sympathy 1–4 (ed. Gemoll 1884).
See also Bouffartigue 2008.

114. See Sorabji 1993; Grant 1999; Gilhus
2006, 37–63; Spittler 2008.

115. See Tatian, Ad Gr. 15.3.

116. Tatian, Ad Gr. 15.3. Compare Sextus
Empiricus, Outlines of Pyrrhonism 2.26, 211;
Math. 7.269; [Galen,] Medical Definitions (19.355
Kühn), cited by Nesselrath 2016, 144 n. 245.

117. Tatian, Ad Gr. 15.3.

118. Tatian, Ad Gr. 15.3, paraphrasing Gen.
1:26, 27: μόνος δὲ ὁ ἄνθρωπος εἰκὼν καὶ ὁμοίωσις
τοῦ θεοῦ.

119. Tatian, Ad Gr. 15.3: λέγω δὲ ἄνθρωπον οὐχὶ
τὸν ὅμοια τοῖς ζῴοις πράττοντα, ἀλλὰ τὸν πόρρω
μὲν τῆς ἀνθρωπότητος πρὸς αὐτὸν δὲ τὸν θεὸν
κεχωρηκότα.

120. Tatian, Ad Gr. 15.6: δαίμονες δὲ πάντες
σαρκίον μὲν οὐ κέκτηνται. See also Smith 2008,
490–92.

121. Tatian, Ad Gr. 14.3: οἳ θνήσκουσι μὲν οὐ
ῥαδίως, σαρκὸς γὰρ ἀμοιροῦσι.

122. Tatian, *Ad Gr.* 8.2: τοῖς αὑτοῖς πάθεσιν οἵσπερ καὶ οἱ ἄνθρωποι κρατηθέντες.

123. On *pathē*, see Shaw 1998, 44–46; Timotin 2016, 280.

124. Tatian, *Ad Gr.* 12.6: μακρὰν δὲ τῆς εὐταξίας εὑρεθέντας.

125. Note the following examples: Puech 1903, 125: "se sont tant éloignés du bon ordre"; Whittaker 1982, 25: "have been found to be far from orderly in their conduct"; Trelenberg 2012, 119: "weit außerhalb der rechten Ordnung befunden wurden"; Aragione 2015, 197: "lontani dal retto ordine"; Nesselrath 2016, 61: "weit entfernt von guter Ordnung erfunden wurden."

126. See LSJ, s.v. εὐταξία. Lampe (1961, s.v. εὐταξία) excludes medical connotations completely.

127. [Plutarch,] *Opinions of the Philosophers* 911b: Ἐρασίστρατος τὰς νόσους διὰ πλῆθος τροφῆς καὶ <δι'> ἀπεψίας καὶ φθορᾶς, τὴν δ' εὐταξίαν καὶ αὐτάρκειαν εἶναι ὑγείαν. Mansfeld and Runia 1997–2018, 1:121–25 date Pseudo-Plutarch to the second century.

128. Galen, *Loc. Aff.* 6.5 (8.451 Kühn): τῷ ἀθλητῇ ῥυσσὸν καὶ προσεσταλμένον ἐστὶ τὸ αἰδοῖον ἐκ τῆς εὐταξίας. See also Secord 2018, 471–72.

129. See Smith 2008, 483–90.

130. See Tatian, *Ad Gr.* 8.2 and 6.

131. Tatian, *Ad Gr.* 2.1–2.

132. Tatian, *Ad Gr.* 25.2: τὸν θεὸν οὐκ οἶδας καὶ ἐπὶ τὴν ἀλόγων μίμησιν μεταβέβηκας.

133. Tatian, *Ad Gr.* 25.1.

134. Tatian, *Ad Gr.* 2.1: τὴν αὐτάρκειαν σεμνυνόμενος.

135. Tatian, *Ad Gr.* 2.1: πολύποδος ὠμοβορία πάθει συσχεθεὶς εἱλεῷ διὰ τὴν ἀκρασίαν ἀποτέθνηκεν.

136. See Plutarch, *Alexander* 50–51.

137. Tatian, *Ad Gr.* 2.2: κλαίων καὶ ἀποκαρτερῶν προφάσει λύπης, ἵν' ὑπὸ τῶν οἰκείων μὴ μισηθῇ.

138. See Mattern 2016, 203–23.

139. Tatian, *Ad Gr.* 23.4.

140. Tatian, *Ad Gr.* 15.7: πνεύματι θεοῦ φρουρούμενοις. See also 16.5.

141. See Strutwolf and Lakmann 2016, 227–36.

142. See Tatian, *Ad Gr.* 20.2; with Plato, *Phaedrus* 246a–248d and Trapp 1990, 154.

143. Tatian, *Ad Gr.* 9.3.

144. Tatian, *Ad Gr.* 19.9: τῶν παθῶν ἂν ὑπάρχῃς ἀνώτερος, τῶν ἐν τῷ κόσμῳ πάντων καταφρονήσεις. τοιούτους ἡμᾶς ὄντας μὴ

ἀποστυγήσητε, ἀλλὰ παραιτησάμενοι τοὺς δαίμονας θεῷ τῷ μόνῳ κατακολουθήσατε.

145. Tatian, *Ad Gr.* 11.1: νόσου παντοδαπῆς ἀνώτερος γίνομαι, λύπη μου τὴν ψυχὴν οὐκ ἀναλίσκει.

146. Tatian, *Ad Gr.* 20.4: τὰ δὲ ὑπὲρ τοῦτον αἰῶνες οἱ κρείττονες οὐ μεταβολὴν ὡρῶν ἔχοντες, δι' ὧν ποικίλαι νόσοι καθίστανται.

147. Galen, *On Mixtures* 1.4 (1.527 Kühn), citing Hippocrates, *Aphorisms* 3.4.

148. Tatian, *Ad Gr.* 20.4.

149. See Puech 1903, 18–36; Heiler 1909, 86–101.

150. E.g., Puech 1903, 36; Whittaker 1982, xii.

151. See Swain 1996, 17–64; Whitmarsh 2005, 41–56; Horrocks 2010, 133–41; Kim 2010, 2017.

152. See Swain 1996, 51–56; Whitmarsh 2005, 43–45; Strobel 2009; Lee 2013; Vessella 2018, 17–26.

153. See Jones 2008, 253–62; Janiszewski, Stebnicka, and Szabat 2015, 298–99.

154. Dedication to Commodus: Photius, *Bibl.* 158.

155. Cornelianus: Janiszewski, Stebnicka, and Szabat 2015, 203.

155. See Horrocks 2010, 138–39; Lee 2013, 288–92.

156. Phrynichus, *Ecl.*, proem (ed. Fischer 1974): Ὅστις ἀρχαίως καὶ δοκίμως ἐθέλει διαλέγεσθαι, τάδε αὐτῷ φυλακτέα.

157. Phrynichus, *Ecl.* 176: Ὀπωροπώλης· τοῦθ' οἱ ἀγοραῖοι λέγουσιν, οἱ δὲ πεπαιδευμένοι ὀπωρώνης ὡς καὶ Δημοσθένης.

158. E.g., Phrynichus, *Ecl.* 64.

159. Phrynichus, *Ecl.* 357.

160. Phrynichus, *Ecl.* 402: πόθεν, Μένανδρε, συσσύρας τὸν τοσοῦτον τῶν ὀνομάτων συρφετὸν αἰσχύνεις τὴν πάτριον φωνήν; See also Tribulato 2014, 200–204.

161. Phrynichus, *Ecl.* 332.

162. See Photius, *Bibl.* 158, with Jones 2008, 254–55.

163. Aristides's *Panathenaic Oration*: Robert 2009, 154–55. Tatian's familiarity with Aristides: Grant 1988, 116–17; Norelli 1998, 102–3.

164. See Oudot 2008.

165. See Aristides, *Or.* 1.335 (ed. Trapp 2017). Translations are my own, though they take inspiration from Trapp's renderings.

166. Aristides, *Or.* 1.7: πρεσβυτάτην εἶναι τῶν ἐν μνήμῃ τὴν πόλιν συμβαίνει καὶ τὴν ἀρχὴν ἀνήκειν εἰς τὸ πλέον τοῦ φανεροῦ καὶ προχείρου λαβεῖν. See also Oudot 2006.

167. Aristides, *Or.* 1.25: πρώτη γὰρ ἤνεγκεν ἄνθρωπον καὶ πρώτη πατρίς ἐστιν ἀνθρώπου.

168. Aristides, *Or.* 1.14: μόνη τὸ τῶν Ἑλλήνων πρόσχημα καθαρῶς ἀνῄρηται καὶ τοῖς βαρβάροις ἐστὶν ἐπὶ πλεῖστον ἀλλόφυλος.

169. Aristides, *Or.* 1.26.

170. Aristides, *Or.* 1.15.

171. See Oudot 2008, 79.

172. Tatian, *Ad Gr.* 1.1: Μὴ πάνυ φιλέχθρως διατίθεσθε πρὸς τοὺς βαρβάρους, ὦ ἄνδρες Ἕλληνες, μηδὲ φθονήσητε τοῖς τούτων δόγμασιν. ποῖον γὰρ ἐπιτήδευμα παρ᾽ ὑμῖν τὴν σύστασιν οὐκ ἀπὸ βαρβάρων ἐκτήσατο;

173. Tatian, *Ad Gr.* 1.1. For Tatian's use of the word *paideia*, see also Gemeinhardt 2016, 254–59.

174. See Herodotus 5.58.2; Jeffery 1967, 157–58.

175. See Aristides, *Or.* 1.2.

176. Tatian, *Ad Gr.* 31.1: εὑρήσομεν γὰρ οὐ μόνον τῆς Ἑλλήνων παιδείας τὰ παρ᾽ ἡμῖν, ἔτι δὲ καὶ τῆς τῶν γραμμάτων εὑρέσεως ἀνώτερα.

177. Tatian, *Ad Gr.* 1.4: τὰς μὴ συγγενεῖς ὑμῶν ἑρμηνείας τετιμήκατε, βαρβαρικαῖς τε φωναῖς ἔσθ᾽ ὅτε καταχρώμενοι συμφύρδην ὑμῶν πεποιήκατε τὴν διάλεκτον.

178. Tatian, *Ad Gr.* 1.4: τῇ παρ᾽ ὑμῖν σοφίᾳ κἂν εἰ πάνυ σεμνός τις ἦν ἐν αὐτῇ.

179. Tatian, *Ad Gr.* 11.2: τὴν εὐγένειαν οὐ σεμνύνομαι. Petersen (2005, 129) misinterprets this passage.

180. See Tatian, *Ad Gr.* 39.1–4.

181. Tatian, *Ad Gr.* 39.4.

182. Plutarch, *On the Delays of the Divine Vengeance* 551c.

183. Diodorus Siculus 1.28.7.

184. See Grant 1988, 119; Nasrallah 2010, 51–76; Andrade 2013, 261–87; 2014, 307–16.

185. For discussion of Syrian identity, see Andrade 2013.

186. See Ritter 2016, 300.

187. See Droge 1989; Pilhofer 1990; see additional details in chapter 4.

188. Tatian, *Ad Gr.* 1.3: οἵτινες ὑφ᾽ ὑμῶν αὐτῶν ἐπαινούμενοι συνηγόρους τοὺς οἴκοι κέκτησθε.

189. Tatian, *Ad Gr.* 31.2: μάρτυρας δὲ οὐ τοὺς οἴκοι παραλήψομαι, βοηθοῖς δὲ μᾶλλον Ἕλλησι καταχρήσομαι.

190. Tatian, *Ad Gr.* 36.2.

191. See Tatian, *Ad Gr.* 36.3–4 = Berossus, *BNJ* 680 T 2 (Breucker 2010) = Juba, *BNJ* 275 F 4 (Roller 2018). See also Nesselrath 2016, 180 n. 570 for Tatian's dependence on Juba, rather than Berossus.

192. See Tatian, *Ad Gr.* 38.1–2 = Ptolemy of Mendes, *BNJ* 611 T 1a (Gambetti 2015).

193. See Tatian, *Ad Gr.* 38.1–2 = Apion, *BNJ* 616 T 11a (Keyser 2015).

194. See Tatian, *Ad Gr.* 37.3 = Menander, *BNJ* 783 T 4 (Naiden 2008). See Naiden 2008 for Menander.

195. See Tatian, *Ad Gr.* 37.1 = Laetus, *BNJ* 784 T 1 and F 1a (López-Ruiz 2009).

196. See López-Ruiz 2009, commentary on T 1; Nesselrath 2016, 181 n. 572.

197. See Waszink 1963, 51–56; Boys-Stones 2001, 99–122.

198. Tatian, *Ad Gr.* 37.1: καὶ τοὺς βίους τῶν φιλοσόφων ἐπ᾽ ἀκριβὲς πραγματευσάμενος.

199. See Opsomer 2008; Keyser 2016, 497–99. See also Lakmann 2017, 163–65, which unfortunately lacks any discussion of Ofellius Laetus's likely identification with the Laetus named by Tatian.

200. *IG* II² 3816. The two inscriptions are published in Nollé 1981. See also Bowersock 1982a.

201. *IG* II² 3816: εἰ κατὰ Πυθαγόρην ψυχὴ μεταβαίνει ἐς ἄλλον, / ἐν σοί, Λαῖτε, Πλάτων ζῇ πάλι φαινόμενος. The inscription from Athens substitutes the word σωζόμενος for φαινόμενος (i.e., "Plato is kept alive to live again").

202. See O'Meara 1989, 9–10; Dillon 1996, 341.

203. Plutarch, *Natural Questions* 911f, 913e.

204. See Damascius, *Problems and Solutions Concerning First Principles* 125.3 = Laetus, *BNJ* 784 F 4 (López-Ruiz 2009).

205. Plato: Riginos 1976, 62–69. Pythagoras: Burkert 1972, 112.

206. Tatian, *Ad Gr.* 29.1.

207. Tatian, *Ad Gr.* 29.2: περινοοῦντι δέ μοι τὰ σπουδαῖα συνέβη γραφαῖς τισιν ἐντυχεῖν βαρβαρικαῖς, πρεσβυτέραις μὲν ὡς πρὸς τὰ Ἑλλήνων δόγματα, θειοτέραις δὲ ὡς πρὸς τὴν ἐκείνων πλάνην.

208. Tatian, *Ad Gr.* 29.2: τῆς τοῦ παντὸς ποιήσεως τὸ εὐκατάληπτον.

209. See Speyer 1970, 51–65; Festugière 1986, 1:319–24.

210. See Festugière 1986, 1:320; Heilen 2010, 48–52.

211. See *BNJ* 790 (Kaldellis and López-Ruiz 2009); Baumgarten 1981; Kokkinos 2012; López-Ruiz 2017.

212. On earlier uses of the same trope in the Near East, see Ní Mheallaigh 2008, with López-Ruiz 2017, 374–75.

213. See Stephens and Winkler 1995, 101–57.

214. Dictys, *A Journal of the Trojan War*, prologue.

215. Note also a similar motif in Philostratus, *VA* 1.3.1, concerning the discovery of a new source of information concerning the life of Apollonius of Tyana, which Philostratus claims was written by Damis. On Damis, see chapter 4.

216. "Phoenician letters"; see Ní Mheallaigh 2012.

217. See Dio Chrysostom, *Or.* 11.37–38.

218. See Vettius Valens 4.11.4, with Komorowska 2004, 248–59.

219. Philo of Byblus, *BNJ* 790 F 1 = Eusebius, *Praep. ev.* 1.9.27, with discussion in López-Ruiz 2017, 371.

220. For a comparison between Tatian and Philo, see López-Ruiz 2017, 384–86.

221. Compare Elze 1960, 11; Millar 1993, 493.

222. Ulpian: Paolucci 2004. Date of Athenaeus: Braund 2000, 13.

223. See Braund 2000, 17; Honoré 2002, 11–13.

224. Athenaeus 1.1e.

225. Athenaeus 3.126f and 9.368c.

226. Athenaeus 3.126a = Philo of Byblus, *BNJ* 790 F 7a = Laetus, *BNJ* 784 F 3b: ἐμπίπλασο, Οὐλπιανέ, χθωροδλαψου πατρίου, ὃς παρ' οὐδενὶ τῶν παλαιῶν μὰ τὴν Δήμητρα γέγραπται πλὴν εἰ μὴ ἄρα παρὰ τοῖς τὰ Φοινικικὰ συγγεγραφόσι Σαγχουνιάθωνι καὶ Μώχῳ, τοῖς σοῖς πολίταις. For the word *chthōrodlapsus*, see Maxwell-Stuart 1981.

227. Athenaeus 3.121e–f.

228. See Janiszewski, Stebnicka, and Szabat 2015, 151–52.

229. See Philostratus, *VS* 2.10 (587): πάλιν ἐκ Φοινίκης γράμματα.

230. See Philostratus, *VS* 2.10 (587–88).

231. Lucian, *The Mistaken Critic* 1, 11. For the identification of the unnamed target with Hadrian of Tyre, see Jones 1972, 478–87.

232. See Whitmarsh 2005, 47–49.

233. Tatian, *Ad Gr.* 26.8: εἰ γὰρ Ἀττικίζεις οὐκ ὢν Ἀθηναῖος, λέγε μοι τοῦ μὴ Δωρίζειν τὴν αἰτίαν· πῶς τὸ μὲν εἶναί σοι δοκεῖ βαρβαρικώτερον, τὸ δὲ πρὸς τὴν ὁμιλίαν ἱλαρώτερον;

234. See Swain 1996, 56–63; Morison 2008, 144–45.

235. Galen, *On the Properties of Foodstuffs* 2.11 (6.584 Kühn): οὗτοι γὰρ εὖ οἶδ' ὅτι τὴν μὲν τῶν Ἀθηναίων φωνὴν οὐδὲν ἡγοῦνται τιμιωτέραν εἶναι φύσει τῆς τῶν ἄλλων ἀνθρώπων.

236. Tatian, *Ad Gr.* 27.9: τί δ' ἂν ὠφελήσειε λέξις Ἀττική;

237. Tatian, *Ad Gr.* 27.9: τὸ γὰρ περὶ τοιαύτην ἀσχολεῖσθαι ζήτησιν νομοθετοῦντός ἐστιν ἔργον ἑαυτῷ τὰ δόγματα.

238. Galen, *On the Properties of Foodstuffs* 2.29 (6.612 Kühn): τῶν δ' οὐδεμίαν μὲν τέχνην ἠσκηκότων τῷ βίῳ χρήσιμον; 2.44 (6.633 Kühn).

239. Fragments of his work are edited in Valente 2015.

240. See Valente 2015, 52–55.

241. See Tribulato 2016, 187–91.

242. Tatian, *Ad Gr.* 1.4: Δωριέων μὲν γὰρ οὐχ ἡ αὐτὴ λέξις τοῖς ἀπὸ τῆς Ἀττικῆς, Αἰολεῖς τε οὐχ ὁμοίως τοῖς Ἴωσι φθέγγονται· στάσεως δὲ οὔσης τοσαύτης παρ' οἷς οὐκ ἐχρῆν ἀπορῶ τίνα με δεῖ καλεῖν Ἕλληνα.

243. Phrynichus, *Ecl.* 332: τῆς ἄλλης Ἑλλάδος, Αἰολέων λέγω καὶ Δωριέων καὶ Ἰώνων.

244. See Lee 2013, 292–94.

245. See Jones 2004, 20–21; Whitmarsh 2010.

246. Tatian, *Ad Gr.* 25.5. See also Norelli 1998, 98; Trelenberg 2012, 224–30.

247. E.g., Philostratus, *VS* 2.27 (619); Galen, *Loc. Aff.* 4.2 (8.225 Kühn); *AA* 2.1 (2.281 Kühn).

248. Tatian, *Ad Gr.* 12.10. See also 35.3 for another reference to "our *paideia*."

249. Tatian, *Ad Gr.* 27.1: σὺ τῆς ἐκείνων ἀντέχῃ παιδείας.

250. Tatian, *Ad Gr.* 26.1: ἑκάστη πόλις ἐὰν ἀφέληται τὴν ἰδίαν αὐτῆς ἀφ' ὑμῶν λέξιν, ἐξαδυνατήσουσιν ὑμῖν τὰ σοφίσματα.

251. See also Georgia 2018.

252. Tatian, *Ad Gr.* 42.2: ἕτοιμον ἐμαυτὸν ὑμῖν πρὸς τὴν ἀνάκρισιν τῶν δογμάτων παρίστημι.

253. See Ritter 2016, 302.

254. For Tatian's reception, see Crawford 2016; Ritter 2016, esp. 288–94.

255. For the terminology of "East" and "West," see Hunt 2003, 177–78; Koltun-Fromm 2008, 16, 29–30. For suggestions about the significance of "sociocultural" arguments and motivations in heresiology, compare Vallée 1981, 24–33.

256. For heresiology as a form of ethnography, see Berzon 2016.

257. See Gemeinhardt 2016, 252.

258. See Irenaeus, *Adv. haer.* 3.23.8.

259. See Eshleman 2011, 198–99.

260. See Antonova 2019, 130–62.

261. Tatian, *Ad Gr.* 42.1: κατὰ βαρβάρους φιλοσοφῶν . . . γεννηθεὶς μὲν ἐν τῇ τῶν Ἀσσυρίων γῇ.

262. See Elze 1960, 26.

263. Justin, *Dial.* 120.6.

264. Tatian, *Ad Gr.* 29.2.

265. Justin, *1 Apol.* 44.8: πρεσβύτερος γὰρ Μωυσῆς καὶ πάντων τῶν ἐν Ἕλλησι συγγραφέων. See also 59.1.

266. Justin, *1 Apol.* 5.4.

267. See Aristides, *Apology* 2.2–4 (ed. Pouderon and Pierre 2003).

268. Justin, *Dial.* 119.4: οὐκοῦν οὐκ εὐκαταφρόνητος δῆμός ἐσμεν οὐδὲ βάρβαρον φῦλον οὐδὲ ὁποῖα Καρῶν ἢ Φρυγῶν ἔθνη.

269. Justin, *1 Apol.* 60.11: παρ' ἡμῖν οὖν ἐστι ταῦτα ἀκοῦσαι καὶ μαθεῖν παρὰ τῶν οὐδὲ τοὺς χαρακτῆρας τῶν στοιχείων ἐπισταμένων, ἰδιωτῶν μὲν καὶ βαρβάρων τὸ φθέγμα, σοφῶν δὲ καὶ πιστῶν τὸν νοῦν ὄντων.

270. Contrast Elze 1960, 25.

271. See Lashier 2014, esp. 18–22; Secord forthcoming a.

272. See Secord forthcoming a.

273. See Slusser 2006.

274. Irenaeus, *Adv. haer.* 3.4.2: *Hanc fidem qui sine litteris crediderunt, quantum ad sermonem nostrum barbari sunt, quantum autem ad sententiam et consuetudinem et conversationem propter fidem perquam sapientissimi sunt et placent Deo.*

275. Irenaeus, *Adv. haer.* 1.pr.3: Οὐκ ἐπιζητήσεις δὲ παρ' ἡμῶν τῶν ἐν Κελτοῖς διατριβόντων, καὶ περὶ βάρβαρον διάλεκτον τὸ πλεῖστον ἀσχολουμένων, λόγων τέχνην.

276. See Secord 2012, 29–32.

277. See Secord 2012, 27–28.

278. Irenaeus, *Adv. haer.* 1.28.1.

279. Irenaeus, *Adv. haer.* 1.24.1.

280. Irenaeus, *Adv. haer.* 1.28.1: ὃς Ἰουστίνου ἀκροατὴς γεγονώς, ἐφόσον μὲν συνῆν ἐκείνῳ, οὐδὲν ἐξέφηνε τοιοῦτον· μετὰ δὲ τὴν ἐκείνου μαρτυρίαν ἀποστὰς τῆς Ἐκκλησίας, οἰήματι διδασκάλου ἐπαρθεὶς καὶ τυφωθεὶς ὡς διαφέρων τῶν λοιπῶν, ἴδιον χαρακτῆρα διδασκαλείου συνεστήσατο. See also 3.23.8.

281. See Martens 2016, 376–87.

282. See Marchiori 2000, 335–37.

283. See Benoit 1960, 50, 59.

284. Tatian, *Ad Gr.* 35.3: Τατιανὸς ὑπὲρ τοὺς Ἕλληνας ὑπὲρ <τε> τὸ ἄπειρον τῶν φιλοσοφησάντων πλῆθος καινοτομεῖ τὰ βαρβάρων δόγματα.

285. See Eusebius, *Hist. eccl.* 5.26.1.

286. For Clement's familiarity with Irenaeus, see Patterson 1997; Eusebius, *Hist. eccl.* 6.13.9.

287. See Clement, *Strom.* 1.21.101.2; 1.21.102.2. See *Strom.* 3.12.81.1–2 (= Whittaker 1982, F 5) for the reference to *On Perfection According to the Savior.* Harris (1924, 15–51) makes an unconvincing attempt to identify this work

with an extant Armenian text. Clement also makes other references to Tatian at *Strom.* 3.12.82.2 (= Whittaker 1982, F 6); 3.13.92.1; Clement, *Ecl.* 38 (= Whittaker 1982, F 8).

288. Clement, *Strom.* 1.21.101.2; 1.21.102.2; with Tatian, *Ad Gr.* 39.4. See also Nesselrath 2016, 20–23.

289. See Eusebius, *Hist. eccl.* 4.29.7.

290. See Clement, *Strom.* 3.12.81.1–2; *Ecl.* 38.

291. See Clement, *Strom.* 3.13.91.1, referencing Julius Cassianus.

292. See Van Den Hoek 1990; Van Den Hoek and Herrmann 2006.

293. Clement, *Strom.* 1.1.11.2: ἀνεπαυσάμην, ἐν Αἰγύπτῳ θηράσας λεληθότα. The teacher in question is evidently Pantaenus, named by Clement at *Ecl.* 56.2. See also Eusebius, *Hist. eccl.* 5.11.1–2; 6.13.2.

294. Epiphanius, *Panarion* 32.6.1: ὃν φασί τινες Ἀλεξανδρέα, ἕτεροι δὲ Ἀθηναῖον.

295. See Steneker 1969, 69–74.

296. See Clement, *Paed.* 1.4.11.1 (Menander); 1.5.14.1; 2.11.117.3; 2.12.122.3–4 (Philemon).

297. Parallels: Clement, *Paed.* 1.4.11.1, with Moeris 62 and Pollux, *Onom.* 2.17 (παιδάριον); *Paed.* 1.5.14.1, with Phrynichus, *Ecl.* 210 (παιδίσκη); *Paed.* 2.11.117.3, with Pollux, *Onom.* 7.86 (κονίποδες).

298. Clement, *Strom.* 2.1.3.1.

299. Clement, *Strom.* 3.12.81.1.

300. Clement, *Strom.* 1.16.75.1: οἱ δὲ Φοίνικας καὶ Σύρους γράμματα ἐπινοῆσαι πρώτους λέγουσιν.

301. Clement, *Protr.* 2.39.9: τῶν τὴν Φοινίκην Σύρων κατοικούντων, ὧν οἱ μὲν τὰς περιστεράς, οἱ δὲ τοὺς ἰχθῦς οὕτω σέβουσι.

302. Athenaeus 8.346c: διὰ τὰ Σύρων πάτρια καὶ ἡμᾶς τῶν ἰχθύων ἀπεστέρησεν.

303. Clement, *Ecl.* 38.

304. For the relatively limited use of the optative in *Against the Greeks*, see Heiler 1909, 58–59.

305. See Jones 2004, 19–20; Andrade 2014, 299–305.

306. See Aristides, *Or.* 1.335; and the previous discussion of this passage.

307. Clement, *Protr.* 6.70.1: πολλά σε καὶ Ἀσσύριοι πεπαιδεύκασι. See also *Strom.* 1.21.102.4.

308. Clement, *Strom.* 1.1.11.2: ὁ μὲν τῆς τῶν Ἀσσυρίων. Nesselrath (2016, 6) rejects the claim that Tatian himself might have been this Assyrian teacher.

309. Clement, *Protr.* 11.112.1: ἡμᾶς ἐπ' ἀνθρωπίνην ἰέναι μὴ χρῆναι διδασκαλίαν ἔτι,

Ἀθήνας καὶ τὴν ἄλλην Ἑλλάδα, πρὸς δὲ καὶ Ἰωνίαν πολυπραγμονοῦντας.

310. Tatian, *Ad Gr.* 35.2.

311. Clement, *Protr.* 11.112.1: τὸ πᾶν ἤδη Ἀθῆναι καὶ Ἑλλὰς γέγονεν τῷ λόγῳ.

312. See Tertullian, *On Fasting* 15.1; [Hippolytus,] *Refutation of All Heresies* 8.16, 10.18; Origen, *On Prayer* 25.4 (= Whittaker 1982, F 8).

313. See Elze 1960, 117 n. 1.

314. See Ritter 2016, 296–98, for the reception of this part of Tatian's work.

315. Origen, *Against Celsus* 1.16.

316. For praise of Tatian alongside references to Irenaeus and Clement, compare Eusebius, *Hist. eccl.* 5.28.4–5.

317. See Hegedus 2007, 125–37; and Crawford forthcoming.

318. For one example, note the discussion of Berzon 2016, 102–16.

319. See Secord 2018, 466–67.

320. See Heyne 2011, 151–53, 160–61; Secord 2013, 222–24; Grant 1983, 535–36.

321. See Eusebius, *Hist. eccl.* 6.24.3.

322. See Aulus Gellius, *NA* praef. 7; and Plutarch, F 179 (Sandbach 1969) = Eusebius, *Praep. ev.* 1.7.16.

323. Clement, *Strom.* 7.18.111.3: πολλὰ γὰρ τὰ δελέατα καὶ ποικίλα διὰ τὰς τῶν ἰχθύων διαφοράς.

324. Clement, *Strom.* 2.2.4.2: αἱ δὴ ὁδοὶ σοφίας ποικίλαι ὀρθοτομεῖν ἐπὶ τὴν ὁδὸν τῆς ἀληθείας.

325. See Petersen 2005, 152–53.

326. Fojtik 2009, 34.

Chapter 4

1. Africanus, *Cesti*, T3 (ed. Wallraff et al. 2012) = Georgius Syncellus, *Ecl. chron.* 439.15–20 (ed. Mosshammer 1984): Ἐμμαοὺς ἡ ἐν Παλαιστίνῃ κώμη, περὶ ἧς φέρεται ἐν τοῖς ἱεροῖς εὐαγγελίοις, Νικόπολις ἐτιμήθη καλεῖσθαι ὑπὸ Ἀλεξάνδρου τοῦ αὐτοκράτορος, Ἀφρικανοῦ πρεσβευσαμένου τὰς ἱστορίας ἐν πενταβίβλῳ συγγραψαμένου. Ἀφρικανὸς τὴν ἐννεάβιβλον τῶν Κεστῶν ἐπιγεγραμμένην πραγματείαν ἰατρικῶν καὶ φυσικῶν καὶ γεωργικῶν καὶ χυμευτικῶν περιέχουσαν δυνάμεις Ἀλεξάνδρῳ τούτῳ προσφωνεῖ. Translations from Africanus are my own, but they take some inspiration from the versions of William Adler.

2. Africanus, *Chronographiae*, T5 = Georgius Syncellus, *Ecl. chron.* 446.3–5 (ed. Wallraff 2007).

3. *Geoponica* 7.14 contains an allusion to the Bible and is attributed to Africanus. But this, like all the authorial attributions in the chapter headings of the *Geoponica*, cannot be trusted. See Rodgers 2009, 203.

4. Africanus, *Cesti*, T 7.48–49 = Michael Psellus, *On Paradoxical Sayings* (Duffy 1992, no. 32 [111.45–46]): ἐκ δὲ ἀποπατήματος τῶν συνελθόντων βοῶν καὶ τοῦ οὔρου ἀποπατεῖν ἄνδρα ποιεῖ καὶ γυναῖκα οὐρεῖν, ὅτε βούλοιτο, καὶ γελᾶν πάμμεγα.

5. See Africanus, *Cesti*, T 1b = *Scholium* on Eusebius, *Hist. eccl.* 6.31.

6. See Guignard 2011, 9.

7. See Roberto 2011, 20 and 186–88, for the dates.

8. For reviews of the evidence, see McKechnie 1999; Barnes 2009.

9. Origen: Eusebius, *Hist. eccl.* 6.21.3–4, as discussed later. Hippolytus: Achelis 1897a, 251–54; 1897b, 189–94; Richard 1963, 79–80.

10. E.g., Jefferson 2014, 36, suggesting that Severus Alexander's mother, Julia Mamaea, was "a devoted Christian."

11. See Mazza 1995, 131, 135–36; Sanzi 2000; Buraselis 2007, 39–47; Roberto 2011, 125, 170.

12. See Levick 2007, 163; Rowan 2012, 9–10.

13. See Hopkins 2018, 475–76.

14. See Kemezis 2014, 277–80.

15. See Halfmann 1979; Mennen 2011, 49–81; Duncan-Jones 2016, 61–75.

16. See Birley 1999, 72; Millar 2006, 191.

17. See many of the papers collected in Swain, Harrison, and Elsner 2007 and now LaValle Norman 2019.

18. See Blois 2001; Millar 2002, 72–75; Marcone 2004. Note also Honoré (1994), who makes a controversial attempt to identify the style of individual jurists in imperial rescripts.

19. See esp. Millar 1999, 105–7.

20. See Honoré 2002, 1–36; Millar 2002, 80–87.

21. See Millar 2002, 72–75.

22. On administrative positions as political appointments, see Lewis 1981, 149–55.

23. See Millar 1999, 98.

24. Ulpian's prefecture: *Codex of Justinian* 4.65.4.1 and Cassius Dio. 80.2.2–4. His death: Blois 2003, 135–45. Severan praetorian prefects: Coriat 2007, 192–98.

25. See Honoré 2002, vii–viii.

26. König and Woolf 2013b, 32.

27. See Millar 2006, 191–200.

28. See Millar 2006, 168–91.

29. See Millar 2006, 191.

30. *Dig.* 50.15.1.2: *Est et Heliupolitana, quae a divo Severo per belli civilis occasionem Italicae coloniae rem publicam accepit.* Compare 50.15.1.3.

31. *Dig.* 50.15.1.pr.: *Foederis quod cum Romanis percussit tenacissima.*

32. *Dig.* 50.15.1.pr.: *Divus Severus et imperator noster ob egregiam in rem publicam imperiumque Romanum insignem fidem ius Italicum dedit.*

33. Italian right: Honoré 2002, 11. Tyre: Millar 1993, 285–95.

34. See Millar 1993, 290–91; Honoré 2002, 13–14.

35. For evidence relating to M. Cn. Licinius Rufinus, the only other Severan jurist besides Ulpian whose home city is known with certainty, see Millar 1999, 92–96.

36. Papinian's possible origins in Syria: SHA *Marcus Aurelius Antoninus (Caracalla)* 8.2, with the conflicting interpretations of Liebs 1997a, 118; and Birley 1999, 164.

37. See Bowersock 1982b.

38. See Andrade 2013, 314–24.

39. See Dickey 2014.

40. See Hall 2004, 192–209, 276–81.

41. See Gregory Thaumaturgus, *Orat. paneg.* 5.68 (ed. Crouzel 1969), with Millar 1999, 106–8.

42. Gregory Thaumaturgus, *Orat. paneg.* 1.7.

43. See Gregory Thaumaturgus, *Orat. paneg.* 5.60; Philostratus, *VA* 7.42.2.

44. Athenaeus 3.121e–f.

45. See Honoré 2002, 90–92.

46. See Lenel 1889, 1:707–18; Liebs 1997c.

47. See *Dig.* 27.1.1.pr. Note also *Dig.* 50.16.103.

48. See Millar 1999, 102.

49. For a passage of uncertain significance locating Modestinus in Dalmatia, see *Dig.* 47.2.52.20.

50. *Dig.* 50.15.1.pr.: *Splendidissima Tyriorum colonia, unde mihi origo est, nobilis regionibus, serie saeculorum antiquissima.*

51. Watson 1985.

52. See Glare 2010, s.vv. *saec(u)lum* 1c, *series* 3.

53. See Yaron 1987; Manthe 1999; both are too confident in assuming that Ulpian knew Aramaic.

54. See Birley 1999, 1–22.

55. See Millar 1993, 292.

56. See Levick 2007, 6–21.

57. Cassius Dio 76.17.1: καὶ γὰρ τοῖς δικαζομένοις ὕδωρ ἱκανὸν ἐνέχει, καὶ ἡμῖν τοῖς συνδικάζουσιν αὐτῷ παρρησίαν πολλὴν ἐδίδου.

58. See Millar 2002, 69.

59. See Honoré 2002, 90.

60. See *Dig.* 48.19.16.6–8. For details on Saturninus, see Liebs 1997b.

61. *Dig.* 1.1.1.pr.-1.

62. See Galen, *Exhortation to the Arts* 14 (1.39 Kühn).

63. *Dig.* 1.1.1.1: *Aequum ab iniquo separantes, licitum ab illicito discernentes, bonos non solum metu poenarum, verum etiam praemiorum quoque exhortatione efficere cupientes.*

64. *Dig.* 1.1.1.1: *Veram . . . philosophiam, non simulatam.*

65. See also Dufault 2019, 2–3.

66. See Lactantius, *Divine Institutes* 5.11.19; and the speculative comments of Honoré 2002, 83.

67. See Icks 2012.

68. Nickname: Cassius Dio 80(79).11.2. Foreign habits and rites: Herodian 5.5.4–5; 5.6.4–6; 5.6.9.

69. Herodian 5.7.5.

70. Africanus, *Cesti*, F 10.50–51 = *P.Oxy.* 3.412.

71. See Millar 2006, 188–91.

72. See Roberto 2011, 30–33.

73. On the praenomen, see Adler 2004, 523–24; Roberto 2011, 32–33.

74. See Imrie 2018 for Caracalla's decree.

75. See *Chronographiae*, T3 = Syncellus, *Ecl. chron.* 439.15–20.

76. See Roberto 2011, 177 for the date.

77. Alexandria: *Chronographiae*, F98 = Eusebius, *Hist. eccl.* 6.31.2. The Dead Sea: *Chronographiae*, F26.13–22 = Syncellus, *Ecl. chron.* 114.13–24 (ed. Mosshammer 1984). Edessa: Africanus, *Cesti*, F 12.20, with Roberto 2011, 46–57.

78. Africanus, *Cesti*, F 12.20.35–47.

79. See Africanus, *Cesti*, F 12.20.1–27.

80. See *Chronographiae*, F 23.18–20 = Syncellus, *Ecl. chron.* 22.6–8.

81. Suphis's book: *Chronographiae*, F46.52–55 = Syncellus, *Ecl. chron.* 63.2–6. Compare *Chronographiae*, F46.5–6 = Syncellus, *Ecl. chron.* 61.11–12. Archival visits in Colonia Aelia Capitolina and Nysa: Africanus, *Cesti*, F 10.49–53 = *P.Oxy.* 3.412. See also *Chronographiae*, T88 = Moses of Chorene 2.10, relating to Africanus's archival research in Edessa, a passage treated skeptically by Walraff 2007, xlviii and 261 n. 1, but accepted by Roberto 2011, 56.

82. See Cassius Dio 75.13.2.

83. Africanus, *Cesti*, T3 = Syncellus, *Ecl. chron.* 439.15–20.

84. Africanus, *Cesti*, F 10 = *P.Oxy.* 3.412. See also Hammerstaedt 2009; Dufault 2019, 84–90.

85. Africanus, *Cesti*, F 10.52–53 = *P.Oxy.* 3.412: ἐν Ῥώμῃ πρὸς ταῖς Ἀλεξάνδρου θερμαῖς ἐν τῇ ἐν Πανθείῳ βιβλιοθήκῃ τῇ καλῇ, ἣν αὐτὸς ἠρχιτεκτόνησα τῷ Σεβαστῷ.

86. See Bowie 2013, 259 n. 109.

87. See Siwicki 2019, a discussion that supersedes all previous speculation about the library and its possible location.

88. See Harnack 1921, 145; Adler 2004, 541.

89. Vitruvius, *On Architecture* 1.1.3: *Et ut litteratus sit, peritus graphidos, eruditus geometria, historias complures noverit, philosophos diligenter audierit, musicam scierit, medicinae non sit ignarus responsa iurisconsultorum noverit, astrologiam caelique rationes cognitas habeat.*

90. Geometry: Africanus, *Cesti*, F7.15.1–2. Philosophy: *Suda* α 4647. Astronomy: *Chronographiae*, F93.67–69.

91. Michael Syrus, *Chronicle* 6.7 (113; ed. Chabot 1899–1924), cited by Adler 2004, 541 n. 86.

92. See Roberto 2011, 178.

93. Contrast Harnack 1921, 145; Granger 1934, 367.

94. See Petrain 2013, 337–38.

95. See Petrain 2013, 339–42.

96. On libraries as "politicized" spaces, see Dix and Houston 2006, 683; Petrain 2013, 346.

97. Suetonius, *Tiberius* 70.2; *Gaius Caligula* 34.2.

98. See Thomas 2007, 92.

99. See Bowie 2013, 244–59.

100. See *Epitome de Caesaribus* 14.4.

101. See Whitehead 2010.

102. See Drijvers 1966.

103. Africanus, *Cesti*, F 12.20.25.

104. See Cameron 2011, 743–82.

105. See Barnes 1978, 48.

106. See Barnes 1978, 57–59; Bertrand-Dagenbach 1990.

107. See SHA *Alexander Severus* 29.2.

108. See Jefferson 2014, 36. See also Granger 1934, 367.

109. Eusebius, *Hist. eccl.* 6.28.1: ἐκ πλειόνων πιστῶν συνεστῶτα.

110. Africanus, *Cesti*, T2 = Eusebius, *Quaestiones evangelicae, apud* Nicetas of Heraclea, *Catena in Lucam* (PG 22:965AB). For similar comments on Africanus's learning,

see also Eusebius, *Praep. ev.* 10.9.26; Socrates, *Ecclesiastical History* 2.35.10.

111. See Nautin 1977, 68–69.

112. See Lange 1976, 15–24.

113. For discussion of the controversy, see the papers collected in Bäbler and Nesselrath 2018.

114. On problems with the chronological evidence in Eusebius, see Bäbler 2018, 198; on Porphyry's selective portrayal of Origen across different works, see Tanaseanu-Dobler 2018, 157–59.

115. See Nautin 1977, 197–202; Digeser 2012, 49 n.1; Riedweg 2018, 33.

116. Eusebius, *Hist. eccl.* 6.1.2. Origen's father: Nautin 1977, 32; Heine 2010, 20; Digeser 2012, 51.

117. Eusebius, *Hist. eccl.* 6.2.13. See Digeser 2012, 51, for the date.

118. See Eusebius, *Hist. eccl.* 6.2.7, 14.

119. See Origen, *Letter to Gregory Thaumaturgus* 2.1 (ed. Crouzel 1969); Gregory Thaumaturgus, *Orat. paneg.* 8.113–14; and Eusebius, *Hist. eccl.* 6.18.3.

120. Ambrose: Jerome, *Letters* 43.1. Compare Epiphanius, *Panarion* 64.3.5. See also Eusebius, *Hist. eccl.* 6.23.1–2; Castagno 2003.

121. Eusebius, *Hist. eccl.* 6.21.3–4.

122. Nautin 1977, 56–57.

123. Eusebius, *Hist. eccl.* 6.21.3.

124. Eusebius, *Hist. eccl.* 6.21.4: πλεῖστά τε ὅσα εἰς τὴν τοῦ κυρίου δόξαν καὶ τῆς τοῦ θείου διδασκαλείου ἀρετῆς ἐπιδειξάμενος, ἐπὶ τὰς συνήθεις ἔσπευδεν διατριβάς.

125. Eusebius, *Hist. eccl.* 6.21.4.

126. Eusebius, *Hist. eccl.* 6.19.15: ἐπιστάς τις τῶν στρατιωτικῶν ἀνεδίδου γράμματα Δημητρίῳ τε τῷ τῆς παροικίας ἐπισκόπῳ καὶ τῷ τότε τῆς Αἰγύπτου ἐπάρχῳ παρὰ τοῦ τῆς Ἀραβίας ἡγουμένου, ὡς ἂν μετὰ σπουδῆς ἁπάσης τὸν Ὡριγένην πέμψοιεν κοινωνήσοντα λόγων αὐτῷ.

127. See Nautin 1977, 411–12 and 436; and Amacker and Junod 2002, 35–38.

128. Rufinus, *Adult. libr. Orig.* 7 (ed. Amacker and Junod 2002).

129. Rufinus, *Adult. libr. Orig.* 7.54–55: *Ego quidem cognovi, ad eos qui Romae erant, sed non dubito quod et ad alios qui per diversa sunt.*

130. Rufinus, *Adult. libr. Orig.* 7.58–59.

131. Rufinus, *Adult. libr. Orig.* 7.63–64.

132. Mobility of sophists: Bowersock 1969, 109. Sophistic cities: Bowie 2004.

133. Philostratus, *VS* 2.8 (579): θορύβου δὲ πολλοῦ καὶ γέλωτος.

134. Galen, *On My Own Books* Prol. 1–3 (19.8–9 Kühn).
135. Nautin 1977, 367–68.
136. See McLynn 2004, 186.
137. Pamphilus, *Apology* 9 (ed. Amacker and Junod 2002).
138. See Eusebius, *Hist. eccl.* 6.36.1.
139. See Pradel 2012; Perrone 2013a, 2013b, 2015.
140. See Perrone 2013a, 84.
141. Origen, *Homilies on 1 Samuel* 5.1.22–23 (ed. Nautin and Nautin 1986).
142. See Staden 1997, 40–44.
143. See Staden 1997, 42–44.
144. Whitmarsh 2007, 38; Eshleman 2012, 199. Note also Ramelli 2004b, 41 ("un contesto cultúrale").
145. E.g., Swain 1999, 185; 2009, 46. Note also the suggestion of Laks (2014, 361) that the third century was "deeply marked by a religious, spiritual and intellectual confrontation between paganism and Christianity."
146. For the suggestion that Diogenes "vive fuori del tempo," see Gigante 1972, 41.
147. See Diogenes Laertius 3.47, 10.29.
148. See Hemelrijk 1999, 304 n. 119.
149. Contrast the suggestion of Mansfeld (1986, 301) that Diogenes was "a local savant largely depending on the not wholly up-to-date public library of an unimportant town in an outlying Roman province." For the argument that Diogenes was from the minor city of Laertes in Cilicia, see also Masson 1995, 227–28.
150. See Diogenes Laertius 9.116.
151. See Floridi 2002, 3–7, a much more positive treatment than the extreme skepticism of House (1980).
152. See Jouanna 2009, 389–90, with the responses of Petit 2009, xliii–xliv; 2014, 277–80. See also Floridi 2002, 5. Miller 2018 also assumes a date of the mid-third century.
153. See Warren 2007, 147: Diogenes was "not the poor prisoner of an outdated set of sources."
154. Diogenes Laertius 1.1: Τὸ τῆς φιλοσοφίας ἔργον ἐνιοί φασιν ἀπὸ βαρβάρων ἄρξαι.
155. See Diogenes Laertius 1.1. See Aronadio 1990, 203–33, for Sotion.
156. Diogenes Laertius 1.3: Λανθάνουσι δ' αὐτοὺς τὰ τῶν Ἑλλήνων κατορθώματα, ἀφ᾽ὧν μὴ ὅτι γε φιλοσοφία, ἀλλὰ καὶ γένος ἀνθρώπων ἦρξε, βαρβάροις προσάπτοντες.

157. Diogenes Laertius 1.4: καὶ ὧδε μὲν ἀφ᾽ Ἑλλήνων ἦρξε φιλοσοφία, ἧς καὶ αὐτὸ τὸ ὄνομα τὴν βάρβαρον ἀπέστραπται προσηγορίαν.
158. See Warren 2007, 141.
159. See Canfora 1992; Ramelli 2004a; Whitmarsh 2007, 38–39. Contrast Warren 2007, 141; Eshleman 2012, 199 n. 97.
160. Eshleman 2012, 191, 194. See also Hope 1930, 110.
161. For Africanus, see *Chronographiae*, F34 = Eusebius, *Praep. ev.* 10.10.1. For Origen, see *Against Celsus* 1.16.
162. For Callinicus, see *BNJ* 281 (Kaldellis 2011). For a review of sophists from this period, see Heath 2004, 52–89.
163. See Porphyry, *Plot.* 7 (Paulinus of Scythopolis and Zethus, an Arabian) and 17 (on Porphyry's name in his native language). Note also the connections of the Etrurian Amelius Gentilianus to Apamea in Syria: Plot. 2–3.
164. See *BNJ* 281 T 1a = *Suda* κ 231; T 2a = *Suda* γ 132 for the example of Callinicus and his rival Genethlius, another native of Petra, who both taught at Athens.
165. See Wallraff 2010, 552–53.
166. See Johnson 2013, esp. 12.
167. Porphyry, *On Aristotle Categories* 119.37–120.3: ὡμολόγηται δὲ καὶ τὰ μαθήματα ὅτι ὀψὲ εἰς τοὺς Ἕλληνας ἦλθεν, οἷον ἡ γεωμετρία καὶ ἡ ἀριθμητικὴ καὶ ἡ ἀστρονομία· ἀλλ᾽ ὅμως ἦν ἐπιστητά, καίπερ τῶν Ἑλλήνων αὐτὰ μὴ ἐπισταμένων.
168. See Gordon 1993.
169. See Richter 2011, 192–98.
170. See Plutarch, *On the Malice of Herodotus* 857e, citing Herodotus 6.53–54.
171. Plutarch, *On the Malice of Herodotus* 857f, citing Herodotus 1.170.3: τὸν μὲν Θάλητα Φοίνικα τῷ γένει τὸ ἀνέκαθεν ἀποφαίνεται βάρβαρον.
172. E.g., Plutarch, *On the Fortune or Virtue of Alexander* 328d.
173. Diogenes Laertius 1.22.
174. Diogenes Laertius 1.22: οἱ πλείους φασίν, ἰθαγενὴς Μιλήσιος ἦν καὶ γένους λαμπροῦ.
175. See Jerome, *Chronica* ad Olymp. 238.4. See also Moreschini 1987; Dillon 1996, 361–79.
176. See Dillon 1996, 247–48.
177. Atticus F 1 (ed. des Places 1977) = Eusebius, *Praep. ev.* 11.2.2: Πλάτων πρῶτος καὶ μάλιστα συναγείρας εἰς ἓν πάντα τὰ τῆς φιλοσοφίας μέρη.
178. Atticus F 1 = Eusebius, *Praep. ev.* 11.2.3.

179. Atticus F 1 = Eusebius, *Praep. ev.* 11.2.4: Πλάτων, ἀνὴρ ἐκ φύσεως ἀρτιτελὴς καὶ πολὺ διενεγκών, οἷα κατάπεμπτος ὡς ἀληθῶς ἐκ θεῶν, ἵν' ὁλόκληρος ὀφθῇ ἡ δι' αὐτοῦ φιλοσοφία.

180. Atticus F 4 = Eusebius, *Praep. ev.* 15.6.3: Πλάτωνι πιστεύομεν οἷς αὐτὸς Ἕλλην ὢν πρὸς Ἕλληνας ἡμᾶς σαφεῖ καὶ τρανῷ τῷ στόματι διείλεκται.

181. See Diogenes Laertius 1.3. See Clinton 1974 for more on the Eumolpidae.

182. See Clinton 2004, 51 and 55.

183. See Philostratus, *VS* 2.20 (600–602); with Clinton 2004, 47–50 and Janiszewski, Stebnicka, and Szabat 2015, 41–42.

184. See Diogenes Laertius 1.3.

185. Diogenes Laertius 1.3: ἀπὸ δὲ τοῦ πατρὸς τοῦ Μουσαίου καὶ Εὐμολπίδαι καλοῦνται παρ' Ἀθηναίοις.

186. See Heath 2004, 93–131.

187. See Menander Rhetor 2 (354.22–355.1).

188. Menander Rhetor 2 (354.22–25): πρὸ ἄστρων ἢ μετὰ τῶν ἄστρων φάσκωμεν, ἢ πρὸ κατακλυσμοῦ ἢ μετὰ κατακλυσμὸν φάσκωμεν οἰκισθῆναι.

189. See Menander Rhetor 2 (354.25–28), with the commentary of Russell and Wilson 1981 ad loc.

190. Menander Rhetor 2 (354.29–30): ὅτ' ἤνθησεν ἡ Ἑλλὰς ἢ ἡ Περσῶν δύναμις ἢ Ἀσσυρίων ἢ Μήδων.

191. Menander Rhetor 2 (354.29–30): πλεῖσται τῆς Ἑλλάδος καὶ τῆς βαρβάρου.

192. See Pausanius 7.23.7–8.

193. Pausanias 7.23.7: ἐγνωκέναι τὰ ἐς τὸ θεῖον ἔφασκε Φοίνικας [καὶ] τά τε ἄλλα Ἑλλήνων βέλτιον.

194. Pausanias 7.23.8: ἐγὼ δὲ ἀποδέχεσθαι μὲν τὰ εἰρημένα, οὐδὲν δέ τι Φοινίκων μᾶλλον ἢ καὶ Ἑλλήνων ἔφην τὸν λόγον.

195. See Baumgarten 1981, 264–65 for the equation of Eshmun with Asclepius.

196. See Athenaeus 3.126f; 4.174e–f; 8.346c; 9.368c; 13.571a; 14.649c; 15.669b, 697c.

197. See Philostratus, *VA* 1.19.2, 3.43.1, 7.14.1, and 8.29.1. Bowie (1978, 1653) argues that Damis was invented by Philostratus.

198. Philostratus, *Heroicus* 1.1.

199. Philostratus, *VA* 1.19.2.

200. See Philostratus, *Heroicus* 53.3.

Conclusion

1. Eusebius, *Hist. eccl.* 6.43.11: πρεσβυτέρους εἶναι τεσσαράκοντα ἕξ, διακόνους ἑπτά, ὑποδιακόνους ἑπτά, ἀκολούθους δύο καὶ τεσσαράκοντα, ἐξορκιστὰς δὲ καὶ ἀναγνώστας ἅμα πυλωροῖς δύο καὶ πεντήκοντα, χήρας σὺν θλιβομένοις ὑπὲρ τὰς χιλίας πεντακοσίας.

2. See Saxer 2004; Corke-Webster 2019, 89–120.

3. See Holliday 2011.

4. See Countryman 1979.

5. See Eusebius, *Hist. eccl.* 6.36.3. See also 7.10.3 for the suggestion, derived from a letter written by Dionysius of Alexandria, that the household of the emperor Valerian was filled with Christians.

6. See Barnes 2009, 19.

7. Eusebius, *Hist. eccl.* 7.13.1.

8. Eusebius, *Hist. eccl.* 7.13.1: πρὸς ἑτέρους ἐπισκόπους . . . τὰ τῶν καλουμένων κοιμητηρίων ἀπολαμβάνειν ἐπιτρέπων χωρία.

9. See Porphyry, *Plot.* 12, with Blois 1976, 185–94.

10. See Blois 1976, 185.

11. Porphyry, *Plot.* 16: τῶν Χριστιανῶν πολλοὶ μὲν καὶ ἄλλοι, αἱρετικοὶ δὲ ἐκ τῆς παλαιᾶς φιλοσοφίας ἀνηγμένοι. See Edwards 2000, 28 nn. 155–56 for this interpretation and translation of the passage.

12. See Porphyry, *Plot.* 16.

13. Porphyry, *Plot.* 16: πρὸς τὸ Ζωροάστρου συχνοὺς πεποίημαι ἐλέγχους.

BIBLIOGRAPHY

Achelis, Hans. 1897a. *Hippolyt's kleinere exegetische und homiletische Schriften*. GCS 1.2. Leipzig: Teubner.

———. 1897b. *Hippolytstudien*. Texte und Untersuchungen zur Geschichte der altchristlichen Literatur 16.4. Leipzig: J. C. Hinrichs.

Adler, William. 2004. "Sextus Julius Africanus and the Roman Near East in the Third Century." *JTS* 55 (2): 520–50.

———. 2009. "The *Cesti* and Sophistic Culture in the Severan Age." In Wallraff and Mecella 2009, 1–15.

———. 2011. "Alexander Polyhistor's *Peri Ioudaiōn* and Literary Culture in Republican Rome." In *Reconsidering Eusebius: Collected Papers on Literary, Historical, and Theological Issues*, edited by Sabrina Inowlocki and Claudio Zamagni, 225–40. VCSup 107. Leiden: Brill.

Allen, Pauline. 2009. *Sophronius of Jerusalem and Seventh-Century Heresy: The "Synodical Letter" and Other Documents*. OECT. Oxford: Oxford University Press.

Amacker, René, and Éric Junod. 2002. *Pamphile et Eusèbe de Césarée: Apologie pour Origène, suivi de Rufin d'Aquilée; Sur la falsification des livres d'Origène*. 2 vols. SC 464–65. Paris: Les Éditions du Cerf.

Amato, Eugenio. 2010. *Favorinos d'Arles: Oeuvres*. Vol. 2, *Fragments*. Paris: Les Belles Lettres.

Amundsen, Darrel W. 1995. "Tatian's Rejection of Medicine in the Second Century." In *Ancient Medicine in Its Socio-Cultural Context*, edited by Ph. J. van der Eijk, H. F. J. Horstmanshoff, and P. H. Schrijvers, 2:377–92. Amsterdam: Rodopi.

Andrade, Nathanael. 2013. *Syrian Identity in the Greco-Roman World*. GCRW. Cambridge: Cambridge University Press.

———. 2014. "Assyrians, Syrians, and the Greek Language in the Late Hellenistic and Roman Imperial Periods." *Journal of Near Eastern Studies* 73 (2): 299–317.

Antonova, Stamenka. 2019. *Barbarian or Greek? The Charge of Barbarism and Early Christian Apologetics*. Studies in the History of Christian Traditions 187. Leiden: Brill.

Aragione, Gabriella. 2015. *Taziano: Ai Greci*. Letture Cristiane del Primo Millennio 52. Milan: Paoline.

Aronadio, Francesco. 1990. "Due fonti laerziane: Sozione e Demetrio di Magnesia." *Elenchos* 11:203–55.

Aujac, Germaine. 2002. *Denys d'Halicarnasse: Opuscules rhétoriques*. 2nd ed. 5 vols. Paris: Les Belles Lettres.

Bäbler, Balbina. 2018. "Origenes und Eusebios' *Chronik* und *Kirchengeschichte*." In Bäbler and Nesselrath 2018, 179–99.

Bäbler, Balbina, and Heinz-Günther Nesselrath. 2018. *Origenes der Christ und Origenes der Platoniker*. Seraphim: Studies in Education and Religion in Ancient and Pre-Modern History in the Mediterranean and Its Environs 2. Tübingen: Mohr Siebeck.

Bagatti, B. 1979. "San Giustino nella sua patria." *Augustinianum* 19:319–31.

Bakker, Egbert J., ed. 2010. *A Companion to the Ancient Greek Language*. Chichester: Wiley-Blackwell.

Baldwin, Barry. 1973. *Studies in Lucian*. Toronto: Hakkert.

Barclay, J. M. G. 2007. *Flavius Josephus: Translation and Commentary*. Vol. 10, *Against Apion*. Leiden: Brill.

Barnard, L. W. 1967. *Justin Martyr: His Life and Thought*. Cambridge: Cambridge University Press.

———. 1968. "The Heresy of Tatian—Once Again." *JTS* 19 (1): 1–10.

Barnes, T. D. 1978. *The Sources of the "Historia Augusta."* Collection Latomus 155. Brussels: Latomus.

———. 1985. *Tertullian: A Historical and Literary Study.* 2nd ed. Oxford: Oxford University Press.

———. 2009. "Aspects of the Severan Empire, Part II: Christians in Roman Provincial Society." *New England Classical Journal* 36 (1): 3–19.

———. 2010. *Early Christian Hagiography and Roman History.* Tria corda 5. Tübingen: Mohr Siebeck.

Barton, Tamsyn. 1994. *Ancient Astrology.* Sciences of Antiquity. London: Routledge.

Baumbach, Manuel, and Dirk Uwe Hansen. 2005. "Die Karriere des Peregrinos Proteus." In *Lukian: Der Tod des Peregrinos; Ein Scharlatan auf dem Scheiterhaufen*, edited by Peter Pilhofer et al., 111–28. SAPERE 9. Darmstadt: Wissenschaftliche Buchgesellschaft.

Baumgarten, Albert I. 1981. *The "Phoenician History" of Philo of Byblos: A Commentary.* Études préliminaires aux religions orientales dans l'empire romain 99. Leiden: Brill.

Beck, Roger. 2004. "Whose Astrology? The Imprint of Ti. Claudius Balbillus on the Mithraic Mysteries." In *Beck on Mithraism: Collected Work with New Essays*, 323–29. Aldershot: Ashgate.

———. 2007. *A Brief History of Ancient Astrology.* Malden, Mass.: Blackwell.

Behr, Charles A. 1968. *Aelius Aristides and the Sacred Tales.* Amsterdam: Hakkert.

———. 1981–86. *P. Aelius Aristides: The Complete Works.* 2 vols. Leiden: Brill.

Benoit, André. 1960. *Saint Irénée: Introduction à l'étude de sa théologie.* Paris: Presses universitaires de France.

Bertrand-Dagenbach, Cécile. 1990. *Alexandre Sévère et l'"Histoire Auguste."* Collection Latomus 208. Brussels: Latomus.

Berzon, Todd S. 2016. *Classifying Christians: Ethnography, Heresiology, and the Limits of Knowledge in Late Antiquity.* Berkeley: University of California Press.

Birley, Anthony R. 1999. *Septimius Severus: The African Emperor.* Rev. ed. London: Routledge.

———. 2006. "Voluntary Martyrs in the Early Church: Heroes or Heretics?" *Cristianesimo nella storia* 27:99–127.

Blakely, Sandra. 2016. "Alexander Polyhistor." In *BNJ*, 273.

Blois, Lukas, de. 1976. *The Policy of the Emperor Gallienus.* Leiden: Brill.

———. 2001. "Roman Jurists and the Crisis of the Third Century A.D. in the Roman Empire." In *Administration, Prosopography, and Appointment Policies in the Roman Empire*, edited by Lukas De Blois, 136–53. Amsterdam: J. C. Gieben.

———. 2003. "Ulpian's Death." In *Hommages à Carl Deroux III: Histoire et épigraphie, droit*, edited by Pol Defosse, 135–45. Collection Latomus 270. Brussels: Éditions Latomus.

Bobichon, Philippe. 2003. *Justin Martyr: Dialogue avec Tryphon.* 2 vols. Paradosis 47.1–2. Fribourg: Academic Press Fribourg.

———. 2005. "Justin Martyr: Étude stylistique du *Dialogue avec Tryphon* suivie d'une comparaison avec l'*Apologie* et le *De resurrectione*." *Recherches Augustiniennes et Patristiques* 34:1–61.

Borg, Barbara E., ed. 2004. *Paideia: The World of the Second Sophistic.* Berlin: Walter de Gruyter.

Bosman, Philip R., ed. 2019. *Intellectual and Empire in Greco-Roman Antiquity.* London: Routledge.

Boudon-Millot, Véronique. 2012. *Galien de Pergame: Un médecin grec à Rome.* Paris: Les Belles Lettres.

———. 2016. "Aelius Aristide et Galien: Regards croisés de l'orateur et du médecin sur la maladie." In *Aelius Aristide écrivain*, edited by Laurent Pernot, Giancarlo Abbamonte, and Mario Lamagna, 393–413. Recherches sur les rhétoriques religieuses 19. Turnhout: Brepols.

Bouffartigue, Jean. 2008. "L'automédication des animaux chez les auteurs antiques." In *Le médecin initié par l'animal: Animaux et médecine dans l'antiquité grecque et latine; Actes du colloque international tenu à la Maison de l'Orient et de la Méditerranée-Jean Pouilloux, les 26 et 27 octobre 2006*, 79–96. Lyons: Maison de l'Orient et de la Méditerranée Jean Pouilloux.

Bowersock, G. W. 1965. *Augustus and the Greek World.* Oxford: Clarendon Press.

———. 1969. *Greek Sophists in the Roman Empire*. Oxford: Clarendon Press.

———. 1979. "Historical Problems in Late Republican and Augustan Classicism." In *Le classicisme à Rome aux I^ers siècles avant et après J.-C.: Neuf exposés suivis de discussions*, 57–78. Entretiens sur l'antiquité classique 25. Geneva: Fondation Hardt.

———. 1982a. "Plutarch and the Sublime Hymn of Ofellius Laetus." *GRBS* 23:275–79.

———. 1982b. "Roman Senators from the Near East: Syria, Judaea, Arabia, Mesopotamia." *Tituli* 5:651–68.

———. 1995. "The Barbarism of the Greeks." *Harvard Studies in Classical Philology* 97:3–14 (= "Les Grecs 'barbarisés.'" *Ktema* 17 (1992): 249–57).

Bowie, Ewen. 1978. "Apollonius of Tyana: Tradition and Reality." *ANRW* 16.2:1652–99.

———. 1982. "The Importance of Sophists." *Yale Classical Studies* 27:29–59.

———. 2004. "The Geography of the Second Sophistic: Cultural Variations." In Borg 2004, 65–83.

———. 2006. "Portrait of the Sophist as a Young Man." In McCing and Mossman 2006, 141–53.

———. 2011. "Men from Mytilene." In Schmitz and Wiater 2011, 181–96.

———. 2013. "Libraries for the Caesars." In König, Oikonomopoulou, and Woolf 2013, 237–60.

Boys-Stones, G. R. 2001. *Post-Hellenistic Philosophy: A Study of Its Development from the Stoics to Origen*. Oxford: Oxford University Press.

———. 2003. "The Stoics' Two Types of Allegory." In *Metaphor, Allegory, and the Classical Tradition: Ancient Thought and Modern Revisions*, edited by G. R. Boys-Stones, 189–216. Oxford: Oxford University Press.

Branham, R. Bracht. 1989. *Unruly Eloquence: Lucian and the Comedy of Traditions*. Cambridge, Mass.: Harvard University Press.

Braswell, Bruce Karl. 2013. *Didymus of Alexandria: Commentary on Pindar*. Schweizerische Beiträge zur Altertumswissenschaft 41. Basil: Schwabe.

Braund, David. 2000. "Learning, Luxury, and Empire: Athenaeus' Roman Patron." In *Athenaeus and His World: Reading Greek Culture in the Roman Empire*, edited by David Braund and John Wilkins, 3–22. Exeter: University of Exeter Press.

Braund, David, and John Wilkins, eds. 2000. *Athenaeus and His World: Reading Greek Culture in the Roman Empire*. Exeter: University of Exeter Press.

Bremmer, Jan N. 2007. "Peregrinus' Christian Career." In *Flores Florentino: Dead Sea Scrolls and Other Early Jewish Studies in Honour of Florentino Garcia Martinez*, edited by Anthony Hilhorst, Emile Puech, and Eibert Tigchelaar, 729–47. Leiden: Brill.

Brenk, Frederick E. 1986. "In the Light of the Moon: Demonology in the Early Imperial Period." *ANRW* 16.3:2068–145.

Brent, Allen. 2006. *Ignatius of Antioch and the Second Sophistic: A Study of an Early Christian Transformation of Pagan Culture*. Studien und Texte zu Antike und Christentum 36. Tübingen: Mohr Siebeck.

Breucker, Geert de. 2010. "Berossos of Babylon." In *BNJ*, 680.

———. 2012. "Alexander Polyhistor and the *Babyloniaca* of Berossos." *BICS* 55 (2): 57–68.

Brockmann, Christian. 2016. "God and Two Humans on Matters of Medicine: Asclepius, Galen, and Aelius Aristides." In *In Praise of Asclepius: Aelius Aristides, Selected Prose Hymns*, edited by Donald A. Russell, Michael Trapp, and Heinz-Günther Nesselrath, 115–27. SAPERE 29. Tübingen: Mohr Siebeck.

Brown, Peter. 1992. *Power and Persuasion in Late Antiquity: Towards a Christian Empire*. Madison: University of Wisconsin Press.

Bru, Hadrien, and Alister Filippini. 2016. "La lettera di Adriano ad Alicarnasso e la cultura storico-antiquaria in età adrianea: Riflessioni sull'iscrizione AE 2012, 1550." *Mediterraneo antico* 19 (1–2): 293–342.

Brunt, P. A. 1979. "Marcus Aurelius and the Christians." In *Studies in Latin Literature and Roman History*, edited by C. Deroux, 1:483–520. Brussels: Latomus.

Bryen, Ari Z. 2013. *Violence in Roman Egypt: A Study in Legal Interpretation*. Empire and After. Philadelphia: University of Pennsylvania Press.

———. 2014. "Martyrdom, Rhetoric, and the Politics of Procedure." *Classical Antiquity* 33 (2): 243–80.

Buck, P. Lorraine. 2002. "The Pagan Husband in Justin." *JTS* 53:541–46.

———. 2003. "Justin Martyr's *Apologies*: Their Number, Destination, and Form." *JTS* 54 (1): 45–59.

Buraselis, Kostas. 2000. *Kos: Between Hellenism and Rome; Studies on the Political, Institutional, and Social History of Kos from ca. the Middle Second Century B.C. Until Late Antiquity*. Transactions of the American Philosophical Society 90.4. Philadelphia: American Philosophical Society.

———. 2007. Θεία δωρεά: *Das göttlich-kaiserliche Geschenk; Studien zur Politik der Severer und zur "Constitutio Antoniniana."* Translated by Wolfgang Schürmann. Akten der Gesellschaft für griechische und hellenistische Rechtsgeschichte 18. Vienna: Verlag der Österreichischen Akademie der Wissenschaften.

Burgess, R. W., and Michael Kulikowski. 2013. *Mosaics of Time: The Latin Chronicle Traditions from the First Century BC to the Sixth Century AD*. Vol. 1, *A Historical Introduction to the Chronicle Genre from Its Origins to the High Middle Ages*. Turnhout: Brepols.

Burkert, Walter. 1972. *Lore and Science in Ancient Pythagoreanism*. Translated by Edwin L. Minar Jr. Cambridge, Mass.: Harvard University Press.

Burstein, Stanley. 2010. "Thrasyllos of Mendes." In *BNJ*, 622.

Califf, David J. 2003. "Metrodorus of Lampsacus and the Problem of Allegory: An Extreme Case?" *Arethusa* 36 (1): 21–36.

Cameron, Alan. 2011. *The Last Pagans of Rome*. Oxford: Oxford University Press.

Canfora, Luciano. 1992. "Clemente di Alessandria e Diogene Laerzio." In *Storia, poesia e pensiero nel mondo antico: Studi in onore di Marcello Gigante*, 79–81. Naples: Bibliopolis.

Capponi, Livia. 2017. *Il ritorno della fenica: Intellettuali e potere nell'Egitto romano.* Studi e testi di storia antica 23. Pisa: Edizioni ETS.

———. 2019. "A Disillusioned Intellectual: Timagenes of Alexandria." In *Intellectual and Empire in Greco-Roman Antiquity*, edited by Philip Bosman, 43–62. London: Routledge.

Cartledge, Paul, and Anthony Spawforth. 2002. *Hellenistic and Roman Sparta: A Tale of Two Cities*. 2nd ed. London: Routledge.

Castagno, Adele Monaci. 1987. *Origene predicatore e il suo pubblico*. Milan: F. Angeli.

———. 2003. "Origene e Ambrogio: L'indipendenza dell'intellettuale e le pretese del patronato." In *Origeniana Octava: Origen and the Alexandrian Tradition; Papers of the 8th International Origen Congress, Pisa, 27–31 August 2001*, edited by Lorenzo Perrone, 1:165–93. Bibliotheca Ephemeridum Theologicarum Lovaniensium 164. Leuven: Leuven University Press.

Cerrato, J. A. 2002. *Hippolytus Between East and West: The Commentaries and the Provenance of the Corpus*. Oxford: Oxford University Press.

Chabot, J. B. 1899–1924. *Chronique de Michel le Syrien, Patriarche Jacobite d'Antioche (1166–1199)*. 5 vols. Paris: Ernest Leroux.

Chaniotis, Angelos. 2004. "Epigraphic Evidence for the Philosopher Alexander of Aphrodisias." *BICS* 47:79–81.

Christesen, Paul. 2007. *Olympic Victor Lists and Ancient Greek History*. Cambridge: Cambridge University Press.

Cichorius, Conrad. 1888. *Rom und Mytilene*. Leipzig: Teubner.

———. 1922. *Römische Studien*. Leipzig: Teubner.

Clarke, Katherine. 1999. *Between Geography and History: Hellenistic Constructions of the Roman World*. Oxford Classical Monographs. Oxford: Clarendon Press.

Clinton, Kevin. 1974. *The Sacred Officials of the Eleusinian Mysteries*. Transactions of the American Philosophical Society 64.3. Philadelphia: American Philosophical Society.

———. 2004. "A Family of Eumolpidai and Kerykes Descended from Pericles." *Hesperia* 73 (1): 39–57.

Cooper, John M. 1999. "Greek Philosophers on Euthanasia and Suicide." In *Reason and Emotion: Essays on Ancient Moral Psychology and Ethical Theory*, 515–41. Princeton: Princeton University Press.

Coriat, Jean-Pierre. 2007. "Les préfets du prétoire de l'époque sévérienne: Un essai de synthèse." *Cahiers Glotz* 18:179–98.

Corke-Webster, James. 2019. *Eusebius and Empire: Constructing Church and Rome in the "Ecclesiastical History."* Cambridge: Cambridge University Press.

Cornell, Tim. 2010. "Universal History and the Early Roman Historians." In *Historiae mundi: Studies in Universal History*, edited by Peter Liddel and Andrew Fear, 102–15. London: Duckworth.

Cosentino, Augusto. 2018. "The Authorship of the *Refutatio omnium haeresium*." *ZAC* 22 (2): 218–37.

Cotton, Hannah M., and Werner Eck. 2005. "Josephus' Roman Audience: Josephus and the Roman Elites." In Edmondson, Mason, and Rives 2005, 37–52.

Countryman, L. William. 1979. "The Intellectual Role of the Early Catholic Episcopate." *Church History* 48 (3): 261–68.

Crawford, Matthew R. 2013. "Diatessaron, a Misnomer? The Evidence from Ephrem's Commentary." *Early Christianity* 4:362–85.

———. 2015. "'Reordering the Confusion': Tatian, the Second Sophistic, and the So-Called *Diatessaron*." *ZAC* 19 (2): 209–36.

———. 2016. "The *Problemata* of Tatian: Recovering the Fragments of a Second-Century Christian Intellectual." *JTS* 67 (2): 542–75.

———. Forthcoming. "'The Hostile Devices of the Demented Demons': Tatian on Astrology and Pharmacology." *JECS*.

Crosignani, Chiara. 2017. "The Influence of Demons on the Human Mind According to Athenagoras and Tatian." In *Demons and Illness from Antiquity to the Early-Modern Period*, edited by Siam Bhayro and Catherine Rider, 175–91.

Magical and Religious Literature of Late Antiquity 5. Leiden: Brill.

Crouzel, Henri. 1969. *Grégoire le Thaumaturge: Remerciement à Origène, suivi de la lettre d'Origène à Grégoire*. SC 148. Paris: Les Éditions du Cerf.

Curty, Olivier. 1995. *Les parentés légendaires entre cités grecques: Catalogue raisonné des inscriptions contenant le terme syngeneia et analyse critique*. Geneva: Libr. Droz.

Delia, Diane. 1991. *Alexandrian Citizenship During the Principate*. Atlanta: Scholars Press.

Denzey, Nicola. 2010. "'Facing the Beast': Justin Martyr, Seneca, and the Emotional Life of the Martyr." In *Stoicism and Early Christianity*, edited by Ismo Dunderberg and Tuomas Rasimus, 176–98. Peabody, Mass.: Hendrickson.

Desmond, William. 2008. *Cynics*. Ancient Philosophies. Berkeley: University of California Press.

DeVore, David J. 2019. "Opening the Canon of Martyr Narratives: Pre-Decian Martyrdom Discourse and the *Hypomnēmata* of Hegesippus." *JECS* 27 (4): 579–609.

———. Forthcoming. *Eusebius of Caesarea and Classical Culture: Philosophy, Empire, and the Formation of Christian Identity*. GCRW. Cambridge: Cambridge University Press.

Dickey, Eleanor. 2014. "New Legal Texts from the *Hermeneumata Pseudodositheana*." *Tijdschrift voor Rechtsgeschiedenis* 82:30–44.

Digeser, Elizabeth DePalma. 2012. *A Threat to Public Piety: Christians, Platonists, and the Great Persecution*. Ithaca: Cornell University Press.

Dihle, Albrecht. 1977. "Der Beginn des Attizismus." *Antike und Abendland* 23:162–77.

———. 2011. "Greek Classicism." In Schmitz and Wiater 2011, 47–60.

Dillery, John. 2003. "Putting Him Back Together Again: Apion Historian, Apion *Grammatikos*." *CP* 98 (4): 383–90.

———. 2015. *Clio's Other Sons: Berossus and Manetho*. Ann Arbor: University of Michigan Press.

Dillon, John. 1996. *The Middle Platonists*, 80 B.C. *to A.D. 220*. Rev. ed. Ithaca: Cornell University Press.

Dix, T. Keith, and George W. Houston. 2006. "Public Libraries in the City of Rome: From the Augustan Age to the Time of Diocletian." *Mélanges de l'École française de Rome: Antiquité* 118 (2): 671–717.

Döring, Klaus. 1979. *Exemplum Socratis: Studien zur Sokratesnachwirkung in der kynisch-stoischen Popularphilosophie der frühen Kaiserzeit und im frühen Christentum*. Hermes Einzelschriften 42. Wiesbaden: Franz Steiner Verlag.

Dowden, Ken. 2013. "Poseidonios." In *BNJ*, 87.

Downing, F. Gerald. 1998. *Cynics, Paul, and the Pauline Churches: Cynics and Christian Origins II*. London: Routledge.

Drijvers, H. J. W. 1966. *Bardaiṣan of Edessa*. Studia Semitica Neerlandica 6. Assen: Van Gorcum.

Droge, Arthur J. 1989. *Homer or Moses? Early Christian Interpretations of the History of Culture*. Hermeneutische Untersuchungen zur Theologie 26. Tübingen: J. C. B. Mohr.

Dubuisson, Michel. 1982. "Remarques sur le vocabulaire grec de l'acculturation." *Revue belge de philologie et d'histoire* 60:5–32.

Dudley, Donald R. 1998. *A History of Cynicism: From Diogenes to the 6th Century AD*. Foreword and bibliography by Miriam Griffin. 2nd ed. (1st ed., 1937). London: Bristol Classical Press.

Dufault, Olivier. 2019. *Early Greek Alchemy, Patronage, and Innovation in Late Antiquity*. California Classical Studies 7. Berkeley: California Classical Studies.

Duffy, J. M. 1992. *Michael Psellus: Philosophica minora*. Vol. 1. Stuttgart: Teubner.

Dulk, Matthijs den. 2018a. *Between Jews and Heretics: Refiguring Justin Martyr's "Dialogue with Trypho."* Routledge Studies in the Early Christian World. London: Routledge.

———. 2018b. "Justin Martyr and the Authorship of the Earliest Anti-Heretical Treatise." *Vigiliae Christianae* 72:471–83.

Duncan-Jones, Richard. 2016. *Power and Privilege in Roman Society*. Cambridge: Cambridge University Press.

Dunderberg, Ismo. 2008. *Beyond Gnosticism: Myth, Lifestyle, and Society in the School of Valentinus*. New York: Columbia University Press.

———. 2013. "Early Christian Critics of Martyrdom." In *The Rise and Expansion of Christianity in the First Three Centuries of the Common Era*, edited by Clare K. Rothschild and Jens Schröter, 419–40. WUNT 301. Tübingen: Mohr Siebeck.

Dupont, Florence, and Emmanuelle Valette-Cagnac. 2005. *Façons de parler grec à Rome*. Paris: Belin.

Eck, Werner. 2014. "Sergius Paullus, der Liebhaber der Philosophie in Lucians *Peregrinus Proteus*." *Rheinisches Museum* 137:221–24.

Eck, Werner, and Andreas Pangerl. 2014. "Eine Konstitution des Antoninus Pius für die Auxilien in Syrien aus dem Jahr 144." *ZPE* 188:255–60.

Edelstein, L., and I. G. Kidd. 1989. *Posidonius I: The Fragments*. 2nd ed. Cambridge: Cambridge University Press.

Edmondson, Jonathan. 2005. "Introduction: Flavius Josephus and Flavian Rome." In Edmondson, Mason, and Rives 2005, 1–33.

Edmondson, Jonathan, Steve Mason, and James Rives, eds. 2005. *Flavius Josephus and Flavian Rome*. Oxford: Oxford University Press.

Edwards, Mark J. 1989. "Satire and Verisimilitude: Christianity in Lucian's *Peregrinus*." *Historia* 38 (1): 89–98.

———. 1991. "On the Platonic Schooling of Justin Martyr." *JTS* 42 (1): 17–34.

———. 2000. *Neoplatonic Saints: The Lives of Plotinus and Proclus by Their Students*. Liverpool: Liverpool University Press.

Elze, Martin. 1960. *Tatian und seine Theologie*. Göttingen: Vandenhoeck & Ruprecht.

Engberg, Jakob, et al. 2014. "The Other Side of the Debate 2: Translation of Second Century Pagan Authors on Christians and Christianity." In *In Defence of Christianity: Early Christian Apologists*, edited by Jakob Engberg, Anders-Christian Jacobsen, and Jörg Ulrich, 229–35. Early Christianity in the Context of Antiquity 15. New York: Peter Lang.

Erbse, Hartmut. 1950. *Untersuchungen zu den attizistischen Lexika*. Abhandlungen der Deutschen Akademie der

Wissenschaften zu Berlin, Philosophisch-historische Klasse 2. Berlin: Akademie-Verlag.

Eshleman, Kendra. 2011. "Becoming Heretical: Affection and Ideology in Recruitment to Early Christianity." *HTR* 104 (2): 191–216.

———. 2012. *The Social World of Intellectuals in the Roman Empire: Sophists, Philosophers, and Christians*. GCRW. Cambridge: Cambridge University Press.

Fazzo, Silvia. 2008. "Nicolas, l'auteur du *Sommaire de la philosophie d'Aristote*: Doutes sur son identité, sa datation, son origine." *REG* 121:99–126.

Fédou, Michel. 1998. "La figure de Socrate selon Justin." In *Les apologistes chrétiens et la culture grecque*, edited by Bernard Pouderon and Joseph Doré, 51–66. Paris: Beauchesne.

Feke, Jacqueline. 2018. *Ptolemy's Philosophy: Mathematics as a Way of Life*. Princeton: Princeton University Press.

Ferguson, Everett. 2009. *Baptism in the Early Church: History, Theology, and Liturgy in the First Five Centuries*. Grand Rapids, Mich.: William B. Eerdmans.

Ferngren, Gary B. 2009. *Medicine and Health Care in Early Christianity*. Baltimore: Johns Hopkins University Press.

Ferrary, Jean-Louis. 1988. *Philhellénisme et impérialisme: Aspects idéologiques de la conquête romaine du monde hellénistique, de la seconde guerre de Macédoine à la guerre contre Mithridate*. Rome: École Française de Rome.

Ferreiro, Albert. 2005. *Simon Magus in Patristic, Medieval, and Early Modern Traditions*. Studies in the History of Christian Traditions 125. Leiden: Brill.

Festugière, R. P. 1986. *La révélation d'Hermès Trismégiste*. 2nd ed. 3 vols. Paris: Les Belles Lettres.

Fields, Dana. 2013. "The Reflection of Satire: Lucian and Peregrinus." *Transactions and Proceedings of the American Philological Association* 143 (1): 213–45.

Fischer, Eitel. 1974. *Die Ekloge des Phrynichos*. Sammlung griechischer und lateinischer Grammatiker 1. Berlin: Walter de Gruyter.

Flemming, Rebecca. 2017. "Galen and the Christians: Texts and Authority in the Second Century AD." In *Christianity in the Second Century: Themes and Developments*, edited by James Carleton Paget and Judith Lieu, 171–88. Cambridge: Cambridge University Press.

Flinterman, Jaap-Jan. 1995. *Power, Paideia, and Pythagoreanism: Greek Identity, Conceptions of the Relationship Between Philosophers and Monarchs, and Political Ideas in Philostratus' "Life of Apollonius."* Dutch Monographs on Ancient History and Archaeology 13. Amsterdam: J. C. Gieben.

———. 2004. "Sophists and Emperors: A Reconnaissance of Sophistic Attitudes." In Borg 2004, 359–76.

Floridi, Luciano. 2002. *Sextus Empiricus: The Transmission and Recovery of Pyrrhonism*. American Philological Association, American Classical Studies 46. Oxford: Oxford University Press.

Fojtik, John Eugene. 2009. "Tatian the Barbarian: Language, Education, and Identity in the *Oratio ad Graecos*." In *Continuity and Discontinuity in Early Christian Apologetics*, edited by Jörg Ulrich, Anders-Christian Jacobsen, and Maijastina Kahlos, 23–34. Early Christianity in the Context of Antiquity 5. Frankfurt: Peter Lang.

Foster, Paul. 2007. "The *Apology* of Quadratus." In *The Writings of the Apostolic Fathers*, edited by Paul Foster, 52–62. London: T & T Clark.

Fowden, Garth. 1993. *The Egyptian Hermes: A Historical Approach to the Late Pagan Mind*. Princeton: Princeton University Press.

Fromentin, Valérie. 2002. *Denys d'Halicarnasse: Antiquités romaines*. Vol. 1. Paris: Les Belles Lettres.

Fürst, Alfons. 2007. *Christentum als Intellektuellen-Religion: Die Anfänge des Christentums in Alexandria*. Stuttgarter Bibelstudien 213. Stuttgart: Verlag Katholisches Bibelwerk.

Gaca, Kathy L. 2003. *The Making of Fornication: Eros, Ethics, and Political Reform in Greek Philosophy and Early Christianity*. Hellenistic Culture and Society 39. Berkeley: University of California Press.

Gambetti, Sandra. 2015. "Ptolemy of Mendes." In *BNJ*, 611.

Garland, Robert. 2006. *Celebrity in Antiquity: From Media Tarts to Tabloid Queens*.

Classical Interfaces. London: Duckworth.

Gemeinhardt, Peter. 2016. "Tatian und die antike Paideia: Ein Wanderer zwischen zwei (Bildungs-)Welten." In Nesselrath 2016, 247–66.

Gemoll, W. 1884. *Nepualii fragmentum* Περὶ τῶν κατὰ ἀντιπάθειαν καὶ συμπάθειαν *et Democriti* Περὶ συμπαθειῶν καὶ ἀντιπαθειῶν. Städtisches Realprogymnasium zu Striegau. Striegau: Druck von Ph. Tschörner.

Georgia, Allan. 2018. "The Monster at the End of His Book: Monstrosity as Theological Strategy and Cultural Critique in Tatian's *Against the Greeks*." *JECS* 26 (2): 191–219.

Gigante, Marcello. 1972. "Chi è Diogene Laerzio?" *Cultura e scuola* 44:38–49.

Gilhus, Ingvild Sælid. 2006. *Animals, Gods and Humans: Changing Attitudes to Animals in Greek, Roman and Early Christian Ideas*. London: Routledge.

Gill, Christopher. 2013. *Marcus Aurelius: Meditations Books 1–6*. Clarendon Later Ancient Philosophers. Oxford: Oxford University Press.

Girgenti, Giuseppe. 1990. "Giustino Martire, il primo platonico cristiano." *Rivista di filosofia neo-scolastica* 82.2–3:214–55.

Gitner, Adam. 2015. "Varro *Aeolicus*: Latin's Affiliation with Greek." In *Varro Varius: The Polymath of the Roman World*, edited by D. J. Butterfield, 33–50. Cambridge Classical Journal Supplement 39. Cambridge: Cambridge Philological Society.

Glare, P. G. W. 2010. *Oxford Latin Dictionary*. Oxford: Clarendon Press.

Gleason, Maud. 1995. *Making Men: Sophists and Self-Presentation in Ancient Rome*. Princeton: Princeton University Press.

———. 2009. "Shock and Awe: The Performance Dimension of Galen's Anatomy Demonstrations." In *Galen and the World of Knowledge*, edited by Christopher Gill, Tim Whitmarsh, and John Wilkins, 85–114. GCRW. Cambridge: Cambridge University Press.

Goeken, Johann. 2012. *Aelius Aristide et la rhétorique de l'hymne en prose*. Recherches sur les rhétoriques religieuses 15. Turnhout: Brepols.

Goldhill, Simon. 2002. *Who Needs Greek? Contests in the Cultural History of Hellenism*. Cambridge: Cambridge University Press.

Gordon, Pamela. 1993. "On *Black Athena*: Ancient Critiques of the 'Ancient Model' of Greek History." *CW* 87 (1): 71–72.

Goukowsky, Paul. 2004. "Diodore de Sicile, Pompéien repenti?" *Comptes rendus de l'Académie des inscriptions et belles-lettres* 2:599–622.

Goulet-Cazé, Marie-Odile. 1990. "Le cynisme à l'époque impériale." *ANRW* 36.4:2720–833.

———. 2014. *Cynisme et christianisme dans l'antiquité*. Textes et traditions 26. Paris: Vrin.

Graf, David F. 2014. "Theodorus of Gadara." In *BNJ*, 850.

Grafton, Anthony, and Megan Williams. 2006. *Christianity and the Transformation of the Book: Origen, Eusebius, and the Library of Caesarea*. Cambridge, Mass.: Harvard University Press.

Granger, Frank. 1934. "Julius Africanus and the Western Text." *JTS* 35:361–68.

Grant, Robert M. 1954. "The Heresy of Tatian." *JTS* 5 (1): 62–68.

———. 1983. "Paul, Galen, and Origen." *JTS* 34 (2): 533–36.

———. 1985. "A Woman of Rome: The Matron in Justin, 2 Apology 2.1–9." *Church History* 54 (4): 461–72.

———. 1988. *Greek Apologists of the Second Century*. Philadelphia: Westminster Press.

———. 1999. *Early Christians and Animals*. London: Routledge.

Green, Bernard. 2010. *Christianity in Ancient Rome: The First Three Centuries*. London: T & T Clark.

Greenbaum, Dorian Gieseler. 2016. *The Daimon in Hellenistic Astrology: Origins and Influence*. Ancient Magic and Divination 11. Leiden: Brill.

Griffin, M. T. 1982. "The Lyons Tablet and Tacitean Hindsight." *CQ* 32:404–18.

Grmek, M. D., and D. Gourevitch. 1994. "Aux sources de la doctrine médicale de Galien: L'enseignement de Marinus, Quintus et Numisianus." *ANRW* 37.2:1491–1528.

Gruen, Erich. 2013. "Did Ancient Identity Depend on Ethnicity? A Preliminary Probe." *Phoenix* 67:1–22.

Guignard, Christophe. 2011. *La lettre de Julius Africanus à Aristide sur la généalogie du Christ: Analyse de la traduction textuelle, édition, traduction et étude critique.* Texte und Untersuchungen zur Geschichte der altchristlichen Literatur 167. Berlin: De Gruyter.

Habicht, Christian. 1994. "Hellenistic Athens and Her Philosophers." In *Athen in hellenistischer Zeit: Gesammelte Aufsätze*, 231–47. Munich: C. H. Beck.

Hadas, Moses. 1931. "Gadarenes in Pagan Literature." *Classical Weekly* 25 (4): 25–30.

Halfmann, Helmut. 1979. *Die Senatoren aus dem östlichen Teil des Imperium Romanum bis zum Ende des 2. Jahrhunderts n. Chr.* Hypomnemata 58. Göttingen: Vandenhoeck & Ruprecht.

Hall, Jennifer. 1981. *Lucian's Satire.* New York: Arno Press.

Hall, Jonathan M. 2002. *Hellenicity: Between Ethnicity and Culture.* Chicago: University of Chicago Press.

Hall, Linda Jones. 2004. *Roman Berytus: Beirut in Late Antiquity.* London: Routledge.

Hamman, Adalbert G. 1995. "Essai de chronologie de la vie et des oeuvres de Justin." *Augustinianum* 35:231–39.

Hammerstaedt, Jürgen. 2009. "Julius Africanus und seine Tätigkeiten im 18. Kestos (P. Oxy. 412 col. II)." In Wallraff and Mecella 2009, 53–69.

Hankinson, R. J. 2008a. *The Cambridge Companion to Galen.* Cambridge: Cambridge University Press.

———. 2008b. "The Man and His Work." In Hankinson 2008a, 1–33.

Harker, Andrew. 2008. *Loyalty and Dissidence in Roman Egypt: The Case of the "Acta Alexandrinorum."* Cambridge: Cambridge University Press.

Harl, Marguerite, and Nicholas de Lange. 1983. *Origène: Sur les Écritures: Philocalie, 1–20; La lettre à Africanus sur l'histoire de Suzanne.* SC 302. Paris: Les Éditions du Cerf.

Harnack, Adolf von. 1921. "Julius Afrikanus, der Bibliothekar des Kaisers Alexander Severus." In *Aufsätze Fritz Milkau gewidmet*, edited by Georg Leyh, 142–46. Leipzig: K. W. Hiersemann.

Harris, Rendel. 1924. "Tatian: Perfection According to the Saviour." *Bulletin of the John Ryland Library* 8:15–51.

Harris, William V., and Brooke Holmes. 2008. *Aelius Aristides Between Greece, Rome, and the Gods.* Leiden: Brill.

Harris-McCoy, Daniel. 2013. "Artemidorus' *Oneirocritica* as Fragmentary Encyclopedia." In *Encyclopaedism from Antiquity to the Renaissance*, edited by Jason König and Greg Wolf, 154–77. Cambridge: Cambridge University Press.

Haupt, Moriz. 1875–76. *Opuscula.* 3 vols. Leipzig.

Hayes, Andrew. 2017. *Justin Against Marcion: Defining the Christian Philosophy.* Minneapolis: Fortress Press.

Heath, Malcolm. 1998. "Was Homer a Roman?" *Papers of the International Leeds Latin Seminar* 10:23–56.

———. 2003. "Theon and the History of the Progymnasmata." *GRBS* 43:129–60.

———. 2004. *Menander: A Rhetor in Context.* Oxford: Oxford University Press.

Hegedus, Tim. 2007. *Early Christianity and Ancient Astrology.* Patristic Studies 6. New York: Peter Lang.

Heilen, Stephan. 2010. "Ptolemy's Doctrine of the Terms and Its Reception." In *Ptolemy in Perspective: Use and Criticism of His Work from Antiquity to the Nineteenth Century*, edited by Alexander Jones, 45–93. Heidelberg: Springer.

———. 2011. "Some Metrical Fragments from Nechepsos and Petosiris." In *La poésie astrologique dans l'Antiquité*, edited by Isabelle Boehm and Wolfgang Hübner, 23–93. Paris: De Boccard.

Heiler, Carl Ludwig. 1909. *De Tatiani Apologetae dicendi genere.* Marburg: Koch.

Heine, Ronald E. 2010. *Origen: Scholarship in the Service of the Church.* Christian Theology in Context. Oxford: Oxford University Press.

Heller, Anna. 2011. "D'un Polybe à l'autre: Statuaire honorifique et mémoire des ancêtres dans le monde grec d'époque impériale." *Chiron* 41:287–312.

Hemelrijk, Emily A. 1999. *Matrona Docta: Educated Women in the Roman Elite from Cornelia to Julia Domna.* London: Routledge.

Herren, Michael. 2017. *The Anatomy of Myth: The Art of Interpretation from the Presocratics to the Church Fathers.* Oxford: Oxford University Press.

Heyne, Thomas. 2011. "Tertullian and Medicine." *SP* 50:131–74.

Hidber, Thomas. 2011. "Impacts of Writing in Rome: Greek Authors and Their Roman Environment in the First Century BCE." In Schmitz and Wiater 2011, 115–23.

Hintzen, Beate. 2011. "Latin, Attic, and Other Greek Dialects: Criteria of ἑλληνισμός in Grammatical Treatises of the First Century BCE." In Schmitz and Wiater 2011, 125–41.

Hogg, Daniel. 2013. "Libraries in a Greek Working Life: Dionysius of Halicarnassus, a Case Study in Rome." In König, Oikonomopoulou, and Woolf 2013, 137–51.

Hollander, William den. 2014. *Josephus, the Emperors, and the City of Rome: From Hostage to Historian.* Ancient Judaism and Early Christianity 86. Leiden: Brill.

Holliday, Lisa. 2011. "From Alexandria to Caesarea: Reassessing Origen's Appointment to the Presbyterate." *Numen* 58:674–96.

Honoré, Tony. 1994. *Emperors and Lawyers.* 2nd ed. Oxford: Clarendon Press.

———. 2002. *Ulpian: Pioneer of Human Rights.* 2nd ed. Oxford: Oxford University Press.

Hooff, Anton J. L. van. 1990. *From Autothanasia to Suicide: Self-Killing in Classical Antiquity.* London: Routledge.

Hope, Richard. 1930. *The Book of Diogenes Laertius: Its Spirit and Method.* New York: Columbia University Press.

Hopkins, Keith. 2018. "Christian Number and Its Implications." In *Sociological Studies in Roman History*, edited by Christopher Kelly, 432–80. Cambridge: Cambridge University Press (= *JECS* 6 [1998]: 185–226).

Horrocks, Geoffrey C. 2010. *Greek: A History of the Language and Its Speakers.* 2nd ed. Chichester: Wiley-Blackwell.

Horst, Pieter Willem van der. 1987. *Chaeremon: Egyptian Priest and Stoic Philosopher.* 2nd ed. Leiden: Brill.

House, D. K. 1980. "The Life of Sextus Empiricus." *CQ* 30 (1): 227–38.

Hunt, Emily J. 2003. *Christianity in the Second Century: The Case of Tatian.* London: Routledge.

Hunter, Richard. 2012. *Plato and the Traditions of Ancient Literature: The Silent Stream.* Cambridge: Cambridge University Press.

Hyldahl, Niels. 1966. *Philosophie und Christentum: Eine Interpretation der Einleitung zum Dialog Justins.* Acta theologica Danica 9. Aarhus: Aarhus universitet.

Icks, Martijn. 2012. *The Crimes of Elagabalus: The Life and Legacy of Rome's Decadent Boy Emperor.* Cambridge, Mass.: Harvard University Press.

Imrie, Alex. 2018. *The Antonine Constitution: An Edict for the Caracallan Empire.* Impact of Empire 29. Leiden: Brill.

Irby-Massie, Georgia L. 2008. "Mētrodōros of Alexandria." In Keyser and Irby-Massie 2008, 554.

Isaac, Benjamin. 2004. *The Invention of Racism in Classical Antiquity.* Princeton: Princeton University Press.

Israelowich, Ido. 2015. *Patients and Healers in the High Roman Empire.* Baltimore: Johns Hopkins University Press.

Jacob, Christian. 2013. "Fragments of a History of Ancient Libraries." In König, Oikonomopoulou, and Woolf 2013, 57–81.

Janiszewski, Pawel, Krystyna Stebnicka, and Elżbieta Szabat. 2015. *Prosopography of Greek Rhetors and Sophists of the Roman Empire.* Oxford: Oxford University Press.

Jażdżewska, Katarzyna. 2019. "Entertainers, Persuaders, Adversaries: Interactions of Sophists and Rulers in Philostratus' *Lives of Sophists*." In *Intellectual and Empire in Greco-Roman Antiquity*, edited by Philip Bosman, 160–77. London: Routledge.

Jefferson, Lee M. 2014. *Christ the Miracle Worker in Early Christian Art.* Minneapolis: Fortress Press.

Jeffery, Lillian H. 1967. "Ἀρχαῖα γράμματα: Some Ancient Greek Views." In *Europa: Studien zur Geschichte und Epigraphik frühen Aegaeis; Festschrift für Ernst Grumach*, edited by William C. Brice, 152–66. Berlin: Walter de Gruyter.

Johnson, Aaron P. 2013. *Religion and Identity in Porphyry of Tyre: The Limits of Hellenism in Late Antiquity*. GCRW. Cambridge: Cambridge University Press.

Jones, Brian W. 1993. *The Emperor Domitian*. London: Routledge.

Jones, C. P. 1972. "Two Enemies of Lucian." *GRBS* 13 (4): 475–87.

———. 1978. *The Roman World of Dio Chrysostom*. Cambridge, Mass.: Harvard University Press.

———. 1986. *Culture and Society in Lucian*. Cambridge, Mass.: Harvard University Press.

———. 1996. "The Panhellenion." *Chiron* 26:29–56.

———. 1999. *Kinship Diplomacy in the Ancient World*. Cambridge, Mass.: Harvard University Press.

———. 2002. "Towards a Chronology of Josephus." *Scripta classica israelica* 21:113–21.

———. 2004. "Multiple Identities in the Age of the Second Sophistic." In Borg 2004, 13–21.

———. 2008. "Aristides' First Admirer." In *Aelius Aristides Between Greece, Rome, and the Gods*, edited by William V. Harris and Brooke Holmes, 251–62. Leiden: Brill.

———. 2012. "Galen's Travels." *Chiron* 42:399–419.

Jouanna, Jacques. 2009. "Médecine et philosophie: Sur la date de Sextus Empiricus et celle de Diogène Laërce à la lumière du *Corpus Galénique*." *REG* 122:359–90.

Kaldellis, Anthony. 2011. "Callinicus of Petra." In *BNJ*, 281.

Kaldellis, Anthony, and Carolina López-Ruiz. 2009. "Philon." In *BNJ*, 790.

Kamesar, Adam. 2009a. "Biblical Interpretation in Philo." In Kamesar 2009b, 65–91.

———. 2009b. *The Cambridge Companion to Philo*. Cambridge: Cambridge University Press.

Kaplan, Michael. 1990. *Greeks and the Imperial Court, from Tiberius to Nero*. New York: Garland.

Karadimas, Dimitrios. 2003. *Tatian's "Oratio ad Graecos": Rhetoric and Philosophy/ Theology*. Scripta minora Regiae Societatis humaniorum litterarum

Lundensis 2000–2001:2. Stockholm: Almquist & Wiksell International.

Karamanolis, George. 2013. *The Philosophy of Early Christianity*. Ancient Philosophies. London: Routledge.

Kaufman, David B. 1932. "Poisons and Poisoning Among the Romans." *CP* 27 (2): 156–67.

Kemezis, Adam M. 2014. *Greek Narratives of the Roman Empire Under the Severans: Cassius Dio, Philostratus, and Herodian*. GCRW. Cambridge: Cambridge University Press.

Kennedy, George A. 2003. *Progymnasmata: Greek Textbooks of Prose Composition and Rhetoric*. SBL Writings from the Greco-Roman World 10. Atlanta: Society of Biblical Literature.

Ker, James, and Christoph Pieper. 2014. "General Introduction: Valuing Antiquity in Antiquity." In *Valuing the Past in the Greco-Roman World: Proceedings from the Penn-Leiden Colloquia on Ancient Values VII*, edited by James Ker and Christoph Pieper, 1–22. *Mnemosyne* Supplements 369. Leiden: Brill.

Keyser, Paul T. 2014. "Chairemon." In *BNJ*, 618.

———. 2015. "Apion of Alexandria." In *BNJ*, 616.

———. 2016. "Mōchos the Phoenician Sage in Ampelius." *Classical Journal* 111 (4): 495–501.

Keyser, Paul T., and Georgia L. Irby-Massie, eds. 2008. *The Encyclopedia of Ancient Natural Scientists: The Greek Tradition and Its Many Heirs*. London: Routledge.

Kim, Lawrence. 2010. "The Literary Heritage as Language: Atticism and the Second Sophistic." In *A Companion to the Ancient Greek Language*, edited by Egbert J. Bakker, 468–82. Chichester: Wiley-Blackwell.

———. 2017. "Atticism and Asianism." In *The Oxford Handbook to the Second Sophistic*, edited by Daniel S. Richter and William A. Johnson, 41–66. Oxford: Oxford University Press.

Kokkinos, Nikos. 2012. "A Note on the Date of Philo of Byblus." *CQ* 62:433–35.

Koltun-Fromm, Naomi. 2008. "Re-imagining Tatian: The Damaging Effects of Polemical Rhetoric." *JECS* 16 (1): 1–30.

Komorowska, Joanna. 2004. *Vettius Valens of Antioch: An Intellectual Monography.* Kraków: Księgarnia Akademicka.

König, Jason. 2005. *Athletics and Literature in the Roman Empire.* GCRW. Cambridge: Cambridge University Press.

———. 2006. "The Cynic and Christian Lives of Lucian's *Peregrinus*." In McCing and Mossman 2006, 227–54.

———. 2009. *Greek Literature in the Roman Empire.* London: Bristol Classical Press.

———. 2011. "Competitiveness and Anti-Competitiveness in Philostratus' *Lives of the Sophists*." In *Competition in the Ancient World*, edited by Nick Fisher and Hans van Wees, 279–300. Swansea: The Classical Press of Wales.

———. 2012. *Saints and Symposiasts: The Literature of Food and the Symposium in Greco-Roman and Early Christian Culture.* GCRW. Cambridge: Cambridge University Press.

König, Jason, Katerina Oikonomopoulou, and Greg Woolf, eds. 2013. *Ancient Libraries.* Cambridge: Cambridge University Press.

König, Jason, and Tim Whitmarsh. 2007a. "Ordering Knowledge." In König and Whitmarsh 2007b, 3–39.

———. 2007b. *Ordering Knowledge in the Roman Empire.* Cambridge: Cambridge University Press.

König, Jason, and Greg Woolf, eds. 2013a. *Encyclopaedism from Antiquity to the Renaissance.* Cambridge: Cambridge University Press.

———. 2013b. "Encyclopaedism in the Roman Empire." In König and Woolf 2013a, 23–61.

———. 2017. *Authority and Expertise in Ancient Scientific Culture.* Cambridge: Cambridge University Press.

Labriolle, Pierre de. 1948. *La réaction païenne: Étude sur la polémique antichrétienne du Ier au Ve siècle.* Paris: L'Artisan du Livre.

Lakmann, Marie-Luise. 2017. *Platonici minores 1.Jh.v.Chr.–2.Jh.n.Chr.: Prosopographie Fragmente und Testimonien mit deutscher Übersetzung.* Philosophia antiqua 145. Leiden: Brill.

Laks, André. 2014. "Diogenes Laertius' *Life of Pythagoras*." In *A History of Pythagoreanism*, edited by Carl A.

Huffman, 360–80. Cambridge: Cambridge University Press.

Lamberton, Robert. 1986. *Homer the Theologian: Neoplatonist Allegorical Reading and the Growth of the Epic Tradition.* The Transformation of the Classical Heritage 9. Berkeley: University of California Press.

Lampe, G. W. H. 1961. *A Patristic Greek Lexicon.* Oxford: Clarendon Press.

Lampe, Peter. 2003. *From Paul to Valentinus: Christians at Rome in the First Two Centuries.* Translated by Michael Steinhauser. Edited by Marshall D. Johnson. Minneapolis: Fortress Press.

Lang, Phillipa. 2016. "Manetho." In *BNJ*, 609.

Lange, N. R. M. de. 1976. *Origen and the Jews: Studies in Jewish-Christian Relations in Third-Century Palestine.* University of Cambridge Oriental Publications 25. Cambridge: Cambridge University Press.

Lans, Birgit van der. 2019. "The Written Media of Imperial Government and a Martyr's Career: Justin Martyr's *1 Apology*." In *Marginality, Media, and Mutations of Religious Authority in the History of Christianity*, edited by Laura Feldt and Jan N. Bremmer, 117–34. Leuven: Peeters.

Lashier, Jackson. 2014. *Irenaeus on the Trinity.* VCSup 127. Leiden: Brill.

Lauwers, Jeroen. 2013. "Systems of Sophistry and Philosophy: The Case of the Second Sophistic." *Harvard Studies in Classical Philology* 107:331–63.

LaValle Norman, Dawn. 2019. *The Aesthetics of Hope in Late Greek Imperial Literature: Methodius of Olympus' "Symposium" and the Crisis of the Third Century.* GCRW. Cambridge: Cambridge University Press.

Le Boulluec, Alain. 1985. *La notion d'hérésie dans la littérature grecque IIe–IIIe siècles.* 2 vols. Paris: Études Augustiniennes.

Lee, John A. L. 2013. "The Atticist Grammarians." In *The Language of the New Testament: Context, History, and Development*, edited by Stanley E. Porter and Andrew Pitts, 283–308. Leiden: Brill.

Leest, J. vander. 1985. "Lucian in Egypt." *GRBS* 26:75–82.

Lenel, Otto. 1889. *Palingenesia iuris civilis*. 2 vols. Leipzig: Ex Officina Bernhardi Tauchnitz.

Levick, Barbara. 1990. *Claudius*. New Haven: Yale University Press.

———. 2007. *Julia Domna: Syrian Empress*. Women of the Ancient World. London: Routledge.

Levieils, Xavier. 2007. *Contra Christianos: La critique sociale et religieuse du christianisme des origines au concile de Nicée (45–325)*. Beihefte zur Zeitschrift für die neutestamentliche Wissenschaft 146. Berlin: Walter de Gruyter.

Lewis, Naphtali. 1965. "Exemption of Physicians from Liturgy." *Bulletin of the American Society of Papyrologists* 2 (3): 87–92.

———. 1981. "Literati in the Service of Roman Emperors: Politics Before Culture." In *Coins, Culture, and History in the Ancient World: Numismatics and Other Studies in Honor of Bluma L. Trell*, edited by Lionel Casson and Martin Price, 149–66. Detroit: Wayne State University Press.

Liebs, D. 1997a. "Aemilius Papinianus." In Sallmann 1997, 117–23.

———. 1997b. "Claudius Saturninus." In Sallmann 1997, 213–14.

———. 1997c. "Herennius Modestinus." In Sallmann 1997, 195–201.

Lloyd, G. E. R. 2008. "Galen and His Contemporaries." In Hankinson 2008a, 34–48.

Long, A. A. 1982. "Astrology: Arguments Pro and Contra." In *Science and Speculation: Studies in Hellenistic Theory and Practice*, edited by Jonathan Barnes et al., 165–92. Cambridge: Cambridge University Press.

———. 2002. *Epictetus: A Stoic and Socratic Guide to Life*. Oxford: Clarendon Press.

López-Ruiz, Carolina. 2009. "Laitos (-Mochos)." In *BNJ*, 784.

———. 2017. "'Not That Which Can Be Found Among the Greeks': Philo of Byblos and Phoenician Cultural Identity in the Roman East." *Religions of the Roman Empire* 3:366–92.

Lössl, Josef. 2016. "Date and Location of Tatian's *Ad Graecos*: Some Old and New Thoughts." *SP* 74:43–55.

Lutz, Cora E. 1947. "Musonius Rufus 'The Roman Socrates.'" *Yale Classical Studies* 10:3–147.

Lyman, Rebecca. 2003. "The Politics of Passing: Justin Martyr's Conversion as a Problem of 'Hellenization.'" In *Conversion in Late Antiquity and the Early Middle Ages: Seeing and Believing*, edited by Kenneth Mills and Anthony Grafton, 36–60. Rochester: University of Rochester Press.

———. 2007. "Justin and Hellenism: Some Postcolonial Perspectives." In Parvis and Foster 2007, 160–68.

MacLeod, M. D. 1979. "Lucian's Activities as a μισαλάζων." *Philologus* 123 (2): 326–29.

Malherbe, Abraham J. 1970. "'Gentle as a Nurse': The Cynic Background to 1 Thessalonians 2." *Novum Testamentum* 12:203–17 (= Malherbe 1989, 35–48).

———. 1981. "Justin and Crescens." In *Christian Teaching: Studies in Honor of LeMoine G. Lewis*. Edited by Everett Ferguson. Abilene: Abilene Christian University, 312–27.

———. 1989. *Paul and the Popular Philosophers*. Minneapolis: Fortress Press.

Mansfeld, Jaap. 1986. "Diogenes Laertius on Stoic Philosophy." *Elenchos* 7:295–382.

———. 1994. *Prolegomena: Questions to Be Settled Before the Study of an Author, or a Text*. Philosophia antiqua 61. Leiden: Brill.

Mansfeld, Jaap, and D. T. Runia. 1997–2018. *Aëtiana: The Method and Intellectual Context of a Doxographer*. 4 vols. Philosophia antiqua 73, 114, 118, 148. Leiden: Brill.

Manthe, Ulrich. 1999. "Assyrius Sermo: Ulp. D.45.1.1.6." In *Mélanges Fritz Sturm: Offerts par ses collègues et ses amis à l'occasion de son soixante-dixième anniversaire*, edited by Jean-François Gerkens, 357–64. Liège: Editions juridiques de l'Université de Liège.

Marchiori, Antonia. 2000. "Between Ichthyophagists and Syrians: Features of Fish-Eating in Athanaeus' *Deipnosophistae* Books Seven and Eight." In *Athenaeus and His World: Reading Greek Culture in the Roman Empire*, edited by David Braund and John Wilkins, 327–38. Exeter: University of Exeter Press.

Marcone, Arnaldo. 2004. "La prosopografia dei giuristi severiani." *Atti della*

Accademia nazionale dei Lincei, Classe di scienze morali, storiche e filologiche, Rendiconti ser. 9a, 15 (4): 735–46.

Marincola, John. 2011. "Romans and/as Barbarians." In *The Barbarians of Ancient Europe: Realities and Interactions*, edited by Larissa Bonfante, 347–57. Cambridge: Cambridge University Press.

Markschies, Christoph. 2006. "Intellectuals and Church Fathers in the Third and Fourth Centuries." In *Christians and Christianity in the Holy Land: From the Origins to the Latin Kingdoms*, edited by Ora Limor and Guy G. Stroumsa, 239–56. Turnhout: Brepols.

Martens, John W. 2016. "The Disability Within: Sexual Desire as Disability in Syriac Christianity." In *Disability in Antiquity*, edited by Christian Laes, 376–87. London: Routledge.

Martin, Dale Basil. 2004. *Inventing Superstition: From the Hippocratics to the Christians*. Cambridge, Mass.: Harvard University Press.

———. 2010. "When Did Angels Become Demons?" *Journal of Biblical Literature* 129 (4): 657–77.

Marx-Wolf, Heidi. 2016. *Spiritual Taxonomies and Ritual Authority: Platonists, Priests, and Gnostics in the Third Century C.E.* Divinations: Rereading Late Ancient Religion. Philadelphia: University of Pennsylvania Press.

Mason, Steve. 2003. *Flavius Josephus: Translation and Commentary*. Vol. 9, *Life of Josephus*. Edited by Steve Mason. Leiden: Brill.

Masson, Olivier. 1995. "La patrie de Diogène Laërce est-elle inconnue?" *Museum Helveticum* 52 (4): 225–30.

Mattern, Susan P. 2013. *The Prince of Medicine: Galen in the Roman Empire*. Oxford: Oxford University Press.

———. 2016. "Galen's Anxious Patients: *Lypē* as Anxiety Disorder." In *Homo Patiens: Approaches to the Patient in the Ancient World*, edited by Georgia Petridou and Chiara Thumiger, 203–23. Studies in Ancient Medicine 45. Leiden: Brill.

Maxwell-Stuart, P. G. 1981. "An Unexplained Syriac Word in Athenaeus." *Glotta* 59 (1): 117.

Mazza, Mario. 1995. "Le religioni dell'Impero Romano: Premesse ad una

considerazione storica della religiosità ellenistico-romana." In *Storia letteratura e arte a Roma nel secondo secolo dopo Cristo: Atti del convegno; Mantova 8–9–10 ottobre 1992*, 109–38. Florence: Olschki.

McCing, Brian, and Judith Mossman. 2006. *The Limits of Ancient Biography*. Swansea: The Classical Press of Wales.

McGehee, Michael. 1993. "Why Tatian Never 'Apologized' to the Greeks." *JECS* 1 (2): 143–58.

McKechnie, Paul. 1999. "Christian Grave-Inscriptions from the *Familia Caesaris*." *Journal of Ecclesiastical History* 50 (3): 427–41.

McLynn, Neil. 2004. "Roman Empire." In *The Westminster Handbook to Origen*, edited by John Anthony McGuckin, 185–87. Louisville: Westminster John Knox Press.

Mendelson, Alan. 1988. *Philo's Jewish Identity*. Brown Judaic Studies 161. Atlanta: Scholars Press.

Mennen, Inge. 2011. *Power and Status in the Roman Empire, AD 193–284*. Impact of Empire 12. Leiden: Brill.

Middleton, Paul. 2013. "Early Christian Voluntary Martyrdom: A Statement for the Defence." *JTS* 64 (2): 556–73.

Millar, Fergus. 1992. *The Emperor in the Roman World*. 2nd ed. London: Duckworth.

———. 1993. *The Roman Near East, 31 B.C.–A.D. 337*. Cambridge, Mass.: Harvard University Press.

———. 1999. "The Greek East and Roman Law: The Dossier of M. Cn. Licinius Rufinus." *JRS* 89:90–108.

———. 2002. "Government and Law: Ulpian, a Philosopher in Politics?" In *Philosophy and Power in the Graeco-Roman World*, edited by Gillian Clark and Tessa Rajak, 69–87. Oxford: Oxford University Press.

———. 2006. "The Roman *Coloniae* of the Near East: A Study of Cultural Relations." In *Rome, the Greek World, and the East*, vol. 3, *The Greek World, the Jews, and the East*, edited by H. M. Cotton and G. M. Rodgers, 164–222. Chapel Hill: University of North Carolina Press.

Miller, James. 2018. *Diogenes Laertius: Lives of the Eminent Philosophers*. Translated by Pamela Mensch. Oxford: Oxford University Press.

Minns, Denis, and Paul Parvis. 2009. *Justin, Philosopher and Martyr: Apologies.* OECT. Oxford: Oxford University Press.

Moles, John. 2006. "Cynic Influence upon First-Century Judaism and Early Christianity." In McCing and Mossman 2006, 89–116.

Montana, Fausto. 2015. "Hellenistic Scholarship." In *Brill's Companion to Ancient Greek Scholarship*, edited by Franco Montanari, Stephanos Matthaios, and Antonios Rengakos, 1:60–183. Leiden: Brill.

Moreschini, Claudio. 1987. "Attico: Una figura singolare del medioplatonismo." *ANRW* 36.1:477–91.

Morgan, Teresa. 1998. *Literate Education in the Hellenistic and Roman Worlds.* Cambridge: Cambridge University Press.

Morison, Ben. 2008. "Language." In Hankinson 2008a, 116–56.

Moss, Candida. 2012. "The Discourse of Voluntary Martyrdom: Ancient and Modern." *Church History* 81 (3): 531–51.

———. 2013. *The Myth of Persecution: How Early Christians Invented a Story of Martyrdom.* New York: HarperOne.

Mosshammer, Alden A. 1979. *The "Chronicle" of Eusebius and Greek Chronographic Tradition.* Lewisburg: Bucknell University Press.

———. 1984. *Georgius Syncellus: Ecloga chronographica.* Leipzig: Teubner.

Mossman, Judith. 2005. "*Taxis ou barbaros*: Greek and Roman in Plutarch's *Pyrrhus*." *CQ* 55 (2): 498–517.

Munier, Charles. 2006. *Justin: Apologie pour les chrétiens.* SC 507. Paris: Les Éditions du Cerf.

Muntz, Charles E. 2017. *Diodorus Siculus and the World of the Late Roman Republic.* Oxford: Oxford University Press.

Musurillo, Herbert A. 1954. *The Acts of the Pagan Martyrs: Acta Alexandrinorum.* Oxford: Clarendon Press.

———. 1961. *Acta Alexandrinorum.* Leipzig: Teubner.

———. 1972. *The Acts of the Christian Martyrs.* Oxford: Clarendon Press.

Mygind, Benedicte. 1999. "Intellectuals in Rhodes." In *Hellenistic Rhodes: Politics, Culture, and Society*, edited by Vincent Gabrielsen, Per Bilde, Troels

Engberg-Pedersen, Lise Hannestad, and Jan Zahle, 247–93. Aarhus: Aarhus University Press.

Nachmanson, Ernst. 1918. *Erotiani vocum Hippocraticum collectio cum fragmentis.* Göteborg: Eranos' Förlag.

Nahm, Charles. 1992. "The Debate on the 'Platonism' of Justin Martyr." *Second Century* 9 (3): 129–51.

Naiden, Fred S. 2008. "Menander." In *BNJ*, 783.

Nasrallah, Laura Salah. 2010. *Christian Responses to Roman Art and Architecture: The Second-Century Church amid the Spaces of Empire.* Cambridge: Cambridge University Press.

Nautin, Pierre. 1961. *Lettres et écrivains chrétiens des IIe et IIIe siècles.* Patristica 2. Paris: Éditions du Cerf.

———. 1977. *Origène: Sa vie et son oeuvre.* Christianisme antique 1. Paris: Beauchesne.

Nautin, Pierre, and Marie-Thérèse Nautin. 1986. *Origène: Homélies sur Samuel.* SC 328. Paris: Les Éditions du Cerf.

Nesselrath, Heinz-Günther. 2016. *Gegen falsche Götter und falsche Bildung: Tatian, Rede an die Griechen.* SAPERE. Tübingen: Mohr Siebeck.

Neugebauer, O., and H. B. van Hoesen. 1959. *Greek Horoscopes.* Philadelphia: American Philosophical Society.

Nicolet, Claude. 1991. *Space, Geography, and Politics in the Early Roman Empire.* Jerome Lectures 19. Ann Arbor: University of Michigan Press.

Nicolotti, Andrea. 2011. *Esorcismo cristiano e possession diabolica tra II e III secolo.* Instrumenta Patristica et Mediaevalia 54. Turnhout: Brepols.

Niehoff, Maren R. 2001. *Philo on Jewish Identity and Culture.* Texts and Studies in Ancient Judaism 86. Tübingen: Mohr Siebeck.

Ní Mheallaigh, Karen. 2008. "Pseudo-Documentarism and the Limits of Ancient Fiction." *AJP* 129 (3): 403–31.

———. 2012. "The 'Phoenician Letters' of Dictys of Crete and Dionysius Scytobrachion." *Cambridge Classical Journal* 58:181–93.

Nollé, J. 1981. "Ofellius Laetus, platonischer Philosoph." *ZPE* 41:197–206.

Norelli, Enrico. 1998. "La critique du pluralisme grec dans le *Discours aux*

Grecs de Tatien." In *Les apologistes chrétiens et la culture grecque*, edited by Bernard Pouderon and Joseph Doré, 81–120. Paris: Beauchesne.

Noy, David. 2000. *Foreigners at Rome: Citizens and Strangers*. London: Duckworth.

Nutton, Vivian. 1971. "Two Notes on Immunities: *Digest* 27, 1, 6, 10 and 11." *JRS* 61:52–63.

———. 1979. *Galen: On Prognosis*. CMG V 8.1. Berlin: Akademie-Verlag.

———. 1984. "Galen in the Eyes of His Contemporaries." *Bulletin of the History of Medicine* 58:315–24.

———. 2008. "The Fortunes of Galen." In Hankinson 2008a, 355–90.

———. 2013. *Ancient Medicine*. 2nd ed. London: Routledge.

Oikonomopoulou, Katerina. 2017. "Miscellanies." In *The Oxford Handbook to the Second Sophistic*, edited by Daniel S. Richter and William A. Johnson, 447–62. Oxford: Oxford University Press.

Oliver, James. 1989. *Greek Constitutions of Early Roman Emperors from Inscriptions and Papyri*. Memoirs of the American Philosophical Society 178. Philadelphia: American Philosophical Society.

O'Meara, Dominic J. 1989. *Pythagoras Revived: Mathematics and Philosophy in Late Antiquity*. Oxford: Clarendon Press.

Opsomer, Jan. 2008. "Ofellius Laetus." In Keyser and Irby-Massie 2008, 586–87.

Oudot, Estelle. 2006. "Au commencement était Athènes: Le *Panathénaïque* d'Aelius Aristide ou l'histoire abolie." *Ktèma* 31:227–38.

———. 2008. "'Dresser un trophée sans verser le sang': Athènes dans la rhétorique du IIᵉ siècle—l'image d'un empire linguistique et ses enjeux." In *Langues dominantes, langues dominées: À la mémoire de Gérard Dallez*, edited by Laurence Villard and Nicolas Ballier, 65–84. Mont-Saint-Aignan: Publications des universités de Rouen et du Havre.

Paolucci, Emanuela. 2004. "Il 'deipnosofista' Ulpiano in Ateneo." *Eikasmos* 15:245–59.

Parker, Holt N. 2007. *Censorinus: The Birthday Book*. Chicago: University of Chicago Press.

Parker, Robert. 1991. "Potamon of Mytilene and His Family." *ZPE* 85:115–29.

Parmentier, Édith, and Francesca Prometea Barone. 2011. *Nicolas de Damas: Histoires; Recueil de coutumes; Vie d'Auguste; Autobiographie; Fragments*. Paris: Les Belles Lettres.

Parvis, Sara. 2007. "Justin Martyr and the Apologetic Tradition." In Parvis and Foster 2007, 115–27.

Parvis, Sara, and Paul Foster, eds. 2007. *Justin Martyr and His Worlds*. Minneapolis: Fortress Press.

Patterson, L. G. 1997. "The Divine Became Human: Irenaean Themes in Clement of Alexandria." *SP* 31:497–516.

Penella, Robert J. 2011. "The *Progymnasmata* in Imperial Greek Education." *CW* 105 (1): 77–90.

Perkins, Judith. 1995. *The Suffering Self: Pain and Narrative Representation in the Early Christian Era*. London: Routledge.

Perrone, Lorenzo. 2013a. "*Origenes rediuiuus*: La découverte des Homélies sur les Psaumes dans le Cod. Gr. 314 de Munich." *Revue d'études augustiniennes et patristiques* 59:55–93.

———. 2013b. "Rediscovering Origen Today: First Impressions of the New Collection of Homilies on the Psalms in the *Codex monacensis Graecus* 314." *SP* 56:103–22.

———. 2015. "Discovering Origen's Lost Homilies on the Psalms." *Auctores nostri: Studi e testi di letteratura cristiana antica* 15:19–46.

Perry, Ben Edwin. 1964. *Secundus the Silent Philosopher*. Philological Monographs 22. Ithaca: Cornell University Press.

Petersen, William L. 1994. *Tatian's Diatessaron: Its Creation, Dissemination, Significance, and History in Scholarship*. VCSup 25. Leiden: Brill.

———. 2005. "Tatian the Assyrian." In *A Companion to Second-Century Christian "Heretics,"* edited by Antti Marjanen and Petri Luomanen, 125–58. VCSup 76. Leiden: Brill.

Petit, Caroline. 2009. *Galien: Oeuvres*. Vol. 3, *Introduction, ou Médecin*. Paris: Les Belles Lettres.

———. 2014. "What Does Pseudo-Galen Tell Us That Galen Does Not? Ancient Medical Schools in the Roman Empire." In *Philosophical Themes in*

Galen, edited by Peter Adamson, Rotraud Hansberger, and James Wilberding, 269–90. Bulletin of the Institute of Classical Studies Supplement 114. London: Institute of Classical Studies.

———. 2018. *Galien de Pergame ou la rhétorique de la providence: Médecine, littérature et pouvoir à Rome. Mnemosyne* Supplement 420. Leiden: Brill.

Petrain, David. 2013. "Visual Supplementation and Metonymy in the Roman Public Library." In König, Oikonomopoulou, and Woolf 2013, 332–46.

Pietrobelli, Antoine. 2019. "Galen's Early Reception (Second–Third Centuries)." In *Brill's Companion to the Reception of Galen*, edited by Petros Bouras-Vallianatos and Barbara Zipser, 11–37. Leiden: Brill.

Pilhofer, Peter. 1990. *Presbyteron kreitton: Der Altersbeweis der jüdischen und christlichen Apologeten und seine Vorgeschichte.* WUNT 2.39. Tübingen: Mohr.

———. 2005. "Das Bild der christlichen Gemeinden in Lukians *Peregrinos.*" In *Lukian: Der Tod des Peregrinos; Ein Scharlatan auf dem Scheiterhaufen,* edited by Peter Pilhofer et al., 97–110. SAPERE 9. Darmstadt: Wissenschaftliche Buchgesellschaft.

Pilhofer, Peter, Manuel Baumbach, Jens Gerlach, and Dirk Uwe Hansen, eds. 2005. *Lukian: Der Tod des Peregrinos; Ein Scharlatan auf dem Scheiterhaufen.* SAPERE 9. Darmstadt: Wissenschaftliche Buchgesellschaft.

Pingree, David. 1986. *Vettii Valentis Antiocheni Anthologiarum libri novem.* Leipzig: Teubner.

Places, Édouard des. 1974. *Numénius: Fragments.* Paris: Les Belles Lettres.

———. 1977. *Atticus: Fragments.* Paris: Les Belles Lettres.

Pouderon, Bernard. 1989. *Athénagore d'Athènes: Philosophe chrétien.* Théologie historique 82. Paris: Beauchesne.

Pouderon, Bernard, and Marie-Joseph Pierre. 2003. *Aristide: Apologie.* With the collaboration of Bernard Outtier and Marina Guiorgadzé. SC 470. Paris: Les Éditions du Cerf.

Pradel, Marina Molin. 2012. "Novità origeniane dalla Staatsbibliothek di Monaco di Baviera: Il *Cod.graec.* 314." *Adamantius* 18:16–40.

Price, S. R. F. 1984. *Rituals and Power: The Roman Imperial Cult in Asia Minor.* Cambridge: Cambridge University Press.

Prostmeier, Ferdinand R. 2016. "Tatians *Oratio ad Graecos* und der Diskurs über 'Religion' in der frühen Kaiserzeit." In Nesselrath 2016, 193–223.

Puech, Aimé. 1903. *Recherches sur le "Discours aux Grecs" de Tatien.* Paris: F. Alcan.

Puech, Bernadette. 1992. "Prosopographie des amis de Plutarque." *ANRW* 33.6:4831–93.

Quass, Friedemann. 1993. *Die Honoratiorenschicht in den Städten des griechischen Ostens: Untersuchungen zur politischen und sozialen Entwicklung in hellenistischer und römischer Zeit.* Stuttgart: F. Steiner.

Rajak, Tessa. 2004. *Josephus: The Historian and His Society.* 2nd ed. London: Duckworth.

Ramelli, Ilaria. 2004a. "Diogene Laerzio e Clemente Alessandrino nel contesto di un dibattito culturale comune." *Espacio, tiempo y forma: Revista de la Facultad de geografía e historia,* ser. 2, *Historia antigua* 15:207–24.

———. 2004b. "Diogene Laerzio e i Cristiani: Conoscenza e polemica con Taziano e con Clemente Alessandrino?" *Espacio, tiempo y forma: Revista de la Facultad de geografía e historia,* ser. 2, *Historia antigua* 15:27–42.

Rankin, David Ivan. 2006. *From Clement to Origen: The Social and Historical Context of the Church Fathers.* Aldershot: Ashgate.

Rawson, Elizabeth. 1985. *Intellectual Life in the Late Roman Republic.* Baltimore: Johns Hopkins University Press.

Rebillard, Éric. 2012. *Christians and Their Many Identities in Late Antiquity, North Africa, 200–450 CE.* Ithaca: Cornell University Press.

Rémy, Bernard. 2005. *Antonin le Pieux 138–161: Le siècle d'or de Rome.* Paris: Fayard.

Richard, Marcel. 1963. "Quelques nouveaux fragments des pères anténicéens et nicéens." *Symbolae Osloenses* 38:76–83.

Richter, C. E. 1830. *Philonis Iudaei Opera omnia.* Leipzig: Schwickert.

Richter, Daniel. 2005. "Lives and Afterlives of Lucian of Samosata." *Arion* 13 (1): 75–100.

——. 2011. *Cosmopolis: Imagining Community in Late Classical Athens and the Early Roman Empire.* Oxford: Oxford University Press.

Richter, Daniel S., and William A. Johnson, eds. 2017. *The Oxford Handbook to the Second Sophistic.* Oxford: Oxford University Press.

Riedweg, Christoph. 2018. "Das Origenes-Problem aus der Sicht eines Klassischen Philologen." In Bäbler and Nesselrath 2018, 13–39.

Riginos, Alice Swift. 1976. *Platonica: The Anecdotes Concerning the Life and Writings of Plato.* Leiden: Brill.

Riley, Mark. 1996. "A Survey of Vettius Valens." http://www.csus.edu/indiv/r/rileymt/pdf_folder/vettiusvalens.pdf.

Ritter, Adolf Martin. 2016. "Spuren Tatians und seiner *Oratio ad Graecos* in der christlichen Literatur der Spätantike." In Nesselrath 2016, 287–303.

Rives, James B. 2009. "Diplomacy and Identity Among Jews and Christians." In *Diplomats and Diplomacy in the Roman World,* edited by Claude Eilers, 99–126. *Mnemosyne* Supplement 304. Leiden: Brill.

Robert, Fabrice. 2009. "Enquête sur la présence d'Aelius Aristide et de son oeuvre dans la littérature grecque du IIᵉ au XVᵉ siècle de notre ère." *Anabases* 10:141–60.

Roberto, Umberto. 2011. *Le Chronographiae di Sesto Giulio Africano: Storiografia, politica e cristianesimo nell'età dei Severi.* Rome: Rubbettino.

Rodgers, Robert H. 2009. "Julius Africanus in the Constantinian *Geoponica.*" In Wallraff and Mecella 2009, 197–210.

Rodriguez, Philippe. 2007. "Chérémon, Néron et l'Égypte hellénistique." In *Neronia VII: Rome, Italie et la Grèce; Hellénisme et philhellénisme au premier siècle après J.-C.,* edited by Yves Perrin, 50–73. Brussels: Collection Latomus.

Roller, Duane W. 2018. "Juba II of Mauretania." In *BNJ,* 275.

Romeo, Ilaria. 2002. "The Panhellenion and Ethnic Identity in Hadrianic Greece." *CP* 97 (1): 21–40.

Ronconi, A. 1996. "*Exitus illustrium virorum.*" *Rivista di archeologia cristiana* 6:1258–68.

Rowan, Clare. 2012. *Under Divine Auspices: Divine Ideology and the Visualisation of Imperial Power in the Severan Period.* Cambridge: Cambridge University Press.

Royse, James R. 2009. "The Works of Philo." In Kamesar 2009b, 32–64.

Russell, D. A. 1981. *Criticism in Antiquity.* London: Duckworth.

Russell, D. A., and N. G. Wilson. 1981. *Menander Rhetor: A Commentary.* Oxford: Clarendon Press.

Russell, Donald A., Michael Trapp, and Heinz-Günther Nesselrath. 2016. *In Praise of Asclepius: Aelius Aristides, Selected Prose Hymns.* SAPERE 29. Tübingen: Mohr Siebeck.

Rutherford, R. B. 1989. *The Meditations of Marcus Aurelius: A Study.* Oxford: Clarendon Press.

Rutledge, Steven H. 2008. "Tiberius' Philhellenism." *CW* 101 (4): 453–67.

Ryholt, Kim. 2011. "New Light on the Legendary King Nechepsos of Egypt." *Journal of Egyptian Archaeology* 97:61–72.

Sacks, Kenneth S. 1990. *Diodorus Siculus and the First Century.* Princeton: Princeton University Press.

Saffrey, Henri-Dominique. 1968. "Ἀγεωμέτρητος μηδεὶς εἰσίτω: Une inscription légendaire." *REG* 81:67–87.

Sallmann, Klaus, ed. 1997. *Handbuch der lateinischen Literatur der Antike.* Vol. 4, *Die Literatur des Umbruchs von der römischen zur christlichen Literatur: 117 bis 284 n. Chr.* Munich: C. H. Beck.

Samama, Évelyne. 2003. *Les médecins dans le monde grec: Sources épigraphiques sur la naissance d'une corps médical.* Hautes études du monde gréco-romain 31. Geneva: Droz.

Sandbach, F. H. 1969. *Plutarch's Moralia: Fragments.* Loeb Classical Library 429. Cambridge, Mass.: Harvard University Press.

Sanzi, Ennio. 2000. "Sincretismo e tolleranza religiosa dell'età dei Severi: Per una tipologia storico-religiosa dei culti orientali del secondo ellenismo." *Studi e materiali di storia delle religioni* 24:109–44.

Saxer, Victor. 2004. "Le progrès de l'organisation ecclésiastique de la fin du IIe siècle au milieu du IIIe siècle (180–250)." In *Histoire du christianisme,* vol. 1, *Le nouveau peuple (des origins à*

250), edited by Luce Pietri, 777–816. Paris: Desclée.

Scarborough, John. 2008. "Thessalos of Tralleis." In Keyser and Irby-Massie 2008, 804–5.

Schepens, Guido. 1999. "Potamon of Mytilene." *FGH* 1085.

Schironi, Francesca. 2009. *From Alexandria to Babylon: Near Eastern Languages and Hellenistic Erudition in the Oxyrhynchus Glossary (P.Oxy. 1802 + 4812)*. Sozomena: Studies in the Recovery of Ancient Texts 4. Berlin: Walter de Gruyter.

———. 2013. "The Early Reception of Berossos." In *The World of Berossos*, edited by Johannes Haubold, Giovanni B. Lanfranchi, Robert Rollinger, and John Steele, 235–54. Classica et Orientalia 5. Wiesbaden: Harrasowitz Verlag.

Schmid, Ulrich B. 2013. "The Diatessaron of Tatian." In *The Text of the New Testament in Contemporary Research: Essays on the Status Quaestionis*, edited by Bart D. Ehrman and Michael K. Holmes, 115–42. 2nd ed. New Testament Tools, Studies and Documents 42. Leiden: Brill.

Schmitz, Thomas, and Nicolas Wiater, eds. 2012. *The Struggle for Identity: Greeks and Their Past in the First Century BCE*. Stuttgart: Franz Steiner Verlag.

Schwartz, Daniel R. 2009. "Philo, His Family, and His Times." In Kamesar 2009b, 9–31.

Secord, Jared. 2012. "The Cultural Geography of a Greek Christian: Irenaeus from Smyrna to Lyons." In *Irenaeus: Life, Scripture, Legacy*, edited by Paul Foster and Sara Parvis, 25–33. Minneapolis: Fortress Press.

———. 2013. "Medicine and Sophistry in Hippolytus' *Refutatio*." *SP* 65:217–24.

———. 2017a. "Galen and the Theodotians: Embryology and Adoptionism in the Christian Schools of Rome." *SP* 81:51–64.

———. 2017b. "Julius Africanus, Origen, and the Politics of Intellectual Life Under the Severans." *CW* 110 (2): 211–35.

———. 2018. "The Celibate Athlete: Athletic Metaphors, Medical Thought, and Sexual Abstinence in the Second and Third Centuries CE." *Studies in Late Antiquity* 2 (4): 464–90.

———. Forthcoming a. "Irenaeus at Rome: The Greek Context of Christian Intellectual Life in the Second Century." In *Irénée entre Asie et Occident*, edited by Agnès Bastit-Kalinowska. Collection des études augustiniennes. Turnhout: Brepols.

———. Forthcoming b. "Medical and Philosophical Ways of Knowing in the School of Justin Martyr." In *The Intellectual World of Christian Late Antiquity: Reshaping Classical Traditions*, edited by Lewis Ayres, Michael W. Champion, and Matthew R. Crawford. Cambridge: Cambridge University Press.

Segre, Mario. 1993. *Iscrizioni di Cos*. 2 vols. Monografie della Scuola archeologica di Atene e delle missioni italiane in Oriente 6. Rome: L'Erma di Bretschneider.

Sharples, Robert W. 2005. "Implications of the New Alexander of Aphrodisias Inscription." *BICS* 48:47–56.

Shaw, Teresa M. 1998. *The Burden of the Flesh: Fasting and Sexuality in Early Christianity*. Minneapolis: Fortress Press.

Sherwin-White, A. N. 1966. *The Letters of Pliny: A Historical and Social Commentary*. Oxford: Clarendon Press.

Sidebottom, Harry. 2007. "Severan Historiography: Evidence, Patterns, and Arguments." In *Severan Culture*, edited by Simon Swain, Stephen Harrison, and Jaś Elsner, 52–82. Cambridge: Cambridge University Press.

Simpson, William Alexander. 2017. *Aristides' "Apology" and the Novel "Barlaam and Ioasaph."* Studia Patristica Supplement 7. Leuven: Peeters.

Siwicki, Christopher. 2019. "Defining Rome's Pantheum." *Journal of Ancient History* 7 (2): 269–315.

Slusser, Michael. 2006. "How Much Did Irenaeus Learn from Justin?" *SP* 50:515–20.

———. 2007. "Justin Scholarship: Trends and Trajectories." In Parvis and Foster 2007, 13–21.

Smelik, K. A. D., and E. A. Hemelrijk. 1984. "'Who Knows Not What Monsters

Demented Egypt Worships?' Opinions on Egyptian Animal Worship in Antiquity as Part of the Ancient Conception of Egypt." *ANRW* 17.4:1852–2000.

Smith, Geoffrey S. 2015. *Guilt by Association: Heresy Catalogues in Early Christianity*. Oxford: Oxford University Press.

Smith, Gregory A. 2008. "How Thin Is a Demon?" *JECS* 16 (4): 479–512.

Smith, Steven D. 2014. *Man and Animal in Severan Rome: The Literary Imagination of Claudius Aelianus*. GCRW. Cambridge: Cambridge University Press.

Snyder, Harlow Gregory. 2000. *Teachers and Texts in the Ancient World: Philosophers, Jews, and Christians*. London: Routledge.

———. 2007. "'Above the Bath of Myrtinus': Justin Martyr's 'School' in the City of Rome." *HTR* 100 (3): 335–62.

Sorabji, Richard. 1993. *Animal Minds and Human Morals: The Origins of the Western Debate*. Cornell Studies in Classical Philology 54. Ithaca: Cornell University Press.

Spawforth, A. J. S. 1978. "Balbilla, the Euryclids, and Memorials for a Greek Magnate." *Annual of the British School at Athens* 73:249–60.

———. 1985. "Families at Roman Sparta and Epidaurus: Some Prosopographical Notes." *Annual of the British School at Athens* 80:191–258.

———. 1999. "The Panhellenion Again." *Chiron* 29:339–52.

———. 2012. *Greece and the Augustan Cultural Revolution*. GCRW. Cambridge: Cambridge University Press.

Spawforth, A. J. S., and Susan Walker. 1985. "The World of the Panhellenion: I. Athens and Eleusis." *JRS* 75:78–104.

———. 1986. "The World of the Panhellenion: II. Three Dorian Cities." *JRS* 76:88–105.

Speyer, Wolfgang. 1970. *Bücherfunde in der Glaubenswerbung der Antike*. Hypomnemata 24. Göttingen: Vandenhoeck & Ruprecht.

Spittler, Janet. 2008. *Animals in the Apocryphal Acts of the Apostles: Early Christianity's Wild Kingdom*. WUNT 247. Tübingen: Mohr Siebeck.

Staden, Heinrich von. 1982. "Hairesis and Heresy: The Case of the *haireseis iatrikai*." In *Jewish and Christian Self-Definition*, vol. 3, *Self-Definition in the Greco-Roman World*, edited by E. P. Sanders, 76–100. Philadelphia: Fortress Press.

———. 1997. "Galen and the Second Sophistic." In *Aristotle and After*, edited by R. Sorabji, 33–55. Bulletin of the Institute of Classical Studies Supplement 68. London: Institute for Classical Studies.

Stander, Hendrik F. 1985/86. "Is Justin Really a Bad Stylist?" *Second Century* 5 (4): 226–32.

Stanton, G. R. 1973. "Sophists and Philosophers: Problems of Classification." *AJP* 94 (4): 350–64.

Stead, Christopher. 1994. *Philosophy in Christian Antiquity*. Cambridge: Cambridge University Press.

Steneker, Heinricus. 1969. ΠΕΙΘΟΥΣ ΔΗΜΙΟΥΡΓΙΑ: *Observations sur la fonction du style dans le "Protreptique" de Clément d'Alexandrie*. Nijmegen: Dekker & van de Vegt.

Stephens, Susan A., and John J. Winkler. 1995. *Ancient Greek Novels: The Fragments*. Princeton: Princeton University Press.

Stern, Menahem. 1976–89. *Greek and Latin Authors on Jews and Judaism*. 3 vols. Jerusalem: Israel Academy of Sciences and Humanities.

Stevens, Benjamin. 2006. "Aeolism: Latin as a Dialect of Greek." *Classical Journal* 102 (2): 115–44.

Straw, Carole. 2002. "'A Very Special Death': Christian Martyrdom in Its Classical Context." In *Sacrificing the Self: Perspectives in Martyrdom and Religion*, edited by M. Cormack, 39–57. Oxford: Oxford University Press.

Strobel, Claudia. 2009. "The Lexica of the Second Sophistic: Safeguarding Atticism." In *Standard Languages and Language Standards: Greek, Past and Present*, edited by Alexandra Georgakopoulou and Michael Silk, 93–107. Farnham: Ashgate.

Strohmaier, Gotthard. 1976. "Übersehenes zur Biographie Lukians." *Philologus* 120 (1): 117–22.

———. 2012. "Lukian verspottet die urchristliche Glossolalie: Ein rätselhafter Satz in Galens

Epidemienkommentaren." *Philologus* 156:166–73.

Strutwolf, Holger, and Marie-Luise Lakmann. 2016. "Tatians Seelenlehre im Kontext der zeitgenössischen Philosophie." In Nesselrath 2016, 225–45.

Swain, Simon. 1996. *Hellenism and Empire: Language, Classicism, and Power in the Greek World, AD 50–250*. Oxford: Clarendon Press.

———. 1999. "Defending Hellenism: Philostratus, In Honour of Apollonius." In *Apologetics in the Roman Empire: Pagans, Jews, and Christians*, edited by Mark Edwards, Martin Goodman, and Simon Price, 157–96. Oxford: Oxford University Press.

———. 2009. "Culture and Nature in Philostratus." In *Philostratus*, edited by Ewen Bowie and Jaś Elsner, 33–46. GCRW.Cambridge: Cambridge University Press.

Swain, Simon, Stephen Harrison, and Jaś Elsner, eds. 2007. *Severan Culture*. Cambridge: Cambridge University Press.

Tacoma, Laurens E. 2016. *Moving Romans: Migration to Rome in the Principate*. Oxford: Oxford University Press.

Tanaseanu-Döbler, Ilinca. 2018. "Die Origeneis des Porphyrios." In Bäbler and Nesselrath 2018, 129–63.

Tarrant, Harold. 1993. *Thrasyllan Platonism*. Ithaca: Cornell University Press.

Taylor, Tristan. 2011. "Magic and Property: The Legal Context of Apuleius' *Apologia*." *Antichthon* 45:149–66.

Tcherikover, Victor A., and Alexander Fuks. 1957–64. *Corpus papyrorum Judaicarum*. 3 vols. Cambridge, Mass.: Harvard University Press.

Tecusan, Manuela. 2004. *The Fragments of the Methodists*. Vol. 1, *Methodism Outside Soranus*. Leiden: Brill.

Temkin, Owsei. 1991. *Hippocrates in a World of Pagans and Christians*. Baltimore: Johns Hopkins University Press.

Terian, Abraham. 1981. *Philonis Alexandrini De animalibus: The Armenian Text with an Introduction, Translation, and Commentary*. Studies in Hellenistic Judaism, Supplements to *Studia Philonica* 1. Chico, Calif.: Scholars Press.

Thomas, Edmund. 2007. *Monumentality and the Roman Empire: Architecture in the Antonine Age*. Oxford: Oxford University Press.

Thomassen, Einar. 2004. "Orthodoxy and Heresy in Second-Century Rome." *HTR* 97 (3): 241–56.

Thorsen, Thea Selliaas. 2012. "Sappho, Corinna, and Colleagues in Ancient Rome: Tatian's Catalogue of Statues (*Oratio ad Graecos* 33–4) Reconsidered." *Mnemosyne* 65:695–715.

Thorsteinsson, Runar M. 2010. *Roman Christianity and Roman Stoicism: A Comparative Study of Ancient Morality*. Oxford: Oxford University Press.

———. 2012a. "By Philosophy Alone: Reassessing Justin's Christianity and His Turn from Platonism." *Early Christianity* 3:492–517.

———. 2012b. "The Literary Genre and Purpose of Justin's *Second Apology*: A Critical Review with Insights from Ancient Epistolography." *HTR* 105 (1): 91–114.

———. 2013. "Justin's Debate with Crescens the Stoic." *ZAC* 17 (3): 451–78.

Tieleman, Teun. 2016. "Religion and Therapy in Galen." In *Religion and Illness*, edited by Annette Weissenrieder and Gregor Etzelmüller, 15–31. Eugene, Ore.: Wipf and Stock.

Timotin, Andrei. 2012. *La démonologie platonicienne: Histoire de la notion de daimōn de Platon aux derniers néoplatoniciens*. Leiden: Brill.

———. 2016. "Gott und die Dämonen bei Tatian." In Nesselrath 2016, 267–86.

Tite, Philip L. 2015. "Voluntary Martyrdom and Gnosticism." *JECS* 23 (1): 27–54.

Toher, Mark. 2017. *Nicolaus of Damascus: "The Life of Augustus" and "The Autobiography."* Cambridge: Cambridge University Press.

Toner, Jerry. 2017. "The Intellectual Life of the Roman Non-Elite." In *Popular Culture in the Ancient World*, edited by Lucy Grig, 167–88. Cambridge: Cambridge University Press.

Too, Yun Lee. 2010. *The Idea of the Library in the Ancient World*. Oxford: Oxford University Press.

Trapp, Michael. 1990. "Plato's *Phaedrus* in Second-Century Greek Literature." In *Antonine Literature*, edited by D. A.

Russell, 141–73. Oxford: Clarendon Press.

———. 2017. *Aelius Aristides: Orations.* Vol. 1. Loeb Classical Library 533. Cambridge, Mass.: Harvard University Press.

Trelenberg, Jörg. 2012. *Tatianos, Oratio ad Graecos: Rede an die Grechen.* Beiträge zur historischen Theologie. Tübingen: Mohr Siebeck.

Tribulato, Olga. 2014. "'Not Even Menander Would Use This Word!' Perceptions of Menander's Language in Greek Lexicography." In *Menander in Contexts,* edited by Alan H. Sommerstein, 199–214. London: Routledge.

———. 2016. "Herodotus' Reception in Ancient Greek Lexicography and Grammar: From the Hellenistic to the Imperial Age." In *Brill's Companion to the Reception of Herodotus in Antiquity and Beyond,* edited by Jessica Priestley and Vasiliki Zali, 169–92. Leiden: Brill.

Tuci, Paolo A. 2017. "Potamon." In *BNJ,* 147.

Vagelpohl, Uwe. 2016. *Galen: Commentary on Hippocrates' Epidemics Book II, Parts I–VI.* With Simon Swain. CMG Supplementum Orientale 5.2. Berlin: Walter de Gruyter.

Valente, Stefano. 2015. *The Antiatticist: Introduction and Critical Edition.* Berlin: Walter de Gruyter.

Vallée, Gérard. 1981. *A Study in Anti-Gnostic Polemics: Irenaeus, Hippolytus, and Epiphanius.* Studies in Christianity and Judaism 1. Waterloo: Wilfrid Laurier University Press.

Van Den Hoek, Annewies. 1990. "How Alexandrian Was Clement of Alexandria? Reflections on Clement and His Alexandrian Background." *Heytrop Journal* 31:179–94.

Van Den Hoek, Annewies, and John J. Hermann Jr. 2006. "Clement of Alexandria, Acrobats, and the Elite." *Rivista di storia del cristianesimo* 3:83–97.

Vanderpool, Eugene. 1959. "An Athenian Monument to Theodorus of Gadara." *AJP* 80 (4): 366–69.

Van Nuffelen, Peter. 2011. *Rethinking the Gods: Philosophical Readings of Religion in the Post-Hellenistic Period.* GCRW. Cambridge: Cambridge University Press.

Vessella, Carlo. 2018. *Sophisticated Speakers: Atticistic Pronunciation in the Atticist Lexica.* Berlin: Walter de Gruyter.

Wallraff, Martin. 2007. *Iulius Africanus Chronographiae: The Extant Fragments.* With the assistance of Umberto Roberto and Karl Pinggéra. Translated by William Adler. GCS, n.F., 15. Berlin: Walter de Gruyter.

———. 2010. "The Beginnings of Christian Universal History from Tatian to Julius Africanus." *ZAC* 14:540–55.

Wallraff, Martin, and Laura Mecella. 2009. *Die Kestoi des Julius Africanus und ihre Überlieferung.* Texte und Untersuchungen zur Geschichte der altchristlichen Literatur 165. Berlin: Walter de Gruyter.

Wallraff, Martin, Carlo Scardino, Laura Mecella, and Christophe Guignard. 2012. *Iulius Africanus: Cesti; The Extant Fragments.* Translated by William Adler. GCS, n.F., 18. Berlin: Walter de Gruyter.

Walzer, Richard. 1949. *Galen on Jews and Christians.* Oxford: Oxford University Press.

Warren, James. 2007. "Diogenes Laërtius: Biographer of Philosophy." In *Ordering Knowledge in the Roman Empire,* edited by Jason König and Tim Whitmarsh, 133–49. Cambridge: Cambridge University Press.

Waszink, J. H. 1963. "Some Observations on the Appreciation of 'The Philosophy of the Barbarians' in Early Christian Literature." In *Mélanges offerts à Mademoiselle Christine Mohrmann,* edited by L. J. Engels et al. 41–56. Utrecht: Spectrum Editeurs.

Watson, Alan. 1985. *The Digest of Justinian.* 2 vols. Philadelphia: University of Pennsylvania Press.

Weijenborg, Reinhold. 1972. "Die Berichte über Justin und Crescens bei Tatian." *Antonianum* 47:372–90.

Wendt, Heidi. 2016. *At the Temple Gates: The Religion of Freelance Experts in the Roman Empire.* Oxford: Oxford University Press.

Westall, Richard. 2018. "In Praise of Pompeius: Re-Reading the *Bibliotheke Historike*." In *Diodoros of Sicily: Historiographical Theory and Practice* in the *"Bibliotheke,"* 91–127. Studia Hellenistica 58. Leuven: Peeters.

Whitehead, David. 2010. *Apollodorus Mechanicus, Siege Matters* (Πολιορκητικά). Historia Einzelschriften 216. Stuttgart: Franz Steiner Verlag.

Whitmarsh, Tim. 2001. *Greek Literature and the Roman Empire: The Politics of Imitation.* Oxford: Oxford University Press.

———. 2005. *The Second Sophistic.* New Surveys in the Classics 35. Oxford: Oxford University Press.

———. 2007. "Prose Literature and the Severan Dynasty." In *Severan Culture,* edited by Simon Swain, Stephen Harrison, and Jaś Elsner, 29–51. Cambridge: Cambridge University Press.

———. 2010. "Thinking Local." In *Local Knowledge and Microidentities in the Imperial Greek World,* edited by Tim Whitmarsh, 1–16. Cambridge: Cambridge University Press.

———. 2013. *Beyond the Second Sophistic: Adventures in Greek Postclassicism.* Berkeley: University of California Press.

Whittaker, Molly. 1982. *Tatian: Oratio ad Graecos and Fragments.* OECT. Oxford: Clarendon Press.

Wiater, Nicolas. 2011. *The Ideology of Classicism: Language, History, and Identity in Dionysius of Halicarnassus.* Untersuchungen zur antiken Literatur und Geschichte 105. Berlin: Walter de Gruyter.

Wilken, Robert Louis. 2003. *The Christians as the Romans Saw Them.* 2nd ed. New Haven: Yale University Press.

Williams, Mary Frances. 2018. "Thrasyllos of Rhodes." In *BNJ,* 253.

Williams, W. 1967. "Antoninus Pius and the Control of Provincial Embassies." *Historia* 16 (4): 470–83.

Wisse, Jakob. 1995. "Greeks, Romans, and the Rise of Atticism." In *Greek Literary Theory after Aristotle: A Collection of Papers in Honour of D. M. Schenkeveld,* edited by J. G. J. Abbenes, S. R. Slings, and I. Sluiter, 65–82. Amsterdam: VU University Press.

Woerther, Frédérique. 2013. *Apollodore de Pergame; Théodore de Gadara; Fragments et témoignages.* Paris: Les Belles Lettres.

Yaron, R. 1987. "Semitisms in Ulpian?" *Tijdschrift voor rechtsgeschiedenis* 55:3–17.

Zeegers-Vander Vorst, Nicole. 1972. *Les citations des poètes grecs chez les apologistes chrétiens du IIe siècle.* Louvain: Publications Universitaires de Louvain.

INDEX